COMBINED OPERATIONS in the Civil War

Rowena Reed

COMBINED OPERATIONS
in the Civil War

Naval Institute Press

ANNAPOLIS • MARYLAND

For Amy

CONTENTS

LIST OF MAPS

PREFACE

Given the importance in modern war of a unified effort by all arms, it is somewhat surprising that no study of combined operations in the American Civil War has been made. Despite the wealth of source material, almost all of which is now available in published form, historians have limited themselves to descriptive accounts of some of these operations—notably Burnside's expedition, the assault on Fort Fisher, and the "siege" of Charleston. The planning of combined movements, their relation to Federal war aims, the effect of technological change on their design and execution, and the multiplicity of economic and political factors influencing the use of combined operations have not been previously examined. Nor has the development of combined tactics received sufficient attention.

I do not claim to have produced a definitive history of this large and complex subject, for it is impossible to fully discuss all aspects of Federal combined operations in a single work. Thorough studies of Union and Confederate logistics, the functioning of various war bureaus, the impact of financial, mercantile, and railway interests on government policy, and the influence of Congressional committees are still needed. The effects of the Federal blockade and trade with the enemy should be reassessed. Key personalities, both civilian and military, deserve examination in greater depth, especially regarding their private interests, professional feuds, business associations, and personal prejudices. These considerations, while necessary to a complete understanding of Civil War combined operations, have not been explored in depth in this work. Faced with a choice between presenting an exhaustive account of one operation, and a more comprehensive examination of the subject as a whole, I chose the latter scheme, hoping to stimulate other scholars to explore the field in greater detail. I have therefore omitted blow-by-blow campaign narratives except when there are no accurate accounts or where it is essential to retell the story to demonstrate an important point.

The reader should note that throughout this book I have used the broad British term "combined", which includes all operations requiring strategic or tactical cooperation between naval and land forces under separate command. The narrower American term "amphibious" is appropriate only to operations involving an actual waterborne landing, while the even more specific "amphibious assault" refers to an engagement requiring tactical cooperation to overcome a fortified position.

Since this study examines both the strategic and tactical application of Federal combined operations, it is organized into three parts, corresponding to the different uses of combined forces at various stages of the war. Part I explains the evolution of combined strategy from Lincoln's proclamation of the blockade in April 1861 until McClellan's removal as commanding general of the United States Army in March 1862. Part II examines the collapse of combined strategy incident to this change of command, its repercussions in the various military departments, and the split between the Army and the Navy over strategic priorities in the middle period of the war. Part III describes the evolution of combined tactics, and the relation of amphibious operations to Union war strategy, from the naval attack on Charleston in April 1863 to the reduction of Fort Fisher in the early months of 1865.

The fundamental sources for this study were the official records of the War and Navy Departments, supplemented by the various reports and minutes of evidence compiled by the Joint Committee on the Conduct of the War. Certain manuscript collections, memoirs, diaries, and standard compilations like *Battles and Leaders* were helpful, although this class of material is, on the whole, less reliable or useful than the official records (with some exceptions, such as the McClellan Papers). Secondary works and participant accounts have been used where documentary sources are insufficient or confusing.

Donald M. Schurman of Queen's University deserves special

acknowledgment for his enthusiastic interest and sustained encouragement. I wish to thank George Reed, Olaf Janzen, W. K. Backhaus, and A. M. Keppel-Jones, who read all or part of the manuscript, for their helpful criticisms and comments, as well as my editor Wilfred McClay of the Naval Institute Press, and my typist, Margaret DeLucca. For locating source material, and for other valuable services, I am especially grateful to George Henderson of the Queen's University Archives, W. A. B. Douglas, Director of the Historical Division of the Canadian Department of National Defense, and to the staffs of the Royal Military College Library, the United States Library of Congress, and the United States National Archives. Financial assistance for research was provided by the Civil War Round Table, the Ontario Ministry of Colleges and Universities, and the Institute of Commonwealth and Comparative Studies.

INTRODUCTION

A MAJOR STRATEGIC problem confronting the United States in the war with the Confederacy was how to employ its almost total naval superiority against a continental enemy. The necessarily defensive tasks of commerce raiding and coast protection during the Revolution and the War of 1812 had not prepared the U.S. Navy for a role as an invader. The limited experience of the Mexican War and minor campaigns against the Indians, while better than no experience at all, had not been sufficient to produce a very exacting approach to military problems or skill in handling large bodies of troops. Nor had the Navy's experiences with blockade during the Mexican conflict or patrol to suppress the slave trade taught its officers how to command whole squadrons of vessels, and exploit their strategic or tactical possibilities. Despite the existence of West Point for fifty years and the recent founding of the Naval Academy, there were still few truly professional officers in either service.

As for combined operations, coastal raids and improvised expeditions in the style of the Seven Years War were not good precedents for the planning and execution of large-scale amphibious movements. Although it has rightly been claimed that General Winfield Scott's landing at Vera Cruz in 1847 showed a much higher degree of organization and logistical efficiency than had ever been attained before in such an operation, it should be remembered that the Mexicans had no strong defenses, that the landing was unopposed, and that the port itself was taken by siege. Nevertheless, it was a step in the right direction. Scott's engineers, who managed this affair, seem to have learned something from it, which may explain why

Army engineers showed more skill in the management of combined operations during the Civil War than did their naval counterparts.

The handicaps of inexperience and a still "amateurish" approach to war might have been more quickly overcome had the Union forces not been burdened by an awkward command structure. At the head of the Army was the senior major general, variously styled the general-in-chief, the commanding general, the commander-in-chief, or simply the major general commanding. This office, filled by executive appointment, had no legal status and its authority was based solely upon the seniority of that individual in the regular army. Field command was determined in the same haphazard manner; that is, the senior officer present with a unit—in this case, including volunteer ranks—was automatically in command if he chose to be. Not surprisingly, arguments over who ranked who were common obstacles to the war effort.

The command structure of the United States Navy was even more primitive. There was no chief of naval operations, nor was any one officer appointed commander of the United States Fleet so that he might consult directly in an official capacity with his Army counterpart. The lack of such an office, not to mention the lack of either an army or a naval staff, was a serious obstacle to efficient combined operations. The highest professional appointment was that of squadron commander (commodore), or flag officer, later designated rear admiral. While the Navy escaped the Army's problem of seniority for operational commands, grades were generally lower in the Navy and their equivalents in Army ranks not always clear. This caused confusion, especially in the West when the Mississippi Squadron was under the authority of the War Department and its officers thus subject to orders from their Army "seniors".

At the top of this whole nebulous structure was the president, the constitutional commander-in-chief who, by tradition, was not expected to command in the military sense, but whose function it was to set war policy and "advise" on the best way to carry it out. The opportunities for misunderstanding here were obviously legion. Yet another amorphous echelon stood between the president and the service chiefs—the Cabinet, principally the civilian secretaries of War and of the Navy. While the Navy secretary, who acted much like a chief of staff, was a valuable official because he was the only coordinating authority between the government and the squadron commanders and, in practice, had charge of policy as well as operations, the post of secretary of War was an anomalous one with no definite powers or responsibilities. Its influence depended almost entirely on what the individual in that office wished to make of it. A weak War secretary, like Simon Cameron, was a useless but minor encumbrance, while a strong personality, like Edwin M. Stanton, was a millstone around the neck of the general-in-chief.

Formulation of Army plans was the responsibility of the commanding general, subject to approval by the president and his Cabinet. Naval plans were devised by the secretary of the Navy or, in the Civil War, by the assistant secretary. Although squadron commanders were often encouraged to submit ideas and plans for specific naval or combined operations, no naval officer presumed to advise on naval strategy or operations as a whole (except for Captain Samuel F. Du Pont, when he was chairman of the Blockade Board). The higher military functions remained the prerogative of the civilian secretary. Furthermore, the secretaries were not required to cooperate or even consult with one another, or with the general-in-chief.

This already confused politico-military chain of command was further complicated by the appointment, by both the president and the Congress, of special boards and committees. Washington swarmed with amateur Napoleons. Regardless of the merits or defects of any particular strategy, without a central planning and control agency, whether military or civilian, it was extremely unlikely that any one strategic idea would emerge in well-defined form and be consistently implemented. It is not surprising that General Scott's famous "Anaconda" strategy has a somewhat elusive quality, or that the Federal high command is often said to have had no plans.

Given this state of affairs, it is perhaps a credit to human resourcefulness that the Union was able to conduct *any* successful military operations, let alone successful combined operations. The South's relative weakness and its own internal problems allowed the Federals to get away with serious mistakes that would have meant defeat against a stronger and better-prepared enemy. There was a positive side to the confusion, however. The same "amateurish" attitude of opportunism that frequently led both political and military leaders to work at cross-purposes was also responsible for initiating some of the most important combined expeditions. The political generals like Butler, Banks, and McClernand, looking for profit, publicity, or just a chance to play soldier, were the foremost proponents of amphibious warfare, and their enthusiasm seems to have compensated to a surprising extent for what they lacked in military skill. Because they had no vested interest in the Army establishment, they often cooperated better than West Pointers with the Navy.

Furthermore, the United States Army had by 1861 produced a small group of officers whose approach to war was nearly as professional as that of as their European counterparts. Foremost among them was Major General George Brinton McClellan, a thoroughly "modern" young soldier of seemingly inexhaustible energy and talent, a student of European army organization and an expert on the employment of the three arms (infantry, artillery, and cavalry) in battle. The appointment of McClellan to succeed Scott as general-in-chief in November 1861 temporarily brought order to the formulation of Federal strategy.

Although he respected the Napoleonic concepts of mass and firepower on the battlefield, McClellan believed that it was no longer necessary (if indeed it was still possible) to destroy the enemy's armies to gain a decisive victory. American geography and the extension of interstate rail lines in the 1850s made a different strategy against the South possible. Deprived of this "nervous system," large armies could not be maintained for extended periods at long distances from their base. Bludgeoning the enemy to death was unsound military logic when he could easily be paralyzed by the disruption of his internal communications.

McClellan also saw, as General von Moltke's later operations would confirm, that the strongest form of warfare under changed conditions was a combination of the strategic offense and the tactical defense. The increased range and accuracy of small arms and field guns was not the only factor diminishing the effectiveness of offensive battlefield tactics. Railways, again, were significant. They not only permitted a large initial concentration of troops in the field; they provided for constant supply and reinforcement from the rear. The enemy's fortified line became more and more extended and long difficult maneuvers by detachments were required to outflank it. Such movements were perilous for an army on exterior lines, because the enemy could either fall on the enveloping column or meet the expected flank attack with a new fortified line. That the Confederates frequently succeeded with flanking maneuvers during the first two years of the war while the Federals generally failed was due almost entirely to superior Southern mobility and discipline. An added factor strengthening the defense was the facility for transporting heavy guns, materials for constructing gun emplacements and field works, and the continuous supply of ammunition—provided the army remained in position. As soon as it attempted to move forward, however, especially with the rapid movements required for effective pursuit, it inevitably became bogged down by its cumbersome transport. Thousands of wagons and heavy caissons plowed the dirt roads into quagmires while the enemy, retiring quickly along his supply lines, drew nearer his depots.

Another invention modified the accepted principle of strategic concentration. The telegraph enabled a skillful commander-in-chief to coordinate the movement of several independent armies against widely separated objectives. Such dispersion not only compelled the enemy to fragment his armies in response, but permitted the employment of larger numbers than limited rail facilities could have maintained on a single front.

But while in the Civil War the Southern rail network was a tempting target and offered a convenient means of advancing on important rail junctions, these same lines, when supporting a Federal advance, would be vulnerable to attack. To counter this threat, it was necessary to detach a large part of an invading field army to guard long rail lines of communication, thus greatly reducing that army's combat strength. The alternative was the use of water transportation, for both logistic and operational purposes. Naval supremacy provided this option for the Union while denying it to the Confederacy.

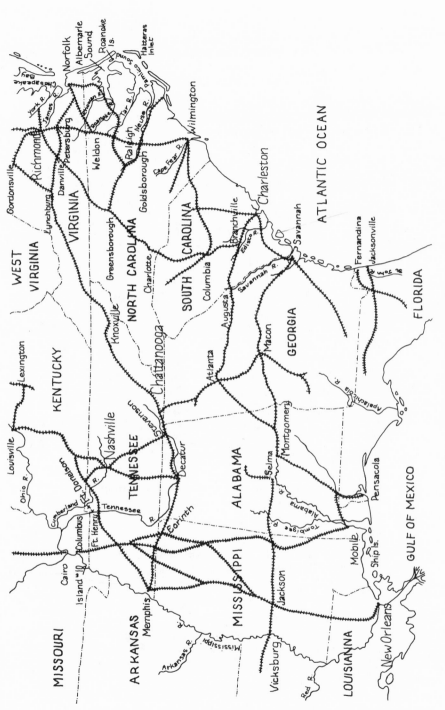

Railroad Map of the Confederacy
1861-1865

Of the men in the Federal high command, professional and civilian, during the first two years of the war only General McClellan envisioned the use of combined operations as the foundation of a comprehensive plan to paralyze the South from within. Perceiving the futility of relying on the slow and uncertain process of blockade, McClellan meant to grasp the enemy by the throat. The destruction of the main Confederate army in Virginia, even if possible, would not be decisive, for as long as Southern resources and the means to move them remained intact, another army could be raised, equipped, and transported to the front in a remarkably short time. Nor would seizing *one* strategic point, (for example, one important rail junction) such as Richmond end the war quickly. The Confederates could evacuate Richmond, fall back along their rail lines into the interior and, placing themselves in more inaccessible positions, prolong the conflict indefinitely.

Instead, McClellan proposed using the great water highways of the South. Penetrating deep into the Confederacy along the Mississippi, the Tennessee, and the Cumberland rivers, Federal armies could seize the great East–West rail lines connecting the Mississippi Valley with the Atlantic and Gulf seaboard, and with Virginia. Pushing into the North Carolina sounds and up the Roanoke and Neuse rivers, they could disrupt Richmond's lines to the Deep South and force the Confederate army in Virginia to disperse for lack of supplies. From their beachhead at Port Royal, South Carolina, Union troops could entrench themselves along the Charleston and Savannah Railroad, threatening both cities and preventing their garrisons from reinforcing one another. Seizure of the rail junction at Mobile would disrupt communications between middle Tennessee and western Mississippi. To free themselves from this death grip, Southern generals would have to hurl their men against strongly fortified positions which could not be invested while protected by Union warships or gunboats.

Had McClellan's brilliant strategy been fully implemented, it would have ended the Civil War in 1862, as intended. Built upon the North's primary assets—larger industrial capacity, greater manpower, and command of the sea—it minimized the South's advantages of more skillful battlefield leadership, better troop discipline, and superior marching and fighting endurance. Equally important, his strategy was compatible with the Union government's war aims—to restore Federal authority in the seceded states as quickly as possible, at the least cost and with the least disruption of social and commercial life.

McClellan's successor as commanding general of the Federal armies, Major General Henry Wager Halleck, not only failed to exploit the strategic potential afforded by Union command of the sea, he actually disapproved of combined operations, and did not follow up McClellan's initial coast expeditions. General Halleck was a respected military theorist, able administrator, and skilled engineer; but, while recognizing the logic of a war of position under Civil War conditions, he was a "continental" thinker, obsessed with the idea of military concentration. To his inflexible mind, coast operations only involved a waste of manpower better employed on the two main land fronts. Not perceiving that the telegraph had rendered the old command system obsolete, he usually left the employment of the various field armies up to their commanders' discretion and refused to "interfere" with their plans—thus allowing their locally based plans to interfere with one another. When he did intervene, it was to promote some eccentric campaign, impossible to execute and of no military value. The result was chaos. Under his disingenuous leadership, operations in the West were misdirected and fragmentary, and his refusal to cooperate with the Navy prolonged the war for at least a year. In the East, because Halleck and the government were obsessed with the safety of Washington, the armies of Generals Pope, Burnside, Hooker, and Meade had to concern themselves solely with General Lee's army. But the Confederate army's skill in field maneuvers destroyed more Union soldiers faster than the Federals could have dispersed them in coast operations.

Although Halleck's replacement by Lieutenant General Ulysses S. Grant in March 1864 seemed to promise a revival of combined operations in the final campaigns, Grant's preferred plan, which had the same object as McClellan's, was never carried out. Government interference with military movements—a pernicious and intractable feature of Civil War operations—and Halleck's still-pervasive influence as Army chief of staff—dictated a continuation of costly, unnecessary, and unproductive land-based offensives. Richmond, like Vicksburg, was taken by siege; Savannah and Charleston by an army marching through the interior upon their rear. Only in the last few months of the war, when the Confederacy was already collapsing under the weight of inefficiency and mismanagement, could Grant break free of a land-based strategy and use Union sea power to give the exhausted enemy the coup de grace.

Ironically, the breakdown of Federal combined operations strategy in early 1862 facilitated the evolution of more sophisticated combined tactics. Prolonging the war gave the Confederacy time to perfect more elaborate defensive systems, while a split between the Union Army and Navy over strategic priorities reinforced the tendency for both services to concentrate on means rather than ends. By 1863, the question of whether Richmond should be taken, or Vicksburg, or Charleston, or Mobile, had become largely irrelevent. The same psychology which, a half-century later, following the breakdown of strategic plans on the Western front, would cause both belligerents to contract their vision to the narrow limits of the battlefield, operated in the Civil War. Victory came to be seen in terms of successfully attacking or defending fortified positions. On land, the only alternative to siege tactics was the expenditure of thousands of men in assaults on works which could seldom be held for lack of sufficient reserves. On the coast and navigable rivers, the alternative was a combined attack.

The necessity for combined tactics was assumed in the planning for expeditions against Hatteras and Port Royal in 1861, before the inherent weakness of early Southern coast defenses proved to the Navy's satisfaction that these works could be reduced by bombardment alone. The proof was deceptive, however, for the relative strength of "ships versus forts" had not actually shifted in favor of the fleet. Well-constructed works could still defy the power of large-caliber naval ordnance while inflicting disproportionate damage on vessels and crews. Initially, the Navy did not attempt to use amphibious assault to take such well-defended seaports as Charleston and Wilmington, where shoals, mines, and ingenious channel obstructions prevented a run-by in the style of Farragut at New Orleans. After General McClellan's departure, the Army was always reluctant to spare troops, and besides, the Navy could obtain more popular acclaim by capturing those cities single-handed.

For civilian policy makers Secretary of the Navy Gideon Welles and Assistant Secretary Gustavus Fox, the concern with public opinion went beyond a mere question of prestige. With England likely to intervene on behalf of the South, a strong fleet was thought essential for national survival; but the fast ships and modern guns needed to challenge the Royal Navy's sea hegemony were expensive and Congressional appropriations were likely to be granted in proportion to the Navy's demonstrated ability to win battles. Although the blockade was lucrative in prize money for officers and crews, it was tedious and undramatic; policing the coast is hardly the stuff of which newspaper headlines, promotions, or national heroes are made. Transporting and assisting the Army was little more glamorous. The Navy's role in the war was especially frustrating to nineteenth-century American sailors raised in the "fighting" tradition of John Paul Jones, Stephen Decatur, and Oliver Hazard Perry.

John Ericsson's new floating batteries, the "monitor" ironclads, although designed to protect American harbors from incursions by the Royal Navy or by Confederate vessels, seemed to offer a better alternative. The dramatic ship engagement in Hampton Roads in March 1862 demonstrated more than the already known fact that armored ships could sink wooden vessels. The powerful batteries at Newport News made no impression on the *Virginia*'s casemate, while the Confederate guns on Sewell's Point likewise failed to damage the *Monitor*. Convinced that the monitors were invulnerable to gunfire, Secretary Welles and his overzealous assistant supposed that several of these marvelous engines of war could steam past any number of heavy shore batteries and threaten any port in North America. They thus ignored Du Pont's repeated warnings that the ironclads' defensive properties did not compensate for their offensive weakness.

The abortive naval attack on Charleston in April 1863, however, convinced the Navy Department of its error. It was the

Union's last attempt to take a fortified position without some Army cooperation. But, while tactical reality dictated a return to combined operations, it did not alter the Navy's (or Army's) strategic thinking. Whatever strategy the Army might choose to pursue against the Confederacy, the Navy was still determined to take the remaining Confederate seaports, and to take them head on. The decision to attack the enemy at his strongest point, instead of at some weak spot in his defensive system, was a new approach to amphibious warfare—an approach which, in the twentieth century, would become the distinctive characteristic of U.S. combined operations doctrine.

For the element of surprise, impossible to attain against strong positions where the enemy had been long prepared, and in the absence of a large attacking army, United States forces substituted overwhelming fire, hoping to crush the defenses or make it too "hot" for the enemy to remain in them. This technique worked against Battery Wagner, where the fleet's fire was used for interdiction, allowing the work to be captured by siege. But it was a tedious method, costly to the assailants in worn-out ships and exhausted men. Furthermore, Union planners had not foreseen the magnitude of the preparations and the huge quantity of materiel required for success; thus, the Union was unable to exploit the initial victory. Nevertheless, the operations against Charleston were an important step in the evolution of combined tactics.

The failure of the first attack on Fort Fisher in late 1864 reemphasized the need for thorough advance planning and preparations, to assure an adequate flow of supplies and reinforcements, continuous fire superiority, and careful coordination of all elements in the assault. As a result, in the second Fort Fisher operation the Union used a technique much more effective than the exhausting combination of interdiction fire and siege—the close support bombardment. But the campaign had a significance aside from this tactical innovation. Because the strategic value of the Cape Fear River was finally appreciated by the Army high command before the second attack, no effort or means were spared to ensure success, to consolidate the position once taken, and to build up forces at the beachhead for a further advance. Thus, for the only time in the war, efficient combined tactics became, in its closing months, the servant of an intelligent combined strategy.

Regrettably, this success came too late to demonstrate the true potential of amphibious warfare. Because the Confederacy was defeated not by a highly mobile and flexible water-based strategy, but instead by a massive plodding territorial invasion, the experience and techniques developed by Union forces during the Civil War were quickly discarded and virtually forgotten.

PART ONE

The Evolution of Combined Strategy

1

THE ANACONDA

THE OUTBREAK of the American Civil War caught both sides unprepared and, paradoxically, the people of both the seceding states and the Union states, if not their governments, anticipated a short conflict. Yet, despite the lack of preparations, it would be wrong to assume, as some historians do, that neither belligerent had formulated any war plans or strategy, however vaguely expressed in operational terms. Because the conflict began as an "insurrection," or in Southern eyes, as a legitimate rebellion against the existing authority of the Federal government, the new Confederate States of America had only to prove that it could maintain its declared integrity as an independent nation by protecting its citizens and their property. This was the Confederacy's main war aim, and it dictated the South's initially defensive strategy. The primary aim of the United States, on the other hand, was to reassert the Federal government's authority over the seceded states; it therefore adopted an offensive strategy.

Since amphibious warfare is almost always an offensive technique, both strategically and tactically, it is not surprising —waterborne capability aside—that combined operations formed no part of the South's original strategic thought. Such operations were an essential element in the initial Federal war strategy, however, and remained so until the summer of 1862. But it would be misleading to suppose that the conception of combined operations remained unchanged from April 1861 until July 1862, or that the United States armed forces began the Civil War with a recognition of their full strategic potential.

The legacy of the past, always a powerful influence on initial operations, was, in this instance, relatively recent experience.

In fact, the first six months of the Civil War might be regarded, from the standpoint of strategy and operations, as a continuation in greatly expanded proportions of the Mexican War. The general-in-chief of the United States Army, Brevet Lieutenant General Winfield Scott, had commanded the land forces in the Mexican War, while prominent senior naval officers like Captain Samuel F. Du Pont had important roles in that conflict. These two men, under whose leadership the initial Union strategy was devised, seemed to assume that what had worked against Mexico in 1847 would work equally well against the Confederacy in 1861. There were many apparent points of resemblance between these two enemies. In both cases, the area of operations was large, with vast regions of difficult, sparsely inhabited terrain; and there were two fairly distinct theaters of war, separated by geographical barriers which precluded exact coordination of military operations. Both had extensive coastlines with only a few important seaports, and a number of navigable rivers penetrating into the interior. Both depended largely on foreign commerce, but neither had a respectable navy nor the means to produce one in a hurry.

Scott's plans, and Du Pont's, reflected these parallels with the Mexican War and the Lincoln administration accepted their strategic ideas almost without question. As the Mexicans were subdued by a combination of blockade, raiding operations, and a seaborne expedition culminating in seizure of the Mexican capital, so the Confederacy would succumb to a like formula of blockade, amphibious forays along the Atlantic and Gulf coasts, and a great combined expedition down the Mississippi terminating in the occupation of the South's largest city and major seaport, New Orleans.

Some coordination of the U.S. Army and Navy was thus made necessary by the nature of the Union government's political aims and the plans drawn up by the War and Navy departments. The expedition to open the Mississippi and capture New Orleans necessarily included a gunboat flotilla, while implementation of the blockade of Southern seaports proclaimed by President Lincoln on 19 April 1861 required the cooperation of Federal troops to seize and hold coaling stations and harbors of refuge for the blockading squadrons on the Atlantic coast, south of Hampton Roads, Virginia.

Still, this traditional concept of interservice cooperation was far from representing a truly integrated combined strategy. Although on occasion it was thought expedient or necessary for the Army to "help" the Navy and vice versa, both services continued to regard their combat roles and objectives as completely separate.

Most of the men who volunteered for the Army under Lincoln's call to the state governors in April 1861 enlisted for three months, and the government had determined on only a small increase of 25,000 in the regular army. Thus General Scott, in formulating his so-called "Anaconda" plan, relied heavily on the blockade to force the Confederate states back into the Union. Moreover, in a memorandum written in March to Secretary of State William H. Seward, Scott had rejected the idea of invading and conquering the South. Not only would such a strategy require a three-hundred-thousand-man army, years of bitter conflict, and a huge national debt, but it would devastate the South and embitter its people for generations. The effect of the blockade, on the other hand, would be indirect and inexpensive; few people would be killed and the economic resources of the South would remain intact. The idea was to "strangle" the Confederacy by closing off all external trade.[1]

To complete the investment on the land side, Federal troops had to hold the line of the Ohio River and gain control of the Mississippi. By the first of May Scott had devised a basic plan for the Mississippi River expedition, to begin in early November. The intervening months would be used to train sixty thousand regular troops and three-year volunteers, build gunboats, and set up depots. Progressing down the river, the combined expedition would turn all of the enemy's fortified posts and shore batteries by water, leaving small garrisons to keep open its line of communications. Finally, the expedition would occupy New Orleans and reduce Forts Jackson and St. Philip below the city, allowing the expeditionary force to link up with the Union squadron blockading in the Gulf of Mexico, thus completing the encirclement of the Confederacy.[2]

On 21 May Scott sent more definite instructions to Major General George B. McClellan, then commanding the Ohio troops, who was expected to prepare and lead the expedi-

Lieutenant General   Major General
Winfield Scott   George B. McCellan
(*National Archives*)   (*National Archives*)

tion. This version of the plan contained significant alterations. While the first plan had envisaged a single waterborne column, the new instructions called for two columns of unequal size, a total of 80,000 men. The smaller waterborne column, preceded and flanked by fast, powerful gunboats, would steam down the river while the larger supporting column marched along the left bank, receiving its bulk supplies by water. Scott acknowledged in this memorandum that the progress of the land column, marching without benefit of rail transport, through difficult country, encumbered with a large baggage train, would be exceedingly slow. Because the river force was to stay abreast the land column, the march would greatly retard the entire expedition. Nevertheless, he insisted upon this mode of operation.[3]

Since he did not state his reasons for changing the original plan, one can only assume that it was prompted by his belief that waterborne landings of small bodies of troops would be insufficient to capture the enemy's fortified river posts—an assumption which was proved sound by the subsequent experience of Federal combined forces on the Mississippi. Whether the second plan was any more practicable than the first, however, is doubtful. A march by 50,000 men over nearly eight hundred miles of boggy ground interlaced with creeks, marshes, and bayous, while the enemy used his railroads to mass on their flanks and rear, invited not only delay and attrition from disease and exhaustion, but disaster at one or more points along the river. Moreover, it would hardly have been possible, even in the winter of 1861, to have reduced *en passant* sizeable fortified towns like Columbus, Vicksburg, Port Hudson, and Baton Rouge, not to mention the expedition's ultimate objective: the metropolis of New Orleans. Thus it was probably fortunate for the Union that the Mississippi River expedition as conceived by General Scott was never attempted. Although preparations began promptly at St. Louis, Cairo, and Cincinnati, other events and considerations intervened during the next four months to change the direction and character of Union grand strategy.

The other half of the Anaconda, the coastal blockade, was, according to the prevalent division of command function, the responsibility of the Navy Department. At about the time Scott issued his final instructions to McClellan regarding the western expedition, the Navy Department's chief clerk, Gustavus V. Fox, soon to become assistant secretary of the Navy and a prime force in the formulation of strategy, received a letter from Alexander Dallas Bache, superintendent of the United States Coast Survey, proposing the establishment of an advisory council to devise specific measures for implementing the blockade. This proposal seems to have been the brain child of Secretary of the Treasury Salmon P. Chase. At that time, the Coast Survey was a bureau of the Treasury Department and, from the beginning of the war, Chase had taken a lively interest in military affairs. He was especially concerned about the economic implications for the Union of the blockade and of Confederate control of southern seaport trade. Bache convinced the Navy to support his proposal, arguing that the Coast Survey could furnish hydrographic charts and other information necessary for the seizure of South Atlantic harbors, and could assist the Navy in sounding and marking the approach channels.[4]

Fox, who was anxious for some aggressive naval action to

compensate for his failure in April to save Fort Sumter, moved quickly to establish this board, and its first meeting was held in Washington around the end of May. The board, variously referred to as the Blockade Board, the Strategy Board, and the Committee on Conference, consisted of the chairman, Captain Du Pont, Major John G. Barnard of the United States Engineer Corps, Professor Bache, and the board secretary, Commander Charles Henry Davis.[5]

Through June and July, the Blockade Board met several times a week. With prodigious energy, it surveyed the characteristics and operational possibilities of the entire Atlantic and Gulf seaboard from Cape Henry just south of Hampton Roads to the Mississippi delta. It produced five reports of observations and recommendations. The first three, dated 5, 13, and 16 July 1861, were the most important.[6] Secretary of the Navy Gideon Welles had instructed the committee to select two points on the South Atlantic coast to be occupied as coaling stations, stores depots, and harbors of refuge.

Going somewhat beyond the range of its directive, the board in its first report recommended two separate expeditions of a different character: one to seize Fernandina, Florida for purposes of the blockade; the other, a "purely military expedition" to occupy some point of greater strategic importance. Both expeditions were to be conducted simultaneously. The main body of the report discusses the advantages of Fernandina. Because this place was not meant to serve as a base for operations on the mainland, the fact that it was situated "on an island, bounded by the ocean on one side, and having on the other an interior, poor and uninviting in all respects, sparse in population, remote from large cities or centers of military occupation, and not easily accessible by railroad or water communications" made it an ideal location for a naval station. The same considerations clearly indicate that no follow-up was possible or envisaged in preparing this expedition.[7]

There is some confusion regarding the other expedition of a "purely military character," however. The second report discusses the respective advantages of occupying Bull's Bay (just north of Charleston harbor), St. Helena Sound (midway between Charleston and Savannah), and Port Royal, South Carolina (just north of Savannah). After an exhaustive examination of these three locations from the standpoint of defense and easy ocean access, the board recommended permanent occupation of Bull's Bay and St. Helena, also as naval stations for the blockade. An operation to capture Port Royal, although considered desirable from the military point of view, was rejected as too ambitious.

Despite its designation of the South Carolina expedition as "military," as distinct from the "purely naval" operation against Fernandina, the committee did not, in fact, make any great distinction between them in selecting the point of debarkation. The same considerations of defensibility and easy access to the sea were paramount in both cases. Nor was there any suggestion of follow-up operations on the mainland against the coastal railroad or against Charleston or Savannah, although all three harbors considered in the second report were admirably situated to serve as bases for such operations.[8]

The third report is interesting in the light of subsequent operations in the North Carolina Sounds. Due to the peculiar nature of this coastline, formed by long seaward sandbars with narrow inlets opening into extensive inland waters, it was thought advisable to close off most of the coast, leaving only two or three points to be watched by the blockading squadron. As to the value of this region for military or other purposes, the board stated that the sole importance of "the sterile and halfdrowned shores of North Carolina" lay in the connection through the sounds with Norfolk and Richmond. But the possibility of using these sounds and their tributary rivers and canals to attack these cities either was not considered or was rejected. Instead, at the suggestion of Assistant Secretary Fox, it was decided to obstruct the channels by sinking old ships loaded with stone, thus isolating the various sounds from the sea and from one another, and interrupting the enemy's coasting trade. The only reference to possible offensive operations in this region is the suggestion that, before closing the most important inlets—Hatteras and Ocracoke—the government should decide whether such operations were desired; the committee, however, advised against them because the region was poor and unhealthy for Northerners.[9]

With the program thus set by the Blockade Board, around the end of July Secretary of War Simon Cameron appointed

Brigadier General Thomas W. Sherman to command the troops requested by the Navy for the expeditions against Bull's Bay, St. Helena, and Fernandina. Although Du Pont was not officially assigned command of the fleet until September, it was already understood that he was to have the job.[10]

In early August, several conferences were held in Washington under the auspices of General Scott. Present, besides Scott, Sherman, and Du Pont, were the Army's chief engineer, Brigadier General Joseph A. Totten, the quartermaster general, Montgomery Meigs, and Sherman's second-in-command, Brigadier General Horatio G. Wright. After studying the first two Blockade Board reports, it was determined, according to Sherman's later testimony,

> that no ulterior operations by land were to be considered in getting up this expedition; that is, any ulterior operations that would probably be demanded by circumstances, were not to be anticipated at that time; and therefore no preparations were to be made for anything of the sort . . . All the preparations to be made were simply with reference to the seizure and occupation of these two important harbors [Bull's Bay and Fernandina]; . . .[11]

The number of troops required for the expeditionary force was estimated at 12,000, and the target date of its departure from New York set for 7 September.

A number of divergent plans, however, had already begun to undermine the simple concept of the Anaconda. General Scott had envisaged no offensives in Virginia; with the Federal capital securely held, the war would be decided elsewhere by indirect means. Brigadier General Irwin McDowell disagreed. A proper West Pointer, McDowell was an able and ambitious professional soldier, with important political connections. In May, two months before Horace Greeley's *New York Tribune* proclaimed "Forward to Richmond!" as the battle cry of an impatient public, McDowell had submitted his own plan for a campaign in Virginia; not, incidentally, to his superior, General Scott, but to Secretary Chase. Reminding Chase that he had been promised field command of the Union army in Virginia, he outlined a plan for seizing and fortifying strategic points close to Washington: Alexandria, the line of the Rappahannock River, and Manassas Junction at the intersection of the Orange and Alexandria Railroad running north from Richmond and the short line through Thoroughfare Gap from Manassas to Strasburg in the Shenandoah Valley.[12]

Although McDowell's plan was obviously defensive and did not appear very ambitious or likely to compromise Scott's basic strategy, it was the initial step in the Federal movement which led to the first battle of Bull Run (Manassas). More important, perhaps, than the actual plan was the undermining of the general-in-chief's authority, a regrettable precedent too frequently copied by successive department commanders, almost always to the detriment of the Union war effort. With this new project in the wind and General McClellan's campaign in western Virginia underway, made necessary by Confederate activity against the Baltimore and Ohio Railroad in mid-May, the U.S. Army suddenly found its hands full, without having yet undertaken a major coast expedition.[13]

Needless to say, this preoccupation with land warfare did not please the Navy, nor did it satisfy Major General Benjamin F. Butler, commanding a small Union force at Fort Monroe, Virginia. Having driven an even smaller Confederate detachment under Colonel John B. Magruder out of Newport News, Butler attempted to exploit this success by breaking up Magruder's fortified camp at Big Bethel where his undisciplined little army was soundly repulsed on 10 June. To salvage his reputation (and for other reasons discussed in Chapter 2) Butler almost immediately submitted a memorandum to his friend, Secretary of War Cameron, informing him that the Confederates were fortifying Hatteras Inlet on the North Carolina coast as a base for Southern privateers, and proposing a combined raid to destroy the forts. In early August, the Navy Department accepted Butler's proposal, agreeing to furnish a squadron to bombard the Hatteras forts.[14]

At this early stage in the war, the U.S. Navy had not succumbed to "bombardment fever." Since the old doctrine that naval gunfire alone could not reduce land batteries was still taken for granted, a cooperating infantry force was presumed essential. Butler was therefore authorized to prepare a detachment of 860 infantry and an artillery company with ten days' rations, to assist the fleet in capturing the works. Once occupied, the inlet would be permanently closed by stone ships in accordance with the Blockade Board's recommendation.[15] Permanent occupation or follow-up operations in the sounds, were ruled out at that time, both by Fox's immediate action to procure the stone hulks and by Butler's orders of 25 August from his new superior now commanding at Fort Monroe, Brigadier General John E. Wool. Butler was instructed in no uncertain terms to return to Fort Monroe with his whole force "as soon as the object of the expedition is attained."[16]

Because the successful capture of the Hatteras forts, the first Civil War combined operation, established a pattern scarcely broken until the summer of 1863, it is important to describe and evaluate its significant features in some detail.

The defenses of Hatteras Inlet consisted of two unfinished works: the main battery, Fort Hatteras, commanding the eastern side of the channel, a 250-foot square earthen redoubt armed with twelve short-range 32-pounder smoothbore cannon; and a smaller earthwork, Fort Clark, situated 700 yards to the east [seaward], armed with two 6-pounders and five 32s. The guns were all *en barbette* separated by light traverses, and a bombproof had been built for the troops. There were, at the time of the attack, 580 men in both garrisons, commanded by Flag Officer Samuel Barron of the Confederate States Navy, with his headquarters at Fort Hatteras.[17]

The Federal plan of attack called for a covering bombardment by a fleet under Commodore Silas Stringham comprising the steam frigates *Minnesota* (flag, 47 guns) and *Wabash* (46 guns), the sloop *Cumberland* (24), the sidewheel steamer *Susquehanna* (15), and the gunboat *Pawnee* (9). While the cannonade was in progress, General Butler would disembark his troops on the open beach approximately three miles north of Fort Clark, covered by the gunboats *Monticello* and *Harriet Lane*, Butler's flagship. The landing craft were surf boats and navy launches procured from the squadron and handled by seamen, some of whom, along with a small marine contingent, would support the infantry in its assault on the forts.

Arriving outside Hatteras bar on 27 August, Butler prepared to disembark while Stringham reconnoitered the approach to the inlet to determine the best bombardment station. It was discovered that the warships, drawing eighteen to twenty feet, could approach no closer than one mile off Fort Hatteras. Since Fort Clark was slightly closer and more exposed, the fleet's fire was concentrated against this work first. The bombardment opened at 10 A.M. on the 28th. Imitating tactics used in the Allied bombardment of Odessa during the Crimean War, Stringham's squadron steamed in a circle to spoil the enemy's aim. Expecting the Federals to approach closer, Flag Officer Barron held the fire of Fort Hatteras for some time since none of its guns could reach the fleet. The defenders in Fort Clark, however, opened almost immediately and in two hours of hot firing expended their ammunition. Because the defenders' guns were small and nearly all their fire fell short, the ships sustained only minor damage. At 12:25, the Confederates abandoned Fort Clark, taking refuge in the main work.

Meanwhile, at 11:30, Butler began disembarking his troops. A heavy surf was breaking on the beach. Two iron boats were swamped and two flat boats broken up. The *Pawnee*'s launch ran aground and could not be got off. Butler himself was about to land when he learned that the remaining boats were stove. Despite the difficulties, 315 men got ashore including some regular artillery and 55 Marines along with two boat howitzers. The men were disorganized, soaked to the skin, and without provisions. At 2 P.M. a Federal company took posses-

Attack on the Hatteras Forts

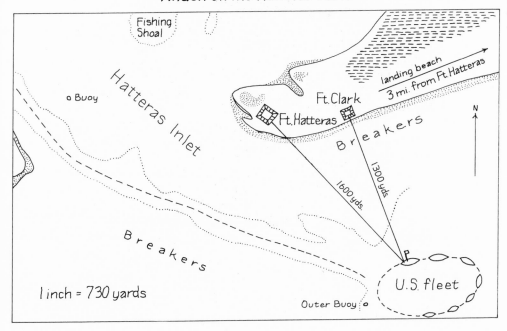

sion of the abandoned Fort Clark and set up the boat howitzers, along with an unspiked cannon from the fort, on the beach commanding the approach to Fort Hatteras via Pamlico Sound.

Stringham continued to bombard Hatteras without much effect. One gunboat trying to pass into the rear of the fort through the inlet was driven off by the Confederate gunners. By 6 P.M. the wind was blowing so hard that the squadron was forced to haul off for the night. The troops, most of whom had remained near the landing point, could not be taken off, nor could provisions be got to them, the men spending a miserable night on the open beach without food. Finding the sea calmer next morning, the Federal warships resumed their bombardment at 8 A.M. At first their broadsides consistently fell short because of the long range. Then the ships fired their pivot guns at extreme elevation producing a plunging fire against the work, which dismounted two guns and threatened to break through the magazine. At 1:30, Fort Hatteras surrendered. Since the garrison had no transport and none could be sent to it because the Union howitzers north of the forts had interrupted enemy communications via the sound, all the men were taken along with the work.[18]

Although physical damage to the fleet and to the forts was insignificant, the attack demonstrated, to the Union Navy Department at least, that shore batteries could be reduced by naval bombardment alone. Due to the foul weather and their lack of experience in landing on an open beach, the "cooperating" troops had proved more of a handicap than an asset, except for the interdicting fire of the boat howitzers, which could have been managed by a handful of Marines. What the Federals did not appreciate was that these forts, improperly sited, poorly constructed, and badly armed, were indefensible against any kind of attack in force. Aside from the fact that Barron's guns could not reach the Federal squadron, the fog and constant dampness on that coast had so soaked the powder in the fort's magazines that it would hardly burn. The exposed situation of the batteries and the threat of isolation and capture demoralized the defenders to such an extent that, in their panic, they neglected to destroy stores and spike the guns before surrendering.[19]

As a *combined* operation, this first Union expedition was a tactical failure; indeed, with a little more initiative the Confederates might have captured the wretched landing party and its light battery during the night of 28 August. The Union's plans for disembarking troops were clearly inadequate, despite prior knowledge that water and wind conditions at Hatteras were seldom ideal for small boats. The failure to land provisions with the first contingent put ashore, or to ensure that the officers accompanied their men in the boats, also demonstrate a gross lack of foresight which marks the expedition as an amateurish operation, in the style of an eighteenth-century raid. It is little wonder that the Navy began to doubt the necessity, or even the desirability, of amphibious operations when it appeared that warships alone could accomplish the same ends more efficiently. Moreover, the publicity attending this first real Northern victory of the war, focused attention on the fleet's offensive capability, a development not at all displeasing to the Navy Department.

Despite the Blockade Board's views, the successful seizure of Hatteras Inlet immediately raised the question of what to do with it. As frequently happens in war, the Navy Department's plans to carry out a limited operation were undermined, even before the forts fell, by the ambitions of the men on the spot. General Butler, who had thought that combined operation were best employed in harassing raids involving no permanent occupation,[20] suddenly decided that Hatteras was an admirable base for further operations and should not fall victim to the "stone fleet" already being prepared by Commander H.S. Stellwagen. Stringham shared this opinion, for another reason: the blockading squadron needed a coaling station south of Hampton Roads, and Hatteras could be held, if properly fortified, by a small infantry force. Consequently, while Butler applied direct political pressure in Washington, Stringham strongly urged Welles to consider the permanent occupation of both Hatteras and Ocracoke Inlets, using the stone fleet only to block less important exits from the inland waters.[21]

Although this was undoubtedly sound strategy from a local point of view and Welles was persuaded of its advantages, it ran afoul of Lincoln's blockade policy. Numerous complaints that the blockade was not being enforced for lack of vessels or of naval initiative worried both the secretary of State whose consular agents in Liverpool, London, and Paris warned of increasing pressure for intervention, and the secretary of the Treasury whose office was deluged with protests from Northern revenue collectors, marine insurance underwriters, and New York and New England shippers interested in stopping illegal commerce and seizure of their vessels.[22]

The administration's problem was simple. If Union success at Hatteras was followed up, even to the extent of holding it as a base, a naval squadron would be required to command the sounds, leaving fewer ships for blockade duty. The Atlantic Squadron was already stretched so thin that some important enemy ports, notably Wilmington, North Carolina, remained almost completely open.

Welles thought the solution equally simple. Before the Hatteras expedition, he had urged that Lincoln abandon the blockade policy proclaimed at the beginning of the war and declare Confederate ports "closed" by act of Congress. This would deny the Southerners belligerent status and the protection of international law. Under existing blockade regulations, Union naval officers were required to warn vessels flying foreign flags and enter the warning in the ship's log. A vessel could be seized only if it attempted to run into a blockaded port after an official warning. Otherwise, the cases were thrown out in the prize courts. Many foreign ships, finding a particular Southern harbor closed, simply proceeded until they found one temporarily unguarded.[23]

Such regulations naturally frustrated the Navy. The country did not understand the problems involved, and newspaper attacks upon the department for its supposed inefficiency embarrassed the government and encouraged its political enemies. Claiming the Federal government's continued authority over all the states and declaring the Confederate States in insurrection, Lincoln might indeed have closed the ports; in July Congress had authorized the president to issue such a proclamation. But Lincoln saw what Welles did not. First, the Confederate port authorities would ignore the proclamation unless it was enforced by direct naval action, a policy requiring the same number of vessels as the blockade. Second, removing the incentive for patrol duty—the prize money from captured ships—would weaken the Navy, since many of the officers and seamen serving with the fleet were in the merchant marine. Finally, such a measure would prove highly unpopular with certain politically and financially powerful Northern merchants covertly engaged in triangular traffic with the Confederacy.[24]

While the politicians thus argued over policy and the strategy necessary to implement that policy, the military situation in the sounds was developing independently. Unaware that neither the Army nor the administration were interested in exploiting Federal control of Hatteras Inlet, Commander S.C. Rowan, commanding the U.S. gunboat *Pawnee*, and Colonel Rush Hawkins, commanding the small army contingent left to garrison the post, were concocting ambitious schemes for extending Union control to the far shores of Albemarle and Pamlico Sounds, culminating in offensives to take Beaufort, and even Norfolk.[25]

Sensing that General Scott was reluctant to detach troops from the army guarding Washington, Rowan urged these offensive schemes upon his immediate superior, Flag Officer Stringham, as necessary defensive measures. The capture of Hatteras had alarmed both the Confederate government and the local authorities. North Carolina troops serving in Johnston's army in Virginia were returning to defend their state. Confederate engineers were fortifying Beaufort and New Berne, and were building shallow-draft gunboats to control the inland waters.[26] With more vessels and a few more soldiers, Rowan and Hawkins could stop this activity before the enemy became strong enough to resist, or worse, to recapture Hatteras. Two more heavily armed fast tugboats to complement the Army's steam tug *Fanny*, some landing barges, and a regiment or two of infantry were all that was required. The requested reinforcements were very meagre, considering the value of the objective, the likely effect on Confederate morale, the diversion of the enemy's main army from threatening the Federal capital, and the interdiction of the whole North Carolina seaboard with its booming coastal trade.[27]

Such arguments convinced Stringham and he was inclined to approve Rowan's initiative. So was General Wool, whose ultimate goal was Norfolk. Although the phlegmatic Scott was predictably disinterested, still confident that the war would be won by blockade if the Confederates were kept out of Washington and Baltimore, Welles was receptive to the idea. The unexpectedly successful bombardment of the Hatteras forts had greatly improved the Navy's press image, at least for the moment. The value of sea power had been dramatically revealed to the nation and the Congress. Appropriations for ironclad vessels were speedily approved. The thankless job of chasing elusive blockade-runners could hardly compare with the more glamorous task of capturing Beaufort or Norfolk. Unlike Fox, Welles was not especially susceptible to grandiose schemes; but the logical extension of Federal combined operations in the sounds appeared to require no great expenditure of means. Nor would it compromise the blockade. On the contrary, it would ultimately free ships currently employed along the North Carolina coast for duty elsewhere.[28]

Lincoln disagreed and, of course, his opinion was decisive. The eventual effect of the projected operations was all very well, provided the war lasted long enough for the effect to be felt. The immediate situation, however, made this assumption uncertain. The British, worried about their textile industry, were actively searching for evidence that the proclaimed blockade was ineffective. Any admission by the Federal government that it could not enforce its authority at sea would probably lead to British recognition of the Confederacy in return for important commercial concessions which would damage Northern business. French recognition would doubtless follow.

The Union's power to implement its policies was equally important at home. Financial credit was closely tied to political credit, and government contracts backed by a shaky administration were not attractive. Nor were the New York financial houses upon which the Federal government depended for operating funds anxious to underwrite what looked like a bad investment.[29] At this point in the war, Lincoln could not afford the risk of sacrificing political goals for military expedients, or abandoning his immediate concerns for long-range objectives, however promising they might seem. It was, therefore, unmistakably impressed upon the secretary of the Navy that it was government policy to strengthen the blockade and that the Navy's first (and, for the moment, only) duty was to enforce this policy. All other plans and projects would have to await a more favorable political climate.[30]

Furthermore, General-in-Chief Scott disapproved of diversionary operations; in fact, he disapproved of all offensive operations. The whole Army was needed to protect Washington. It was not fit for the field, as the Bull Run debacle had demonstrated. Besides, he was now convinced that to win its independence and foreign recognition, the Confederacy must take the offensive; its armies must invade the North before they melted away from inactivity or lack of supplies. The North's proper strategy was to wait, and when the Southerners found they could not take Washington or other Northern cities, they would give up.[31]

This proper West Point doctrine might have worked if the blockade had been really effective, if the South had contained no "bitter-enders" in the army or government, or if President Jefferson Davis had followed the advice of his fellow West Pointers to launch an immediate invasion of the North with an inexperienced army, badly supplied and inadequately armed. Unfortunately for the Union, Davis was not permitted to adopt the "correct" military strategy during the first year of the war. The governors of the Confederate border states and their Congressmen felt that the new nation could not survive unless it protected its citizens and their property. This meant guarding the frontiers, erecting permanent fortifications, and following a defensive strategy for Southern field armies.[32]

On 16 September, Stringham, disgusted with the Navy Department's criticism of the blockade and vaguely aware that his ideas were unwelcome in Washington, offered his resignation, which Welles gratefully accepted. The secretary had already concluded that the long South Atlantic seaboard was too much responsibility for one head and he intended dividing the command into two squadrons as earlier recommended by the Blockade Board.[33] Also, he had been anxious for some time to replace the aging seniors on the Navy list with younger, presumably more energetic officers. The men selected to command the North and South Atlantic Blockading Squadrons, Captains Louis M. Goldsborough and Samuel F. Du Pont, were considered the most capable and experienced of their rank; more important, both agreed that the Navy's first duty was

North Carolina
Sounds

blockade.[34] To further discourage the advocates of amphibious operations, Commander Rowan was ordered transferred to the Potomac River Squadron as of 5 October. But the change came just too late to prevent a minor disaster to the combined Union force in the sounds. Of seemingly insignificant proportions at the time, this reverse would soon require a far greater expenditure of time and means than Rowan and Hawkins ever intended.

Roanoke Island, which lies between Pamlico and Albemarle sounds and commands the communicating channel, was the strategic key to the region. Upon discovering that the Confederates were erecting batteries on its southwestern shore, Colonel Hawkins decided to drive them off before the defenses were completed and armed. On 29 September, with Rowan's approval, he detached 300 men to occupy an advanced position at Chicomicomico, forty miles north of Hatteras, where they could observe enemy activity. Expecting six tugboats requisitioned on 5 September to arrive at any moment, Rowan did not anticipate any problems in maintaining this force or controlling the waters of Pamlico Sound. In fact, he supposed that the vessels would permit Hawkins to transport enough reinforcements from Hatteras to drive the Southerners off the island and occupy their unfinished works.

But the tugs did not arrive. Rowan had discovered on 26 September that the only two sent him were seized by Captain J.S. Chauncey, who was in charge of the Union squadron blockading outside Hatteras bar. While Rowan negotiated for the tugs, the Union troops at Chicomicomico waited for their supplies; finally, in desperation, on 1 October Hawkins dispatched his only armed boat, the *Fanny*. Seeing their opportunity, three weak Confederate gunboats stationed in Pamlico Sound closed in on the *Fanny*, forcing her aground near Loggerhead Inlet. They captured the vessel intact, with her crew and some welcome provisions. Rowan in the *Pawnee* returned to Hatteras with the tugboats on the same day, only to discover that forty of Hawkins' isolated soldiers were now prisoners, the rest of them dispersed, and that the Confederate squadron with the addition of its valuable prize now outnumbered his own, forcing him to take refuge within range of the Hatteras forts.[35]

The last act in this farce of mismanagement was played out on the following day. Commander Stellwagen finally appeared before Hatteras, still under imperative orders to sink the stone ships. Having made several heroic and entirely futile attempts to approach the inlet with his ponderous charges through the heavy surf, during which hawsers parted, men were thrown overboard, and his own ships stove in several places, he gave up in disgust, wiring the Navy Department that the whole idea was absurd and impossible and asking for a new command. He also warned Welles that, unless reinforced, the Federals must either evacuate Hatteras or be captured by the enemy, whose navy controlled the sounds and was mounting an offensive to retake the forts.[36]

The decision to hold Hatteras Inlet threatened to compromise Du Pont's expedition. Before the attack on Hatteras, Wool had requested more troops for his department; now it appeared that, unless reinforcements were sent to Hatteras, the Federal victory which had begun to pull the nation out of its depression following Bull Run might end in a humiliating retreat. In mid-September, at the urging of General McClellan, now commanding the Federal army in Virginia, Scott ordered General Sherman to report to Washington with the troops raised for the South Atlantic coast expedition. But Lincoln promptly overruled the general-in-chief. On 18 September, the same day Du Pont was officially given command of the South Atlantic Blockading Squadron, the president informed both Cameron and Welles that this expedition, so long in preparation and at such great expense, was in no circumstances to be given up.[37]

In any case, by 14 October the situation at Hatteras had stabilized. The Confederates had not moved. On 6 October Wool had sent reinforcements to the garrison along with a new commander, Brigadier General J.K.F. Mansfield, who replaced Hawkins. Scott had also supplied several light-draft steamers and more artillery. On the 14th, Mansfield reported Hatteras safe from attack, adding that, in his opinion, which Scott valued, the inlet was "no base for operations into the interior. All such commands, unless very strong, would be exposed to be cut off from supplies and it was a very circuitous route." He personally saw no point in disturbing the peaceful inhabitants of a few little towns.[38] Neither did the general-in-chief.

Oddly enough, with the final approval of his expedition to the South Atlantic coast, Du Pont began to entertain serious doubts about the result. It was one thing to propose and plan a major combined operation, but quite another to be given full responsibility for its execution. In early September, he had confessed to his wife that he was struck by the "extent of the responsibility put upon me" and suggested that he would have declined the command and remained on shore duty, except that "no service on shore, however useful, could be considered anything after the war." By 17 October, he openly admitted to her that he feared failure. Although as chairman of the Blockade Board he had rejected operations against Port Royal as too ambitious, and Welles's instructions of 12 October left the choice of destination to him and General Sherman, the Navy Department made it clear that, since the expedition had greatly expanded beyond the original conception, the country would expect some important result.[39]

Although Du Pont felt compelled to attack Port Royal, the fleet and stores ships which sailed from New York on 18 October to rendezvous with Sherman's troop transports in Hampton Roads were still divided into two separate divisions, one heading for Bull's Bay and one for Fernandina. While awaiting late arrivals and fair weather, the whole subject of objectives and methods was thoroughly discussed among the army and naval commanders. After much debate, it was decided to attack Port Royal, then Fernandina.[40] Du Pont later claimed that it was Sherman who doubted the fleet's fire capability against forts; however, Du Pont himself had been extremely worried about this problem ever since Welles and Fox urged him to attack Port Royal. On 18 September, he informed the secretary that he had little confidence in the squadron's offensive power and that because of the shoals he might be unable to use his large frigates like the flagship *Wabash* against the forts in the way that Stringham had done at Hatteras. He insisted upon having the U.S. steam sloops *Pawnee, Iroquois, Mohican,* and *Seminole,* each carrying at least one 11-inch gun, accompanied by three or four new gunboats. And because,

Brigadier General
Thomas W. Sherman
(*Library of Congress*)

Captain (later Rear Admiral)
Samuel F. Du Pont
(*National Archives*)

in his opinion, even this force along with the Army might prove insufficient, he also demanded and got a battalion of 300 Marines.[41]

Having selected the target, Du Pont decided to take the forts guarding the entrance to the harbor by combined tactics. In his anxiety to be prepared for anything, he had in August asked the constructor at the Philadelphia Navy Yard for advice about proper landing boats for the Army. After searching the Navy Department files on combined operations in the Mexican War, Thornton A. Jenkins advised him to use broad-beam shallow-draft whale boats and sent Du Pont drawings and specifications for them. Many such craft were built by the Navy, and Sherman also procured several New York ferry boats (double-enders, especially useful as landing craft); thus, a total of 500 boats were available, enough to carry a considerable number of men and field guns ashore in the first wave. Because Sherman's soldiers were totally inexperienced in amphibious warfare, a series of landing exercises was begun off Old Point Comfort, near Fort Monroe, on 25 October. These revealed many defects in organization and procedure which Sherman hoped to correct before reaching Port Royal.[42]

On 29 October the expedition, made up of fifty vessels including transports, sailed from Fort Monroe expecting to reach its destination in four days. Du Pont was still worried that he would have to reduce the harbor defenses by bombardment. "We have considerable power to carry on *offensive* warfare," he wrote Fox; "that of *endurance* against forts is not commensurate."[43] Because Du Pont depended on the troops to secure at least one side of the channel to protect his vessels from cross-fire, additional landing exercises were conducted at sea on the 30th. These showed a great improvement over the first maneuvers, partly restoring Du Pont's confidence in the whole enterprise.[44] But some fears persisted, and they were well founded; indeed, had it not been for the Confederates' own mismanagement in building up the Port Royal defenses, the battle might well have gone in just the way that Du Pont had feared.

The entrance to Port Royal harbor at the mouth of Broad River is flanked by several islands; the largest, Hilton Head

The USS *Wabash*

on the southwest side of the channel, consists of flat but mostly dry land unusual for this section of the coast. Across the river to the northeast is Bay Point (the southern end of St. Phillips Island), a small patch of solid ground separated by a large swampy area from St. Helena Island to the north at the entrance to the Beaufort River. The shortest distance between St. Helena and Bay Point is two and one-half miles.[45]

Before leaving to assume a field command in Virginia around the end of May, Confederate General P.G.T. Beauregard, then commanding at Charleston, carefully examined the South Carolina coast designating sites for coast defenses. Beauregard, one of the highest ranking officers in the Confederate Army, though an indifferent field officer, was a superb engineer. Having examined the Port Royal area in some detail, he pronounced the harbor entrance indefensible by shore batteries and advised that none be built. Governor Francis Pickens of South Carolina, naturally displeased with this assessment, persuaded the general to change his mind, but Beauregard insisted when approving the project that any works constructed must be very heavily armed and, because of poor communications, strong enough to withstand attack without reinforcement.[46] Having drawn the plans for two forts, the main work (Fort Walker) on Hilton Head Island and a smaller battery (Fort Beauregard) on Bay Point, General Beauregard turned the project over to Major Francis D. Lee of the Confederate States Engineers.

Work began in early July but, because of a labor shortage, the plantation owners being unwilling to provide the requested number of hands for more than a few days at a time, the forts were still unfinished at the time of attack. Armament was a more serious problem. Beauregard had designed Fort Walker to mount seven 10-inch columbiads *en barbette* in the water battery, each separated by a heavy earthen traverse to protect it from enfilade. The demand on the Confederate Ordnance Bureau for seacoast artillery during the first six months of the war was so pressing, however, that so many large guns could not be obtained; thus Major Lee was forced to substitute twelve smaller cannon, only one of them rifled, plus a single 10-inch columbiad, for the originally projected armament. Because the parapets and bastions were complete before the ordnance arrived in September, there was insufficient space on the waterfront for all the guns intended to compensate by volume of fire for their smaller caliber, unless the traverses were dispensed with. This expedient was adopted, leaving all thirteen guns vulnerable to enfilade; a long traverse was built behind the battery to guard against reverse fire.

Two 8-inch Navy howitzers on improvised carriages were placed in embrasure at the south (right) flank bastion, since this was thought to be the direction from which an approaching fleet would attempt to enfilade the main battery. Another 8-inch howitzer intended for the north (left) flank bastion arrived with no carriage and was not mounted at the time of the engagement. Two small carronades which had also been sent without carriages were dug into the sand flanking the sea front to guard against landing parties and two 12-pounders were placed to sweep the front of the glacis. For defense against infantry attack, the Confederates had planned lines of rifle pits about two miles south of the work. These were never completed, however, nor was a projected battery at the entrance to Skull Creek, west of the island. This waterway could lead shallow-draft gunboats into the rear of the whole position, allowing the Federals to cut off the garrison's retreat to the mainland.[47]

Fort Beauregard on Bay Point, commanding the approaches to the Broad and Beaufort rivers, was a smaller open earthwork, also incomplete, with four fronts all on the water. Its armament, also thirteen guns, was quite respectable for that time, consisting of one 10-inch and one 8-inch seacoast gun, five 42-pounders, five 32s, and a 6-inch rifle. Due to the great width of the channel, however, only the rifle had sufficient range to support Fort Walker against an attack by warships.[48]

For three days the Federal expedition, in almost perfect formation, sailed down the coast on schedule. Having passed through the dangerous sea off Cape Hatteras into the calm waters off South Carolina with their awkward troop transports and stores ships still intact, the sailors began to relax, and the soldiers, sick and nervous in strange and uncomfortable quarters, quit grumbling. Suddenly, just before noon on 1 November the wind hauled around to the southeast and increased within hours to gale velocity. Driving rain and fog reduced visibility to a few hundred yards, and the ships lost all formation, each striving to keep from being driven ashore, and a few desperately battling to stay afloat.

When the weather cleared, Du Pont's flagship was alone, the rest of the squadron having been dispersed. But during the course of the day on 3 November most of the fleet reappeared, and the following morning, having gathered twenty-five of his ships and with more coming in sight, Du Pont anchored off Port Royal bar, ten miles seaward of the harbor entrance. The only loss incurred by the Navy during the storm was to the USS *Isaac Smith*, whose crew had been forced to toss overboard her broadside battery, which included some of the few 30-pounder rifled cannon in the squadron, in order to stay afloat.

The Army was not so fortunate. While the U.S. Coast Survey vessel *Vixen* sounded the bar and shoals and marked the channel to the inner roadstead, and the large warships maneuvered into position on the 5th, General Sherman received some distressing reports. The vessels carrying most of the landing craft had been driven ashore on the 2nd, and two ships loaded with live cattle for the Army had sunk after their crews were rescued. The steamer *Belvidere*, carrying horses, had been forced to return to Fort Monroe, having thrown a number of her unfortunate charges overboard. The USS *Union*, loaded with gunpowder, had sunk the previous night. Worst of all, the quartermaster ship *Ocean Empress* was driven aground and wrecked, her crew reaching shore only to become prisoners. Contrary to Sherman's explicit instructions, much of the Army's artillery and all of its ordnance stores, along with all but one hundred rounds of small-arms ammunition per man (three million rounds), had been loaded by the quartermasters aboard this one vessel. Even the molds for casting bullets were lost.[49]

A final conference was held aboard the *Wabash* on the 6th. Sherman and his staff were humiliated and despondent. Without landing craft and ammunition, there could be no combined operations; the Army would be useless in capturing the forts. The fleet had to attack alone, the very prospect Du Pont had so greatly feared for months.[50] Perhaps Du Pont would have felt more confident if he had the Marine battalion, but the transport *Governor* carrying this unit had not yet arrived, and there were rumors that she had foundered. The *Isaac Smith*'s captain, Lieutenant J.W.A. Nicholson, came across the *Governor* on the 2nd and took her in tow until the blockading sloop *Sabine* arrived on the scene and took the Marines aboard. Nicholson reported with his vessel to Du Pont on the 4th indicating that, although the Marines were probably safe, they had lost their ammunition and equipment and would, in any case, arrive too late to help the Navy.[51] There was no alternative to reducing the forts by naval gunfire.

The attack opened at 8:30 A.M. on 7 November. The *Wabash* led the main squadron, ten ships carrying 123 guns, up the channel in column, bearing midway between the forts and out of range of every gun except the two rifles, one in each work; the flanking squadron, five gunboats carrying 34 guns, steamed close abreast. Du Pont's plan of attack called for all vessels to proceed to a point two and one-half miles north of Fort Beauregard, then the main squadron would turn southeast, steaming slowly past Fort Walker at a distance of 800 yards. Meanwhile, the gunboat squadron, remaining at the northern extremity of the circle, would endeavor to keep down the fire of Fort Beauregard and dispose of a few weak Confederate vessels which Flag Officer Josiah Tattnall had assembled at the mouth of Skull Creek to harass the fleet. The main squad-

Attack on Forts Walker and Beauregard

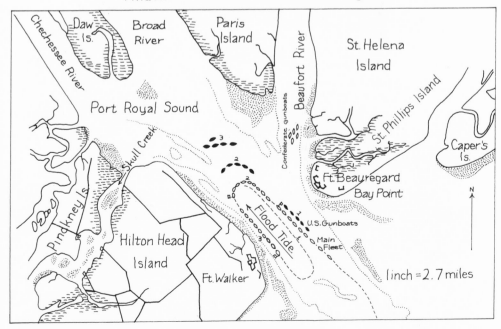

ron would make as many circuits as necessary, at decreasing range, to silence Fort Walker.[52]

On executing the first turn to the south, officers aboard the *Wabash* noticed that the fort's armament was unprotected against enfilade from the north. Du Pont immediately signalled the fleet to open on that flank, and as they passed, each ship in turn poured a terrific fire into the work. Soon after, Commander Daniel Ammen in the gunboat USS *Seneca*, having chased Tattnall's tiny squadron into the Beaufort River, also observed this weakness in Fort Walker; several of the Federal gunboats opened fire in this direction, while the others concentrated, with little effect, on Fort Beauregard. Once more the main squadron made the circuit, this time coming within 550 yards of Fort Walker. As it started north a third time at about 11:30, a white flag was observed over the work and the fleet ceased fire.[53]

Inside Fort Walker all was chaos. Although surprisingly little damage had been done to either the fort or the U.S. fleet, the defenders had experienced great difficulty with their own armament. Many guns were furnished with the wrong size ammunition, while others exploded due to mechanical accident after only a few rounds. Finding all but three cannon useless, and afraid of being cut off, the garrison quickly retreated to the mainland, bringing away their small arms, field guns, and provisions. They were not interfered with.[54]

Du Pont later claimed that he knew nothing about Skull Creek and blamed the Coast Survey for not indicating it on the charts. However, the charts drawn up for the Blockade Board in June 1861 clearly show this creek with a depth of water sufficient for some of the light-draft gunboats. Commander Ammen admitted that the fleet knew about Skull Creek, but maintained that its course was too tortuous for rapid pursuit.[55] Nevertheless, since it took the defending force several hours to get off the island after surrendering the fort, one wonders if a pursuit might not have been worth the attempt. The Navy Department certainly thought so, but it did not press the matter; after all, Du Pont had taken two forts and a fine harbor by naval power alone and was the hero of the hour. Consequently, this first minor indication of his overcautious disposition was ignored.

The garrison in Fort Beauregard remained at its post until 3:30 P.M. firing a few random shots which went unnoticed as the Marines hoisted the United States flag over Fort Walker. Deciding they could no longer affect the situation in the harbor, having received no orders, and fearing capture by Federal landing parties, the defenders spiked the guns, fired the magazine, and retreated through the swamps, arriving in Beaufort next morning.[56]

Du Pont's famous attack on the Port Royal defenses was well-managed and deserved the acclaim accorded it in the North. But while it is not too surprising that the simple fact of victory clouded the vision of Fox, Welles, and others in the Federal Cabinet, many historians seem to have inherited this peculiar myopia. Despite the success of this engagement, several points can not be too strongly emphasized. In the first place, Du Pont did not choose, nor would he have afterwards chosen, naval bombardment as the mode of attack; it was his least preferred tactic. Second, he did not know, when adopting the formation for his attack, that Fort Walker's water battery was open to enfilade, nor did he know that the guns in Fort Beauregard could not reach the fleet in mid-channel. To close the range before this was known would have meant severe damage to the squadron, had Fort Walker been armed as its designer intended.

Like the attack on Hatteras, the capture of Port Royal was not a combined operation in the tactical sense, although the Army was present to secure what the Navy had taken. The battle is nonetheless important to the history of Civil War combined operations for two reasons. Coming so soon after the Hatteras expedition, it reinforced, whether by accident or design, the pattern set by the first. Once again, it had been the Navy's role to reduce the shore defenses by bombardment, and the Army's to stand in the wings, ready for the occupation. This was a bad beginning for integrated amphibious operations, a very hard lesson to unlearn in the later stages of the war.

The other point of importance concerns the strategic effect and the strategic role of combined operations, whatever their tactical character. A large fleet and a fair-size army had secured a permanent foothold at a vital spot on the enemy's coast. This waterborne force pointed straight at the soul—if not the heart—of the Confederacy, Charleston, and to another place of only slightly less value, Savannah. How skillfully the Federals would use the mobility and power conferred by command of the sea, and to what end, remained to be defined.

2

THE ARMY TAKES THE INITIATIVE

THE APPOINTMENT of Major General George B. McClellan to succeed Scott as general-in-chief on 1 November 1861 marks a turning point in the development of Federal grand strategy. Although, as we have seen, Scott had a general plan for slowly strangling the Confederacy, he did not attempt to integrate land and naval operations. Expeditions designed to seize coastal stations to support the blockade had remained a wholly naval responsibility. The use of the Army in a grand march down the Mississippi to New Orleans—Scott's only idea for military operations—was killed in the old general's mind by the debacle at Bull Run. His one remaining thought was to save the Federal capital.

Thus for three months the Union and Confederate main armies stood on the defensive, and only the naval expeditions against Hatteras and Port Royal prevented a complete stalemate. McClellan's appointment changed everything. Under his direction the Federal Army formulated a comprehensive plan, in which combined operations, previously conducted in a haphazard manner with only limited objectives, became the essential ingredient.

Ever since McClellan's assignment in July to command the Army of the Potomac, he had grown increasingly critical of both the condition of the Army and the absence of an overall war plan. While agreeing with Scott's idea for a Mississippi River expedition, he realized that more was required. The South would not succumb to slow strangulation because the war might not last long enough for that strategy to have any effect. Moreover, the United States has traditionally been unable to sustain a protracted war unless its forces are continually engaged in conspicuous action leading to an unbroken series of victories. A major defeat, and certainly a prolonged conflict, would worsen the already rampant sectional and political factionalism in the North, allowing the Confederacy to win its independence by default. Some way had to be found to achieve rapid and effective control over a huge theater of operations, much of it undeveloped, with very poor land communications and few resources to sustain large armies. The Federal Army was further handicapped in offensive operations by the almost unbroken mountains chains separating the east coast states from the West.

While American geography largely determined the strategic problem, McClellan's revolutionary military concepts developed from an extensive knowledge of history, a lively interest in the changes technology was introducing into the art of war, and a rare opportunity to keep abreast of the latest European ideas and experience.

A great admirer of Frederick and to a lesser extent of Napoleon, McClellan had studied Baron Henri Jomini's accounts of their campaigns and, like his fellow West Pointers, was thoroughly familiar with Jomini's treatises on war. But he esteemed Jomini less as a theorist than as a practical soldier, the brilliant staff officer whose keen perception and well-formulated plans had produced Napoleon's most impressive victories. Thus McClellan was not seduced into rigidity by Jomini's tight theoretical constructs, but instead sought to emulate his flexibility and skill in devising strategies to fit specific military conditions. To McClellan, Napoleon's later campaigns after Jomini had left his service reflected the decline of his generalship. Attempting to compensate for bad plans, he threw away his best officers and men in ever more costly battles to achieve tactical victories of small strategic importance. In short, Napoleon, unlike Frederick, lost sight of the true object of war—which is, by skillful maneuver and with maximum economy, to render the enemy incapable of fighting, or to convince him that he can not win.[1]

As for technology, McClellan's observations in the Crimea impressed him with the effects of increasing firepower, especially of artillery. In 1855 he and two other American army officers were sent as a commission to the Crimea and to report on the organization, equipment, and methods of European armies.[2] Their first-hand observation of the siege of Sevastapol, and their reading of Todleben's account of the siege, which McClellan translated for his fellow observers, demonstrated to them the tactical advantage held by defenders protected by strong works.[3] Because of its destructive effect on the assailant, however, modern ordnance also improved the chances for strategic victory. If the aggressor could seize vital points by surprise and fortify them quickly with field works mounting heavy guns, the enemy would be forced to attack despite the tactical disadvantage, or lose the war.

Two concurrent technological advances, on the other hand, seemed to weaken the strategic offensive for an army invading on exterior lines. The railroad and the telegraph permitted the defenders to concentrate faster and in greater force at the point of attack. Although the lessons of the first strategic employment of railways in the 1859 campaign in northern Italy were inconclusive, McClellan's own experiences, both as a railroad executive and during his campaign in West Virginia, had taught him their potential, and their vulnerability, as lines of communication. Because rail transportation was essential for moving troops and heavy equipment rapidly over long distances through the rugged and sparsely settled regions of North America, rail junctions and depots became points of concentration and new strategic targets.[4]

The last, and perhaps most important, influence on McClellan's thinking was his appreciation of sea power, not simply to drive the enemy's navy from the oceans or destroy his commerce, but also to throw invading armies quickly and unexpectedly against strategic points, and then to maintain these armies until victory was attained. His service in the Mexican War, when he was attached to Scott's army as a lieutenant of engineers, introduced him to combined operations. While General Zachary Taylor's column wasted away in the desert, exhausted and short of supplies from a long overland march, Scott's force, with the aid of American naval supremacy, quickly seized the vital port of Vera Cruz. A short advance from this base to Mexico City ended the conflict.

In some respects the use of sea power in the Crimean War provided an even more convincing example, because in that war the Allies fought a major European nation of vast extent possessing a large, well-equipped army. Having failed to gain command of the sea, or to recognize its importance, Napoleon had been compelled to march deep into Russia in 1812. In no other way could the Russians be made to fight or give up the struggle. He forced them into battle, but on their terms and, having gained his objective at great cost, found that it produced, not the enemy's surrender, but the collapse of his own army.[5]

The 1854 campaign was different. Instead of invading armies swallowed up in the Russian hinterland, sea power allowed Britain and France to select the theater of operations, forcing the Russians to fight there. Despite excessive casualties resulting from poor leadership or failure to appreciate the tactical strength of the defensive, the Allies eventually took their objective and caused the Russians to sue for peace because the establishment of secure sea communications allowed the Allies to build up their men and materiel, and to employ heavy guns which could not have been transported by land.[6]

That the object of war is to force the enemy to give up, that this object is more easily and cheaply attained by strategy than combat, that more powerful weapons required maneuvering the enemy into assuming the tactical offensive, that railroads created new objective points and increased the possibilities of maneuver for both sides but tied armies to fragile supply lines, and that combined operations afforded an invading army the means to adopt the strategic offensive without risk to its communications—these elements were the foundation of McClellan's grand plan to defeat the Confederacy.

His basic concept was simple. The South depended upon two primary rail networks to move its armies and supply them in the field: the lines running east from the Mississippi Valley, and those running along the eastern seaboard. Comprising the first group were the roads from Memphis through Chattanooga, Atlanta, and Augusta to Charleston, and a parallel route, incomplete north of Mobile, running from Louisiana through Vicksburg, Selma, Montgomery, and Macon to Savannah. Cross-lines joined these two main roads with each other, and with Mobile via Columbus and Corinth on the west, and Montgomery and Atlanta on the east. Two other north–south lines

McClellan's Strategic Plan November 1861

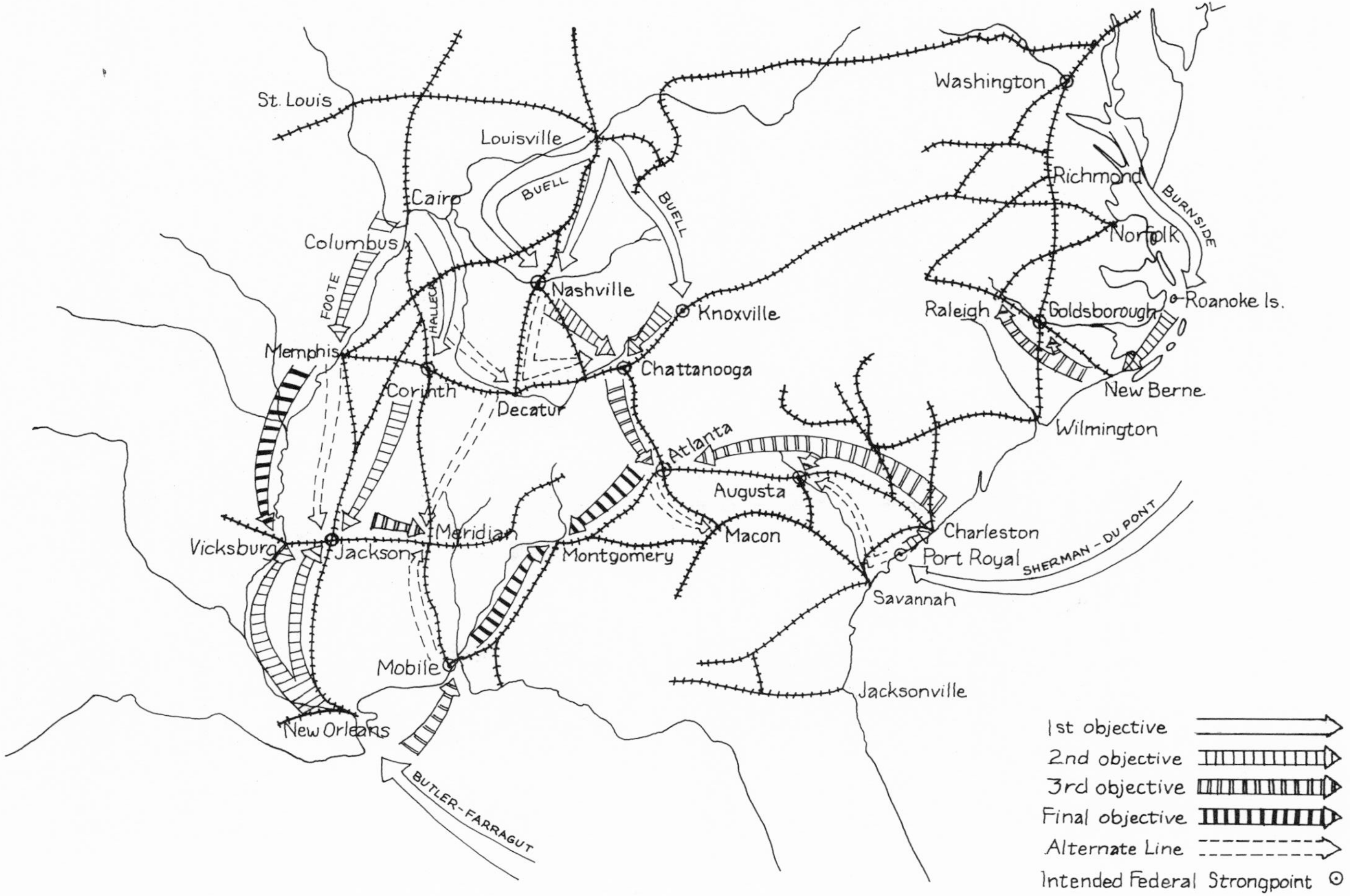

Legend

- **1st objective**
- **2nd objective**
- **3rd objective**
- **Final objective**
- Alternate Line
- Intended Federal Strongpoint ⊙

Map Labels

BURNSIDE
Richmond
Norfolk
Roanoke Is.
Goldsborough
New Berne
Raleigh
Wilmington
Washington
SHERMAN – DU PONT
Charleston
Port Royal
Savannah
Jacksonville
Knoxville
Chattanooga
Atlanta
Augusta
Macon
BUELL
Nashville
Montgomery
Louisville
Decatur
Cairo
BUELL
HALLECK
Corinth
Meridian
Mobile
BUTLER – FARRAGUT
St. Louis
Columbus
FOOTE
Memphis
Jackson
Vicksburg
New Orleans

connected Memphis with New Orleans through Jackson, and a shorter line ran from Louisville through Nashville, joining the Memphis and Charleston road at Decatur.[7] The coastal network was less complex. The main line connected Savannah, Charleston, Wilmington, Goldsborough, Weldon, Petersburg, and Richmond. Branch lines joined seaports like Beaufort and Norfolk with this road. A short railway ran from Branchville (on the Memphis and Charleston line, between Augusta and Charleston) to Charlotte, North Carolina; but until completion of the Piedmont extension in May 1864, this road did not connect to the north with the line from Greensborough to Richmond through Danville. One other southern railroad was of great strategic importance; indeed, it was probably the most vital artery in the Confederacy because it was the only direct link between Virginia and the West. This was the Virginia and Tennessee line, running through the mountains from Chattanooga through Knoxville, Lynchburg, and Danville to Richmond.

To paralyze the South's internal lines of communication, it was not enough to occupy their end points; the roads had to be grasped in the middle, preferably at their junction with connecting lines. Federal seizure of Goldsborough, Charleston, Branchville or Augusta, Knoxville, Nashville, Decatur, Corinth, Selma or Montgomery, and Jackson would disrupt all long-distance rail movement and fragment the Confederate armies into small detachments, unable to support each other and forced to supply themselves from the immediately surrounding country. Or if already concentrated to oppose a threatened Federal movement against one or two points, the enemy's large masses would be cut off from their supplies and must disperse or regain these points by costly assaults on fortified positions. A few such battles, if the Southerners attempted them at all, would soon convince their leaders to return to the Union. If they did not have the sense to see at once that they were beaten, it would still be physically impossible for them to win, for they would either waste away or be slaughtered before the Federal entrenchments.

Significantly, all of these strategic points except Knoxville were accessible by water. Movement by road was impracticable; by rail too slow and uncertain because the enemy could destroy the lines as he retired. Consequently, McClellan, using the Union's superior navy, would take the points by combined operations.[8] As commander of the Army of the Potomac, McClellan outwardly opposed Sherman's expedition (and, indeed, all "dispersion of force"), and convinced Lincoln to give him the chief command in place of Scott's choice, General Halleck, with the argument that the decisive battle must be fought against General Joseph E. Johnston's army in its entrenchments at Manassas. However, it is clear from other evidence and from his actual orders that this argument was both a ploy to gain government support, and a justification of his demand for an army of 240,000 men. Once in overall command, he could use these troops to implement his true strategy.[9]

Long before he had the power to command any force except the Army of the Potomac, which Scott insisted must remain before Washington, McClellan laid the groundwork for the coast expeditions. Throughout the month of August he maintained contact with the Blockade Board through his chief engineer, Brigadier General John G. Barnard. Although not mentioned in the Board's official reports, his ideas on combined operations influenced its thinking. One naval member, Captain Charles Henry Davis, was especially impressed by McClellan's strategic concepts, and was more enthusiastic about capturing Charleston and Savannah than seizing coaling stations for the blockade. On 4 September, Davis discussed the whole question of combined strategy during a private dinner at McClellan's house. It was agreed that, in addition to Sherman and Du Pont's expedition, a special amphibious division of New England seamen commanded by McClellan's old friend and railway associate Major General Ambrose E. Burnside would be raised for operations against Beaufort and Goldsborough from the Federal base at Hatteras Inlet.[10]

McClellan's main object for promoting this expedition was to gain a large and secure base for operations against the Wilmington and Weldon Railroad. The Neuse River, accessible via Pamlico Sound, was navigable for light-draft vessels to just beyond Raleigh, Burnside's ultimate objective. A branch line from Beaufort ran through the town of New Berne and, following the Neuse, crossed the Wilmington and Weldon road at Goldsborough. Thus, having occupied New Berne and the mouth of the Neuse, Burnside would have two parallel lines of communication for his advance on Goldsborough and Raleigh.[11] To secure the base at New Berne, it would be necessary to reduce Fort Macon and occupy Beaufort harbor and the southern terminus of the branch railroad at Moorehead City. If Burnside was unable to reach Goldsborough, he was to return to the coast and prepare an expedition against Wilmington while awaiting the necessary reinforcements, or attempt a raid on the Weldon road at some other point, such as Weldon, which could be easily approached via Albemarle Sound and the Roanoke River.[12]

The Navy's objectives were not so clear. In his statement of operational intentions to Assistant Secretary Fox on 4 December, Flag Officer Louis M. Goldsborough surmised that the Confederates attached great importance to Roanoke Island because "it commands the approach, by water, to Norfolk, from the Eastward." Although it would appear that even at this early date the Union Navy's main interest was in capturing Norfolk from the Carolina sounds, Goldsborough stated that he intended to block up the Dismal Swamp Canal at its lower end.[13] This act would, of course, prevent Federal waterborne forces from approaching Norfolk from this direction.

Such an apparently senseless idea can be explained only by Goldsborough's overly defensive mentality—a quality exhibited even more blatantly in Hampton Roads a few months later. The reason for blocking the shortest water approach to Norfolk seems to have been to prevent enemy vessels using this route for attacking the Union squadron. In December 1861 this notion might not have appeared as fantastic as it seems now, for the Union Navy had known for some months that the Southerners were converting the old USS *Merrimack* into an ironclad warship. But the Navy Department, having the plans of the old vessel, should have realized that the weight of armor plating could only increase her former draft, which was already too great for the canal. Aside from his intention to obstruct the canal, Goldsborough's plans followed McClellan's except for the river operations, which would be arranged with Burnside after New Berne and Beaufort had been taken.

The details of the Federal capture of Roanoke Island on 8

February 1862 are well known and not especially important to the history of Civil War combined operations. Because
the defenses were designed solely to prevent the passage of
warships between Pamlico and Albemarle sounds, Burnside's
landing was unopposed. The capture of the defending force
was a regular infantry action, unsupported by the fleet.[14]

Nevertheless, an interesting feature of this operation, one
which presaged, in exaggerated form, the Union's later combined operations, was the large volume of naval gunfire required to silence the Confederate Fort Bartow on Pork Point.
This nine-gun earthwork was manned only by the crew of the
gunboat CSS *Beaufort* and was open to reverse fire; yet it took
the Union fleet of sixteen gunboats two days to silence this
fort by close bombardment. In the process of reducing this
puny fortification, Goldsborough shot away his entire supply

The USS *Morse* at White House, on the Pamunkey River, 1862.
Converted from New York harbor ferry to gunboat, the *Morse*
participated in the Roanoke Island expedition and served on
Virginia rivers for the remainder of the war, guarding Federal
bases, raiding enemy supplies, and supporting the campaigns
of McClellan, Butler, and Grant.

of ammunition.[15] The high volume of fire (compared with prewar requirements) needed to contend favorably even with badly designed works, was a problem repeatedly encountered during the first year of the war; yet the Union Navy continued to provide insufficient stores of ammunition to its squadron commanders engaged in bombardment. The need to resupply after reducing enemy defenses delayed immediate follow-up operations on several occasions, and gave the enemy time to reconsolidate and recover his morale.

Such was the case with the Burnside expedition. Although all important points in the North Carolina sounds eventually fell into Union hands, no significant progress into the interior via the rivers was made until much later in the war. Because the Confederates despaired of recovering the sounds without

Major General Ambrose E. Burnside
(*National Archives*)

a strong naval force, they concentrated on defending the river approaches to the Wilmington and Weldon Railroad; the Union's delay in exploiting the capture of Roanoke Island gave the Confederates time to construct and man these defenses. If, for example, the Union fleet had entered Albemarle Sound with sufficient ammunition, a combined force might have proceeded at once up the Roanoke River, then completely open, and destroyed the railway bridge at Weldon.[16] Or a force might have moved immediately to close off the Dismal Swamp Canal. When this latter operation was finally attempted in mid-April, the enemy was prepared and the Federals were repulsed.

As it was, Burnside never reached the town of Goldsborough. After he had consolidated his control over the sounds, taken New Berne, and reduced Fort Macon, his orders were changed. When the Union government decided to confine McClellan's command to the Army of the Potomac, and ordered him to operate with his army against Richmond via the lower Chesapeake, Union strategy was also altered.[17] Had McClellan retained command of the whole Union Army, the objective of Burnside's expedition would probably have remained the same. Although possession of the North Carolina coast was possibly of some advantage to the Union, the capture of Goldsborough and Raleigh early in the war would have prevented any large-scale operations by the Army of Northern Virginia for lack of supplies; in conjunction with an offensive by the main Federal army, the Confederate armed forces might have been compelled to evacuate the entire state, including their capital.

Burnside's expedition, like the others, has been discussed separately to avoid confusion. Nonetheless, it should be remembered that the specific object of any particular expedition was less important than its role in relation to McClellan's grand strategic design. The success of each part of the plan may have depended to some extent on local circumstances, but the success of the whole depended on larger considerations of policy and command. Because Burnside's expedition, like the others, was interrupted after attaining only its preliminary objectives, the true offensive power of combined operations remained unrecognized and control of the coast of North Carolina has been seen ever since as the sole purpose of this enterprise.

We have observed that the expedition by Du Pont and Sherman to the South Atlantic coast was initiated by the Navy for naval purposes only. Because General McClellan did not have the authority in September and October to promise Sherman the reinforcements needed to move against his ultimate objectives, the expeditionary force had remained organized into two divisions with the ostensible intention of occupying Bull's Bay and Fernandina. The decision to take Port Royal instead of Bull's Bay came after the expedition had reached Fort Monroe. From McClellan's standpoint Port Royal was the best base for operations against Savannah, Charleston, and the railway connecting these cities.

But, although the Army and the Navy finally agreed on the initial point of attack, the operational concepts of the two services remained essentially different. Nor is it easy, even when strategic differences do not exist, to convert an instrument designed to perform one function into a workable tool for another. In the case of the follow-up to the Port Royal expedition, such a conversion proved impossible.

The capture of Port Royal was only the first stage, it will be recalled, of the Navy's plan to seize two South Atlantic harbors for the blockading squadron. Immediately after securing Hilton Head Island against counterattack, the expedition was to proceed against Fernandina. The Navy Department was determined to carry out the original plan before considering any follow-up operations desired by the Army.

But the fleet was not ready. Du Pont had shot away three-fourths of his ammunition, over two thousand rounds, in reducing Fort Walker, and there was no reason to suppose that Fort Clinch guarding the approach to Fernandina would require a less intensive bombardment, since the Army was still unprepared to take the place by assault.[18]

While the bulk of Sherman's troops waited aboard the transports for the fleet to replenish its ammunition, Du Pont suddenly found himself burdened with a weightier problem. Two stone fleets which Fox had sent down for obstructing the main ship channels at Savannah and Charleston arrived, along with an order from the Navy Department to sink them at once.[19] But the capture of Port Royal had altered the situation.

In Confederate General Thomas Drayton's abandoned headquarters on Hilton Head Island, Du Pont had found a chart showing all of the water defenses and gun positions around Savannah. By 10 November, naval reconnaissance had discovered that the enemy had entirely abandoned the outer approaches. Since Federal vessels now controlled these approaches, the port of Savannah was already closed to blockade-runners. Du Pont was too correct an officer, however, to disregard an imperative order, obsolete or not. Consequently, on 5 December he had the stone ships sunk in the most important entrances to Charleston harbor: the main ship channel, and all but one accessory channel.[20]

Meanwhile, General Sherman's troops had grown restless. Having survived the hurricane en route to Port Royal, they had remained several more weeks aboard uncomfortable vessels. Moreover, his regiments were not composed of the best material; untrained and undisciplined, to a large extent they comprised the dregs of the North's urban population, and, except for Brigadier General Isaac I. Stevens, a gifted and conscientious professional, the officers were little better. Learning that the Fernandina expedition had been postponed until the stone fleets had been disposed of, Sherman finally disembarked his motley army, setting some of them to work on an extensive system of fortifications for Hilton Head Island.[21] Others found more unsavory employment. The white inhabitants of the sea islands off the South Carolina coast had fled at the approach of Du Pont's armada, leaving their slaves and most of their goods behind. This rare opportunity to loot and destroy would have tempted the best-disciplined soldiers. To men from the 'slums' of Boston and New York, the lure was irresistible. Until severe disciplinary measures, including several executions, had restored a degree of order, these regiments were useless for any military movements.[22]

Other problems plagued the commanding general. Transportation was the most serious. Because no extensive follow-up was considered in the original plan, the Federal government, in an effort to avoid the expense of buying troop transports, had chartered private steamers. The cost per day for a sufficient number of vessels to accommodate Sherman's 12,000 men and their materiel was enormous, but Sherman had promised to release them fifteen days after his initial landing on the enemy's coast. Moreover, two of the Army's four shallow-draft steamers had sunk during the storm and the remaining two were forced by damages to put in at other points along the coast. Since only light-draft vessels could negotiate the shallow, marshy waters between the sea islands and the mainland, troop movements and reconnaissance were limited by the small number of cotton barges General Stevens could collect from the abandoned plantations.[23] This army had no cavalry; because mainland operations or raids on the railroads were not anticipated, none had been provided. And to top matters off, Sherman's guns and ordnance stores had been lost at sea.

Given this state of affairs, it is hardly surprising that the rapid capture of Port Royal was not immediately followed up either by the projected expedition to Fernandina or by a coup de main against Savannah, Charleston, or the railroad. By December the latter possibility, the one McClellan had envisaged as the ultimate objective for Sherman's army, was no longer being considered.

Time was all-important. In November, having cracked the thin shell of the enemy's coast defense system, the whole of South Carolina and Georgia lay open to Federal invasion. Except for Fort Pulaski, Savannah had no real defenses. Charleston's harbor forts were inadequately armed and manned, and its "back door" via the Stono River, James Island, and the North Edisto River, was unguarded.[24] Augusta, Georgia, vital for Confederate arms production and a key rail junction, was unfortified and was readily approachable via the Savannah River; the river itself was unobstructed and there were no batteries to impede a Federal advance. The small Confederate force of four thousand men was strung out along the coast from Georgetown, South Carolina to Brunswick, Georgia. On paper there were less than 14,000 soldiers to defend the entire state of South Carolina, and most of those actually present for duty were untrained militiamen carrying obsolete weapons. The vital railroad connecting Savannah and Charleston was irregularly patrolled by five hundred state cavalry.[25] But in November, as we have seen, the Federals were in no condition to profit from the enemy's weakness.

By mid-December this situation had markedly changed. On 5 November, after learning that Du Pont's huge expedition had

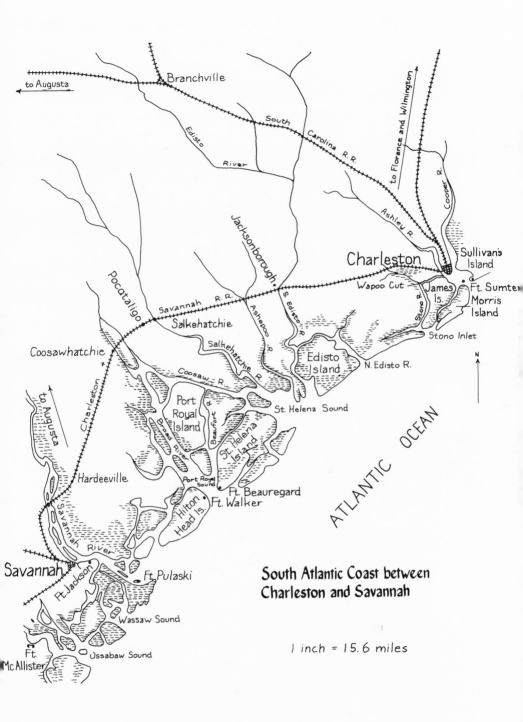

South Atlantic Coast between
Charleston and Savannah

1 inch = 15.6 miles

put to sea, President Davis formed the states of South Carolina, Georgia, and Florida into a new department and assigned its command to General Robert E. Lee. Acting as the president's unofficial chief of staff, Lee was given authority to institute any military measures he saw fit to defend the region, and Davis demanded that the state governors cooperate fully with all Lee's requests for support. An experienced engineer, Lee quickly perceived the futility of the peripheral system of coast defense.[26] As he later explained to the adjutant general:

> Wherever his [the Federal] fleet can be brought to bear no opposition to his landing can be made except within range of our fixed batteries. We have nothing to oppose to its heavy guns, which sweep over the low banks of this country with irresistible force. The farther he can be withdrawn from his floating batteries the weaker he will become, and lines of defense, covering objects of attack, have been selected with this in view.[27]

Moreover, because the inhabitants had fled, the littoral between Savannah and Charleston was useless to the Confederate war effort.

Lee's alternative system was simple and effective, and was designed primarily to protect the railroad. Because troops were scarce and the road accessible at many points, a continuous line of guards and blockhouses was judged impracticable. Instead, Lee organized a mobile defense. Besides the main troop concentrations at Charleston and Savannah, detachments were stationed at Pocotaligo (Lee's headquarters) and Coosawhatchie, the latter forces only two or three hours from either city by rail. In addition to regular infantry, small light units of cavalry, mounted infantry, and horse batteries were based at these points to guard against raids on unprotected sections of the line. Thus the whole Confederate force could be rapidly concentrated at Charleston, Savannah, or any point between.[28] Such a defensive system neutralized to a large extent Federal superiority in numbers and, due to the shortness of the Confederates' interior line, countered Union sea mobility with an even greater mobility by rail.

To strengthen the defenses of the most important harbors, Lee decided to leave the lesser ports unprotected. Only the

General Robert E. Lee
(*National Archives*)

entrances to Cumberland Sound and Brunswick and the approaches to Savannah and Charleston were to be held and further fortified. Preparations were begun for obstructing the Savannah River below Augusta and for connecting the rail terminals at that city. The existing gap in the coastal railroad was closed by bridging the Ashley River south of Charleston.[29] In addition to the main defenses, there were earthworks with two or three guns, located at favorable sites a few miles up the smaller rivers. The weakest points were the large rivers, principally the Edisto, which could easily lead a sizeable enemy force into the rear of Charleston; hence the need to protect the railroad at all costs.[30]

This more rational and integral Confederate coast defense system was not seriously challenged until the summer of 1862. That there was no major Federal thrust in this area was not due to want of activity and certainly not to a lack of plans. If anything, there was too much activity and too many plans. The energy showed by both the Army and the Navy in coastal sorties and reconnaissance produced few results, because it was random, uncoordinated, and not tied to any particular intention.

As for plans, during November and December General Sherman submitted four major alternatives: 1) to open another harbor in accordance with his original instructions from the War Department; 2) to seize Beaufort, South Carolina as a base for moving a strong force against the railroad at Pocotaligo; 3) to take Savannah; and 4) to capture Charleston. The last two proposals each involved several options. Savannah might be taken by a coup de main, or by a systematic advance including, as a first stage, either the reduction of Fort Pulaski by siege artillery emplaced on Tybee Island, or the neutralization of the city's defenses via the small waterways leading from Savannah and Wassaw Sounds into the Savannah River just below Fort Jackson.[31]

The last scheme, which Sherman personally favored, required a large number of boats and full naval cooperation. Although the general informed the War Department of his needs as early as 17 November, the boats never arrived, and having kept the chartered steamers for thirty-two days instead of the agreed fifteen—thereby paying their purchase price several times over—he was finally obliged to discharge most of them on urgent demand from the quartermaster general.[32] Nor were the naval commanders anxious at first to cooperate. Having organized the expedition for purposes of the blockade, they resented the Army's attempt to change or enlarge its objectives. On 11 November, Du Pont told Assistant Secretary Fox that he was anxious to get off to Fernandina as soon as possible; otherwise, "the soldiers will absorb the fleet." He described Sherman's troops, rightly enough, as "depredators and freebooters", good for nothing except robbing Negroes. Even Davis, Du Pont's fleet captain, whom McClellan had relied upon to support combined operations, complained that the troops were no good and their officers lacked initiative.[33]

Had the Navy been anxious to cooperate, Du Pont's squadron was spread too thin. Lee's new defense policy had left openings which the Federal ships quickly filled; thus, instead of occupying the two ports envisaged in the original plan, by the end of the year the fleet occupied seven in South Carolina and Georgia alone. While the Navy Department may have been satisfied with this state of affairs, Du Pont was not. The measures for strengthening the blockade which had seemed so simple and sensible the previous summer in Washington had proved self-defeating. The very last thing his squadron now needed was a few more ports. Although the department was still anxious to add at least Fernandina to his list of responsibilities, Du Pont had already begun to take a second look at the Army and was considering the possibilities for combined attacks on some place of real importance.

In late December, having received no reply from the War Department or General McClellan regarding his proposals for capturing Savannah, Sherman submitted two plans for taking Charleston, prepared by his chief engineer, Captain Quincy A. Gillmore. According to the first plan, the Army would land on Morris and Sullivan's islands and reduce Fort Sumter by bombardment, thus permitting the fleet to pass into the inner harbor. The alternative involved operating along the Stono River. Occupation of James Island would turn the harbor defenses, and land batteries established on the island's northern end could shell the city. In either case, the enemy would probably evacuate the place, allowing it to be used, in accordance with McClellan's plan, as a base for operations into the interior.

The second approach was more direct but less certain. Recognizing James Island as the weakest point in Charleston's defenses, the Confederates had placed strong batteries near the northern end of the island and had obstructed the Stono below Wappoo Cut. A larger Union force would be needed to implement this plan; Sherman estimated requirements of twenty thousand infantry, one thousand cavalry, two field batteries, thirty siege guns, and two or three pontoon bridges. The main attack on James Island would be supplemented by a naval demonstration in Bull's Bay and a raid to cut the railroad south of the city. The first alternative looked better to the Army, but it required a degree of naval cooperation that Du Pont was neither willing nor able to give. Besides, all channels at Charleston (except Maffitt's close along Sullivan's Island, which was too shallow for warships) had been blocked up by Fox's stone ships, and it would take months for these hulks to dredge out a new channel.[34]

Thus, ironically, by obeying the department's order to sink these vessels, Du Pont had not only allowed the Confederates time to perfect their defensive arrangements, but had locked himself out of Charleston with no damage to the enemy, whose shallow-draft blockade runners easily passed over the obstructions at high tide.[35]

Consequently, at the end of December, Du Pont and Sherman agreed to direct their attention to some kind of offensive against Savannah. Although the general had earlier decided that the only feasible operation was the destruction of Fort Pulaski by land bombardment, and had ordered a siege train, the promise of active naval cooperation enlarged the possibilities. Sherman's favorite plan—getting behind the outer defenses via the inlets and creeks—was revived.[36] On 1 January 1862 the Federals began a systematic reconnaissance of the creeks and marshes leading into the Savannah River above Fort Pulaski. Next day, Sherman informed McClellan that he intended to make a major movement

> on the north side of [the] Savannah River, thus occupying the road to that city, the whole country between Broad River and Savannah River, and the southern end of the

railroad, and at the same time, if found practicable, the islands in the river north of Pulaski.[37]

This ambitious undertaking required great energy and both services eagerly cooperated in the reconnaissance and preparation.

Having discovered an artificial channel called Wall's Cut, obstructed by pilings, which led into the Savannah River north of Jones's Island, the topographical engineers on 14 January removed the obstructions and reported twelve to fifteen feet of water in the cut. This information confirmed the possibility of a coup against the city. A conference was held the following day aboard the *Wabash*, with Du Pont, Davis, Captain C.R.P. Rodgers, General Wright, and Captain Gillmore present. All agreed that an attack should be attempted; one combined force would enter the Savannah River via Wall's Cut, while a second debouched into the river from the south through Wassaw Sound and the Wilmington River. The two forces would unite north of Elba Island, attack Fort Jackson, and bombard the city.[38]

Two days later Du Pont called the attack off. The plan, in the opinion of his officers, was too intricate and hazardous. Only two gunboats could be brought to bear upon Fort Jackson. Judging by his experience at Fort Walker, Du Pont rightly

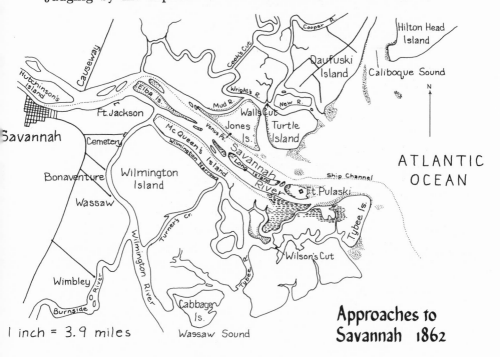

1 inch = 3.9 miles

Approaches to Savannah 1862

concluded that their fire would not be sufficient to silence the work. He had also learned that the channel was too narrow for the vessels to avoid enemy fire rafts. Sherman then suggested that the Navy attempt no bombardment; instead, it would simply land his troops and some field batteries in the rear of the fort. But Du Pont refused to risk his ships unless victory was certain, and the general could not change his mind.[39]

This decision left Sherman back where he started. With no boats, he could not execute the above plan; without cavalry, he could not raid the railroad, as suggested by General Stevens; and until the siege train arrived, he could not blow down Fort Pulaski. In disgust, he informed the quartermaster general on 5 February that, because his material was not sent and the Navy had refused to go through Wall's Cut when it was first opened, the Confederates had now strengthened the city's defenses to the point where a coup was impossible. Since the Army could do nothing without siege equipment or transport, it was going to Fernandina with the Navy.[40]

Du Pont's predicament was little better. Because combined operations against Savannah were considered too risky for the likely gain, and the Army did not have enough troops for an attempt on Charleston via the Stono or the North Edisto, he too fell back upon the original plan of seizing Fernandina. Otherwise, he could do nothing but administer the blockade, a choice not acceptable to the Navy Department. As long as a fort remained in enemy hands, Assistant Secretary Fox could not let it alone.[41]

These important strategic decisions were made while General McClellan was seriously ill. Since 20 December he had seen none of Sherman's reports or requisitions, most of which lay in the adjutant general's office. When well enough to attend to business around mid-January, he was overwhelmed by urgent problems in the West and with final arrangements for Burnside's expedition. Still, seeing Sherman's correspondence for the first time on 12 February, he was not especially disturbed. Until the western armies had taken their objectives, it was as well to stay out of Savannah and Charleston anyway, since interior operations were not yet practicable and, with all the Confederate railroads intact, Federal occupation forces might be driven out of these bases before their land defenses could be fully completed. But now that Fort Henry had fallen, and the western armies in Tennessee were on the move, McClellan wanted Sherman to seize Savannah. He thus decided to send the boats requested from Philadelphia, along with a siege train and some cavalry. Subsequent reinforcements of ten thousand infantry were also promised.[42]

Upon learning that a coup de main against Savannah was no longer possible, the general-in-chief ordered Sherman to reduce Fort Pulaski by bombardment. This would ensure control of the harbor, relieve the Navy, "and render the main body of your force disposable for other operations." Although McClellan did not strongly oppose the Fernandina expedition since it would require little time, the real strategic goal for Sherman's army was Charleston. Its defenses were not yet complete and the Navy could be persuaded that this city was a prize "well worthy of our greatest efforts and considerable sacrifices." As a base of operations toward Atlanta it was in some respects superior to Savannah. The route via Branchville was more direct and struck the railroad further to the north. For logistical purposes the harbor was more spacious. Finally, its land approaches were easier to defend.[43]

Although regarded by McClellan as only interim measures to keep the troops occupied until something important could be attempted in that theater, the destruction of Pulaski and the revival of the Fernandina expedition satisfied both the War and the Navy departments. On 21 February the first installment of siege guns and engineering material arrived; on the following day several Union gunboats entered the Savannah River above the fort, completing its investment. By 9 April the batteries and roads on Tybee Island were finished; on 10 April, at 8 A.M. Gillmore's guns opened and Fort Pulaski, its 7½-foot-thick masonry walls having been breached at the then amazing range of 1500 yards, surrendered at 2 P.M. on the 11th.[44]

The long-awaited expedition to Fernandina was a fitting anticlimax to the whole campaign. On 3 March, when Du Pont's fleet, accompanied by Wright's division, sailed into the harbor, the forts were empty; the enemy had long since gone. Immediately after the fall of Fort Donelson, Confederate War

Secretary Judah P. Benjamin had ordered that all the troops on the Florida coast, except for the garrison at Apalachicola which guarded the river route into central Georgia, be sent to aid Johnston in Tennessee. For the Union, then, it was a hollow victory. After spending tedious months lounging about the vacant houses, chatting with the few remaining local residents, and conducting small unproductive forays into the interior, the Federals in turn evacuated the east Florida coast.[45]

For the next year and a half, attention in the Department of the South would be focused on the capture of Charleston. But it was not by combined operations that the first great attempt to seize the "birthplace of the Confederacy" would be made—nor would it be carried out by General Sherman, nor in accordance with General McClellan's grand strategy. On 11 March McClellan was removed from the chief command; on the 31st Sherman was superseded in the Department of the South by Major General David Hunter—just before his laborious preparations to reduce Pulaski bore fruit. It was a cruel blow to a skillful and conscientious soldier, but one made necessary by the government's consolidation of the western armies under General Halleck's command; since Hunter ranked his new superior, he could not remain in the old Department of Kansas. This change of field commanders was most unfortunate, as we shall see when we examine the attempt to capture Charleston in early 1863.

In assessing the reasons for the failure of this large expeditionary force to accomplish anything very significant after its capture of Port Royal, Du Pont and Sherman agreed that the main difficulty was the lack of proper advance planning and preparations to exploit their initial success. Sherman thought unity of command would have solved most of the problems and that, in the future, the senior officer of either service should command the whole.[46] While it cannot be denied that interservice differences and a shortage of men and materiel handicapped the Federal offensive, these reasons are not sufficient to account for the failure. Sole operational authority would not have given the commander of the combined force a free hand; he would, in fact, have been caught in an even worse position vis-a-vis various civilian policy makers. No single field commander could have reconciled the disparate aims of the president, the general-in-chief, the Cabinet, the War Department, and the Navy Department. In attempting too much—to seize coaling stations, to tighten the blockade, to exploit the economic resources of the region, to occupy and patrol the coast, to protect former slaves and Union sympathizers, to cut the railroad, and to capture cities having permanent defenses—the expeditionary force inevitably accomplished very little.

Nor should the timely and energetic defensive measures taken by the Confederates be underrated. Without Lee's concept of an interior mobile defense, the Federals might well have blundered their way into Savannah, Charleston, and even Augusta. When they saw that their positions could not be held, the Confederates had the good sense not to wait around to be captured. The burden of protecting the coast was left to the attacker, who soon found that limited victories are often little better, and sometimes worse, than temporary defeats. Had the attack on Port Royal failed, the Federals might have learned much sooner how to plan combined operations, and the Confederacy might not have corrected its faulty coast defense system in time to prevent major invasions of the type General McClellan had in mind.

But though this Union expeditionary force did not take advantage of the enemy's initial weakness and confusion by seizing places of great strategic importance, the course of the campaign had not been unalterably set before March 1862. In fact, the prospect for fruitful combined operations and their systematic exploitation was better at that time than during the preceding months. The Navy had become frustrated by merely policing the coast and was anxious to cooperate in an attack on Charleston; the defenses of this harbor and city were well known and the Army had devised several workable plans for cooperative action. The troops were better trained and disciplined, Union material resources were certainly greater, and both the general-in-chief and the Navy Department had promised reinforcements. The real failure of combined operations on the South Atlantic coast was not determined in November 1861, but five months later when McClellan, the driving force behind Federal amphibious strategy, was removed.

One other coast expedition became part of McClellan's

strategic plan, although he had nothing to do with its inception and did not at first approve of it. From the previous chapter it will be recalled that, although General Butler had convinced the administration to retain Hatteras Inlet after the capture of the forts, he was unable to get troops from Scott for follow-up operations in the North Carolina sounds. Consequently, with the backing of Secretary of War Cameron, he decided to raise his own army. The decision had scarcely been made, however, when he learned that the situation at Hatteras had deteriorated and that McClellan had already authorized General Burnside to organize an amphibious division for that purpose. Butler then convinced Cameron to try an expedition to the Eastern Shore of Virginia. Although nothing came of this venture, probably because its military object was obscure, it gave Butler some justification for raising troops.[47]

General Butler was an enterprising individual. More than just a good lawyer, he was a self-made man, former school teacher, inventor, politician, and, above all, a financial wizard. His Yankee horse sense made him a natural merchant, and like all good businessmen he believed that what was best for profit was best for the country. From the beginning of the war he had his own ideas about defeating the Confederacy. His methods may seem a bit peculiar at first glance, and he was never able to convince the Federal government to sanction all of them officially; but in some ways they were more reasonable than the hybrid measures actually adopted.

To Butler, the blockade was a mistake. It only benefited the South, making it self-sufficient and greatly inflating the value of its primary export commodity, cotton. The Confederacy was thus able to finance its war effort and obtain foreign credit. Instead of keeping goods out of the South, the Federal government should allow Northern merchants to flood the market, especially with luxuries, and take out cotton and tobacco in payment. This trade would quickly depress the price of cotton, bankrupt the Southern economy, finance the Federal war debt by custom duties and licenses, and benefit Northern industry.[48]

The U.S. Treasury Department was inclined to agree, but such proceedings would more likely provoke a foreign war than would any other action by the Northern government. While Butler saw this risk and even considered it a good thing (reasoning that another war, especially with England, would bring the seceded states rushing back into the Union) the administration was not so sanguine about the outcome.[49] The U.S. Navy was not prepared to fight the world's leading naval power; nor was the Army, which was frantically trying to update its obsolete coast defenses. Moreover, world opinion might construe any official policy of trade with the enemy as an indication that the war was being fought for economic gain instead of principle.

Although Butler's ideas could not be fully implemented, the secretary of the Treasury saw nothing wrong with issuing licenses to ship goods to ports under Union control or allowing agents to seize or buy cotton and tobacco within Federally occupied territory, as long as these shippers and agents swore loyalty to the United States and certified that the merchandise was not consigned to Confederate sympathizers. Where it ended up, or where the cotton came from, was the responsibility of local dealers and no concern of the Federal government.[50]

In light of the Treasury Department's attitude, there was nothing to prevent the ambitious Butler from seizing a port, obtaining licenses for his agents, and pursuing his own strategy against the Confederacy while making a few dollars both for the national treasury and for himself. While recruiting in the New England mill towns, particularly his home town of Lowell, Massachusetts where he owned half of a textile company, Butler saw that the cloth manufacturers were anxious to obtain cotton at almost any price. They were being ruined by the blockade and by competition from English companies whose suppliers ran the blockade at will. The states of the Deep South bordering the Gulf of Mexico were the best source for the rough grade of raw cotton these firms wished to buy.[51] So, toward the end of November, Butler sent the first contingent of his New England division, two thousand men under Brigadier General J.W. Phelps, to Ship Island in the Gulf midway between Mobile Bay and the Mississippi delta. Phelps was instructed to fortify the island and, while waiting for the rest of the division, size up the coast for a favorable point from which to ship cotton.[52]

None of this fit into McClellan's original scheme. But if

Butler insisted upon going to the Gulf, his force could be used to the general-in-chief's advantage. McClellan had devised no expedition against Selma or Montgomery, places that Butler could reach via the Tombigee or the Alabama rivers after seizing Mobile. Another possibility was an expedition into Texas to cut off the supplies, especially of horses, which passed from this state through Louisiana and then by rail from Vicksburg to the east. In December McClellan asked Butler to submit plans for both alternatives.[53]

The naval leaders had already decided on another objective for this expedition, however, and McClellan was never able to change their minds. While Butler was preparing his commercial venture with the approval of his boyhood friend, Assistant Navy Secretary Fox, who also held shares in the textile mills, Captain David D. Porter appeared in Washington on 12 November, fresh from the Gulf blockade with a proposal to reduce the forts below New Orleans with a mortar flotilla. While he was in Turkey buying camels for the Army during the Crimean War, Porter had observed the Allied bombardment of the Kinburn forts and was impressed—wrongly, as it turned out—by the destructive effect of mortar bombardment.[54] Aside from his business interests Fox was, as usual, wildly enthusiastic about any idea likely to glorify the Navy. Enlisting the support of Senator James Grimes of Iowa, a member of the Naval Affairs Committee, whose constituents, along with the citizens of Illinois, Michigan, Indiana, and Ohio, were loudly clamoring for the government to open the Mississippi, the main prewar outlet for western bulk produce. Fox and Grimes persuaded Welles and Lincoln to consider the proposal as an adjunct to McClellan's plan for an expedition down the river from Cairo, Illinois.[55]

At a meeting attended by Welles, Fox, and Porter at McClellan's house that evening, the question was discussed in detail. Fox came armed with a memorandum from General Barnard, who had designed the New Orleans defenses, "proving" that Fort Jackson could be easily destroyed by mortar fire, which would then allow wooden warships to pass Fort St. Philip and reach New Orleans.[56] Since only a small army contingent would be required to occupy the forts, Butler's two regiments aboard the USS *Constitution* at Boston would suffice.

McClellan was skeptical. The forts might not fall so easily. If they did, at least ten thousand men would be needed to garrison them and the city itself. An even larger force would be needed to exploit the victory, either by attacking Mobile or by moving up the river on some important point. The mere occupation of New Orleans would not contribute to his plan for paralyzing the South's communications.[57]

Still, if the Navy Department insisted and the president approved the expedition, McClellan would not oppose it, not to begin with anyway. It could perhaps be diverted later to a more important point. Besides, since McClellan's strategy depended so heavily on cooperation with the Navy, it would have been unwise to reject too many of its favorite projects. But the general-in-chief was not prepared to endorse the expedition at that time, nor to furnish troops. Porter was certainly convinced that the Navy could handle the operation alone and that the soldiers on Ship Island, whom McClellan agreed could remain there, were sufficient to garrison the forts. Butler, however, was not especially pleased that the 10,000-man army he had raised in New England for service in the Gulf would probably be used to reinforce Burnside or Sherman.

The man selected to command the fleet in the New Orleans expedition, Flag Officer David G. Farragut, was certainly dissatisfied. Farragut, who had observed high-angle naval bombardment during the Mexican War, considered mortar boats entirely useless. Although he had assured the Navy Department in December that his ships could run past the forts and capture the city by a coup de main, this was hardly his preferred mode of attack.[58] From the day of his promotion to flag rank until the end of the war, Farragut was a firm advocate of combined operations. He would willingly sacrifice ships to gain an important object if there was no other choice, but the presence of a cooperating infantry force, he believed, could secure the same end with smaller risk and was therefore the best method of dealing with fortifications. Although it was possible in most cases to run by works, such a tactic established no permanent control and left the fleet without support, vulnerable to being cut off.

In the end it was not Farragut but General Barnard, the Army's liaison with the Navy Department, who persuaded

McClellan to approve the expedition. Barnard used three principal arguments. First, the Federals could achieve surprise, a point always attractive to McClellan. General Beauregard, he said, had pronounced New Orleans safe against attack from the south, so the Confederates were preparing to oppose a thrust from the north. Second, the administration and the Navy insisted on carrying out this expedition and it would not be politically wise for the Army to oppose them. Finally, McClellan could easily fit the operation into his overall strategy by using it to capture the railroad junctions at Jackson and Mobile.[59]

The last argument was decisive. McClellan's instructions of 23 February clearly indicate his reason for finally approving the expedition. After taking New Orleans and securing its approaches from the east, Butler was to proceed up the river to Baton Rouge, his ultimate object being to "seize and hold the railroad junction at Jackson, Mississippi," and to capture all rolling stock in the area. Then, in cooperation with Farragut, Butler was to take Mobile harbor and "control the railway terminus at the city." To accomplish these ends, McClellan promised Butler substantial reinforcements after New Orleans fell.[60] It is interesting to compare this document with Farragut's confidential instructions of 20 January from the Navy Department. Having reduced the forts and forced the Confederates out of the city, the fleet was to push on up the Mississippi taking the defenses at Baton Rouge, Vicksburg, and Memphis from the rear.[61] These instructions accorded well with the first part of Butler's orders, the operation against Jackson—but not with the plan to take Mobile. After McClellan's removal from command and the capture of New Orleans, this disjunction of orders would create great confusion, to the enemy's advantage, both on the Mississippi and at Mobile.

The coast expeditions and their intended follow-up operations were essential components of McClellan's plan. But the Federal forces penetrating the South from the Atlantic and Gulf seaboards formed only half of a gigantic machine designed to paralyze the enemy's internal communications. The other half comprised the western armies. Based on the line of the Ohio River, these two forces were to pierce the South like giant spikes driven between Missouri and the Alleghenies, meeting the coastal columns at vital points within the heart of the Confederacy. As in the other Union expeditions, both western armies were to rely as much as possible on water lines of operation and were to employ river flotillas for reconnaissance and fire support.

While western operations under McClellan's command may be termed "combined" only in a loose sense, they were responsible for the collapse of the entire plan. McClellan's failure to solve the "Western problem" marked the beginning of the end for his combined operations strategy, and led to his removal from the chief command. Indeed, events in Tennessee during the opening campaign permanently influenced Federal prosecution of the war, including the subsequent use of combined operations.

3

TENNESSEE

To AVOID CONFUSION, it is a common practice in written accounts to separate military strategy—movements designed to defeat the enemy's organized forces or to seize points of operational importance—from the larger political and economic war aims of the belligerents. Strategy as operations is a useful definition. By recounting and examining battles and campaigns the war historian may analyze their military significance. Such a distinction, although always somewhat artificial, can usually be drawn with minimum violence to the facts. But in examining McClellan's plans for the West this is not possible, because both political and military considerations gave rise to them, determined their direction, and ultimately decided their fate and that of their chief architect.

Standard accounts of western strategy in early 1862 make the situation appear simple. The Confederate forces under General Albert Sidney Johnston held an advanced line from Columbus to Bowling Green, which covered Nashville. In February, part of General Halleck's command under Brigadier General Ulysses S. Grant and Flag Officer Andrew H. Foote took Fort Henry on the Tennessee and Fort Donelson on the Cumberland, driving a wedge into the center of Johnston's line and forcing him back on his main position guarding the Memphis and Charleston Railroad. This classic military maneuver is so well known that it might seem to require no further examination. But while most accounts retell what happened accurately enough, their view of the campaign usually presumes certain intentions; i.e., that Grant's movement was meant to be the main thrust, and that the object of the western armies was to break the enemy line which happened to run close to the Tennessee border. Neither assumption is correct.

Except for Major General Henry W. Halleck, an avid disciple of Jomini who had recently published an updated version of Jomini's theories, neither the high command, nor the Cabinet, the Congress, or the president were interested in fronts of operation. Meaningless in itself, the enemy's line was important only for what it covered—to McClellan, the great rail junctions of Nashville, Chattanooga, Decatur, and Corinth; to the Federal government, the state of Tennessee.

Looking at an operational or communications map of the South, it is natural to think of the Confederacy as theaters of war, or regions, and to forget that it comprised separate states with definite geographical and administrative boundaries.[1] But both national governments in the "War Between the States" were, of course, well aware of it. The State of Tennessee—as distinct from its territory accidentally situated on the frontier of the Confederacy—was especially valuable to both sides. Tennessee supplied more Confederate soldiers than any other state except for Virginia, and its most important city, Nashville, was one of a handful of Southern industrial centers important for the production of war materiel. The mountainous eastern counties held nearly two-thirds of the Confederacy's mineral wealth and its only large operating salt, lead, copper, and niter mines at the beginning of the war.[2]

For the Northern government, these facts alone justified a major effort to detach Tennessee from the Confederacy and restore it to the United States. But there was an equally important incentive. Upon seceding from the Union, all of the Confederate States except Missouri and Tennessee withdrew their representatives from the United States Congress. Missouri, divided in sympathy but too distant and sparsely settled to become the scene of major conflict, maintained two sets of federal legislators. Tennessee split. One senator, Andrew Johnson, and Representative John Maynard, both from the region east of the Cumberland Mountains, remained in Washington to represent their antisecession constituents, while the rest of Tennessee sent senators and representatives for the whole state, including the dissident eastern counties, to the Confederate Congress.

Johnson and Maynard's continued presence in Washington

was invaluable propaganda. As long as a fragment of Tennessee's Federal delegation remained, the Lincoln administration could claim that Tennessee had never really left the Union.[3] Moreover, these leaders could mobilize the citizens of east Tennessee against the secessionists, encouraging them to obstruct Confederate activities in the area by destroying depots, burning bridges, and sabotaging mines. With a little aid, these people might even recover Nashville and set up a pro-Union state government, thus substantiating Lincoln's claim to the whole of Tennessee. If this proved impracticable, firm Union military control of east Tennessee might encourage the formation of a separate state, as had occurred in the counties of western Virginia.[4]

Lincoln's politically based strategy for the West—"a joint movement from Cairo on Memphis; and from Cincinnati on East Tennessee"—accorded with General McClellan's military ideas. In his first strategic memorandum to General-in-Chief Scott while commanding the Department of the Ohio, McClellan had suggested sending a column of 80,000 men against Nashville; this force could then move toward Montgomery, uniting with a second column pushing through Charleston and Augusta. The ultimate objective of the combined armies might be an attack on Pensacola, Mobile, or New Orleans, planned in conjunction with naval attacks on these ports.[5]

Once in command of the Army of the Potomac and aware of the administration's views, McClellan modified his suggestions for western strategy. On 4 August he recommended operations to secure Missouri, along with an advance down the Mississippi to Memphis, and a movement "into Eastern Tennessee, for the purpose of assisting the Union men of that region and of seizing the railroads leading from Memphis to the East." It was the same concept on a larger scale. The coast expeditions remained an essential part of the plan. But instead of marching one army through central Tennessee to join another army moving in from the South Atlantic coast, his plan would require several armies moving south from the line of the Ohio and uniting at strategic points along the railroads with the combined expeditions moving in from the coast. Split into two columns for east Tennessee and Nashville, the army could reunite at Chattanooga, march on Atlanta in conjunction with the expedition from Charleston, and proceed to Montgomery, linking up with an expedition from Mobile. After gaining control of Missouri the second western army, supported by a strong gunboat squadron, would push down the Mississippi and take New Orleans.[6] The other coast expedition, led by Burnside, was expected to seize the coastal railroad at Goldsborough, North Carolina; this would prevent the enemy from using his forces in Virginia to oppose the Union column marching through South Carolina and Georgia. The New Orleans expedition further extended the plan. But, although McClellan altered his strategic objectives to accord with the Federal government's political priorities, it should be kept in mind that he wanted these points for military reasons. Despite his expressed interest in relieving the "loyal men of Eastern Tennessee," he actually desired an advance on Knoxville so that he could gain control of the Virginia and Tennessee Railroad.

Lincoln had earlier attempted to force a move into east Tennessee. Although a large expedition was impossible for several months, a small force under Brigadier General William Nelson was organized in early October to carry out what amounted to a glorified raid on the railroad. Nelson was to march from Cincinnati up the Licking River, cross the Cumberland Mountains, and descend on Lebanon in the Clinch River valley northeast of Knoxville. Like most hastily prepared and unsupported operations in enemy country, this one accomplished practically nothing. Nelson forgot about the railroad in his eagerness to envelop a small Confederate force at Piketon under Colonel J.S. Williams. Failing in this endeavor and having fallen into an ambush at Ivy Creek Pass, he nevertheless induced Williams to retreat, but could not follow because of fatigue and lack of supplies. Overtaken by winter in the mountains, he was compelled to abandon the area. He left some Union supporters in eastern Kentucky, who had destroyed several railroad bridges in anticipation of his advance, to the not-so-tender mercy of the Confederate authorities, who hung as traitors all the "bridge-burners" they could catch.[7] Such half measures were worse than nothing. Even the remarkable tenacity with which the mountain people clung to the Union could be strained only so far, and it was unwise to encourage an insurrection before substantial Federal forces were in position to take advantage of it.

Immediately upon taking command, McClellan asked the advice of Brigadier General William T. Sherman, commanding the Ohio Department, about the situation in the West, suggesting more ambitious operations.[8] Sherman's response was discouraging. There were, on paper, 70,000 Union soldiers in Ohio, but this disorganized force was "too small to do good and too large to sacrifice." Although the Confederates could maintain only 30,000 men on the line Bowling Green-Nashville-Clarksville, Bowling Green was reported to be strongly fortified. McClellan's proposed march from Louisville through Cumberland Gap to Knoxville presented almost insurmountable logistical problems; it would require three rail lines, all vulnerable, and beyond Lexington and Lebanon, there were no railways at all, and only a few bad roads.[9]

On 4 November, after consulting the new general-in-chief, Lincoln reorganized the western department. General Halleck replaced Major General John C. Frémont, and the eastern boundary of his command, called the Department of the Missouri, was fixed at the Cumberland River. The area east to the Virginia border was designated the Department of the Ohio and placed under Brigadier General Don Carlos Buell. The dividing line between these departments, deliberately chosen to give Buell access to the Cumberland for his eventual move on Nashville, actually proved an obstacle to Federal operations at a later date.

Buell was considered one of the best soldiers in the Army and McClellan selected him for this command, which he regarded as second in importance only to his own, with absolute confidence. Before leaving for Ohio, Buell held full consultations with McClellan which should have left no doubt about the general-in-chief's intentions; these were further confirmed in his initial written instructions of 7 November. Although McClellan agreed with Buell that, "everything being equal," the primary objective for the Army of the Ohio would be Nashville, he could not ignore the political factors involved. He had decided that the main operation should be against Knoxville, not only because the Federal government insisted upon protecting the Unionists of east Tennessee, but because their presence

Major General Don Carlos Buell   Major General Henry W. Halleck
(*Library of Congress*)   (*Library of Congress*)

would assist the Army's advance toward Chattanooga, producing greater strategic results in a shorter time.[10]

Buell disagreed. Ominously, however, he said nothing at
that time, preferring to wait until he had examined the local
situation. The above instructions, reiterated on 12 November,
unfortunately included what amounted to a discretionary order.
Having stated that the Knoxville movement *must* be carried
out as soon as possible, McClellan added that if, in Buell's
opinion, the government had overestimated Union sympathy
in east Tennessee, he was "perfectly free to change the plan
of operations."[11] Buell was not slow to exercise this option.

Although the occupation of Knoxville was an important part
of his overall strategy, McClellan must have recognized that
it might not be possible to get there. More than any other Civil
War general, he knew that railways were necessary for moving
large forces any distance through difficult country. The West
Virginia campaign had further emphasized this point, and his
basic strategy of paralyzing the Confederate armies by seizing
the Southern rail system was founded upon it. Realizing that
railroads, too, were vulnerable, he wished to use water lines

wherever possible. Buell's contention that he could neither move nor supply a large army over two hundred miles of mountain wilderness on a few dirt roads was unanswerable. But while as a conscientious soldier, McClellan could not order the impossible, he knew that the government did not understand logistics and expected the generals to do it somehow.

Buell was not accountable to the politicians. Throughout the month of November, he played upon his superior's predicament and good military sense to weaken McClellan's resolve for an expedition into east Tennessee. Instead, he proposed to divide his 65,000-man army into three columns: one to hold the Confederates at Bowling Green, the second to move past this point through Gallatin on Nashville, and the third to march from Lebanon via Somerset toward Knoxville. In cooperation with the Nashville advance, two columns from Halleck's command should move up the Tennessee and Cumberland Rivers, land, and unite near the state border. Halleck should also make a strong demonstration against Columbus on the Mississippi.[12]

McClellan disapproved of this plan in only one particular. In his view, Buell should use only two columns—15,000 men for east Tennessee and 50,000 for a strong attack on Nashville. He would arrange for gunboats, and would attach Brigadier General C.F. Smith's division at Paducah to Buell's command for the river operations. Having finally decided to support the Nashville scheme, McClellan realized that the move must be made quickly and forcefully to be successful.[13] The rapid capture of the city would be Buell's only excuse for disregarding his initial instructions, and McClellan's justification to the Federal government for changing the campaign plan.

To ensure that his strategy for the conquest of Tennessee was approved, however, Buell had neglected to inform McClellan of the actual state of his army. The ambitious operational proposals and the confident tone of his dispatches gave the impression that he was prepared to move at once; McClellan, therefore, supposed that he could fend off government pressure for the east Tennessee expedition long enough to get Buell in motion toward Nashville.[14] True, the plan was complex, in that it required a simultaneous movement by part of

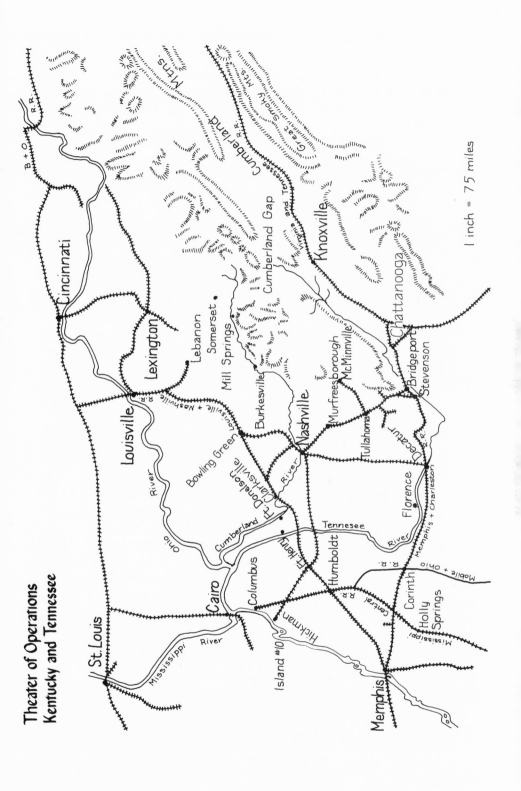

Theater of Operations
Kentucky and Tennessee

1 inch = 75 miles

B + O. R.R.

Cincinnati

Louisville

Lexington

Lebanon
Somerset
Mill Springs

Cumberland Mtns.

Great Smoky Mts.

Tennessee and Ten. R.R.

Cumberland Gap

Knoxville

Chattanooga

Bridgeport
Stevenson

Louisville + Nashville R.R.

Bowling Green

Burkesville

Nashville

Murfreesborough
McMinnville

Decatur

Tullahoma

Ohio River

Cumberland River

Ft. Donelson
Clarksville

Tennessee River

Florence

Memphis + Charleston

Ft. Henry

Humboldt

Mobile + Ohio R.R.

Corinth
Holly
Springs

Cairo

Columbus

Hickman

Island #10

Central R.R.

Mississippi R.R.

St. Louis

Mississippi River

Memphis

Halleck's command; but McClellan was also assuming a state of readiness that did not exist.

Grant's combined attack on Belmont, Missouri in early November, ill-conceived and nearly disastrous in execution, had been hailed in the North as a great victory, and the Federal administration falsely interpreted it as the vanguard of a great push down the Mississippi River. That it was actually a shoestring operation involving raw troops "covered" by two undermanned wooden gunboats was not mentioned. Seizing a long-awaited and short-lived opportunity to take the offensive before his new superior arrived, Grant had initiated the attack without instructions. He did not even inform the responsible naval commander until the attack was over, correctly supposing that Commodore Foote would declare the western flotilla totally incapable of a major operation. In this peculiar hiatus between Army commanders in the Department of the Missouri, Grant had not technically disobeyed orders and, despite a well-deserved repulse by Confederate forces, he managed to return with over half of his troops and the two slightly damaged boats.[15] The only result of his premature foray, aside from encouraging the Confederates to strengthen their defenses on the upper Mississippi, was to give the Washing officials and General McClellan the false idea that Halleck's command was prepared to take the offensive.

Although angry with Grant for usurping his authority, Foote did nothing to correct this misimpression; and Halleck, on his arrival in St. Louis, was preoccupied with cleaning up the mess his predecessor had left behind. General Frémont's enthusiastic incompetence, instead of pacifying an already unstable region, had inflamed Missouri into open civil war. Military strategy and logistics had been neglected, as isolated and unsupported detachments were sent in all directions chasing elusive raiding parties. The soldiers were unpaid, and the quartermaster department hopelessly muddled. Large quantities of stores and arms had been stolen by profiteers, and Frémont had kept no proper accounts of expenses and government contracts. On the political front, his antislavery proclamations and speeches, which ran counter to the administration's official policy, converted many rural inhabitants who had previously been pro-Union or neutral into Southern sympathizers, while inciting the impatience of the large abolitionist German population in the towns. Halleck found St. Louis in such a condition of riotous anarchy that he was forced to declare martial law.[16]

The new department commander's first concern, therefore, was not to prepare for the Mississippi River expedition or coordinate his movements with Buell's, as McClellan wished, but to stabilize his base and prevent Missouri from falling into the hands of invading Confederate armies, or of Frémont's partisans who ignored the Federal government's war aims and clamored for the restoration of their hero. This monumental task, which kept Halleck in St. Louis for four months, made it impossible for him to report regularly to the adjutant general in Washington. Moreover, Halleck was a superb administrator of stoic disposition, who was not prone to complain about his responsibilities. While this concept of duty was one of his most admirable qualities, it had the effect of leaving McClellan in the dark about conditions in his department.

Buell also failed to report regularly, but for a different reason. If the government became aware that he could not move immediately on Nashville, it would renew pressure on him to advance into east Tennessee. Unaware that McClellan had approved the Nashville scheme, Johnson and Maynard wrote Buell directly on 7 December, urging him to hurry his preparations for the Knoxville expedition, pointing out that both McClellan and Lincoln had promised to give this operation top priority.[17] They received no reply.

But Buell could not stall indefinitely. One of McClellan's last acts before being stricken with typhoid on 20 December was to demand that Buell report the condition of his command to the adjutant general. On the 23rd Buell replied to McClellan personally. Revealing that he had "only" 57,000 effectives and that these were short of good officers and a competent staff, he complained that the other 23,000 listed in the returns were undisciplined and fit only to be depot guards; moreover, many of their officers were absent without leave. Unless veteran reinforcements were sent, his army could not undertake an offensive before spring without Halleck's full cooperation.[18]

McClellan had approved the Nashville plan on the assumption that Buell could move in December and that Halleck's support, while desirable, was not essential. Now he knew that

Buell was unprepared to advance in any direction without cooperation from another command—and there was still no word from Halleck. By the 29th Johnson and Maynard suspected they had been deceived. Descending in fury upon the president, they excited his natural sympathy by relating horrible tales of loyal Tennesseans, without arms to defend themselves and their families, being driven from their homes and hunted like beasts in the forest. Lincoln knew nothing of McClellan's overall plan and was, as yet, unwilling to consider himself a military expert; instead, he pleaded with his prostrate general-in-chief to do something. Too ill to write, McClellan dictated a short urgent telegram ordering Buell, for political reasons, to send arms into east Tennessee.[19]

Buell had no choice but to obey, and at once he instructed Brigadier General George H. Thomas to prepare a column for a march toward the Cumberland Gap. Still, he disapproved, and in a long, involved reply, Buell tediously reiterated his logistical problems, of which his sick and harassed superior was only too aware, and demanded large reinforcements. Lincoln himself tried to fill the vacuum left by McClellan's illness, sending numerous inquiries to Buell and Halleck about their preparations and suggesting cooperation in a forward movement. It was a discouraging experience for the president, who got his first lesson in the friction of war. He urged both commanders to communicate directly with each other and act in concert—Buell against Bowling Green and Knoxville; and Halleck against Columbus.[20]

Buell told the president that his army was not ready to advance on Bowling Green, nor had he heard from Halleck. Arranging cooperation was McClellan's responsibility. As for east Tennessee, Thomas was delayed for lack of transport. Besides, he had never approved of this expedition; the order to Thomas was issued solely to satisfy the government and General McClellan, who thought it important. The best strategy was to strike the hinges of the Confederate line—Bowling Green and Columbus. Because only an insignificant enemy force occupied east Tennessee, it was pointless to go there.[21]

Halleck replied that he had no knowledge of the campaign plan, he had heard nothing from Buell, his hands were full in Missouri, and he was not ready to take the offensive. An attack on Columbus with his available force would be suicide. Moreover, Lincoln's strategy was wrong, for separate unsupported movements, even if carried out simultaneously, would everywhere fail. "All military authorities," he instructed the president, "condemn operations on exterior lines against an enemy in a central position." This error had produced McDowell's disaster at Bull Run. Even Smith at Paducah and Buell at Louisville, approaching Nashville on different lines, would allow the enemy to defeat them separately. The proper strategy was to wait until Federal forces could be concentrated to smash with overwhelming force through the Confederate center from an interior position. Such a plan was as yet impossible, and premature thrusts at the periphery would only exhaust and demoralize the Union armies, while encouraging the enemy.[22]

These negative responses depressed the president, angered Johnson and Maynard, and embarrassed McClellan. Rushing to McClellan's house with Buell's dispatch of 5 January concerning east Tennessee, Lincoln again called him from his sick bed to force some action from his strong-willed subordinates. McClellan was understandably shocked, not to discover Buell's real view, but to find that, knowing the government's priorities, Buell had openly opposed the president. Buell's misplaced candor had hardly improved the Army's relations with the administration, and McClellan fired off an incisive telegram in an attempt to repair the damage. Political considerations aside, Buell would have to understand that McClellan's *military* plans required possession of the railroad at Knoxville. Compared with this objective, Bowling Green and Nashville were of secondary importance. If Buell was prepared to move on Bowling Green at once, with or without Halleck's cooperation, he could do so; if not, he must secure east Tennessee, then worry about Nashville.[23]

While arguments over policy and strategy were going on in Washington, events in the West built up a momentum of their own. Two days before Buell's controversial critique arrived, Lincoln induced McClellan to order some movement in support of Buell. The president was still under the impression that the Army of the Ohio was about to proceed against both Bowling Green and Knoxville according to the plan approved in December, although he had received Halleck's discouraging reply about cooperation. McClellan suggested a demonstration against Columbus plus a combined expedition up the Cumberland, "in sufficient force to defeat any possible opposition." Halleck overreacted, complaining that withdrawing troops from Missouri before February for a major offensive would lose the state permanently to the Confederacy. He might make a feint, but no real attack.[24] Actually, an important movement was already taking place on the Tennessee. Initiated by General Smith, with Halleck's approval, a reconnaissance force moved toward Fort Henry. For months Smith had been convinced that the enemy was building up to attack his base and subsequently to conquer the Ohio Valley. According to deserters, General Johnston's army would converge on Paducah from three sides. Reports that the Southerners were constructing heavily armed ironclad gunboats far up the Cumberland gave credence to this idea.[25]

Since reporting the situation to Halleck on 23 November, Smith had kept a sharp eye in this direction, sending Lieutenant Commander S. Ledyard Phelps in the gunboat USS *Conestoga*, temporarily attached to Smith's command, up the rivers whenever possible to observe enemy activity. On 10 December Phelps confirmed the report of two gunboats being built on the Cumberland; one at Clarksville, the other at Nashville. To protect this valuable property, the Confederates had strung chains across the river at Dover and had begun erecting a heavy battery, Fort Donelson, a few miles below the town. Several more boats were reported in progress above Fort Henry on the Tennessee, the most dangerous of which was the *Eastport*, a large fast vessel likely to prove formidable if properly armed. Phelps recommended an immediate advance on both rivers before the Confederates could complete what he and Smith assumed were offensive preparations.[26] This suggestion could not be implemented in December, however, because the Union flotilla was not ready.

Although Smith could not have known it, attacking Paducah or any other Union stronghold was the last thing the Confederates would have considered at that time. General Johnston had barely 30,000 soldiers to defend the whole Tennessee line. As early as 27 October, he had correctly guessed McClellan's strategy for the West, warning Secretary of War Benjamin that, without large reinforcements to defend Bowling Green and secure its flanks, he would have to evacuate it to cover Nashville as soon as the enemy approached or broke through the river defenses.[27] Indeed, the only uncertainty for Johnston was why the Federals were waiting so long to take advantage of their superior resources. By January he had begun to hope, if not for victory, at least for a possible stalemate. More arms were arriving from Europe and from the South's new ordnance factories, Forts Henry and Donelson were nearly complete and armed with a few heavy guns, the defenses of Bowling Green and Columbus could withstand an attack of less than three-to-one superiority, and the state governors were at last responding to his urgent call for men. The South's greatest deficiency was on the water. Without a shipyard, naval constructors, skilled workmen, adequate marine engines, or iron for plating, the South was hopelessly outclassed in gunboat production. Conversion of existing vessels required months of labor under the most unfavorable conditions, and shore batteries, even when buttressed by obstructions and primitive mines, might not be enough to stop a Union flotilla.[28]

Smith's division, accompanied by the wooden gunboats *Lexington, Tyler*, and *Conestoga*, approached within two and one-half miles of Fort Henry. On 27 January he reported that there were two thousand Confederate troops in the vicinity and expressed the opinion that two ironclad gunboats could destroy the work. Encouraged, Halleck was already planning to convert Smith's reconnaissance into a major operation when he received Lincoln's War Order of 27 January, demanding that all Federal armies advance against the enemy on 22 February. Still fully occupied in St. Louis, Halleck gave Grant and Foote responsibility for implementing this order and asked for their assessment of the situation. Foote replied on the following day that Grant and he could be certain of success against Fort Henry if given four ironclads and enough troops for permanent occupation.[29]

But events were moving faster than Halleck anticipated. A fingerlike thrust into enemy country, unless it was a raid, was dangerous even if the Union commanded the river. The Confederate army around Bowling Green might cross the Ohio above Paducah, cutting Grant off from his base, or fall on his left flank from the direction of the Cumberland. Halleck had therefore ordered Smith to examine the roads between Smith-ville and Dover, and those east of the Cumberland, to deter-mine if the ground was firm enough to support enemy troops supplied by water. Although Smith's report had not arrived on the morning of 29 January and Halleck advised Foote and Grant to wait for orders, two telegrams from McClellan re-ceived later that day changed his mind. One contained impor-tant information: according to McClellan, Confederate General Beauregard and his corps were about to leave Virginia to re-inforce General A.S. Johnston. In the other, McClellan endorsed Halleck's plan to move the bulk of his army up the Tennessee and Cumberland rivers, instead of down the Mississippi.[30]

As has been observed before, Halleck opposed multiple lines of operation. Turning Columbus, instead of attacking it, would not only permit Halleck to concentrate his army in the center, but would place it within supporting distance of Buell. From McClellan's standpoint, possession of the rail junction at Decatur, which was accessible via the Tennessee, was more important to his overall strategy than the capture of either Columbus or Memphis. Although the Mississippi River expedi-tion, one of Lincoln's pet projects, might have to be carried out eventually, a firm grip on the Memphis and Charleston Railroad would force the Confederates to withdraw from the upper Mississippi, thus making a combined operation against Memphis easier.[31]

Consequently, although Halleck had scheduled the full-scale push up the Tennessee for mid-February to forestall a sup-posed Confederate invasion plan, McClellan's approval of his proposal, along with the information about Beauregard, prompted him to act immediately. Buell was advised on 30 November that Grant and Foote had been ordered to seize and hold Fort Henry and burn the railroad bridge above this point. Despite his advice to McClellan on the same day that gunboats should be sent up both rivers at once, and take advantage of unusually high water to destroy bridges, Buell strongly pro-tested Halleck's "precipitous haste" in attacking Fort Henry. A raid was one thing, but a serious assault on a fortification, involving a division or more of infantry, was another. Buell informed Halleck and McClellan that he could support Grant only by marching his entire army against Bowling Green—which he was not prepared to do. Because the town was heavily fortified, a demonstration would not fool the Confederates; they would continue to withdraw troops to reinforce the river lines unless menaced by a vastly superior force. There was another reason for Buell's opposition. A large part of his army, under General Thomas, was at Somerset and Burkesville on the upper Cumberland.[32]

Under renewed pressure from Lincoln and McClellan on 13 January, Buell finally dispatched an expedition toward Knoxville.[33] Thomas was in the process of establishing an advanced depot at Somerset when the Confederate force defending Cumberland Gap, under Major General G.B. Crittenden and Brigadier General Felix Zollicoffer, learned of Thomas' activity and moved down along the north bank of the river. The Confederates intended to cross to their fortified camp at Mill Springs, from which point the Federals could be prevented from passing over the river. By the time they arrived opposite Mill Springs, however, heavy rains had so swollen the Cumberland that they could not cross until boats were brought from Nashville. Discovering Thomas's camp a few miles to the north, Crittenden and Zollicoffer decided to attack the camp on 19 January, before Thomas could discover them, and fall upon the troops in the act of crossing.

The details of the resulting engagement, called Mill Springs or Logan's Crossroads, are unimportant, but its effect—the defeat and dispersion of Crittenden's army—decisively altered Federal strategy in the West.[34] Oddly enough, the victory, which cleared the Cumberland Gap and eliminated the able and popular General Zollicoffer of east Tennessee, did more harm than good to the Union cause. Since the only enemy between him and Knoxville had been driven off, Thomas concluded that it was senseless to proceed with the expedition, especially in view of the difficulty he would encounter in getting supplies into the region and crossing the mountains. Instead, he moved his army further down the Cumberland to Burkesville, thinking that if Foote's gunboats could reach this point, their combined forces could attack Nashville from above. Buell agreed with Thomas, and thus was not interested in Halleck's operation against Fort Henry. The gunboats should steam up the Cumberland without the burden of troops, run by Fort Donelson, destroy the railroad bridge at Clarksville, and unite with Thomas above Nashville.[35]

Because the orders for the Fort Henry expedition had already been given and besides, Foote's flotilla was officially attached to Halleck's command, McClellan rejected Thomas's proposal. Buell thereupon resumed his earlier plan, to move in full strength against Bowling Green while Halleck turned the position from the west via the rivers. Thomas's army, however, remained at Burkesville until 6 February. Buell believed that Halleck's movement would doubtless force the enemy out of Bowling Green, while his own advance, he informed McClellan, would be slow and difficult, even without interference from the enemy. Simply rebuilding the railroad from Green River to the town would require at least ten days.[36]

If Buell saw nothing incongruous in this reasoning, Halleck did. Throughout February, until the Union occupation of Nashville on the 25th, Halleck tried to convince McClellan that Buell's strategy was wrong. Since the enemy could be turned out of Bowling Green and Nashville, it was not necessary to march an army against either place. Moreover, after the Confederates had withdrawn there would be ample time to rebuild the railroad from Louisville. The correct strategy, he maintained, was to concentrate all Union forces, including Buell's, on the Tennessee for a grand push through the center of the enemy line.[37] While Halleck's plan was simpler than Buell's and he presented it more forcefully and persistently to the Washington authorities, it contained a serious flaw.

The error in Halleck's reasoning concerned the evacuation of Nashville. Buell himself admitted that the Confederates had to leave Bowling Green to defend the river lines, especially since Thomas's command at Burkesville menaced their right flank. Union possession of the Tennessee and Cumberland rivers, however, would not necessarily force Johnston out of Nashville. To isolate the city, McClellan pointed out, it was necessary to cut or occupy the Memphis and Charleston road at Stevenson, not just at Decatur. With the Virginia and Tennessee line still open, the Confederates could reinforce Nashville from Virginia and the Atlantic seaboard, and from the Deep South through Mobile.[38]

Halleck claimed that Nashville would be of no importance once the Federals had penetrated deep into the state, seized the Memphis and Charleston at Corinth and Decatur, and forced the enemy to evacuate Columbus.[39] This claim had some military merit, but it entirely disregarded political considerations. Lincoln insisted on the occupation of Nashville in force, for only then could a legitimate Union government be established and Tennessee be officially reclaimed by the United States. McClellan objected to Halleck's plan for two other reasons, both of them involving east Tennessee: first, because one massive army in west Tennessee could not link up with any of the coast expeditions; second, because Thomas' failure to move on Knoxville after his success at Mill Springs had outraged Johnson and Maynard and mystified the president. Buell was again violating his instructions, and moving away from east Tennessee. McClellan was able to pacify the politicians and get Buell temporarily off the hook only with the argument that, because of logistical problems on the route through Cumberland Gap, it was faster and more certain for the Army of the Ohio to advance on Chattanooga via Nashville. This plan would ultimately give the Federal government both a state capital and east Tennessee.[40]

Unfortunately, Halleck was not apprised of these political imperatives. His plan—for Buell to operate against Fort Donelson on the Cumberland while Grant pushed up the Tennessee, with the two armies then uniting below Dover for a move against Decatur—was simply rejected by the president and secretary of War. The government's approval of Buell's advance via Bowling Green was for reasons which Halleck, given no explanation, never understood. One thing was certain, even before the attack on Fort Henry, however. If Grant's 15,000 men had to go it alone, Buell must move against some other objective at the same time.[41]

Grant and Smith might be sure that a few gunboats could drive an army from earthworks; but, as an engineer, Halleck was skeptical. He believed that these unwieldy experimental vessels mounting two or three cannon could do little except disperse infantry in the open or frighten civilians; he had no use at all for the mortar boats being hurriedly completed at Cairo. His later claims notwithstanding, Commodore Foote had scarcely more confidence in the motley Union fleet, agreeing entirely with Halleck about the mortars (despite Phelps's opinion, after several fairly close inspections of Forts Henry and Donelson, that high-angle fire was necessary to silence these works).[42]

Foote and Halleck might have considered themselves fortunate to possess a "navy" at all. Indeed, the trials of the western flotilla demonstrate why combined operations are so difficult, and why it took so long to develop a method for designing and preparing such operations. A few dynamic men of exceptional ability could sometimes cut through the tangle of red tape and find their way through the maze of trivia, by sheer energy, determination, and unconventional procedures. But few wars are conducted by men of very exceptional ability. Although most generals and admirals, like legislators and presidents, are professionally competent, they often lack initiative—the resourcefulness to deal with new situations and meet unexpected requirements. So formal doctrines, rules, techniques, and procedures are developed, and serve as indispensable guides to the average capable officer attempting to do his job effectively. But formal doctrine and standard procedures for getting up combined operations did not exist during the Civil War. Consequently, given the chaotic and somewhat primitive nineteenth-century organizational and command structure in both services, such projects were in constant danger of foundering on some petty detail or bogging down in a mire of bureaucratic confusion.

Although he enjoyed the high esteem and confidence of the Navy Department for his aggressiveness and fighting ability, Commodore Foote had discovered that this kind of credit bought no gunboats, or anything else required for the infant river navy. At Welles's insistence, the western flotilla was initially attached to the Army, and remained under its jurisdiction until the summer of 1862. On taking command in September 1861, Foote learned that the seven ironclads ordered from St. Louis firms by his predecessor, Commander John Rodgers, and approved by General Meigs, the quartermaster general, were to be completed before 10 October. But because McClellan's successor in the West, General Frémont, had signed contracts for two more gunboats, thirty-eight mor-

 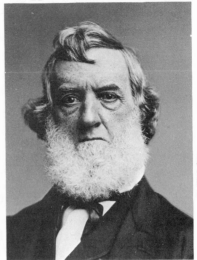

Rear Admiral Andrew H. Foote
(*National Archives*)

Secretary of the Navy
Gideon Welles
(*National Archives*)

tar boats and assorted other vessels, the yards became overloaded. Production was further slowed by the conflicting ideas of the private riverboat builders and the constructor sent out by the Navy Department. And since neither naval architects nor commercial shipbuilders had any experience in designing ironclads, their initial efforts were less than satisfactory. Foote found on inspecting the boats under construction that they were badly designed. The gunboats' draft, even without armor, exceeded specifications, and they were down at the stern. The mortar "rafts" were worse; great awkward wooden boxes, whose decks would be submerged under the weight of 13-inch mortars. All of these vessels required extensive alterations, which Foote could not approve without funds.[43]

On 1 November Meigs peremptorily informed Foote that the government could pay only for the original seven gunboats authorized by the War Department; thus, Frémont's contracts would not be honored. Unfortunately, instead of turning out the vessels one by one, the yards had attempted to build nine ironclads and thirty-eight mortar boats simultaneously, so that all boats were in a state of partial completion. After the work already done had been paid for, only enough money remained to finish four or five of the gunboats, and none of the mortars or tugboats included in the contracts.[44]

Because neither the War nor the Navy departments seemed willing to assume responsibility for the project, McClellan took matters into his own hands. The push into Tennessee, just as vital as the other half of his combined operations strategy, seemed hopelessly stalled for want of a river fleet. Early in December he authorized Foote to complete and arm the nine gunboats (eight of them ironclads) still in the contractor's hands, arranged for credit, and advised the Army Ordnance Bureau to provide the specified armament as a top priority.[45]

But the solution to one problem precipitated another. The boats were useless without crews. Having repeatedly been refused assistance by the Navy Department, even while Welles promoted him to flag officer, Foote persuaded Halleck to supply him with a regiment from St. Louis to man the new gunboats. This arrangement fell apart, however, when the soldiers, discovering that they were to serve without their officers and enlist in the Navy, refused the duty. Frustrated, Foote again requested men from Assistant Secretary Fox in late December. Fox simply referred the matter to the secretary of War, who referred it to McClellan, who referred it back to Halleck.[46] In desperation, having ordered the movement against Fort Henry on 29 January, Halleck instructed Grant to detail men temporarily for this duty. But Grant discovered that his men would not serve without their officers either, and he could not detach them without demoralizing his command. Thus having attempted every expedient, including unproductive recruiting campaigns in Cincinnati, Chicago, and Cleveland, Foote was required to commence the expedition with only four ironclads operating with half crews.[47]

The capture of Forts Henry and Donelson, seen from the perspective of subsequent events, is often cited as a good example of the offensive power of combined operations. But this judgment needs to be qualified. Both attacks were, to a large extent, opportunistic, carried out for a variety of purposes, with no support and inadequate means. That they succeeded is less important than *why*. The decisive Union advantage at Fort Henry was certainly not the supposed destructive power of naval gunfire. It was good luck—a risky element upon which to base operational plans.

Halleck's fears were justified. Ironclads had never been tested against earthen fortifications, and Fort Henry had repeatedly been described as a formidable work. Neither Grant nor Foote knew, before or after the attack, that the fort was manned by inexperienced gunners, that the unusually high level of the river had flooded the magazines, that the ordnance most effective against armor—a converted 32-pounder rifle and a 10-inch columbiad—were rendered useless near the beginning of the action by explosions and mechanical accidents, and that the fort was not "silenced" by the Federal gunboats, but because the garrison feared their own ordnance more than they did the enemy. It has been argued that high water allowed the gunboats to shoot directly into the fort, accounting for the supposed success of direct fire against an earthwork. But the facts do not sustain this conclusion. Contrary to prior Federal reports, Fort Henry was not a barbette battery; its guns were mounted in embrasure. According to the engineers' reports there was very slight damage. Only one shell entered an embrasure and even this, while killing three men, failed to dismount the gun.[48]

Grant was absent during the bombardment, however, and since he was no engineer, he attached little significance to the lack of physical damage to the work. Success was sufficient cause, in his mind, for complete confidence in the flotilla. The general had scarcely arrived at Fort Henry before he set out to capture Fort Donelson. At first, he intended to follow the short land route used by most of Henry's defenders to escape to the Cumberland. But cavalry patrols revealed that the road could not transport artillery. Instead, he moved up the Cumberland by water, landed below Donelson, and attempted to isolate the fort while the gunboats battered it into submission.[49] The trouble with this plan was Grant's overestimation of the fleet's fire capability.

Despite the rapid surrender of Fort Henry after a two-hour cannonade, Foote was not pleased with the action. The gunboats held up badly even under feeble fire from the fort. Several ironclads were extensively damaged and had to be returned to Cairo for repairs. In fact, the flag officer was so pessimistic about his victory at Fort Henry that he refused to attack Donelson.[50]

Halleck now found himself in the very predicament he had sought to avoid by cooperating with Buell. His left was exposed, and unless Donelson was taken immediately, Grant's foothold up the Tennessee might be lost. Since Buell's force was still too far north to engage the enemy, Johnston was able to reinforce the fort with 10,000 men from Bowling Green. Even though Foote was finally persuaded to expose his gunboats to destruction, Grant's force still was too small. Yet the attack had to be made.[51]

Halleck's fears for the safety of Grant's force and the fate of his strategy were exacerbated by the failure of the naval attack on Donelson. While the repulse of the flotilla surprised only Grant, and possibly the enemy, Foote and Halleck were unprepared for a defeat of such magnitude. All four ironclads and one of the two wooden gunboats engaged were badly damaged.[52] Since at least one vessel was needed to patrol the Tennessee, only a single boat remained in the Cumberland by the evening of 14 February. Eight hurriedly completed mortar rafts had been towed to the river mouth but could not be brought upstream against the current. The Union infantry were thus left in a precarious position without fire support. Although his thirty thousand infantry had surrounded the line of Confederate rifle pits outside the fort on 13 February, the perimeter was two miles long and Grant enjoyed only a slight numerical superiority.[53]

That the enemy might break out of the encirclement was a minor worry compared with the danger of losing command of the river. The Union's control of the Cumberland provided the only link between the armies of Grant and Buell, and prevented Confederate movements between Clarksville and Dover. Time seemed all important; if Grant could hold on for a few days until the patched-up ironclads could again steam up the river, the Southerners would have to surrender Donelson or defeat Grant's army. Halleck's apprehensions may appear unrealistic, for without vessels to command the rivers, Johnston's entire line north of the Memphis and Charleston was indefensible. But we should remember that Halleck had no accurate knowledge of his opponent's strength, nor was he aware that, for lack of materials, the Confederates had been unable to finish their two gunboats being built above Nashville.[54]

In fact, the decision to evacuate Donelson was made a week before the Federals approached the fort. With Beauregard's approval, Johnston had issued contingency orders to withdraw his forces from Bowling Green, Clarksville, and Nashville, and concentrate them at Murfreesborough on the railroad southeast of Nashville. The Confederate troops at Columbus on the Mississippi would retreat, first to the recently prepared defenses at Island Number 10, then to Fort Pillow, and ultimately to a

Foote's river flotilla attacking Fort Donelson, 14 February 1862 (*Navy Department*)

line just north of Memphis. To allow heavy guns, ammunition, and stores to be salvaged from the advanced posts, and the valuable machinery from the Nashville foundry shipped further south, it was decided to hold Fort Donelson as long as possible.[55] The sacrifice of 15,000 men captured along with the work was not part of this plan, nor was it supposed that the fort would fall so quickly. This Confederate disaster was due almost entirely to the collective incompetence of Major Generals William Floyd, Gideon Pillow, and Simon Buckner. Aside from the notorious failure of these officers to exploit their break through the right of the Union encirclement on 15 February, there was no urgent reason for surrendering the fort on the 16th.[56] Although the Confederates had evacuated Bowling Green on the previous day, Buell was not in position to follow up immediately, and the Federal ironclads had not reappeared in the river.

The premature surrender of Donelson, while a relief from

his immediate anxiety, took Halleck by surprise and upset his calculations. Unable to persuade Buell to adopt the line of the Cumberland for his main advance on Nashville, McClellan had ordered him to reinforce Grant by water. After considering the matter for several days, Buell dispatched General Nelson's division. This large unit, commanded by a former naval officer, was considered especially suited for river operations. But Nelson got no further than Smithland on the Ohio River; when Buell learned on 16 February that Fort Donelson had surrendered, he informed Halleck that he was recalling this division for his advance on Bowling Green, which the enemy had just abandoned.[57]

Halleck was furious. He had counted on Nelson to protect Grant's left, which was again exposed from the direction of Clarksville. Moreover, Buell's intransigence was throwing away a golden opportunity, for the Confederates had made a fatal mistake, and their center was now wide open. With Nelson on the Cumberland, Grant could move up the Tennessee all the way to Corinth and seize the Memphis and Charleston before the enemy could transport enough troops from Columbus or Nashville to defend it. If Buell would not send Nelson, maybe he would come around to the Cumberland himself. Buell was receptive to this suggestion from Halleck, but only on condition that his own army maintain its original line while he personally commanded Grant's force in a joint move on Nashville. Because Halleck naturally declined this proposition, Buell refused to relieve Grant on the Cumberland and even urged Halleck to occupy Clarksville, thus extending Grant's operations still further from his base—actually into Buell's department.[58]

Before the fall of Forts Henry and Donelson, the conflicting ideas of the western army commanders were a nuisance for the general-in-chief but did not greatly delay or upset his plans. Neither army could have advanced very far, except toward Knoxville, until the flotilla was ready. Once the offensive was in progress, however, this dispute, perhaps inevitably, erupted into a crisis. Had Buell and Halleck agreed on strategy or had McClellan imposed his will on either general from the outset, the divided command, its boundary bisecting the theater of operations, might not have mattered.

Government interference added to the problem. In late January the secretary of War had sent his assistant, Thomas Scott, to inspect both departments. A former army colonel, Scott seemed the ideal person to bring order out of impending chaos. Actually, Stanton could not have selected a worse agent. Scott's service experience made him prone to offer ill-considered judgments on military matters which were properly the province of the general-in-chief. Moreover, he was so gullible that all ideas supported by reasoned arguments seemed equally attractive. Thus, after interviewing Halleck in St. Louis, Scott enthusiastically endorsed the general's strategic plans, recommending that the War Department give him authority to carry them out. No sooner had he arrived in Louisville, however, than everything took on a different aspect. Captivated by Buell's efficiency and self-assurance, and even more by the glorious political results likely to result from a triumphal entry into Nashville, he advised Stanton to support Buell in every possible way, and give Buell's command priority over Halleck's in the allocation of arms, equipment, and reinforcements.[59] Scott's untimely intervention, instead of reconciling the strategic dispute, compounded it, for each general was encouraged to hold fast to his own ideas, at the expense of McClellan's overall scheme, in the expectation of unqualified support from the War Department.

It finally dawned on McClellan that by focusing only on military results he had allowed the power struggle between his two stubborn subordinates to undermine his authority. As long as the campaign was progressing, he was inclined to dismiss differences of opinion as trivial. But his failure to insist that Buell carry out his instructions to cooperate against the river defenses, or at least make a demonstration in favor of Grant, allowed Halleck to claim the victories at Henry and Donelson exclusively for his own army, and to demand a reward from the government. The reward Halleck had in mind was overall command in the West.[60]

No one could justly accuse Halleck of personal ambition, which is precisely why that ambition was dangerous to McClellan, and eventually fatal to McClellan's strategy. Control of all western armies would allow Halleck to implement his own plan for conquering Tennessee, a plan which he told

McClellan could not possibly go wrong. To this doctrinaire disciple of Jomini, it was inconceivable that other ideas might have equal merit in the particular context of the Civil War, especially in the western theater.[61]

McClellan did not take this proposal for a unified command seriously enough. The government was relying on Buell to liberate east Tennessee. Halleck's plan was unacceptable because it would pull the Army of the Ohio away from Chattanooga. Therefore, the administration would never concentrate all the western troops in his hands. McClellan was confident that the military and political results of Buell's occupation of Nashville would more than equal the prestige of Grant's victories. Still, he decided it was time to assert his authority over both armies to get Halleck's troops off Buell's line.[62]

Halleck was happy to oblige, for he had never approved of operations against Nashville. Besides, he was becoming increasingly nervous about Grant's extended communications and the Federal base at Cairo. On 17 February his chief of staff, General Cullum, reported that fifteen Confederate troop transports accompanied by several gunboats had passed Memphis four days before. They were headed, he thought, for Columbus with the intention of attacking Cairo and Paducah. With part of the Federal flotilla immobilized in the dockyard and the rest up the Cumberland with Grant, both places were unprotected. McClellan's instructions of 18 February, forbidding Halleck's command to proceed up the Cumberland beyond Clarksville, thus coincided with Halleck's own order for nearly all of his troops and gunboats to return to Cairo in anticipation of the expected enemy offensive.[63]

By the time this last order reached the front, Grant and Foote were on their way to Nashville. On 19 February Smith's division occupied Clarksville on the heels of the retreating Confederates. Before proceeding against Nashville, however, where they might meet opposition, Foote, who had only two patched-up ironclads and eight mortar rafts at his disposal, thought it prudent to bring up the rest of the squadron. On reaching Cairo, Foote was shown Halleck's order to evacuate the Cumberland. Dismayed that the ultimate prize was about to be forfeited and convinced that Halleck did not understand how easy it would be to seize the city, he decided to disregard the order. But Cullum, acting on blanket authority from his chief, refused to release the boats. After several fruitless appeals to both General Halleck and the Navy Department, Foote and Grant reluctantly abandoned their advance on Nashville and prepared to return to base.[64]

By 25 February, however, all of the problems which had plagued western operations from the outset seemed to have disappeared. On the 24th Nelson's division, advancing up the Cumberland, had occupied Nashville, and Buell's advance arrived the following day. The enemy had gone. Lincoln remarked that he was well satisfied with Buell's "cautious vigor" and with McClellan's management of the campaign. Foote's gunboats patrolled the Tennessee as far south as Florence, Alabama, protecting Federal recruiters and cotton agents. At Cairo, Halleck's command was preparing a combined operation to hurry the Confederates out of Columbus and attack their positions at Island Number 10 and New Madrid.[65]

The coast expeditions were also progressing. Burnside and Goldsborough had taken Roanoke Island and were extending Federal control in the North Carolina sounds. Butler's army had arrived at Ship Island, and Farragut's fleet was gathering in the Gulf of Mexico. On the South Atlantic coast, Sherman was pushing his reconnaissances closer to Savannah and Charleston, collecting artillery and stores, and preparing detailed plans to capture one of these cities as soon as reinforcements became available. It seemed that nothing could now interfere with the successful execution of McClellan's strategy.

But old controversies are not so easily extinguished. They smoulder just below the surface of events, ready to burst forth with renewed energy at the slightest provocation. If Buell had not been content to rest on his laurels, or at least had kept quiet, all would have been well. Having won the long-contested prize, however, he seemed to forget that Nashville was only an intermediate stop on the road to Chattanooga. McClellan found it as difficult to get Buell out of the place as it was to get him in. Even before the city was occupied, McClellan had urged Buell to push on toward Murfreesborough, thus denying the enemy time to prepare a new defensive line or to effect a junction with the force withdrawing from Columbus. Aside from the military results to be gained, Lincoln would tolerate no more temporizing on this matter. He intended to have east Tennessee one way or another.[66]

At first, McClellan was encouraged by Buell's reports. The Army of the Ohio was closely pursuing the enemy and its advance units were apparently in contact with Johnston's rear guard. In light of this information, McClellan ordered a immediate full-scale advance on Murfreesborough. Buell could not obey. He had, in fact, totally misrepresented the situation. On 6 March he informed McClellan that he could make no significant progress for several weeks. Part of his army was still north of the Cumberland, and the railroad from Bowling Green had to be rebuilt to bring up supplies, since the departing enemy had left none in Nashville.[67] These were legitimate excuses for delay, and the government might have been willing to accept them—if Buell had been more cooperative in the past, and had not so often evaded McClellan's instructions for less compelling reasons.

The final straw for Lincoln was Buell's attempt to meddle in politics. No one had asked his opinion regarding the administration of middle Tennessee; yet, in the haughty tone of a conqueror, he told the president that it was inadvisable to appoint a civilian "military governor" for the state. He, Buell, did not approve, especially of Lincoln's choice, Senator Johnson; the Army was capable of looking after Federal interests in the occupied territory and Johnson's presence would only make its job more difficult.[68]

The administration suddenly had enough of Buell's "cautious vigor." Under prolonged aggravation, most men of easy disposition eventually reach a state of determination against which no argument will prevail. For months, the president had reserved his opinion of Buell, accepting McClellan's persuasive justifications for his conduct. But now his mind was made up. Halleck's proposal for a unified Western command, which he had never ceased urging upon both McClellan and the government, suddenly appeared attractive.[69]

It has been said that McClellan's friendship for Buell was the main motive for his opposition to the administration on this question. While it can not be denied that McClellan's command style was distinctly personal and that he surrounded himself with cliques of trusted associates and intimate friends

—a state of affairs hardly peculiar to McClellan or to the Civil War—his favoritism for certain men was no accident. Buell was a good soldier, and his army was superbly trained and disciplined; such capable officers, rare in the Federal service, should not be demoted. Nor would McClellan approve the consolidation scheme, for he knew of Halleck's fixation with concentration of force and fronts of operation. A strong-willed general whose views so markedly conflicted with his own and with the government's, at least regarding east Tennessee, was not the proper instrument to carry out his grand strategic design. In command of one army, Halleck was very useful; in command of several, he would be difficult to control.[70]

But McClellan was playing a risky game with the politicians, a game he seemed bound to lose. His opponents, led by Secretary of War Stanton, simply bided their time, meanwhile setting up the machinery for the reorganization and corresponding with Halleck through political, rather than military, channels. On 9 March Buell was promoted to major general in order to give him sufficient rank to command one of the three armies Halleck wanted placed under him. Two days earlier, Stanton had virtually assured Halleck that the government would give him command in the West.[71] Although in a final effort to avert a showdown, Halleck warned McClellan that he would regret siding with Buell against the unification scheme, even Halleck did not foresee the magnitude of the repercussions for McClellan and the Union war effort as a whole.[72]

Unknown to either general, the government had already concluded that it could only unify the western departments, and solve the long-standing problem of military support for east Tennessee, by getting rid of McClellan. On 9 March, he rode out of Washington at the head of the Army of the Potomac for a reconnaissance of the Confederate positions at Manassas. The politicians immediately seized their opportunity, and two days later, a copy of the reorganization order (Lincoln's War Order #3) was delivered to McClellan's camp. It announced his removal from the chief command, the restriction of his authority to the Army of the Potomac, and the appointment of General Halleck to command all Federal armies in the West.[73]

Another clause in the order had special significance; in fact, it was probably this feature, more than the controversy with

Buell, which induced Lincoln to demote McClellan. East Tennessee had been the president's top priority since the war began and remained so until it was securely occupied by Union troops in 1864. General Frémont had spent the months since his removal from the Department of Missouri agitating for a new command, and his efforts had the active (indeed, almost fanatical) support of the large German population in the North. A delegation of financiers and businessmen from New York had descended upon the president in January, demanding that Frémont and his former second-in-command, Brigadier General Franz Sigel, be given important assignments. A secret association of German–American friends of emancipation and of Generals Frémont and Sigel was formed in Washington early in the war. The Army Provost Marshal and McClellan's intelligence agents had discovered this "fifth column" and had kept a close watch on its activities. After its champion was ousted from Missouri, this group began to talk wildly about carrying out a coup d'etat to set up Frémont as dictator, at least for the duration of the war.[74]

Something had to be done to counter this menace; but McClellan was unalterably opposed to any command for Frémont or promotion for Sigel. They were incredibly bad generals, more of an asset to the Confederacy than to the Union.[75] But despite their demonstrated ineptitude, Lincoln could not afford to give their supporters continued grounds for agitation. Restoring Frémont to command would put an end to this very real threat to his government. Since the command had to be important enough to satisfy Frémont's partisans, Lincoln hoped to solve two problems at once. He thus created a new department for Frémont called the Mountain Department, extending from Knoxville to the Shenandoah Valley and including a 30,000-man army with a division for Sigel; in return, Frémont promised to capture Knoxville, seize the Virginia and Tennessee Railroad and occupy east Tennessee.[76] With Frémont pushing in that direction, it did not seem to matter much that Halleck would immediately pull Buell off his intended line toward Chattanooga to concentrate on the Tennessee and Mississippi Rivers.

But although the president was aware of, and thus attempted to mitigate, the implications of his decision for the western

Abraham Lincoln

theater, he failed to recognize the larger military consequences of removing the general-in-chief. The effect of War Order #3 was nearly disastrous for the Union. At one blow, McClellan's grand strategy for winning the war in 1862 was wrecked. Outside the context of his master plan, the coast expeditions made little sense as offensive ventures; without a long-range objective, they degenerated into mere raids and shooting contests with forts. Their purpose was seldom clear, either to those who planned them, or those whose lives and reputations were at stake.

Moreover, a wide dispersion of manpower was effective only so long as Federal strategy was based upon a pattern of combined operations. When this pattern was disrupted and the Army, under General Halleck, returned to the old doctrine of strategic concentration, this dispersion of force was a severe handicap for the Union. Existing coastal lodgments, intended only as the first stage in McClellan's plan to penetrate the Confederacy from all directions, could not for political reasons be given up, even though they no longer had any military value.

Despite these retrospective observations, however, the course of the war was not unalterable in March 1862, for Lincoln's decision was not irreversible at that time. In fact, he seems to have thought of McClellan's demotion as a temporary measure to solve urgently pressing political problems. The office of commanding general of the United States Army was left vacant for four months, and McClellan continued to wear the three stars of his former command. If the Peninsular offensive—a kind of test case for combined operations—had succeeded in capturing Richmond or driving the Confederates from Virginia, Lincoln would probably have restored McClellan to the chief command, and the cracks in the Federal war machine which had developed in Tennessee would have been speedily repaired.

What happened in the Peninsula was the climax of Federal combined operations strategy, its most vigorous expression, and must be examined in that light. Many historians claim that the test of any military idea or technique is the simple fact of its success or failure in action; but surely this view is misleading and naive. War is a complex enterprise, and because of a variety of unforeseen or unalterable circumstances, the best generals and the best plans do not always bring victory.

4

ON TO RICHMOND

ALTHOUGH HIS operational schemes were being shaped and reshaped during the fall and winter of 1861, General McClellan did not intend to use the main army offensively in Virginia (if at all) until the preliminary movements of other Federal armies had seized the western railroads and the lines south of Richmond.

For months the Army of the Potomac remained immobile before Washington, waiting for Confederate General Joseph E. Johnston's force, in peak condition after its victory at Bull Run, to waste away from sickness, desertion, and inactivity. And indeed, a winter spent in the open, in a region stripped of supplies, did almost destroy the Confederate army without a battle. The detachment of the North Carolina troops to defend against Burnside in January further depleted its strength. Union intelligence reports, submitted almost daily, remarked on the very low morale and poor physical condition of Johnston's men.[1] McClellan carefully avoided any movements that might signal his intention to advance, thus lulling the Southerners into a false sense of security so that they would not withdraw to new positions before he was ready to attack.[2]

While this strategy was militarily sound, it did not take into account the inevitable political pressure for conspicuous action. Until January 1862, staving off a Cabinet which was divided on strategic priorities proved comparatively easy. The Northern press was kept reasonably satisfied by McClellan's energy in organizing the Army of the Potomac, by his construction of an elaborate fortifications system for Washington, and by the naval successes at Hatteras and Port Royal. McClellan's confinement to bed with typhoid fever in December and his resulting absence from headquarters created a leadership vacuum. In the absence of a chief of staff, all of his orders as general-in-chief were issued through Army Adjutant General Lorenzo Thomas. But because McClellan had not taken Thomas into his confidence regarding plans for the Army of the Potomac, no one knew whom to consult for instructions or information. The Federal war effort thus seemed to enter a state of "suspended animation," while domestic and foreign problems pressed upon the Union government with increasing force.

Although the immediate crisis of open war with Great Britain over the *Trent* affair had passed, British intervention in some form was becoming more probable, according to reports from the U.S. embassy. The so-called Confederate "blockade" of the Potomac below the national capital was an especially favored subject for ridicule in the foreign press, while the Union's own blockade of Southern seaports seemed no more effective than it had six months before.[3] Johnston's army was still secure in its entrenchments at Manassas and Centreville, less than thirty miles from Washington. As far as the Federal government knew, the general-in-chief had no immediate or long-range operational plans for the main army.

This was not the case. As early as November, McClellan mentioned to General Barnard the possibility of landing the army on the south bank of the Rappahannock River, and seizing West Point, at the head of the York River, as a base of operations against Richmond—the so-called "Urbanna Plan." McClellan had formulated no definite plan at that time, however. On 1 December, under pressure from the State Department and Congress to move the Army of the Potomac, Lincoln suggested *his* favorite strategy. The army would advance in three columns: one marching from Alexandria on the direct road to Richmond, another landing just south of the Occoquan to seize the crossings of that river, and the third threatening the main enemy position at Centreville. Uniting below the Occoquan, the first two columns would move to Brentsville and seize the Orange and Alexandria Railroad where it crossed Broad Run. McClellan did not point out the defects of this scheme in detail; instead, he replied rather cryptically that his mind had "actively turned toward another plan of campaign

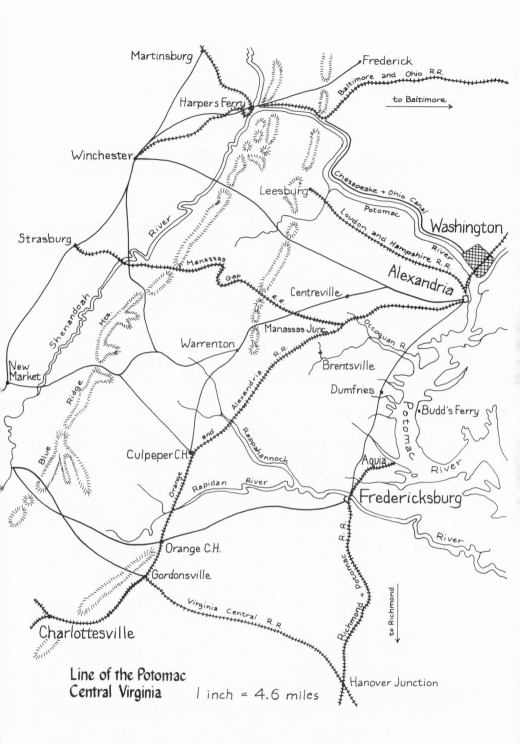

Line of the Potomac
Central Virginia   1 inch = 4.6 miles

that I do not think at all anticipated by the enemy nor many of our own people," and informed the president that the move might be possible by 15 December.[4]

This overly optimistic estimate of the time required to organize a large-scale combined operation was based solely on a report of the available water transport, submitted to McClellan on 28 November. Counting Burnside's vessels already assembled at Annapolis, the Federals could transport 50,000 men; in addition, the barges which Barnard planned to purchase from the Pennsylvania canal companies could accommodate another 15,000.[5] But an amphibious operation, especially a landing with two or more corps, involves more than loading troops aboard assorted transports and dumping them somewhere on the enemy's coast. At this stage the Urbanna movement was only an idea, not yet an operational plan.

McClellan's request for a staff appreciation of the idea produced a masterful analysis by the Prince de Joinville, then serving as an aide-de-camp. Although this long memorandum was a strategic assessment rather than a detailed plan, it made McClellan realize that more careful thinking was needed before he could decide on the best offensive line. Without recommending any particular scheme, Joinville examined the advantages and disadvantages of all the possibilities open to the Army of the Potomac, the relative military and political value of various objectives, the time and resources required to attain them, and the probable reaction of the enemy.

Above all, he stressed the problems and risks involved in carrying out successful combined operations, and the absolute necessity for thorough planning and preparation for all phases, especially the critical (but often neglected) follow-up. McClellan would not only have to obtain enough of the right kind of transports, organize them as self-contained divisions and brigades (complete with landing craft, ammunition, stores, medical supplies, etc.), and assemble a fleet for convoy and fire support; he would also have to foresee what would be needed to get the army from the landing point to its ultimate objective.[6] Moving troops by land, crossing rivers, and reducing fortifications would require horses and wagons, bridge equipage, and siege guns or warships to shell water batteries. If McClellan intended to use the York River Railroad, he would have to procure rolling stock, and perhaps rails, in advance and have this material ready for shipment aboard suitable vessels when it was needed.

Otherwise, an advance on Richmond by any water line, including the Rappahannock, would be exceedingly slow. The army would not be able to move from its beachheads, although it might successfully defend them; then the element of surprise would be lost and the enemy, using his railways, would have ample time to concentrate in front of the Union position and construct new fortifications. Or given sufficient resources, the Confederates might contain the beachheads with a small force while taking the offensive across the Potomac into Maryland from their positions at Centreville and Leesburg. Butler

Major General George B. McClellan and his staff. At the right (r. to l.) are the exiled Bourbons the Comte de Paris, claimant to the French throne, and his brother, the Prince de Joinville. As staff intelligence officer, the Comte de Paris provided accurate information on enemy strength during the Peninsular campaign. (*National Archives*)

and Stringham had seized Hatteras in an improvised operation, but its defenses were easily isolated by water. Besides, Hatteras was an object of small importance; the capital of the Confederacy would not fall to such a poorly executed expedition. Allowed time to react, the enemy would be able to concentrate all his available forces to defend the city.

McClellan therefore had two choices in devising a plan to operate against Richmond by the river lines. It would have to be either a lightning campaign prepared beforehand to the smallest detail, designed to paralyze the enemy and seize the objective before he could respond; or a deliberate advance, using sheer numbers to overwhelm the enemy or maneuver him out of successive positions.[7] Although Joinville expressed no preference for either method, his clear definition of alternatives and requirements provided an invaluable outline of the problem.

The reasons for the delay were not explained to Congress or the administration. Perhaps because he had such a low opinion of politicians anyway, and resented civilian control, McClellan thought they would not accept the need for thorough preparation—and even if they did understand, their alarm about immediate problems was so great that, to save a few months, they might throw away any chance to end the war in one blow, in favor of a less elaborate operation.[8] Nor did he explain the Urbanna plan to the government; he had already informed Lincoln that he had a plan to be implemented as soon as possible, and this assurance, in his view, should have sufficed.

Besides, his mind was not made up. The Navy was pushing hard for an attack on Norfolk to take the navy yard before the Confederates could finish converting the *Merrimack* into an ironclad warship.[9] The idea of reaching West Point via the York River instead of the Rappahannock also had to be considered. Joinville had pointed out that it might be necessary to drive Magruder out of the Yorktown defenses as part of the Urbanna plan, in order to open a more convenient supply line and prevent Magruder from attacking the army's left flank during its march from Urbanna to West Point. The quickest way to do this was by fleet bombardment which meant full naval support, a difficult and time-consuming proposition.

Before any of these ideas could be acted upon, while Mc-Clellan was still confined to his sickbed, the quartermaster general seized the initiative for the government. Meigs was disturbed about the mounting Federal debt; unless some action was taken soon, the administration's credit would be ruined and the war lost through the Federal government's inability to finance it. At his request, Lincoln convened the Cabinet on 4 January 1862 to discuss strategy with some of McClellan's divisional generals.[10] Two officers presented plans. General McDowell recommended a direct attack on Richmond from Alexandria, via Fredericksburg. Brigadier General William B. Franklin, McClellan's good friend and confidant, without revealing his direct knowledge of the general-in-chief's intentions, argued for the Urbanna expedition. However, Assistant Secretary of War Thomas Scott said he could provide transportation for only 12,000 men (one division), thus ruling out the latter plan until more shipping could be obtained.[11]

Since the Cabinet had reached no decision on operations, on 10 January Lincoln asked McDowell and Franklin to draw up a plan. Franklin suggested that before proceeding they consult Secretary of the Treasury Chase, with whom McClellan had discussed the Urbanna plan. The following day, the president appointed a special council composed of the new secretary of War, Edwin M. Stanton, Postmaster General Montgomery Blair, Chase, Thomas Scott, and the two generals. After discussing the plan for two days, they accepted it, asking Meigs to provide water transport for 50,000 men.[12]

But the government had no assurance that this was really McClellan's plan. He could always claim that Franklin and Chase misunderstood him. Consequently, the council went to McClellan's house on 13 January. McClellan excused himself on the grounds that this council was "irregular" and he refused to discuss strategic questions. The real reason for his reticence was that he had still not decided upon a plan. Burnside's expedition to the North Carolina coast, scheduled for the last week in December, was delayed until mid-January, the amount of time required for Flag Officer Goldsborough to assemble a fleet from the blockading squadron. As long as the situation remained fluid, McClellan preferred to make no direct statement of his intentions. He rightly suspected that once the government officials had been informed of any particular plan they would hold him to it, regardless of subsequent military developments. Moreover, it was still too early for a decisive campaign. In a private and confidential interview arranged by Stanton the following evening, McClellan told a reporter from the New York *Herald* that he had not determined upon a definite plan for the Army of the Potomac because Halleck and Buell in the West, Sherman in South Carolina, and Burnside on the coast, had yet to take their objectives. If these preliminary movements succeeded, the Confederates in Virginia could not escape to reorganize; Johnston would have to keep Richmond as his base, and the capture of that city would then prove decisive.[13]

The administration was equally determined to force McClellan into a firm commitment. Since the council failed to find out anything, Lincoln issued an ultimatum giving McClellan fifteen days to submit his own plan. A critical development on the international scene (or, more accurately, the secretary of State's interpretation of a crisis, based on alarmist reports from London) induced the president to act sooner. The U.S. ambassador warned that, unless a major Union offensive had been set in motion when Parliament convened on 4 March, Britain would recognize the Confederacy.[14] Lincoln thereupon issued his famous General War Order #1 of 27 January, demanding that all Federal armies advance against some objective, regardless of the state of their preparations, on 22 February. Because he still wished to leave the choice of objective for the Army of the Potomac up to its commander, he did not insist upon any particular plan at that time, including his own for an attack on the line of the Occoquan.

But even this preposterous order did not provoke a response. The fifteen days expired and McClellan remained silent. There was now only one way left to force his hand. On 31 January Lincoln issued a special war order requiring the Army of the Potomac to advance before 22 February and seize "a point upon the railroad southwestward of what is known as Manassas Junction." McClellan knew the game was up and reacted with customary swiftness. That evening he appeared at the executive mansion to discuss his intentions with the president. After hearing the general's outline of the Urbanna plan,

Lincoln insisted that it be submitted in writing to the secretary of War. Returning home, McClellan drafted the document that night but did not send it immediately.[15] Perhaps he hoped that Lincoln would change his mind, and be satisfied with a verbal explanation.

This last-ditch attempt to avoid putting anything on paper inevitably failed. While the president himself might have accepted such assurance, the Cabinet, especially the secretary of War, would not. Lincoln thereupon wrote McClellan again on 3 February submitting a list of questions as to why the general's proposed line of operation was better than his, and agreeing to accept the Urbanna plan if these questions were satisfactorily answered. McClellan revised the draft of 31 January to include answers to the president's questions and sent the final version to Stanton that day.

His primary argument was not that an advance across the Occoquan, leading to a general engagement or an attack on Johnston's main position, might produce another Bull Run. Contrary to most historical accounts, McClellan was not misled by his intelligence agents, working under the famous railroad detective Allen Pinkerton, into supposing that the Confederate army outnumbered his own. Pinkerton's latest reports estimated a maximum of 60,000 enemy troops at Manassas and Centreville. And he knew all about the "Quaker guns"; a recent report revealed that there were several forts on the heights at Centreville with no guns in them, the Confederates instead using *"logs put up shaped like guns* and *painted black on the outer ends."*[16] McClellan acknowledged that, since "nothing is certain in war," the Southerners might win a battle in spite of the odds. But this was a consideration of little importance in choosing the best line of operations. It was the strategic, not the tactical, result of a Federal victory that mattered:

Assuming the success of this operation, and the defeat of the enemy as certain, the question at once arises as to the importance of the results gained. I think these results would be confined to the possession of the field of battle, the evacuation of the line of the Upper Potomac by the enemy, and the moral effect of the victory—important results, it is true, but not decisive of the war, nor securing the destruction of the enemy's main army; for he could fall back upon other positions and fight us again and again, should the condition of his troops permit. If he is in no condition to fight us again out of the range of the intrenchments at Richmond, we would find it a very difficult and tedious matter to follow him up there, for he would destroy his railroad bridges and otherwise impede our progress through a region where the roads are as bad as they well can be, and we would probably find ourselves forced at last to change the whole theater of war, or to seek a shorter land route to Richmond, with a smaller available force, and at an expenditure of much more time than were we to adopt the short line at once. We would also have forced the enemy to concentrate his forces and perfect his defensive measures at the very points where it is desirable to strike him when least prepared.

The Urbanna plan, on the other hand, would produce important, if not decisive results. Moving rapidly, McClellan would seize Johnston's base, forcing him out of the Centreville entrenchments to recover it. "He [Johnston] must do this; for should he permit us to occupy Richmond, his destruction can be averted only by entirely defeating us in battle, in which he must be the assailant." If Johnston chose not to fight for the capital, "Norfolk would fall, all the waters of the Chesapeake would be ours, all Virginia would be in our power, and the enemy forced to abandon Tennessee and North Carolina." Not only was a movement by water necessary to close in on Richmond quickly, it was the one line that permitted full employment of Union naval superiority. And if the rapid move from Urbanna should fail, "we could, with the co-operation of the Navy, cross the James and throw ourselves in the rear of Richmond, thus forcing the enemy to come out and attack us, for his position would be untenable with us on the southern bank of the river." Finally, aside from the fleet's offensive power, it would be an important defensive asset in case of a reverse:

Should we be beaten in battle, we have a perfectly secure retreat down the Peninsula upon Fort Monroe, with our flanks perfectly covered by the fleet. During the whole movement our left flank is covered by the water. Our right is secure for the reason that the enemy is too distant to reach us in time. He can only oppose us in front.[17]

Having been finally compelled to inform the government of his intentions for the Army of the Potomac, McClellan went on to reveal, for the first time officially, his grand strategic design. The plan was flexible enough to accommodate an offensive against Richmond. Should the campaign prove successful, but without ending the war, he explained to Stanton:

Our position would be, Burnside forming our left, Norfolk held securely, our centre connecting Burnside with Buell, both by Raleigh and Lynchburg, Buell in Eastern Tennessee and Northern Alabama, Halleck at Nashville and Memphis.

The next movement would be to connect with [T.W.] Sherman on the left, by reducing Wilmington and Charleston; to advance our centre into South Carolina and Georgia, to push Buell either towards Montgomery, or to unite with the main army in Georgia, to throw Halleck southward to meet the naval expedition from New Orleans.

We should then be in a condition to reduce, at our leisure, all the southern seaports; to occupy all the avenues of communication, to use the great outlet of the Mississippi; to re-establish our government and arms in Arkansas, Louisiana and Texas; to force the slaves to labor for our subsistence, instead of that of the rebels; to bid defiance to all foreign interference. Such is the object I ever had in view; this is the general plan which I hope to accomplish.[18]

Satisfying Lincoln, whose logical mind grasped McClellan's well-reasoned arguments, was difficult enough; but although the president never formally approved the Urbanna plan, he apparently accepted it, pressing McClellan no further about plans and dropping all discussion of his own. The Joint Committee on the Conduct of the War was a more formidable antagonist. Ostensibly organized to inquire into the Ball's Bluff incident, the committee was formed on 2 December, when Congress reconvened after its fall recess and was empowered with wide authority to examine all aspects of the war. Under strong administrations, Congress had often found it necessary to assert its power under the Constitution; the most effective way to do so was to investigate the actions of the elected executive and his agents. Thus, the Joint Committee, comprising some of the most influential and determined members of the Senate and House of Representatives, was as much the watchdog of the Lincoln administration as of the Army command.

But Lincoln knew how to satisfy the congressional inquisitors and McClellan did not. While the president always treated them with the respect due to equals and patiently answered all of their questions as fully and openly as possible, the general regarded them at first with indifference, and finally with barely disguised contempt.[19] His extensive study of, and admiration for, European military systems had made him intolerant of political "interference," especially from men without military education or experience. He never recognized the right of any civilian other than the president, in his role as commander-in-chief, to "meddle" in Army affairs. Furthermore, like all great commanders, McClellan highly valued the element of surprise and therefore did not wish to divulge his plans to anyone except his closest confidants.

While his attitude toward secrecy was obviously proper, his manner toward Congress was not. A more politically astute general with a greater respect for American institutions (even if he did not entirely approve of them) would have acknowledged that the committee members, right or wrong, were as anxious as he to perform their duty to the country. Regarding security, McClellan might have explained his plans in such a general way that the enemy could not have discovered his exact intentions. His refusal, under the plea of secrecy, to give any information especially annoyed the committee's chairman, Senator Benjamin F. Wade, who resented the implication that congressmen were less to be trusted with military secrets than Army officers, or even the foreign princes and observers on McClellan's staff. The general's arrogant posture made the accidental fact of his illness on 20 December, the day before he was to meet with the committee, seem a bit too convenient.[20]

Although McClellan was not well enough to attend to official business until mid-January, he was not too ill to worry about the proceedings of the Joint Committee. During the last week in December, almost all of the Army of the Potomac's divisional generals, and even some brigadiers and lower-ranking officers, were questioned about McClellan's plans and asked for their advice on the proper employment of his main force. The most conscientious officers naturally refused to question their chief's judgment or offer any opinion on operational questions. Others, however, volunteered or were persuaded to express their views under close examination.

The object was not, as McClellan feared and many historians claim, to discredit him. The committee's minutes indicate that it was mainly trying to find out what was going on and to discover a possible remedy for problems that might not await McClellan's recovery. It seems not to have occurred to the congressmen—any more than their right to interfere with the Army occurred to McClellan—that such well-intentioned questioning might embarrass professional soldiers and injure the general-in-chief. Brigadier General Fitz John Porter, a long-time regular and one of McClellan's closest friends, who knew more about McClellan's plans than anyone else in the Army, flatly refused to answer any questions extending beyond the scope of his own command. But General Franklin took the precaution of conferring with McClellan before testifying; thus, unable to appear personally, McClellan was able to "leak" certain of his ideas unofficially. Perhaps he thought Franklin's testimony, revealing the general outline of the Urbanna plan, would satisfy the committee and that he could avoid a direct confrontation altogether.[21] If so, he was disappointed.

So was the committee. It had expected to find a consensus within the Army of the Potomac. Instead, those officers willing to offer advice produced more confusion than enlightenment. Not surprisingly, Brigadier General Frederick W. Lander, commanding the line of the Baltimore and Ohio Railroad, and Brigadier General William S. Rosecrans, commanding in West Virginia, suggested turning Johnston's left flank via Harpers Ferry and Winchester, and operating up the Shenandoah Valley in cooperation with the forces in West Virginia. General McDowell, whose attack at Manassas had produced the first Union defeat, wanted another try at crashing in the now heavily fortified center of Johnston's line around Centreville.

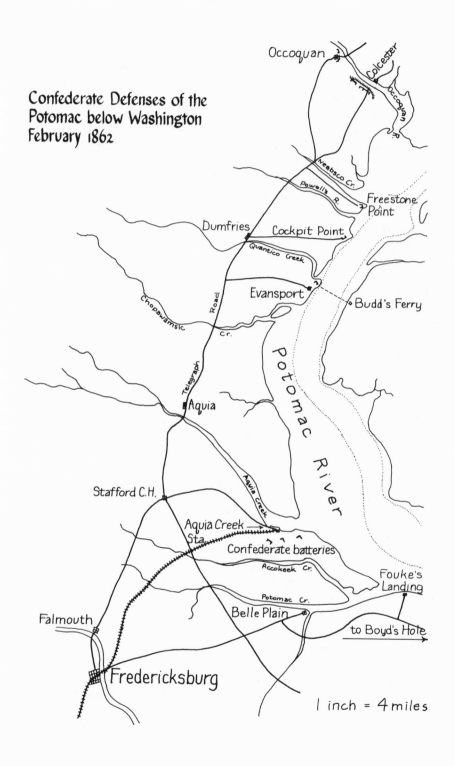

Confederate Defenses of the
Potomac below Washington
February 1862

Occoquan

Colcester

Occoquan

Neabsco Cr.

Powell's R.

Freestone
Point

Dumfries

Cockpit Point

Quantico Creek

Chopowamsic

Road

Evansport

Budd's Ferry

Cr.

Potomac River

Telegraph

Aquia

Stafford C.H.

Aquia Creek

Aquia Creek
Sta.

Confederate batteries

Accokeek Cr.

Fouke's
Landing

Falmouth

Potomac Cr.

Belle Plain

to Boyd's Hole

Fredericksburg

1 inch = 4 miles

Brigadier General Joseph Hooker, whose division held the extreme Union left along the Potomac below Washington, thought it better to outflank the enemy's right opposite his own position. Brigadier General Samuel Heintzelman recommended a combined movement against Richmond via the James or the York, or both. Although Heintzelman's plan came closest to the one actually carried out in the spring, he had no knowledge whatever of McClellan's intentions and said so; therefore his opinion had no more weight than that of the others.[22]

By the second week in January, Wade decided that only McClellan's own testimony could clear up the confusion. Congress was impatient for a report on the progress of the war, or at least to hear some definite plans for the large and very expensive Army of the Potomac. The campaign season in Virginia was already over, the roads were almost impassable, the problems which existed in November remained unsolved, the financial resources of the Federal government were nearly exhausted, the international situation looked continually worse—and no battles had been fought.[23]

Finally, on 15 January, McClellan "conferred" with the committee. Unfortunately, there is no record of his testimony. The committee agenda simply indicates a discussion of several hours about "various matters connected with the conduct of the present war." Although McClellan informed Lincoln it was rough going but he had "come away with my skin," he probably did not impress the committee favorably or tell them very much. His immediate response suggests that the discussion centered around opening the Baltimore and Ohio Railroad, and that the committee insisted upon, and got, the general's assurance that he would act promptly.[24]

Having previously broken this road and carried off twenty-five miles of track west of Harpers Ferry, Confederate General Jackson's small command in December had destroyed Dam Number 5 on the Chesapeake and Ohio Canal, thus interrupting the coal supply to Washington and Baltimore. Since the Mississippi River remained closed, the westerners were already angry because the government had not reopened the B & O. Until midwinter, the Pennsylvania Central Railroad had been able to absorb most of the excess traffic, but it was becoming clear by January that this road could not handle the job alone.

Continuous heavy traffic prevented maintenance of the line, and accidents were more frequent and costly. The B & O president, J.W. Garrett, pressed Lincoln and influential Congressional friends (including Senator Wade, whose home state of Ohio was hurt most by the B & O's closing) to cooperate in reopening the road. Without a large military force to guard the line, the company's effort to restore the tracks and rebuild the bridges was useless because the Confederates destroyed them again as fast as they were repaired.[25]

Immediately after his conference with the committee, McClellan telegraphed Lander and Major General Nathaniel P. Banks, commanding the right of the Union line at Frederick, Maryland, for advice about the best way to protect the road. Both replied that Jackson must be driven off and Winchester occupied. Seizing and holding Winchester required that a large force be pushed into the lower Shenandoah Valley. Because such a move would directly threaten the rear of Johnston's main position at Centreville, it would probably bring on a battle. Realizing that he could not refuse to carry out this operation, even though it meant a premature offensive, without risking his removal from command, McClellan, who always saw favorable possibilities in any development, decided to expand the necessary movement on Winchester into a major campaign.[26]

Concentrating the army against the enemy's left flank alone was dangerous. Because the Federals could not cross the upper Potomac in strength except at Harpers Ferry, they could approach Winchester along only one line of march. Unless his attention were engaged elsewhere, Johnston could throw his whole army into Winchester, or attack Harpers Ferry, or move across the Potomac below this point to cut off Union communications with Washington.[27] The Navy, as well as the administration, had been badgering McClellan for months to capture the Confederate batteries at Freestone and Cockpit points on the lower Potomac. Hooker was anxious to try a combined operation from his camp across the river at Budd's Ferry. McClellan would let him land his division, take the batteries, and secure the crossings of the lower Occoquan, which would permit Heintzelman's division to cross the Occoquan. The joint force might then move either against Johnston's communications, via Brentsville and Catlett's Station, or toward Fredericksburg. Johnston would not turn to fight Banks and Keyes on his left leaving his more vulnerable right open to attack. If the situation developed favorably, supporting divisions could be pushed through Harpers Ferry and landed up the Occoquan at Aquia, or even up the Rappahannock if necessary. Johnston might be trapped; he would certainly be hard-pressed to extricate his army as an organized force, and he would have to abandon his materiel and stores.[28]

Since Hooker's attack would necessarily be a combined operation, he was asked to consult with Lieutenant Commander R.H. Wyman of the Potomac Flotilla, and submit a plan. Captain R.S. Williamson of the topographical engineers thought the Navy could easily reduce the batteries by bombardment, but that a very large initial force would be needed to hold a beachhead on the Virginia shore. The Confederates were estimated to have 8,000 troops around Dumfries, 3,000 at the mouth of the Occoquan, 6,000 on the Brentsville road, six and one-half miles from Dumfries, another 12,000 for immediate support at Fredericksburg, and a total of seventy field guns.[29]

Hooker submitted his first scheme on 27 January. He intended to land a brigade at Aquia and assault the batteries there in front with two regiments in column; this would be followed on the next day by the landing of his other two brigades near Powell's River or Neabsco Creek. The latter force would march up the Colchester Road, taking in reverse the defenses near the mouth of the Occoquan. He thought the move would cause Johnston to fall back towards Richmond.[30]

This plan contained serious flaws. The brigade at Aquia, even if it took the enemy works by frontal assault in daylight, which was doubtful, would be isolated from the main force, with a superior enemy between. Its left would be open to attack from Fredericksburg. The flotilla would be divided into squadrons, leaving fewer vessels to cooperate in attacking the defenses on the Occoquan and protecting the rear of the main column by keeping the enemy from crossing Powell's River from the south. Finally, Wyman doubted that the Confederates could be surprised unless the landing was made at some point above the Occoquan. Since such an action "would merely

reinforce our left wing and leave the right of the enemy unbroken," a larger assault force would be required.[31]

By 18 February, Hooker had devised a different plan. He
intended to disembark his whole force at Fouke's Landing or
Boyd's Hole below Aquia Creek. There were no batteries here,
and the flotilla could protect the ground forces a mile and
one-half to two miles beyond the beach. A short march would
bring the army to Fredericksburg on the extreme enemy right,
turn all the batteries, isolate the defenses on the lower Occoquan, and threaten the rear of Major General W.H.C. Whiting's
command at Dumfries. Hooker's expectations were even more
sanguine. The move, he thought, "would compel the enemy in
the north to fall back without his railroads, enable us to take
Richmond, or, if considered of more importance, capture
Magruder's command [at Yorktown]."[32]

But this plan, although better, was also unacceptable. The
landing had to be in strength—a minimum of three divisions
—and it required extensive preparations, a very large number
of boats, and sufficient land transport to permit a rapid move
on Fredericksburg. And since the crossings of the Occoquan
would not be secured, the position could not be connected
with the left of the main Federal army, thus leaving a gap of
some thirty miles which the Confederates, using the railroads,
could exploit to isolate and overwhelm Hooker's force before
it could be sufficiently reinforced by water. Besides, this was
to be a diversion in favor of the primary movement to secure
Winchester and open the B & O, rather than the main attack
on Richmond, which would occur later on a more promising
line, after Congress had been satisfied. Perhaps the campaign
could be made into something decisive but, against the cautious and ever-watchful Johnston, this could not be counted
on in advance.

The final plan, arranged between Wyman and Hooker on
20 February, was therefore on a smaller scale and had more
limited objectives. Under cover of the gunboats, three brigades
would land and systematically destroy the battery at Cockpit
Point with gunfire. Hooker would meanwhile shell the enemy's
infantry supports from the Maryland shore with his recently
arrived Whitworth rifles. The division would then move down
the Virginia bank of the Potomac under the flotilla's protection,

and cross Quantico Creek in boats. It was thought that a combination of bombardment and assault would dispose of the batteries at Shipping Point above Evansport in a few hours. This move would place Whiting's force at Dumfries on Hooker's flank instead of his rear; but Whiting would be unable to attack or dispute the crossing of Quantico Creek as long as Hooker hugged the shore and the gunboats could interdict any position Whiting might assume to stop him at the river lines.[33]

Regrettably, the lessons that could have been learned from this combined attack, especially regarding the Navy's ability to silence open earthworks with gunboats, lessons which might have changed the course of the Peninsular campaign, were never learned. The grand movement of the Army of the Potomac, so long and impatiently anticipated by Congress, the administration, and the public, and begun so vigorously with the crossing of Banks's advance guard at Harpers Ferry on 26 February, came to a crashing halt the next day. The cause was so apparently trivial that McClellan found it embarrassing to explain the problem to the secretary of War. Because of frequent and sudden flooding on the upper Potomac at that season, the pontoon bridge at Harpers Ferry had to be replaced by a more solid structure to accommodate the army's artillery and baggage. Barnard had assured McClellan that such a bridge could be easily constructed from heavy boats brought into the river from the Chesapeake and Ohio Canal. The engineers had not bothered to measure the locks, however, and it turned out that the boats were too wide to enter the river. McClellan at once wired Stanton that the movement had to be suspended until the railroad bridge was reconstructed. Although the secretary was disgusted, suggesting sarcastically that perhaps the locks could be widened to accommodate the boats, McClellan rightly estimated that it would take longer to rebuild the locks than the bridge and that in either case the enemy would have ample time to fortify Winchester.[34]

The consequences were swift and final. The three divisions of Brigadier Generals Erasmus Keyes, W.F. Smith, and George McCall which had been ordered up to Harpers Ferry by rail, were sent back to their old camps and Hooker was instructed to call off his attack on the river batteries. A conveniently negative report from Barnard, who had just reconnoitered the

Confederate positions opposite Hooker from the water, was used to justify the cancellation of Hooker's operation to the Navy Department. The real reason was not the risk of this combined operation, but the failure of the main attack on Winchester.[35] The one accomplishment of this aborted campaign was the very result McClellan was most anxious to avoid. The Army of the Potomac's preparations to advance in force up the Shenandoah valley alerted Johnston to the vulnerability of his exposed position at Centreville, while the threat to his right on the lower Potomac caused his precipitous withdrawal to the Rappahannock, in order to cover Richmond.[36]

After revealing his hand, McClellan naturally wanted to play it. Immediately upon dispatching the order to Hooker, he informed his chief of staff, Brigadier General R.B. Marcy, that he had decided to adopt the Urbanna plan for a combined movement up the Rappahannock. Having forced McClellan to advance, against his judgment, the government then prevented him from moving any further by setting unnecessary conditions. Both the administration and the Navy Department insisted that the Confederate "blockade" of the Potomac had to be raised before the Army could operate against Richmond from the lower Chesapeake. They did not accept McClellan's perfectly sound argument that the troops could embark safely at Annapolis and that their mere presence in the Rappahannock would force the Confederates to abandon the batteries. From Fox's standpoint, a dramatic fleet bombardment would cast the spotlight on the Navy, while its role in transporting the Army to turn the enemy positions by strategic maneuver would not be appreciated by the public. Moreover, he was anxious to test the *Monitor*'s ability to withstand shore bombardment.[37]

Neither Lincoln, nor the Joint Committee, nor the press could seem to understand that this blockade was more apparent than real. Not only was the navigation of the river never closed, even to slow-moving sailing ships, but in six months' firing, the Confederates failed to hit anything.[38] Furthermore, the Southerners had never intended to "close" the Potomac, and their shelling of the heavy traffic passing up and down the river was mere target practice. The batteries were built and sited solely to cover the Confederate line at the

Occoquan, Dumfries, Aquia, and Fredericksburg against anticipated landing operations. Whiting, Holmes, and Brigadier General N.G. Evans, commanding the Aquia District, manifested a fear of amphibious invasion, amounting almost to panic. Instead of the 27,000 troops McClellan had supposed were available to throw Hooker back into the river, the Southerners did not have enough men even to contain a Federal beachhead until Johnston sent reinforcements. Less than a third of this number were deployed below the Occoquan, including Holmes's command at Fredericksburg, and many of those men were cavalry and artillerists manning the batteries.[39] Hooker's division of 12,000 men, landing as a concentrated force, would have easily overcome any resistance the enemy might have offered anywhere along this section of the line. Although McClellan appreciated the potential of combined operations and should have inferred the real purpose of the Confederate works from their location, this perception would not have changed his plans very much. Although the enemy's

Shelling the Aquia batteries, 1 June 1861. Throughout the war, the Potomac Flotilla guarded the water approach to the Federal capital and cooperated in Army operations against Fredericksburg and Richmond.

weakness was not known, the realization that his dispositions were designed to repel landings would probably have discouraged any plans for an attack across the river.

To destroy the Potomac batteries by bombardment, the Navy Department wanted warships, not gunboats. But again, a confusion of purposes interfered. About the time Hooker's operation was cancelled, McClellan promised General Wool that the *Monitor* would be sent to Hampton Roads as soon as she was ready. Wool was momentarily expecting the Confederate ironclad *Virginia* and Magruder's command on the Peninsula to launch a combined attack on Newport News as a preliminary to the capture of Fort Monroe.[40]

Lieutenant John Worden, the *Monitor*'s captain, taking the ironclad for a trial run in New York harbor on 27 February, encountered so many problems that he had returned the ship to the navy yard for alterations. On 1 March he sailed for Hampton Roads, but the vessel broke down again after a few miles. Worden finally cleared the harbor at 4 o'clock on the afternoon of 6 March—just in time to miss Welles's urgent telegram ordering the *Monitor* into the Potomac to shell the batteries. The secretary thereupon telegraphed Commander J.H. Marston, the senior naval officer in Hampton Roads, telling him to prepare the frigates *Cumberland, Congress*, and *St. Lawrence* to sail for Washington at once and to order Worden, on his arrival, to bring the *Monitor* also.[41] It is interesting to conjecture what might have happened had these instructions been carried out. But Welles had second thoughts about concentrating the fleet in the Potomac with the Confederate ironclad about to emerge from Norfolk; thus, early on the 8th, he suspended the order until Fox had consulted Wool personally and reported on the situation in the Roads.[42]

Having left on the Baltimore boat at 3:30 that same afternoon, Fox arrived too late to save the Union frigates, but just in time to greet Worden and watch the famous fight between the *Monitor* and the *Virginia* the next day. All thought of destroying the Potomac batteries was forgotten in the ensuing panic. The bombardment turned out to be unnecessary anyway. By coincidence, Johnston chose the same day as Flag Officer Buchanan to make his move. Following a carefully arranged plan, General Evans spiked the guns, abandoned the batteries, and withdrew his command behind Aquia Creek just as Johnston, completing the evacuation of the main Confederate position, reached Rappahannock Station. The move was so well managed that the Federals did not discover until the next day, after shelling the Potomac batteries for an hour without reply, that the enemy had gone.[43]

A third significant event occurred on 8 March. At the government's insistence, McClellan's divisional commanders assembled at his Washington house to decide on a campaign plan. The result was an important split between senior and junior officers. McDowell, Heintzelman, and Brigadier General Edwin V. Sumner voted for a direct attack on the Confederate army, still thought to be manning the fortifications at Centreville and Manassas. Brigadier General Erasmus D. Keyes was the only senior officer favoring the Urbanna Plan, on condition that the Potomac batteries were destroyed before the plan was implemented. The other six divisional commanders voted for the expedition up the Rappahannock and an attack upon Richmond from West Point.[44]

The administration was obviously unhappy with the vote. McClellan was immediately ordered to organize the army into corps on the pretext that such organization was standard military practice for large armies.[45] Lincoln insisted that the four resulting *corps d'armée* be commanded by the senior generals, McDowell, Sumner, Heintzelman, and Keyes, all but one of whom disapproved of the plan of operations. McClellan could take small comfort in the one exception since he recognized even then that Keyes was totally incompetent as a corps commander.[46]

Still, the Urbanna movement had been approved. As long as Johnston remained around Manassas, it was a good plan. But again, as at Harper's Ferry, no sooner had a definite decision been reached than the whole situation changed. This time a combination of factors was responsible. The 9th of March was a trying day for McClellan. First, Hooker informed him that the Confederates had abandoned the Potomac batteries and were concentrating their forces at Fredericksburg. Then he learned that Johnston had evacuated Manassas and Centreville. Finally, Fox's reports from Hampton Roads, although grossly exaggerating the *Monitor*'s performance in the battle with the *Virginia* that day, made it clear that the James River could not be used to transport supplies for his army. The second contingent phase of the Urbanna plan—the move to the south side of the James for an attack on Petersburg in cooperation with Burnside—was impossible unless the Navy could open that river.

At this point, there was little time for revising plans, however. Johnston had gone, but where? While it was probable that he had fallen back toward Richmond, he might have divided his army, sending part of it over the still intact Virginia and Tennessee Railroad to attack Buell in Nashville.[47] The administration expected McClellan to "pursue" the flying foe, although how he was to manage this without first corduroying the mud holes which passed for roads in Virginia at that season was not explained to him.

McClellan might have carried out his reconnaissance in force towards Manassas with less display, but it is doubtful that the politicians would have been satisfied with anything less than the capture of Johnston's army, or Richmond, or perhaps both. Besides, McClellan rightly considered Johnston's withdrawal a victory—however incomplete and premature— for his strategy, and was proud that it had been accomplished without losing a man.[48] He could not then understand, and never understood completely, that this was precisely the cause of the government's growing dissatisfaction with his leadership. To civilians, and even to many soldiers who had studied Napoleon's campaigns, war meant marching up and down the country chasing the enemy, fighting, assault, fierce combat with cold steel, huge casualty lists, and bloody battle trophies. What kind of general sat calmly in his headquarters sending telegrams, moving armies and squadrons about on a continental map like pieces on a chessboard, winning a war by strategy instead of fighting? And what kind of general, despising the trusty wagon train, sent troops in all directions by rail and water to points where there was no enemy, instead of attacking him where he was? Few Americans could conceive of warfare in such terms or on such a scale in the 1860s.[49]

Of course, the army's advance to Johnston's old positions produced no military result. Its only consequence, other than

providing the government justification for confining Mc-
Clellan's command to the Army of the Potomac, was that the
difficulties of the march made water communications more attractive to the divisional generals who had opposed the Urbanna
plan. The roads, as reported, were terrible. Stoneman's cavalry
division, "following" the enemy rear guard through the thick
woods and soggy ravines south of Manassas, managed to
reach Cedar Creek but could go no further. With the river
behind him rapidly rising, and his men having used up their
provisions, Stoneman was hardly able to make it back to his
depots, although unmolested by the enemy. McDowell, in particular, rejected the overland march to Richmond which he
had been advocating for two months; he and Franklin were
now anxious to try amphibious operations.[50]

On 11 March, after completing his reconnaissance and conferring with McDowell, McClellan announced that he had
decided definitely on the Urbanna movement approved by the
meeting on 8 March, and had ordered the transports to Washington that morning. The plan was to embark Fitz John
Porter's division, which included the regulars and the reserve
artillery first, followed immediately by the divisions of Mc-
Dowell and Franklin.

Next day, however, Stanton insisted that McClellan carry
out Lincoln's order to form four army corps. That order had
been suspended at the general's request until he had completed his reconnaissance. Stanton further insisted upon another council of war among the president's designated corps
commanders before any move was made. McClellan replied
that Porter was already embarking, but agreed to delay his
departure and call a meeting for the following morning, 13
March, at Fairfax Court House to review the whole question
of operational plans. Such a meeting was perhaps a necessary
evil. The government obviously trusted the opinion of Mc-
Clellan's senior subordinates since it had foisted them upon
him instead of allowing him to choose those who were more
"modern" and capable, regardless of their rank; thus, it might
more cheerfully approve their plan of campaign.[51]

Although all four corps commanders had been converted
to the indirect approach, they still considered the Urbanna
plan too hazardous and uncertain, since Johnston had changed

his line. Hooker and Wyman reported that the enemy was fortifying Fredericksburg and building gunboats on the Rappahannock.[52] Instead, they favored basing the army at Fort Monroe and operating up the Peninsula between the York and the James.

This was not a new idea. In his memorandum of December, Joinville had suggested it as an alternative, or corollary, to the Urbanna plan. If it proved impossible to turn the river defenses, the army could always lay siege to Yorktown. Major General James Shields, in reply to McClellan's request for an opinion in January, had also advised besieging Yorktown, estimating that this would require only six weeks and would provide good experience for the men. Moreover, because of the disastrous effect on new troops of a reverse, he warned McClellan to proceed systematically against Richmond, taking no risks, and using artillery and naval gunfire as much as possible, instead of assault.[53] This advice would appear less remarkable from an engineer or a general known as methodical and cautious; but Shields was an old infantryman, a veteran of both the Mexican and Indian wars, who had a reputation for extreme aggressiveness. That such a man would advocate caution and the use of siege tactics supports McClellan's preference of strategy to combat.

Nevertheless, McClellan did not really like the Peninsular plan. In his memorandum of 3 February, McClellan mentioned this alternative very briefly and with obvious disapproval. He especially disliked the idea of besieging Yorktown. The greatest assets of combined operations—mobility and surprise—would be thrown away in a systematic advance up the Peninsula. The army might as well repair the Fredericksburg railroad and lay siege to Richmond, the main objective, instead of Yorktown. But if the enemy positions on the York River could be turned, the offensive would take on a far different aspect.[54]

Because McClellan opposed a protracted campaign, the council of war specified four conditions under which they recommended moving the Army of the Potomac to the Peninsula. The most important prerequisites were that the *Virginia* must be "neutralized," and "that a naval auxiliary force can be had to silence, or aid in silencing, the enemy batteries on the York River."[55] As usual, McClellan preferred to leave his options open until all the available resources were known. He did not, therefore, express any opinion, but simply sent Mc-Dowell to Washington with the corps commanders' views. Stanton immediately protested that the document submitted did not indicate what McClellan's decision was, and he insisted that the general either endorse the council's report or submit his own plan.[56]

Since he had no definite opinion from Fox regarding the Confederate ironclad nor from the Navy Department concerning further cooperation, McClellan delayed replying to the secretary's demand for a week with the result that, while Lincoln approved the council's decision, he added two more conditions to the original four—that a detachment be left to guard Manassas Junction, and that Washington be left "entirely secure."[57] Although these latter conditions would eventually prove his undoing, McClellan did not consider them very important at that time. The crucial question in his mind was naval cooperation.

The lines of operation against Richmond available to the Army of the Potomac were, of course, determined by the extent of the support guaranteed by the fleet. Without any support besides the Potomac flotilla already operating with Hooker around Evansport, McClellan might have to send nearly the whole army from Aquia against Fredericksburg, leaving a detachment at Fort Monroe to threaten Norfolk and prevent Johnston from receiving reinforcements from that quarter. With partial cooperation, that is, the promise of a few of Goldsborough's gunboats to cover McDowell's landing, the Urbanna plan would be more attractive, after all. Full cooperation, including a promise to reduce the Yorktown defenses if necessary, would make the York River plan certain to yield rapid and probably decisive results.

At the time, McClellan did not know that the government preferred the first alternative, regardless of the available naval support, because the line of march from Fredericksburg to Richmond "covered" Washington. He supposed that his sound military arguments against Lincoln's plan of 31 January to operate in this direction had convinced the president and secretary of War. There were fifteen railway and road bridges between Fredericksburg and Richmond, all of which would

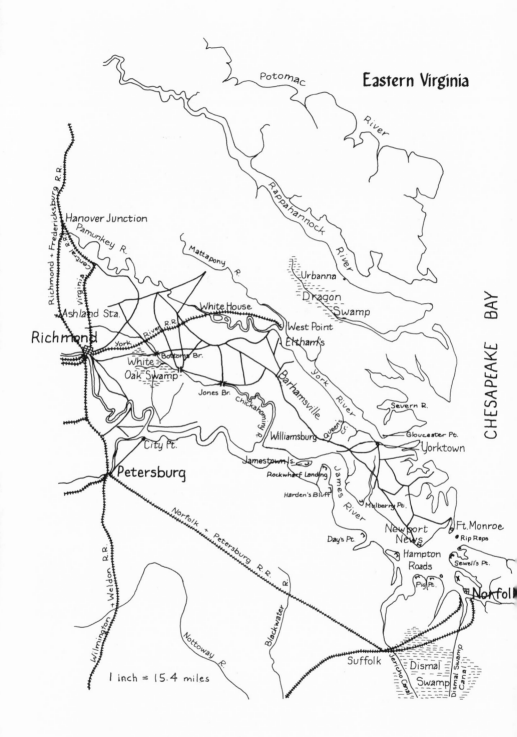

Eastern Virginia

Potomac River

Rappahannock River

Richmond + Fredericksburg R.R.

Hanover Junction

Pamunkey R.

Virginia Central R.R.

Ashland Sta.

Richmond

York River R.R.

White House

Mattapony R.

Urbanna

Dragon Swamp

West Point

Eltham's

Bottom's Br.

White Oak Swamp

Jones Br.

Chickahominy R.

Barhamsville

Williamsburg

Queen's

York River

Severn R.

Gloucester Pt.

Yorktown

CHESAPEAKE BAY

Jamestown Is.

Rockwharf Landing

Harden's Bluff

James River

Mulberry Pt.

City Pt.

Petersburg

Norfolk + Petersburg R.R.

Newport News

Day's Pt.

Ft. Monroe

Rip Raps

Hampton Roads

Sewell's Pt.

Pig Pt.

Norfolk

Wilmington + Weldon R.R.

Blackwater R.

Nottoway R.

Suffolk

Jericho Canal

Dismal Swamp

Dismal Swamp Canal

1 inch = 15.4 miles

have to be rebuilt as the army advanced.[58] Crashing in the right of the new Confederate line on the Rappahannock would produce one of two results, both bad for the Federal army. Johnston would either pull away from the railroad to the west, lying off on the flank and breaking McClellan's communications with cavalry, or he would withdraw slowly towards Richmond, burning bridges and harrassing the Federal right which would be unprotected by natural obstacles or a gunboat squadron. By the time McClellan approached Richmond, if his army had not wasted away, he would find the main Confederate army reinforced from all over the South, concentrated behind works far stronger than those at Centreville, and armed with *real* guns of heavy caliber being rapidly manufactured at Richmond's Tredegar Iron Works.[59] Since a siege would be almost impossible under such conditions, the Union army would be forced to withdraw toward Washington and adopt a line of operations based on water communications, having wasted the whole 1862 campaigning season and given the South a moral victory which would probably lead to European intervention.[60] McClellan would, therefore, undoubtedly have rejected the first alternative in any case, except as a temporary expedient until the Navy was prepared to cooperate.

Assuming he would receive full support from the Navy Department, McClellan devised a contingency plan for the third alternative. On 14 March, I Corps (under McDowell) was reorganized to include Franklin's division. This division contained the engineer brigade which would be required for a large-scale landing and had been trained for amphibious operations. He would place McDowell in the van, a post designed to appeal to that officer's self-esteem, and send him up the York to land directly at West Point. This plan would achieve that end even faster than the Urbanna plan. As soon as McDowell had seized the base and released his transports, the other army corps, meanwhile having been sent to Fort Monroe, would follow. If the fleet proved unable to reduce the York River batteries by bombardment, McDowell's corps could land above Yorktown, turning the defenses so that the vessels could run by.[61]

Although the question of naval support is vital to a proper understanding of McClellan's plans and preparations and their subsequent failure, it is difficult to discover exactly what the Navy Department promised him regarding the York River batteries. Only two remnants of correspondence reflecting the abundant negotiations on the subject appear in the official naval records. The first is a note from Welles to Stanton on 14 March, refusing McClellan's urgent request of the previous evening that part of Du Pont's large warship squadron at Port Royal be sent to Fort Monroe for combined operations in the York or the Rappahannock. The other is a letter dated 24 March in which Fox leaves the decision to cooperate with the Army up to Flag Officer Goldsborough's discretion.[62] Fox's confidential papers include no discussion of the Peninsular preparations, and Welles's diary contains no entries between the beginning of March and the middle of August 1862. (The Army records and McClellan's papers provide no conclusive evidence on this important point.)

Under examination by the Joint Committee in 1863, Fox and Goldsborough denied that the Navy ever promised direct support in reducing the Yorktown defenses, although Goldsborough did admit that he had agreed to land I Corps and supply a few gunboats for fire support. Fox, with whom the primary arrangements were made, not only denied the department's guarantee of any aid, but maintained that he had no knowledge of McClellan's plans, supposing that if the general intended any bombardment or landing operations, the army preferred to make its own arrangements and carry them through without the fleet.[63]

Fortunately those responsible for removing most of the documentation on this question were not very thorough. Enough pieces remain to indicate that Fox certainly lied and Goldsborough told half of the truth. The only explicit statement that the Navy Department promised unconditional cooperation against the York River batteries is contained in a letter from General Keyes to his friend, Senator Ira Harris, dated 7 April 1862. Complaining bitterly of the Navy's failure to honor its agreement with the Army, Keyes explained that he had approved the Peninsular plan during the council of war on 13 March only after personally requesting and receiving that department's promise to shell the Confederates out of Yorktown, if necessary.[64]

Although a dispatch from McDowell to McClellan in the Army records dated 18 March states that his negotiations with Fox resulted in a promise of full support, his telegrams in the McClellan Papers make it clear that this statement referred only to provisional and limited arrangements for convoying and landing I Corps somewhere on the coast of eastern Virginia.[65] Barnard's discussions with Goldsborough and Fox further confuse the picture. Having seen Fox in Washington, Barnard was apparently referred to Goldsborough, whom he visited in Hampton Roads on 20 March. A Cabinet meeting to settle the whole issue, scheduled for the 21st, was postponed until his return the following day. Fox's arrangements regarding I Corps were to receive definite approval at this meeting.[66]

The critical nature of the fleet support question is reflected in McClellan's anxiety over the Cabinet meeting. In a memorandum to Stanton on 19 March outlining the York River plan in response to the Secretary's complaint about the council of war, McClellan stated as an absolute necessity for the rapid success of this plan "that the Navy should at once throw its whole available force, its most powerful vessels, against Yorktown," and requested an immediate decision from the Navy Department.[67]

For some reason, the Cabinet discussion was not reported to McClellan until the 28th. Before leaving Fort Monroe, however, Barnard communicated the substance of his talks with Goldsborough and Wool. Goldsborough's promises appeared encouraging to Barnard, but were actually contradictory and vague. He had first asked Barnard to secure reinforcements from McClellan to allow Burnside to take Norfolk via the Chowan while he and Wool threatened the city from the Roads. If this was impossible, he agreed to land part of McClellan's army on the Poquosin River to turn the Confederate positions below Yorktown, "carry" Yorktown, and cooperate in combined attacks on Richmond *and* Norfolk. Although the Army could not expect the Navy to furnish large vessels simultaneously for the landing and bombardment of the river batteries, he implied that the ships could handle these tasks in sequence. He further suggested, however, that instead of a fleet bombardment, McClellan should land McDowell's Corps on the Severn River, taking the Gloucester defenses in the rear. From this point, Yorktown could be reduced by land batteries and only small gunboats would be required to keep open the York River to West Point.[68]

Despite Barnard's sanguine interpretation of these confused and tentative arrangements, it must have been apparent to McClellan that Goldsborough did not want to use his powerful warships in the York, nor had he dropped the idea for an unnecessary operation against Norfolk.[69] In any case, McClellan did not wait for the Cabinet decision to prepare alternate arrangements. On the 22nd he informed his chief of artillery, Brigadier General William Barry, that it might be necessary for the Army to use vertical fire against the heavy earthworks at Yorktown because "it is possible we cannot count upon the Navy to reduce Yorktown by their independent efforts, [and] we must therefore be prepared to do it by our own means."[70]

Barnard's report on the Cabinet conference and his further conversations with Fox merely confirmed McClellan's impression that Goldsborough would not remove his large vessels— the 47-gun frigate *Minnesota* and the smaller *San Jacinto* (16 guns)—from Hampton Roads, that the Navy Department would not order Du Pont to detach any warships from the blockade, and that the Army would have to make do with a maximum of seven wooden gunboats. Barnard doubted a dozen such vessels could produce enough concentrated fire to silence the enemy water batteries and therefore recommended relying on amphibious operations, adding that he had also instructed his engineers to consult with Goldsborough about taking Norfolk "in case anything should interfere with the full execution of the original plan."[71]

This last statement should have warned McClellan that his trusted chief engineer was the wrong man to have acted as his agent in negotiating with the Navy Department or the government. Barnard had all along favored an attack on Norfolk over any other combined plan, having initially suggested it to Welles and Fox—a fact McClellan did not discover until after the Peninsular campaign. He actually disapproved of McClellan's entire plan to approach Richmond via the lower Chesapeake, secretly agreeing with the Cabinet that the army's offensive line should directly cover Washington.[72] Had Mc-

Clellan chosen another agent, one who understood and agreed with his strategic ideas, or had he conducted the negotiations in person, he might well have secured the desired cooperation. At least he would have been better informed.

Logically, the promise of partial cooperation should have revived the Urbanna plan. But closer study revealed that the swampy terrain between Urbanna and West Point was unsuited to the passage of a large army and its baggage. Interposing the Army of the Potomac between Johnston, now at Fredericksburg, and Magruder in the Peninsula was too dangerous anyway. In the unlikely event McClellan was not attacked on his flank and could reach Richmond before Johnston, he could hardly remain there long without communications, and the possibility of being besieged in the enemy's capital to satisfy the politicians was not inviting. To maintain a safe base near Richmond now that the James River was closed by the *Virginia*, McClellan had to open the York to Union supply vessels. To accomplish this purpose, he had to compel the Confederates to evacuate their works at Yorktown and Gloucester whose batteries, on opposing banks seven-eighths of a mile apart, commanded the narrow channel. As long as the Confederates held Norfolk and the James River, Magruder's force could not be cut off by an isolated move on West Point. But if McClellan moved fast enough, he might shut it up in Yorktown.[73]

Consequently, even though the Navy may have refused full cooperation, McClellan chose the third alternative. Maps of the Peninsula prepared by General Wool's topographical engineer, Captain T.J. Cram, made the final plan appear practicable.[74] The defenses of the lower Peninsula at Big Bethel, Ship Point, and Howard's Bridge would be turned by landing Hooker's division on the Poquosin River and Cheeseman's Creek.[75] To hold Magruder in front, McClellan would advance three corps from Fort Monroe straight up the Peninsula. In case the Confederates withdrew toward Yorktown, the Federal corps forming the left wing, moving via the Young's Mill road, was to seize the Halfway House between Yorktown and Williamsburg. This would cut off the enemy's line of retreat, preventing reinforcements from Johnston's army, and keep Major General Benjamin F. Huger at Norfolk from reaching Magruder in time. If Magruder tried to withdraw up the York, Union gunboats waiting below the narrows could pursue and shoot up the transports. If he crossed over to the Gloucester side, McClellan would immediately push I Corps up river to destroy the Confederate depot and establish his new base at West Point. In the unlikely event that Magruder could sustain his army and hold on at Yorktown, the fleet might be persuaded to force the channel and shell him out of his works with reverse fire. If not, McDowell could take Gloucester via the Severn and use the siege train to destroy the fortress.[76]

The plan appeared foolproof. We do not know, and will probably never know definitely, if the Navy actually promised McClellan full cooperation, although Keyes's letter, Fox's false testimony, and the missing naval documents raise a strong suspicion that there was something to hide, perhaps an embarrassing commitment to force the York River with warships if McClellan requested it. But regardless whether such a commitment was made, McClellan's attempts to secure it wasted several precious weeks, caused him to base the final plan on I Corps' amphibious capability, and delayed the departure of this corps from Alexandria. The delay, it turned out, was more unfortunate than anyone could have predicted.

PART TWO

The Collapse of Combined Strategy

5

YORKTOWN

ALTHOUGH McClellan's plan to take Richmond by a rapid move via York River and the railroad failed, the first stage of the Peninsular campaign demonstrates the offensive power and flexibility of his combined operations strategy. That the campaign did not result in the fall of the Confederate capital or the destruction of a large part of Johnston's army was not due to unsound strategy, but to the failure of resources and lack of interservice cooperation at the right time.

As soon as McClellan's intention to advance by the Peninsula became known to the Confederate government, General Lee was recalled from the Carolinas and placed in charge of the Richmond defenses. Anticipating that his opponent would use combined operations to outflank the Yorktown and Williamsburg lines, he advised Magruder on 26 March to prepare to withdraw all the way to the Pamunkey River if Union vessels attempted to force the York River and land in his rear. Meanwhile, Magruder was to select suitable defensive positions on the upper James and lower Pamunkey to delay the Federals at their beachheads until Richmond's fortifications could be strengthened.[1]

General Joseph Johnston, soon to command all of the military and naval forces confronting McClellan on the Peninsula, had always opposed holding Yorktown. Supremely cautious, though superb on the defensive, he was very sensitive to being outflanked and invariably favored timely evacuation of any place likely to prove a trap for his army. Davis had overruled Johnston's proposal to abandon the Peninsula before McClellan showed his hand, and ordered him to send reinforcements to Magruder once it appeared that the Federal movement was

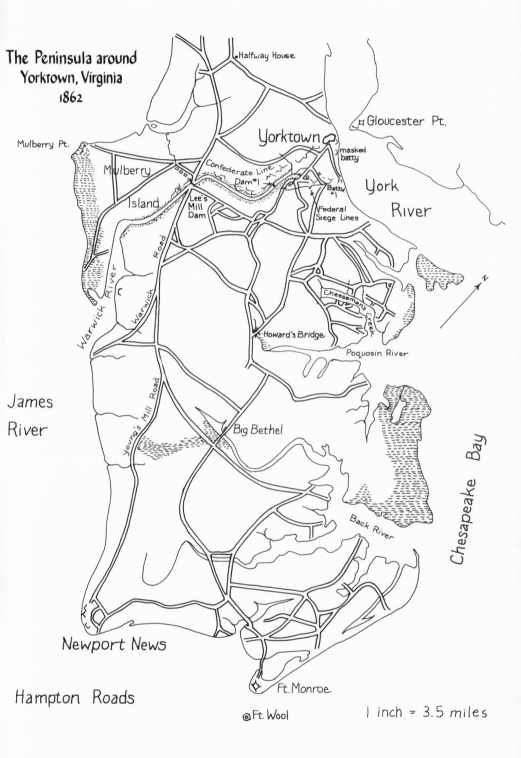

The Peninsula around
Yorktown, Virginia
1862

Halfway House

Gloucester Pt.

Mulberry Pt.

Yorktown

masked
batty

Mulberry

Confederate Line
Dam #1

Batty
#1

York

River

Island

Lee's
Mill
Dam

Federal
Siege Lines

Warwick River

Warwick River

Road

Cheeseman's Creek

Howard's Bridge

Poquosin River

Young's Mill Road

James
River

Big Bethel

Chesapeake Bay

Back River

Newport News

Ft. Monroe

Hampton Roads

Ft. Wool

1 inch = 3.5 miles

not a feint and that Confederate communications west of
Richmond and with the Shenandoah Valley were secure. However, the advance of two Union corps from Fort Monroe on
4 April brought a hurried order for Magruder to withdraw
from Yorktown.[2]

But Magruder disobeyed orders. Although he had only eleven
thousand men to hold the entire Confederate line from Mulberry Island on the right to Yorktown and the detached work
at Gloucester on the left, he had prepared his defenses with
great skill. Unknown to McClellan, Cram's maps were wrong.
The Warwick River, emptying into the James below Mulberry
Island, did not run northwest as shown on the maps, but
straight across the Peninsula to within a mile of Yorktown's
right bastion. The river ran through a low-lying, heavily wooded
area and Magruder had improved upon this natural obstacle
by constructing dams which turned the small stream into a
formidable and impassable water barrier. Detached redoubts
for interlocking fire defended the space between its headwaters
and the town. Instead of disposing his troops equally along
the line, Magruder stationed small detachments at strongly
fortified batteries covering the dams and held the rest of his
force in reserve to oppose a crossing at any threatened point.
To prevent the line being turned by the right, the Confederate
gunboat *Teazer* was stationed within the river mouth to cover
the approaches to the Lee's Mill Dam crossing on the Warwick
(Young's Mill) Road.[3]

During their advance from Fort Monroe, the Federals began
to suspect that the maps were inaccurate. Roads were not
where they should have been.[4] Marching up the Warwick road
toward its objective at Halfway House, Keyes's IV Corps in the
advance ran up against the Warwick River on the afternoon
of 4 April. A quick reconnaissance revealed the great strength
of Magruder's line at this point and Keyes at once informed
McClellan of this unpleasant surprise. Another surprise,
equally unpleasant, reached McClellan's headquarters at
Cheeseman's Creek on the 5th. A telegram from the adjutant
general announced Lincoln's decision to recall McDowell's
corps from its embarkation point at Alexandria and station it
before Washington. Brigadier General James S. Wadsworth
commanding the Washington defenses and Major General

Ethan A. Hitchcock, Stanton's special military advisor, had become increasingly nervous as they watched successive divisions of McClellan's army disappear down the Potomac. They convinced Stanton and the president that McClellan had violated his instructions by failing to leave behind a sufficient covering force for the capital.[5]

The unfortunate delay in obtaining naval cooperation had forced McClellan to postpone embarking McDowell's corps, the best and strongest in the Army of the Potomac, until last. He intended holding it as a unit aboard the transports ready to be thrown upon West Point the moment York River was open or, as indicated, landed on the left bank of the river below Gloucester or up the Severn to take the Gloucester Point batteries from the rear. The loss of Franklin's division of this corps was an especially hard blow.[6] It will be recalled that Franklin, like Burnside and Fitz John Porter, was an early advocate of combined operations and McClellan's confidant in formulating his strategic plans. During the Joint Committee hearings in December, he had skillfully argued the case for waterborne landings to surprise the enemy. Now, just when the army's advance was stopped short, because the hitherto unsuspected barrier of the Warwick made it impossible to invest Yorktown, McClellan was deprived of his only amphibious assault division.

The very contingency for which McClellan had so vigorously attempted to secure an advance promise of full fleet support was now a fact. Yorktown had to be reduced by bombardment. A few broadsides from a frigate like the USS *Minnesota*, still in Hampton Roads, if they could not demolish the works, would at least have driven the Southerners from their guns long enough for part of the fleet to run by. Yorktown was an old fort armed largely with medium-caliber smoothbore artillery. The upper works lacked adequate traverses and bombproofs. All of the best guns, disposed in the water batteries, were mounted *en barbette* and faced down or across the river.[7] Stringham's attack on the Hatteras forts and Du Pont's bombardent of Fort Walker had demonstrated how quickly a garrison could be driven out of such obsolete works or forced to surrender by a well-directed enfilade fire.

But powerful warships were not to be had. Even before

Rear Admiral Louis M.
Goldsborough
(*Navy Department*)

Brigadier General
Fitz John Porter

McClellan arrived on the Peninsula to confer personally with
Flag Officer Goldsborough on 2 April, the contingency plans
for fleet fire support had gone awry. One of Lincoln's prerequisites for approving the decision to base the Federal army
on Fort Monroe was that the ironclad *Virginia* be destroyed
or neutralized. Visions of the Confederate ram sallying out of
Hampton Roads for a cruise up the Potomac or a foray against
New York haunted the administration, while the possibility
of her entering the York to burn valuable transports and supply ships appalled both these ships' private owners and the
Army command.[8]

Although both sides pronounced the historic contest between
the *Monitor* and *Virginia* in Hampton Roads a victory for their
respective ships, and historians have traditionally judged it a
draw, Union naval officers fully perceived the *Monitor*'s unique
advantage on that day. Anticipating a possible confrontation
with the Confederate ironclad, the *Monitor*'s 11-inch guns
were supplied with solid wrought iron and brass shot to crush
her opponent's armor. The *Virginia*, on the other hand, expecting a repeat engagement with wooden vessels, carried only

The CSS *Virginia* (*Navy Department*)

shell. The impact of these shells fired at point-blank range from the Confederate's 7-inch rifles suggested the probable effect of a solid bolt at that range on the *Monitor*'s eight-inch turret armor.[9] The lucky circumstance which found the combatants equal in firepower and invulnerability on 9 March was not likely to recur in a future contest. Returning to Norfolk for repairs to the *Virginia*'s prow, damaged in ramming the USS *Cumberland*, Lieutenant Catesby ap R. Jones, an ordnance officer who had succeeded Buchanan as her captain, took on a large supply of steel-pointed solid projectiles before again venturing into the Roads.[10]

While Jones strengthened his ship for the next encounter with the *Monitor* and prepared boarding parties to capture her if she could not be sunk, the Federal Navy was concocting various schemes to deal with this menace. Not aware that for all her power as a floating battery, the *Virginia* was unseaworthy due to faulty engines and bad steering, Goldsborough's one thought was to prevent the destruction of more fragile blockaders. He assumed an aggressive posture, massing all of the most powerful warships on his station, and privately owned fast steam launches like the *Vanderbilt*, off Old Point Comfort to run over the *Virginia* if she appeared. The measure of his confidence in the Navy's ability to sink this one enemy ship, however, is revealed by his plan to obstruct the mouth of the Elizabeth River and bottle her up in Norfolk.[11]

Although Assistant Secretary Fox with his usual optimism had assured McClellan that the *Monitor* could "handle" the

Virginia unaided, he did not promise to throw down the gauntlet. Any such aggressive renewal of the fight that Fox may have had in mind was nullified by executive order. Lincoln would not allow *Monitor* to take "unnecessary" risks. To the president, more was at stake than Goldsborough's wooden walls. At his insistence, Federal engineers had loaded canal boats with stone to be sunk in the Potomac should the *Virginia* pass out of the Roads.[12]

Pressed by Lincoln's fear of risking the *Monitor* on the one hand and by McClellan's entreaties for naval fire support on the other, Goldsborough's solution was to resurrect the Norfolk plan. This would open the James, freeing his squadron for duty in the York. It might even make McClellan's Peninsular operations unnecessary since the Confederates would surely evacuate both the Warwick and Williamsburg lines once Federal vessels commanded the James. Besides, taking Norfolk would restore the Navy's property, wipe out the painful memory of abandoning a still intact navy yard to the enemy, and stop the construction of more "Merrimacs" and Confederate gunboats still on the stocks. The more Goldsborough thought about Norfolk and the possibilities for promotion inherent in this alternative, the more attractive it became.[13]

His ally, General Wool, still commanded the Department of Virginia and was equally anxious to revive his pet project. Unfortunately for McClellan, this obstreperous old soldier had been next in rank to General Scott in the prewar regular army. On Scott's retirement, Wool might reasonably have expected the top job. Lincoln's experience with an aged general-in-chief during the first six months of the war, however, induced him to select a younger, more vigorous man. Indeed McClellan was so much younger and had been elevated over the heads of so many senior line officers that Wool refused to serve under him.[14] To keep peace within the military establishment, Lincoln's order of 1 November 1861 appointing McClellan general-in-chief had specifically exempted Wool's department at Fort Monroe. Safely confined to what then appeared a backwater of the eastern theater of war and commanding a small number of badly trained troops, Wool was not expected to make trouble. McClellan's removal as general-in-chief and the transfer of active operations to the Peninsula forced Lincoln to demand the old general's cooperation. Instead, Wool disapproved of McClellan's whole plan as too grandiose, criticized his line of approach to Richmond as misdirected, and suggested a descent on Norfolk and Suffolk. This would require a much smaller force and, since it would take place wholly in his department, Wool would command it, leaving the bulk of the Army of the Potomac under McClellan free to cover the capital.[15]

Although the idea appealed to the nervous Washington administrators, Lincoln and Stanton were not yet ready to overrule the commanding general. Unable to secure Wool's cooperation in carrying out McClellan's plan and unwilling at that point to remove the old veteran, Lincoln placed the Department of Virginia and Fort Monroe under McClellan's command. But Stanton, while not favoring the Norfolk operation over the Peninsular plan, saw possibilities in a separate command for Wool. The secretary had begun to distrust McClellan. The general's plans were so meticulous and on such a grand scale; he was always asking for more and better equipment, more men, better guns. Since he took charge in November, large numbers of troops had been raised and vast amounts of money spent. There had been abundant plans and promises of movement, yet the Federal army in Virginia was not one step closer to Richmond than it had been in July. Stanton was not a military man and was therefore no judge of McClellan's competence. But Wool was a soldier. His letters were brief and to the point, unlike McClellan's lengthy disquisitions. Moreover, he was on the Peninsula and could observe and report conditions there to Washington.[16] While under McClellan's command, Wool could not report directly to the secretary. With this in mind, Stanton moved to have Wool restored to his independent position. He succeeded. McClellan had scarcely begun to move up the Peninsula when he discovered, to his amazement, that he no longer commanded his base.[17]

Wool was now free to consult Goldsborough directly about a combined attack on Norfolk. Goldsborough also had balked at an earlier proposal to place his squadron under McClellan's command. Direct communications from Army quartermasters wounded his professional dignity and he complained to Welles that all "requests for cooperation"—not orders—from Stanton and McClellan must be issued through the proper naval authorities. Naturally, he would cooperate with the general as the Navy Department ordered, but only so far as it did not conflict with his primary duty—keeping the squadron alert to deal with the *Virginia*. And the best way to deal with the *Virginia* might well involve capturing Norfolk.[18]

Examination of the problem in more concrete terms, however, revealed the Confederate position to be unusually strong on the water side. Wooden vessels could not, of course, enter the Roads and Lincoln had ruled out the idea that the *Monitor* attempt a coup de main against the city. This left two possibilities: a landing on the Norfolk peninsula which would be very difficult and impossible to execute while the Confederates held the strong works at Sewell's Point, Craney Island Point, Pig Point, and Fort Norfolk; or an attack upon the land side via Suffolk.[19]

Norfolk's only land communication with the rest of Virginia was a narrow strip carrying the railway through Suffolk to Petersburg. The ground lying between Albemarle Sound and this neck was an impassable swamp; but by ascending the Blackwater River from the Sound, a Federal force could penetrate to within a few miles of Suffolk, seize the strip of land and the railroad while Goldsborough and Wool distracted Huger with an attack on the shore batteries, and bag the whole crowd. Burnside's amphibious division, which had controlled Albemarle Sound since February, was available for the move on Suffolk. Goldsborough asked the administration, now directing Federal strategy, to reinforce Burnside with forty thousand men. Although the plan was clearly out of the question without detaching still another corps from McClellan, Lincoln was tempted to try it without reinforcements. Even if Norfolk was not taken, Burnside's 10,000 men and numerous gunboats would doubtless frighten the enemy and prevent troops in North Carolina from reinforcing Lee in Richmond, thereby helping McClellan's campaign.[20]

General McClellan did not see the administration's interference in the same light. He had already ordered Burnside to reduce Fort Macon guarding the Neuse River. His intention, it will be recalled, was for Burnside to follow up this operation with a move on Goldsborough, cutting the Wilmington and Weldon Railroad south of Petersburg. He still considered expeditions against Norfolk a waste of effort. Anyone with a modicum of military sense—and McClellan credited Generals Lee and Johnston with as much professional sagacity as himself—could see that Norfolk was a trap. Without a move on Suffolk from the Sounds, Norfolk could be isolated. As soon as the Confederates evacuated the Warwick line and the Federals controlled Jamestown Island, a Union flotilla could push up the James, and a detachment from the Army of the Potomac could be transferred to the south side of the river to cut communications with Raleigh and Petersburg. The fall of Yorktown inevitably would involve the evacuation of Norfolk.[21]

The converse was not true. As long as the Confederates held Hampton Roads, and their batteries at Mulberry Point and Jamestown Island commanded the river, a Federal force at Suffolk could not prevent the passage of troops and supplies across the river. Norfolk would have to be attacked. Meanwhile, all stores for the Union forces at Suffolk would have to be transported by the tortuous water route through Albemarle Sound, the Chowan, and the Blackwater, and then hauled overland from the river to the town. Even if Norfolk succumbed under these circumstances, the victory would not place the Federals in a more favorable position to attack Richmond. The Confederates would still hold the York and north bank of the James. Unless the Weldon road was cut, an advance from Suffolk on Petersburg could be easily stopped.[22]

If Goldsborough could not, in the event, get Lincoln's approval for his Norfolk project over McClellan's protest, and would not detach his large vessels from the duty of watching the Confederacy's miniature "fleet in being," he at last agreed to provide the Army of the Potomac with a squadron of four gunboats commanded by Captain J.F, Missroon. This officer had acquired a considerable reputation in the Navy as a "fighter" and had served with Du Pont at Port Royal. The Navy Department ordered Missroon to comply willingly and energetically with McClellan's smallest request and it expected great things of him.[23] Before the Yorktown operations were over, Welles and Fox would have reason to regret their judgment.

No one could claim that Missroon's gunboats were formidable vessels of war. Armed with only four Dahlgren smoothbores, their engines were barely sufficient to move them against the York River's deep and powerful current, and their boilers were unprotected.[24] Still, Missroon might have *attempted* something; but as soon as he arrived in the river, without even testing the Yorktown and Gloucester batteries, he concluded that his flotilla could accomplish nothing against them and that bringing his vessels within range to shell the enemy would only result in their being blown out of the water. He even refused to confer with McClellan at his headquarters, stating that he could not trust his inexperienced officers with the squadron.[25]

It looked increasingly like McClellan was stuck with a siege. Having ordered up the siege train on 5 April, he was still reluctant to employ regular approaches, except as a last resort. Despite his education and skill as an engineer, he preferred maneuvering to burrowing an opponent out of a position. Perhaps his observations at Sevastopol had taught him that sieges are expensive and tedious. Perhaps combined pressure from the Joint Committee, the State Department, the Cabinet, and the Northern press convinced him that only a conspicuous (if precipitous) movement would satisfy the country and quiet the incipient agitation in some quarters for a new commander.[26]

Whatever the reasons, McClellan tried every expedient to avoid a siege. After conducting personal inspections along the whole line, he sent General Barnard on the 9th to restudy Magruder's works with an eye to carrying a weak point by assault. The chief engineer's report was discouraging.[27] Further consultation with Missroon revealed that the squadron commander would not attempt to run the channel defenses, even at night, unless the Army first silenced the water batteries. Goldsborough strongly urged the Severn landing, detailing additional gunboats for this enterprise and promising to run past Yorktown if the Gloucester works were captured.[28] Without the I Corps, McClellan was reluctant to attempt this move. But if the Navy favored the plan, perhaps the government could be persuaded to send McDowell after all. In case this expedient proved fruitless, McClellan had one more device. This was the second Federal ironclad, the *Galena*, nearly ready to put to sea. Urging Fox and Commander John Rodgers, her captain, to hurry completion of this vessel, he pointed out that the success of his campaign might well depend on her presence in the York River.[29]

With the progressive disappearance of Johnston's army at Fredericksburg to join Magruder in Yorktown, the Washington administration relented. McClellan could not have McDowell's whole corps since one never knew when the Confederates might reappear close to the capital; but he could have Franklin's division. This would allow him to turn the enemy out of

Federal supply base at Yorktown, 1862. (*National Archives*)

Gloucester and open the river. McClellan immediately wired Rodgers to meet Franklin at Alexandria and remain with the division to supervise its debarkation and see that Goldsborough's gunboats provided adequate fire support for the troops in case of opposition. He asked Franklin to come to headquarters for a conference as soon as he could get away.[30]

Before Franklin reached the Peninsula, however, a new difficulty arose. Missroon reported that the Confederates were constructing more gun emplacements on their upper works at Gloucester to prevent an assault from the rear. They had also ferried infantry units across the river at night. Missroon suggested an alternate site for Franklin's landing, a large open beach three and one-half miles below Gloucester Point. This beach was apparently unguarded and the Confederates, prepared for a move on the Severn, might have been taken by surprise.[31]

McClellan was enthusiastic. When Franklin arrived at Cheeseman's Creek on the 14th, the two generals, in small boats, reconnoitered this beach and another some five miles below Gloucester. While the lower beach was further removed from enemy view, it was also further from the objective. More important, shoal water would keep the gunboats from approaching as close to shore. But a landing on the upper beach would probably meet early opposition—if not at the water line, at least before the assault force could establish an effective defensive perimeter. Moreover, Franklin was not prepared to land his men on an open beach, for he was not equipped to land them as a balanced fighting unit. Although the gunboats could furnish some fire support, naval gunfire at this point in the war was much too inaccurate for a close bombardment, even if the troops had been trained to endure it. And Missroon's often-expressed distrust of his own vessels and their officers must have communicated itself to the Army command.

In view of probable opposition to Franklin's landing and the time required for thorough preparations, McClellan increased his efforts to secure naval support. If Missroon could not be persuaded to run the batteries at night and Goldsborough would not order him to do so, the gunboats might at least have prevented enemy work parties from constructing new defenses on the Gloucester side. Missroon's complaints that his 11-inch smoothbores could not reach the enemy's rifled batteries without unduly exposing the ships was countered by McClellan's appeal to the flag officer for a vessel mounting a 100-pounder (6.4-inch) Parrott rifle. The gunboat *Sebago* was immediately dispatched and joined Missroon's squadron in the York River on the 14th.[32]

It was easier to pry a few more vessels out of Goldsborough, however, than to get Missroon to use them. The night before the *Sebago* arrived at the Cheeseman's Creek anchorage, McClellan had asked that the squadron shell the Confederate picket stations on the shore below Gloucester. Missroon excused himself, remarking that he was unwilling to risk such fragile ships to certain destruction in a contest with fifty heavy cannon. As though his previous apprehensions were not enough, he was further frightened by an incident that same night. A Negro laborer escaping from Gloucester in a canoe came on board the flagship and reported that the batteries there were even more formidable than Missroon had imagined. They were commanded, he said, by "Jeff" Page, late of the U.S. Navy, who boasted that his guns were so accurate they could "kill a dog at a mile."[33] So profound was the squadron commander's fear for his ships that when Lieutenant Commander O.C. Badger, sent to aid McClellan by Commander Wyman of the Potomac Flotilla, had shot off his twelve rifled 50-pounder shells at the Yorktown works on the 15th, he complained that Missroon refused to permit him to fire the *Anacostia*'s 9-inch guns even at night, "fearing that we may be crippled, and that in assisting us he may get some of his own vessels crippled." His excuse this time was that he had to save the gunboats to assist General Franklin.[34] Until Missroon was relieved on 30 April, he continued to use Franklin's landing, which could be regarded as an Army project, to avoid responsibility for continued inaction. By 14 April, McClellan realized that nothing could induce Missroon to move; that no number of ships or naval guns would accomplish anything under his command.[35]

Since the gunboats could not, or would not, stop the enemy from reinforcing Gloucester or extending picket stations in the direction of the beach, Franklin's preparations had to be more elaborate. This would take time, and McClellan realized that

the time for an assault was rapidly running out. By the 15th
Yorktown's defenders had received only 16,000 reinforcements
from Johnston's army—D.H. Hill's command which had arrived on the 11th—but McClellan was puzzled by the delay and
knew the remainder would be arriving any moment.[36] Daily
reconnaissances of Magruder's line along the Warwick revealed
that the weakest point was in the center at Dam Number One.
On 16 April, the 2nd Division of Keyes's corps assaulted this
position. It was a close battle—the Federals never knew how
close—but the attack was repulsed. The next day McClellan
bowed to the inevitable and began constructing siege Battery
Number One on the right of the first parallel. The guns selected
for this redoubt, five 100- and two 200-pounder (8-inch)
rifles would bear on the Yorktown wharf, the water batteries
on that side, and the Gloucester Point works. The naval officers had all along insisted that the Army must reduce these
works before the fleet would run by and McClellan was now
convinced that they meant what they said, and that he must
hereafter rely on his own resources. The soldiers would also
aid Franklin; they had had enough of Missroon and his gunboats.[37]

Despite elaborate contingency planning, the Army of the
Potomac was stopped before Yorktown by a complex of accidents unparalleled in the Civil War. A commanding general
might expect poor maps, unreliable allies, public pressure,
government interference, professional jealousy, and an alert,
intelligent enemy in any campaign. He does not usually con-
front all these obstacles at once, however, and he generally
has time to adjust to one setback before encountering another.
A less resourceful and energetic man might have given up and
returned to Washington with the whole army and its baggage,
starting a new campaign that summer along the government's
preferred line of operation. But McClellan knew his strategy
was right. The Confederates' stubborn defense of the Peninsula
and its flanking water highways was proof of their sensitivity
to attack from this quarter.

A plan based on water communications is only feasible, however, if naval forces are available and willing to cooperate.
Fox, always sensing the proper time to tack to the wind of
popular opinion, was alarmed by the Navy's falling press im-

age. But even while urging Goldsborough to cooperate completely with McClellan, he was covering his tracks. Denying that the Navy had promised the Army any cooperation only convinced Goldsborough that he was free to decide the matter for himself.[38] On his several trips to Hampton Roads, Fox avoided McClellan's camp; thus he reported to Washington only what he saw in the Roads, and Goldsborough's alarm about Norfolk. Of the situation at Yorktown, he was blissfully ignorant. McClellan could not be entirely certain of support from the War Department either. General Hitchcock, visiting Goldsborough as Stanton's agent, agreed with Wool that McClellan's massive move on Richmond was more show than substance, that troops should be provided to take Norfolk, and that McClellan should have operated against the enemy down the railroad from Washington. Stanton himself was not ready to pass premature judgment on the campaign; being angry with the Navy for its independent attitude, he was inclined, for the moment, to side with McClellan. The Army might yet pull off a grand strategic victory on its own.[39]

McClellan could give little thought to administrative quarrels in Washington. He was preoccupied with his immediate problems before Yorktown. While brilliant results might no longer be possible, he was still confident that the Army of the Potomac could gain a major victory, either by turning the enemy out of Richmond or forcing him into a desperate fight for the capital against superior numbers and from a disadvantageous position.[40] But it would take more time; and time was important. The Confederates were concentrating more troops around Richmond every day, withdrawing forces from Georgia and the Carolinas. McClellan could perhaps console himself with the thought that the larger the army opposing him at Yorktown, the more easily part of it might be cut off by a rapid move up the river on its rear. Before this move was possible, however, he would have to take the enemy shore batteries. Franklin had to attack Gloucester before he could land at West Point.

In the absence of adequate naval fire, Franklin's division had to get its own artillery ashore quickly, before the enemy could bring up his field guns to command the beach. This kind of landing had not been tried before. Butler's troops landed without heavy artillery or stores in the surf outside Hatteras Inlet; they literally were "dumped" on the beach in the traditional haphazard manner, the men jammed into the boats, regiments and brigades intermixed and separated from their officers and their ammunition. Even if so many boats had not broken up in the surf or veered away from the landing point, the least opposition would have transformed a fiasco into a disaster. Sherman's expeditionary corps had disembarked in a leisurely manner at the wharves on a friendly shore, the enemy having evacuated Hilton Head Island after the Navy drove them from the forts. Burnside's operation, while a bit more sophisticated in design, had an entire fleet for fire support. When it became apparent that the Confederates would not oppose him on the beach, Burnside was free to land in the old style and his more imaginative expedients were never tested in action.

The only military men who knew about boats were the engineers. Lieutenant Colonel Barton Alexander, the man who had prepared the engineer equipage for the Army of the Potomac and had trained its two regiments of volunteer engineer troops (the 15th and 50th New York), was a ranking officer in the regular engineers. He had acquired a reputation before the war as the builder of the Minot's Ledge lighthouse and was praised by his superior, General Barnard, for his practical ingenuity, energy, and knowledge of the latest developments in European military engineering. While supervising lighthouse construction, Alexander had acquired considerable skill in the handling of heavy equipment on all types of beaches.[41] The appointment of his best engineer to organize Franklin's operation indicates its importance in McClellan's mind.

Alexander joined Franklin on 20 April and a few days later accompanied his new chief, General McClellan, and Commander Rodgers on a further detailed reconnaissance of the beach below Gloucester. Having selected and sounded the exact landing point, Alexander set about solving the many problems of landing troops and artillery in the quickest, most efficient manner.[42] The product of his fertile mind was a self-contained assault force equipped with its own primitive landing craft.

The first problem was landing the guns. In consultation with

Captain Richard Arnold, Franklin's Chief of Artillery, Alexander designed special shallow-draft platforms using two 14 x 80-foot canal barges overlaid with planking brought with the division in case the need for it should arise. A whole battery of artillery could be placed on one of these platforms while another carried enough horses to move it onto the beach. For landing infantry, the large sturdy French batteaux forming the bridge train were used.[43] These boats accommodated about forty men with their knapsacks, haversacks, arms, and ammunition. The assault wave would consist of 2,000 men and one or two field batteries, followed by a second wave of infantry. After landing the first battery, the artillery raft would become a floating wharf for discharging stores from light-draft steamers.

Getting the men into the boats was another problem. Alexander had first planned to allow the sailors aboard the Army transports to manage this. But a few trials in Cheeseman's Creek revealed that a more effective system was required. He had observed that, when the troops were made to climb down the ship's side into a boat, each man waited for the previous man to finish his descent before beginning his own:

> In this way it was found that fully half a day would be consumed in landing the men from some of the larger transports, although they had plenty of boats to carry them at one trip, and they could have been landed in an hour if proper facilities for getting from the vessel into the boats had been provided.[44]

His solution was placing gangplanks anchored on the transport's deck reaching to the gunwales on both sides of the batteaux, permitting the troops to file into the boats. Gangplanks were also prepared for moving the guns from their floating platforms onto the shore.

Equipment was not Alexander's sole concern. Untrained troops can botch a landing using the most ingenious equipment. While waiting for the pontoons, Franklin's division practiced landing and unloading artillery, getting into and out of the transports and batteaux, and forming up in line of battle on the beach south of Cheeseman's Creek. Alexander found that, after two or three such attempts, the men became quite expert at these exercises and could handle both the guns and themselves with ease.[45]

While Franklin was preparing to land without naval assistance, McClellan had not entirely given up the idea of interservice cooperation. He was especially anxious to stop enemy reinforcements from reaching the Yorktown wharf and passing over the river. But he did not know what to do about Missroon. Since he was not under McClellan's command, the general could neither remove him nor order him to proceed against his judgment. Goldsborough might be able to send another ship or two in a week's time, but McClellan had the uneasy impression that the Flag Officer's mind was somewhere else.[46] He was right.

For more than a month, the country and the government had anxiously waited for something to develop in Hampton Roads. The Confederates did not move, however, and Goldsborough could not make them move without risking his ships against orders from Lincoln and Welles. Strangely enough, the more vessels Goldsborough accumulated, the less secure he felt. As the fleet moved further away from the *Virginia*, she appeared more powerful. The Confederates were baffled by the Federals' bizarre behavior. The *Virginia*'s new commander, Flag Officer Josiah Tattnall, anticipating a massive attack at any moment, was unaware that the Union fleet's sole concern was how it might escape this "monster" if she chose to attack.[47] In a glowing commendatory letter to Goldsborough, Welles approved the Flag Officer's dispositions and praised him for not risking the fleet, remarking that if the *Virginia* did not oblige by coming out to be destroyed, "her power will be restricted to narrow limits and where it will be comparatively harmless."[48] It apparently never dawned on Welles or Goldsborough that their overreaction allowed a single enemy vessel to protect the Confederacy's only navy yard, close the main approach to Richmond, and neutralize a large Federal fleet and an army of 120,000 men. Fortunately for the South, General Lee's proposal to send the *Virginia* into the York River was not adopted. As early as 12 April, Magruder recognized that he could hold the Peninsula against numbers of better than three to one merely by allowing the *Virginia* to cruise about the Roads in a threatening attitude, which encouraged the Union Navy to worry itself into complete paralysis. When General Johnston took command on the 18th, he continued this policy with remarkable success.[49]

By mid-April Goldsborough's nerves were so bad that, having discovered an enemy plan to shell the important Federal naval station at Newport News, he assured Welles that his squadron would not be drawn into the Roads to protect it, justifying his decision with the extraordinary statement that "the place is no longer of any material consequence to us."[50] The Department seems to have lost its wits. All kinds of fantastic schemes were taken seriously. A certain H.K. Lawrence, Esq. offered to blow up the Confederate ram for a reward of $500,000 if he succeeded and $1800 if he failed, the government to provide powder, transportation, and use of the Washington arsenal. Welles thought the idea worth considering and actually asked this enterpriser to submit a written proposal for approval by the Navy Department. Lieutenant Commander Badger advised the Naval Ordnance Bureau to use "liquid fire" for repelling boarding attempts on the *Monitor*. He found that Captain Henry A. Wise, the bureau chief, had anticipated him and had already sent Goldsborough a large supply of shells filled with this material. Although totally ineffective against armor, some of the stuff might filter down inside the *Virginia* causing her crew to abandon ship.[51]

To make matters worse in Goldsborough's mind, his Norfolk expedition seemed doomed before it began. Wool was, of course, more than anxious to cooperate, but he had only 10,000 troops in his tiny department and most of them were already occupied guarding McClellan's supply lines. Brigadier General Jesse Reno's division of Burnside's force, sent on the 17th to destroy the locks on the Dismal Swamp Canal, hopefully as a first move toward isolating Norfolk, was driven off on the 20th by a handful of the enemy.[52]

Goldsborough thought the secretary did not fully appreciate his predicament. Deserters had informed him that the Southerners were building another ironclad and five more gunboats at the Norfolk yard. If the *Monitor* could not challenge the *Virginia*, it was a safe assumption that the USS *Galena*, when she arrived, could not handle the new ram. He pleaded with Welles to let him take Norfolk. While the secretary was sympathetic and told Stanton that he considered the capture of Norfolk next in importance to the fall of New Orleans, Fox was closer to the president and tried to warn the Flag Officer, belatedly, that Lincoln expected him to cooperate with McClellan. The country, he told Goldsborough, did not appreciate the situation in Hampton Roads and could not understand why the Navy did not run the Yorktown batteries. Lincoln was discouraged, and saw in the *Galena* the last hope for breaking the deadlock.[53]

McClellan had come to see matters in the same light. The *Sebago*'s rifled gun had not stiffened Missroon's backbone. In fact, under increasing pressure from the commanding general and his siege director, General Porter, to bombard the water batteries, he actually lied to McClellan. The *Sebago*'s first encounter with the enemy's "masked battery"—a one-gun work located about three-quarters of a mile below Yorktown— was extremely brief. Having barely moved within range, Missroon told McClellan, the Southerners proceeded to put their first two shots right through his vessel, just missing the boilers. Assuming that the Confederates had triangulated the river and were firing at fixed range, he immediately hauled off, since "a single shot in the midship section" would have proved fatal. Gunboats, he explained, could never equal such remarkable precision of fire; thus, McClellan's shore batteries must do the job.[54] At best, Missroon exaggerated what had happened. His official report reveals that the *Sebago* was never hit. But the shells came awfully close, he told Goldsborough, actually "throwing water over her and all passing in close proximity."[55]

Had the *Sebago* remained in the channel, she could not have accomplished much. The rifle's carriage was worn out and there were no more 100-pounder shells at Fort Monroe. Although Goldsborough anxiously telegraphed the Naval Ordnance Bureau for a large supply of ammunition and four more Parrott guns, they arrived too late for the final attack on Yorktown.[56]

Because the *Galena* was expected within a week and Franklin's preparations for landing had scarcely begun, McClellan formulated a new plan, or at least a new sequence for the existing plan. Franklin's landing would now coincide with the

The USS *Galena*

opening of the Army's siege guns, rapidly being placed in position. Under cover of this bombardment in front, the *Galena* would pass the water batteries, take them in reverse, and enfilade the enemy's line of retreat from Yorktown.[57]

Goldsborough agreed that the *Galena* should run the channel and thought she might succeed "if sufficiently plated." But when he actually inspected the ship on her arrival in Hampton Roads on the 24th, Goldsborough changed his opinion. "She is," he informed Fox, "a most miserable contrivance—entirely beneath naval criticism."[58] Miserable or not, she was the Navy's only hope for redeeming itself in the eyes of the Army and the government. Unfortunately, the *Galena* could not be immediately dispatched to York River. Her machinery, damaged on the trip from New York, required a few days for repairs. On the 28th, she was still in the Roads. Further inspection convinced Goldsborough that the ship might prove more lethal to friend than foe. Exposed nuts lined her gun deck ready to fly around with every concussion and she had to be fitted with a shield of boiler iron to protect the gun crews.[59]

Missroon did not have to see the *Galena* to know she could effect nothing against the batteries. He warned Goldsborough on the 22nd that although Fox had assured McClellan that the *Galena* could pass up the river with impunity, he thought she would be destroyed.[60] No one listened any longer to Missroon, however. (On 23 April he asked to be relieved, for his own sake and "the Navy's honor.") By the first of May Alexander's preparations were nearly complete and so were the Army's siege batteries.[61] While further alterations still kept the *Galena* in Hampton Roads, a change clearly had come over the York River squadron. Commander William Smith, Missroon's replacement, had scarcely begun his duties when he ordered Lieutenant Commander Nicholson in the USS *Marblehead* to engage the Yorktown batteries. This vessel carried a small supply of "Birney incendiary shell" along with their inventor who had asked Smith to shoot them into the town as an experiment. After firing three rounds, the *Marblehead*, within range of the enemy guns, was nearly hit, but Nicholson did not withdraw until he had shot off all of the incendiary shells and several Parrott shells, and then only at Birney's request.[62]

Smith visited McClellan the following day to arrange the Navy's part in the coming attack. It was decided that the gunboat squadron, along with the *Galena*, would pass Yorktown immediately after the siege batteries opened, running through at night to avoid casualties. Goldsborough objected to this plan. Smith's offensive spirit could not suddenly counteract a month of Missroon's alarmist reports. Goldsborough still insisted that the Gloucester works must be taken before the gunboats could risk such a move.[63] Fortunately for Smith, who was caught in the middle of this argument, the enemy resolved it.

Had the Federals realized the true state of affairs in Yorktown, they could have taken the place in half the time and with a fraction of the effort expended.[64] While Missroon was certainly right that the Confederate works, especially those on the water, were scientifically placed and admirably constructed, he never pushed his reconnaissances close enough to discover that they were miserably armed. The earthworks at Gloucester were unfinished and mounted only eight guns, none larger than 32-pounders. Besides two columbiads in Yorktown's upper fort which bore on the river, there were nine guns in the water batteries below the town, all old-pattern smoothbores.[65] The most effective piece of ordnance bearing on the channel was the rifle in the "masked battery," whose accuracy had so impressed Missroon. A converted 32-pounder, it pointed straight down the river and was skillfully concealed among the bushes and earthen ramparts of an old Revolutionary War redoubt.[66] But it was only one gun.

The artillery shortage in Yorktown was so great that, by 24 April, Confederate Major General D.H. Hill, appointed on the 15th to command the Yorktown and Gloucester defenses, complained that he had only one rifle left to keep vessels out of the channel. "Should the gunboats now pass us," he told Secretary of War George W. Randolph, "all our transports in the river will be lost and the army starved." Hill was certain he knew what McClellan was about. "He is either waiting for a formidable mortar and siege train," he advised Randolph, "or he is waiting until more ironclad vessels are made. In the latter case he expects to reduce Yorktown from the water side." Hill had already urged a massive concentration to crush McClellan in his position before Yorktown, even if this involved exposing the rest of the Confederacy to occupation and losing the South's major seaports. "By attempting to hold so many points," he warned, "we have been beaten in detail, and are losing all that we have been trying to hold." As for the Yorktown lines, Hill admitted that the fall of Gloucester would be a serious blow, "but ironclad boats in the river would be much more so."[67]

The quantitative inferiority of the Confederate ordnance was compounded by its poor quality. This was particularly important in the river defenses. The old smoothbores, however large in caliber or weight of projectile, had insufficient accuracy to prevent gunboats from passing the works. The few rifles were defective and their shells unreliable, bursting at the mouths of the guns or not exploding at all. While Missroon was concluding that he must avoid the enemy's superior artillery by moving to a lower anchorage, Hill was planning to stop gunboats with infantry. Since the distance from the shore to mid-channel was less than a half-mile opposite the wharf, he suggested stationing a company of Texas sharpshooters at this point to pick off the crews of Union vessels attempting to run by.[68]

Hill's gloomy telegrams alarmed the Richmond government. On 28 April the Cabinet considered advising evacuation of the

Peninsula. Davis was not ready to accept this recommendation, because losing Yorktown meant losing Norfolk. Johnston should hold on at least until Huger had removed the valuable property and stores from the town and the navy yard.[69] Johnston, who had never wanted to defend Yorktown, would have been pleased to leave at once; but the roads, he told Lee, were getting worse every day as the result of spring rains. As long as he felt he could avoid being caught, Johnston would hold on. Two days later he suspected any delay might prove fatal. He agreed with Hill that McClellan must be waiting for ironclad vessels; these would permit him to beat Johnston's army in a race for Richmond.[70]

The opening of McClellan's right siege battery on the 30th and the aggressive behavior of the Federal squadron on 1 May decided the question. Battery Number One's first few rounds caught the Confederate transports in the midst of discharging troops and stores at the Yorktown wharf. Thus, Johnston could no longer use the river for his supplies. Some of the *Marblehead*'s incendiary shells set the town's wooden buildings on fire.[71] It was clearly time to leave.

Johnston managed the evacuation with great skill. The Federals suspected nothing until the afternoon of the 2nd when some of Keyes's officers on the left of the line noticed that the enemy pickets had disappeared from their front. This observation was not reported to headquarters. Then the Confederate rear guard staged a pyrotechnic display on the night of the 3rd, firing off nearly all of the ammunition in Yorktown since they could not carry away the fortress guns.[72] Early morning of the 4th brought silence. The deadlock was finally broken, and McClellan was free to move.

It will be recalled that Franklin's division had been held aboard its transports ready to disembark at the beach below Gloucester on receiving the signal for a general attack. Now that the Confederates had evacuated Yorktown, McClellan could have sent Franklin immediately to West Point. Suspecting that the enemy might have placed obstructions covered by shore batteries higher up the York, the gunboat USS *Chocura* was dispatched on reconnaissance the morning of the 4th. The vessels returned that afternoon reporting a white flag flying over the charred Confederate depot at West Point, no troops visible, and no batteries or obstructions in the river.[73]

Several of the best Civil War historians, including the Comte de Paris, have been unable to explain why McClellan did not send the assault division directly to West Point on the 5th. Although the evidence on this question is admittedly inadequate, it seems likely that Alexander had the right explanation. Stoneman's cavalry division, sent to cut off Johnston's rear guard, took the wrong route and when General Hooker, leading III Corps on the Yorktown road, caught up with the Confederates before the Williamsburg entrenchments early on the 5th, he immediately brought on an engagement to prevent their getting away. But Hooker's failure to reconnoiter the ground or wait for his supports, however understandable, resulted in a bloody repulse. General W.F. Smith's division arriving soon afterwards was thrown into disarray, and by the time the senior corps commander, General Sumner, arrived on the field around 1 P.M., he was unable to restore order.

The Confederates had not intended a serious defense of the Williamsburg lines, and Major General James A. Longstreet was well along the road to Richmond. When he learned that the rearguard had held the position against such superior numbers, however, he countermarched his division and arrived back in Williamsburg by mid-afternoon. Upon seeing the disordered condition of the Federal units, Longstreet attacked and drove them away from the works.[74]

McClellan had heard the guns from the direction of Williamsburg since dawn. When he learned the true situation at around 3 P.M., he left for the front, after ordering Commander Smith to prepare two gunboats for sailing at a moment's notice. Arriving at Sumner's field headquarters, he quickly restored order and examined the enemy entrenchments. It was at once apparent that the left of their line could be enfiladed by gunboats stationed in Queen's Creek, a small stream flowing into the York; so McClellan sent back for the *Marblehead* and the *Maratanza*. While awaiting the boats, the Union signal corps established a station close to the battlefield for directing the ships' fire upon the works.[75] McClellan now knew that an assault division would not be required at Williamsburg and ordered Franklin to move on West Point the following morning.[76] From the sequence of events, it seems likely that Alexander is correct in contending that McClellan held Franklin's division at Yorktown until he was certain of driving the Confederates from Williamsburg.[77] Longstreet did not wait for Smith's gunboats to open fire; their mere appearance in Queen's Creek induced him to evacuate the place and continue his retreat to the Chickahominy. As the Federal troops entered the works on the morning of the 6th, Franklin's division passed up the river.[78]

Preparations for the Gloucester landing were utilized to advantage by the division at Eltham's plantation opposite West Point. Within an hour the assault wave, ferried by detachments of the 15th New York engineer regiment, had landed and in three hours there were 8,000 men ashore, with their equipment and provisions, formed into battle order with pickets extended into the woods beyond the beach. Each brigade landed in succession, care being exercised to keep regiments and their officers together. Meanwhile, the first three artillery batteries were brought ashore and a wharf assembled. Most of the division's guns and all of its troops were put on the beach, with their ammunition and stores, in ten hours.[79]

The Army of the Potomac had finally reached its objective at West Point, but the delay was fatal to McClellan's plan. The enemy had been given ample time to construct defenses and to mass his forces around Richmond. Nor could a part of Johnston's army be cut off, for the wily Confederate did not stop to smash the Federal beachhead. Supplies in the neighborhood were inadequate and Johnston knew that Franklin would immediately be supported by another division of Sumner's II Corps already en route to West Point. Worse, McClellan's mobility allowed him to gain the head of navigation on the Pamunkey River at White House. A Union army established on the York River Railroad would not only threaten communications between Johnston's army and the Confederate force facing McDowell at Fredericksburg but would open the door to Richmond. Johnston's one thought was to get in front of McClellan.[80]

Fortuitous circumstances favored his movement. As Franklin's division disembarked, Major General Gustavus Smith, commanding the advance guard with the Confederate reserve, was halted on the road north of Barhamsville waiting for his

wagons and caissons to close up. Observing the Federals pushing skirmishers into the woods beyond the beach, he promptly
attacked on the morning of the 7th, driving them back under
cover of the gunboats.[81] Franklin was thus prevented from
expanding the beachhead until all of his artillery and infantry
supports had landed. The Army of the Potomac's main body
forming the left wing, exhausted by the unexpectedly heavy
fighting at Williamsburg, was delayed several days awaiting
supplies and by worsening road conditions. When McClellan's
more mobile right wing reached White House on the 12th,
Johnston's army was firmly positioned behind the Chickahominy River with its left center across the railroad at Fair
Oaks Station.[82]

Notwithstanding their skillful and successful delaying defense against great odds, from the moment the Army of the
Potomac arrived at Fort Monroe the Confederates lost the
initiative.[83] Even though Richmond was still unoccupied, they
had been maneuvered out of the Peninsula and their important naval establishment at Norfolk had just fallen into enemy
hands. A large and well-equipped army having a permanent
way for bringing forward heavy guns and reinforcements was
planted a few miles from the capital, Virginia's Eastern Shore
was isolated, Burnside had moved within striking distance of
the vital rail links into the Carolinas, and Federal gunboats
patrolled the James.

6

THE JAMES RIVER LINE

As EXPECTED, McClellan's move up the Peninsula forced the Confederates out of Norfolk, opening the James River line to Union operations. The day Norfolk fell, the Army of the Potomac's left wing established contact with Franklin's beachhead. McClellan at once announced his intention to dispense with the York River Railroad and transfer his base to the James. This line would permit naval support for an advance right into Richmond, as well as cooperation with Burnside's force to the south.[1] At least this was McClellan's intention. But the change of base was not accomplished until the first of July, after the Confederates had attacked the Army of the Potomac on the upper Chickahominy and captured its depot at White House. At that point it appeared, not a sagacious move for employing the combined Union land and naval forces at the enemy's most vulnerable point, but a desperate expedient to save a beaten army.

Two developments upset the commanding general's calculations. The problems confronting the Navy in the James River were followed almost immediately by renewed government interference with his dispositions.

Even before Norfolk fell, Federal troops were in possession of Mulberry and Jamestown Islands and Union gunboats could have pushed up the James. The day McClellan entered Yorktown, he had asked that the *Galena* be sent up river immediately. But the Navy delayed too long. Goldsborough's continued reluctance to engage the *Virginia* and Wool's refusal to land his troops until the fleet had silenced the shore batteries allowed the Confederates to hold Norfolk for a week after the fall of Yorktown. By the time they withdrew on the

10th, most of the valuable property, stores, and heavy artillery had been removed and the navy yard demolished.[2]

The best cannon from the Norfolk forts, sent to Richmond and Petersburg, were placed in hastily improvised works on the upper James and Appomattox Rivers. The unfinished iron-clad *Richmond* with her ordnance stores, plus two incomplete gunboats, left Norfolk under tow on the 6th. One piece of valuable property not taken to Richmond was the *Virginia*; her draft was too great. Attempts to lighten her exposed the wooden hull below the casemate to penetration and she was blown up on the 11th. Her battery had already been removed, however, and carried up river in the gunboats *Beaufort* and *Raleigh* where it would soon make up the armament of a formidable elevated earthwork at Drewry's Bluff on the right bank of the James, eight miles below Richmond. After destroying the vessel, her crew took the train to Petersburg, arriving in Richmond on the 12th.[3] The Confederate ram, in a different guise, was about to shoot it out with the Federal ironclads after all.

Had Rodgers moved up the James on the 4th as McClellan requested he would have met no opposition. The Confederates had not succeeded in obstructing the river, nor had they erected any fortifications above City Point. Early in February, Briga-dier General R.E. Colston had advised placing obstructions at Jamestown Island or above to prevent Federal vessels going "all the way to Richmond." The Confederate defeats at Hat-teras and Port Royal had convinced him "that earthen forts are insufficient defenses against fleets." Captain J.R. Tucker of the Confederate States Navy agreed, and advised preparing stone cribs and pilings interlaced with Maury "torpedoes" (electric mines) which could be sunk at a moment's notice in the shallow channel above Trent's Reach fifteen miles below the city.[4]

A week later General Lee ordered the Confederate Engineer Bureau to implement this good advice and the work progressed rapidly. By 25 March the river had been cross-sectioned and some of the pilings and cribs fixed to the bottom. But the same torrents of rain which retarded McClellan's peninsular movements engulfed the engineers' edifice and work was sus-pended. At the end of April as Johnston prepared to evacuate Yorktown, he expected an immediate move by the Federal Navy

Jefferson Davis

General Joseph E. Johnston
(*Valentine Museum*)

on Richmond and urged Lee to complete the barrier. Nevertheless, when Rodgers' flotilla reached City Point on 13 May the obstructions were still unfinished.[5]

Johnston's withdrawal from the Peninsula had produced panic in the capital. In view of the inadequate defenses on the James River side, the Confederate government prepared to evacuate both Richmond and Petersburg. The provost marshal in Petersburg received frantic instructions to destroy all tobacco, cotton, and public property the moment the Federals appeared. The president of the Richmond, Fredericksburg and Petersburg Railroad was directed to ready all rolling stock in the area for a quick move south. The government archives and Confederate treasury notes were crated up awaiting an order to transport them to Danville. Although General Johnston vehemently objected, insisting that he could not maintain his army if driven beyond the city, the Commissary Department, after consulting Davis and Lee, informed him that ninety days' supplies would be sent to a point on the railway southwest of Richmond.[6]

The *Virginia*'s crew arrived just in time. Under the skillful eye of Captain S.S. Lee, who worked continuously for two days and nights, they erected a series of detached gun emplacements on the 200-foot high bluff above the river. Although these were field fortifications, the guns, one 10-inch and four 8-inch naval guns plus two rifled 32-pounders, were well protected by earthern traverses and bombproofs. Their elevation above the river provided for plunging fire onto the decks of enemy vessels, an effect the Union navy had been spared since Foote's losing contest with Fort Donelson in February.

The obstructions which the Confederate engineers had assembled at this point along with several old hulks loaded with stone were quickly sunk in the channel directly beneath the bluff to hold the ships under the guns. The gunboats *Patrick Henry* and *Jamestown* were positioned in the narrow gap left in the barricade for passing ships down the river. A line of sharpshooters under Lieutenant J.T. Wood was stationed in riflepits along both banks to fire into the ports and disable the Union gunners. To complete the defensive preparations, and especially to guard against a landing in force, Brigadier General William Mahone's infantry brigade was ordered to support the Drewry's Bluff work, now called Fort Darling.[7]

Suspecting that the Southerners were preparing him a warm reception, Rodgers was in a hurry to reach Richmond. But he was impeded by an order to destroy all of the shore batteries as he moved up river, meanwhile landing Marines to spike the guns and blow up the magazines. This appears to have been Goldsborough's idea and he got Lincoln's approval contrary to the views of the Navy Department. Goldsborough had no faith in McClellan's operations and old General Wool, as usual, agreed with him. In the likely event of McClellan's retreat to Fort Monroe, the Confederates would reoccupy these works, he thought, unless they were totally destroyed. Then too, Goldsborough would not risk sending stores and ordnance vessels to Rodgers until this was accomplished. Meanwhile, the *Galena* had to draw supplies from the naval stores ships at West Point, McClellan's assistance being required for transporting them across the Peninsula to Jamestown Island.[8]

At this point, Goldsborough could have solved the problem himself, as Rodgers might reasonably have expected, since he had also been ordered to reach Richmond as soon as possible.

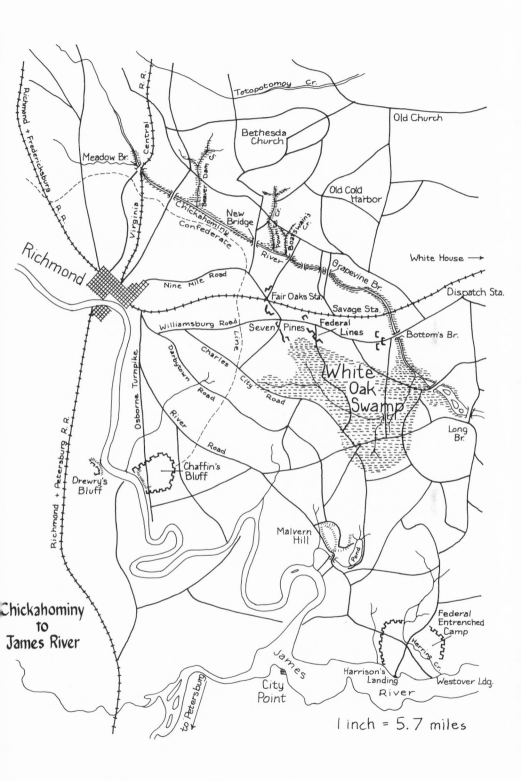

By 11 May, Norfolk was in Federal hands and the *Virginia* was gone. No Confederate forces remained below City Point except small garrisons manning the forts on the right bank below Jamestown Island, and the Federal Navy completely commanded Hampton Roads. Although he continued tying up powerful vessels armed with 100- and 200-pounder rifles which could have driven the Confederates out of these works in an hour, it is difficult to imagine from what quarter Goldsborough now feared an attack. Yet as late as the 14th he upbraided Rodgers for disobeying orders and refused to silence the shore batteries himself, complaining that Rodgers' action had deranged his fleet dispositions in the Roads.[9]

Rodgers attempted to comply with the order but found that his smoothbore guns expended too much ammunition trying to silence the enemy's rifles and he could not put men ashore without running aground. In spite of his caution, the *Galena* stuck fast several times. The Confederates had prudently changed all the channel markers. Sand clogged her valve-pipes and condenser, making it impossible to run the engines while aground, and she had to wait for high water to float free. Since it was soon apparent that he would never get above City Point that way, Rodgers silenced one battery below Jamestown Island and ran past the enemy works at Harden's Bluff and Rock Wharf Landing.[10]

Arriving at Jamestown Island on the 9th, he learned that the river for seven miles below Richmond was too shallow for the *Galena*'s draft, so the *Monitor* would be required for shelling the city into submission. He was thus further delayed waiting for the *Monitor* and her consort, the small iron revenue steamer "E.A. Stevens" (USS *Naugatuck*), to join the squadron. Goldsborough thought it essential to hold these vessels in Hampton Roads until the *Virginia* went down.[11] It apparently never occurred to him that a ship can not survive without a base and must either surrender or be scuttled.

Six precious days had thus elapsed when the Union flotilla, consisting of the *Monitor, Galena, Naugatuck, Port Royal*, and *Aroostook*, reached City Point, but Rodgers' trouble had only begun. The James above this point is full of shoals and extremely tortuous. The *Galena*'s experience running aground warned Rodgers that the river must be sounded before he progressed further. While these were being taken, the *Virginia's* ex-crew were just starting work on the Drewry's Bluff fort 33 miles above. It was a close race despite the delays, but the Confederates won.

Goldsborough's judgment was correct in one particular. The *Galena* was not shotproof. Because ironclads were still experimental, however, Rodgers was determined to give her a thorough test in action. Leading the Union squadron toward the fort on the morning of the 15th, the *Galena* anchored almost directly beneath the bluff and opened fire around 7:45 at a range of 600 yards, the wooden vessels and the *Naugatuck* remaining 1300 yards below. Lieutenant William Jeffers took

Broadside view of USS *Galena* after engaging the Confederate batteries at Drewry's Bluff, Virginia on 15 May 1862
(*Library of Congress*)

the *Monitor* above when it became apparent that the Confederates were concentrating on the *Galena*, but finding that he could not elevate her guns sufficiently to bear on the battery, soon dropped back downstream. The obstructions and the extreme narrowness of the river made it impossible to spoil the enemy's aim by keeping the ships in motion as Stringham and Du Pont had done during earlier artillery duels with forts.

After three hours' fighting, the *Galena* was riddled. Thirteen shot and shell penetrated her port armor, lodging in the wood backing. One 10-inch solid projectile passed almost entirely through the ship burrowing into the starboard bulkhead. An 8-inch shell perforated the gun deck leaving a large hole, killing and wounding gun crews with fragments of twisted iron. Another of the same caliber exploded in the steerage. The smokestack was shot full of holes, the knees and planks on the port side broken, and the armor started. Still, Rodgers would not call off the fight. His guns were serviceable and he intended to fire until he had expended his last round.[12] A lucky shot changed his mind.

Captain Tucker in the *Patrick Henry*, anchored in the line of obstructions, had been watching for an opportunity. With his ship broadside to the fort and preoccupied with the batteries on the hill, Rodgers failed to notice the two Confederate gunboats. At about 11 o'clock an 8-inch shot from the *Patrick Henry* passed through the *Galena*'s bow gun port, setting the ironclad on fire. Smoke pouring from the ports announced the end of the contest and Rodgers, with the rest of the Federal squadron, limped downstream to City Point.[13]

Besides the severe damage to the hull, the *Galena* lost thirteen men, and eleven were badly wounded. The *Monitor* was uninjured but due to the comparatively long range at which she fired, her non-rifled guns made little impression on the fort. The wooden gunboat *Port Royal*, anchored about a mile below the bluff, became an occasional target for the Confederate gunners. Lieutenant George U. Morris, her commander, was amazed at the accuracy of their fire. His ship was twice penetrated below the water line by 8-inch shells forcing him to haul off for repairs. The *Port Royal* was an especially favored mark for Wood's sharpshooters. Although all of the Union vessels were considerably annoyed in this manner both approaching and retiring from the fort, the bullets actually passed through the gunboat's side, one of them striking Morris in the leg.[14]

An undoubted tribute to Confederate energy and ingenuity, the engagement was a discouraging setback for the U.S. Navy. It not only spoiled Goldsborough's plans for attacking Wilmington and postponed Fox's projected expedition against Charleston; it also meant that Army cooperation was necessary to take Richmond or any other well-defended port. Despite Navy Department insistence that the "experiment" was invalid because of the *Galena*'s inferior armor protection, the lesson greatly impressed the professional officers involved. Rodgers advised landing the Army of the Potomac ten miles below Richmond on both banks of the James or, even better, a combined attack on Petersburg. Jeffers thought it "impossible to reduce such works, except with the aid of a land force." Goldsborough told Fox that the Navy could not remove the obstructions without first taking the fort and that the Confederates had built a similar work below it on the left bank of the James at Chaffin's Bluff. "Without the Army," he concluded, "the Navy can make no headway to-wards Richmond."[15] The repercussions from Drewry's Bluff were felt as far away as Charleston. Patrolling outside the bar, Flag Officer Du Pont pondered the problem of cracking harbor defenses which suddenly appeared more forbidding and Rodgers, less than a year later, would experience the strange sensation of having been through it all before.

The local effect of the squadron's defeat was belated, but increased, interservice cooperation. McClellan was worried when he had not heard from Rodgers by the 14th. Regardless of the railway, the York River line looked less promising every day. The Chickahominy bottomlands were a sea of mud, slowing the army's advance to a crawl. The last twenty miles—from White House to Richmond—looked even worse than the first seventy-five and McClellan was troubled by the thought that he might have to repeat the siege of Yorktown on an even larger scale.[16] The news of Rodgers' repulse reached Army headquarters on the 17th. While trying to remain optimistic, McClellan reminded Stanton that he no longer controlled any troops except his own and that the government had not informed him officially of the objects to be attained by other military and naval forces operating in eastern Virginia. The Navy's coup de main against Richmond had failed. If the administration wanted the place taken, the Army and the fleet should operate on the same line and his army would need reinforcements, because of the incidence of sickness and fatigue in a warm, wet climate.[17]

McClellan could hardly have anticipated the effect Rodgers' repulse and his own request for more troops would produce on the official mind, nor the ingenious scheme the government was even then devising to aid him while protecting Washington. If Lincoln had either agreed unconditionally to send McDowell's corps or some equivalent force, or had refused reinforcements altogether, McClellan could have transferred his base to the James on the 18th when he learned that the river was open below Drewry's Bluff. Although Goldsborough suggested another bombardment, Rodgers and Jeffers would have none of it; so Goldsborough bowed to the necessity of sharing the glory with the troops. On the 19th he conferred with McClellan at his camp about a combined attack on Fort Darling. If this preliminary venture succeeded, the whole Army of the Potomac could reach the James in two or three days by crossing the Chickahominy at Bottom's Bridge. While the movement was in progress, McDowell could distract Johnston from the direction of Fredericksburg.[18]

It was a sound plan. But even as he explained it to Goldsborough, McClellan must have suspected that something would go wrong. On the 18th, Lincoln had promised that I Corps would cooperate against Richmond or join McClellan's force in the field, but only on two conditions. McDowell could not come by water; he had to march down the railroad from Fredericksburg to avoid uncovering Washington. Further, McClellan was ordered to extend his right flank in the direction of the railroad to establish communications with McDowell's column. Adding insult to injury, Lincoln specified that McDowell would retain his independent command while "cooperating" with the Army of the Potomac in the field. This last condition understandably perplexed both generals. McClellan thought the telegraph operator must have mistransmitted the president's words. He patiently explained that, under military law, as the senior officer, he would automatically command McDowell's force as soon as it joined the main army in active operations, and asked for a clarification. Did Lincoln really intend using his authority as commander-in-chief, which Mc-Clellan granted was his constitutional right, to place both McDowell and himself in such an awkward and unworkable position? This misunderstanding, if such it was, continued until 21 May when the president explicitly acknowledged that McClellan must indeed have sole field command, insisting only that I Corps join him by marching down the railroad.[19]

There seemed no further impediment to a combined attack on Richmond. As soon as the Army of the Potomac had crossed the Chickahominy and McDowell arrived, McClellan intended to extend his line across White Oak Swamp detailing a division on the extreme left to help Goldsborough take Fort Darling. Rodgers' flotilla would then protect the Army's flank as it marched into Richmond along the left bank of the James. The main body would continuously press Johnston in front, pinning him to the city's northeastern perimeter, while the combined force entered by the "side door." Meanwhile, Burnside would move on Goldsborough and Raleigh, cutting the enemy's main rail lines and blocking his escape south. Johnston would be forced west of Richmond and pushed back into the mountains where his army could be bottled up and starved into submission. If he chose to fight, he would be smashed by superior artillery emplaced behind strong entrenchments.[20]

Goldsborough wished to move at once, but the Army of the Potomac had yet to cross the Chickahominy, and McClellan could not concentrate on the south bank until his right flank was secure. Brigadier General Joseph R. Anderson's Confederate division was still around Fredericksburg and the rail connection with the Shenandoah Valley via Hanover Junction remained in Southern hands. Major General "Stonewall" Jackson's force, thought to be 30,000 strong, was in the valley and might appear on the Union flank within a day. Lincoln promised that McDowell's corps would begin its move south on the 26th and asked that McClellan assist him by cutting the Virginia Central and the Fredericksburg and Richmond Railroads in Anderson's rear. Continued bad weather prevented Fitz John Porter's V Corps from completing this task until the 28th, however, by which time Anderson had safely pulled back to Ashland Station.[21]

But if the Army of the Potomac moved slowly, it was inexorably inching toward Richmond. By the 20th its front had reached the north bank of the Chickahominy. The Confederates seemed helpless to stop the Federal advance. Johnston thought that an assault was the only hope of saving the capital, since the Chickahominy was his last good defense line; but he could not, of course, attack until at least part of McClellan's force was across the river.[22] Agreeing with McClellan that an assault on entrenched lines should only be attempted when all else failed, Lee had already decided to employ an "indirect approach" of his own. Jackson, though outnumbered, was ordered to make a demonstration against Banks's Corps in the Valley with the hope of alarming the Washington authorities enough to delay McDowell's advance until Anderson could withdraw from Fredericksburg.[23] Neither Lee nor Jackson foresaw the sensational results of this diversion, not the least of which was the final ruin of McClellan's strategic plans and the disappearance of the Federal army and fleet from eastern Virginia.

On 23 May, as the opening move of the famous "Valley Campaign," Jackson fell upon General Banks at Front Royal, destroying his outposts and driving him back on Winchester.[24] Lincoln at once informed McClellan that McDowell's scheduled movement to join the Army of the Potomac was "suspended" until Jackson could be disposed of. Knowing that Jackson, with only 15,000 men, was pursuing Banks's broken brigades toward the Potomac, it seemed a simple matter to throw the two corps of Frémont, then operating in western Virginia, and McDowell at Fredericksburg in his rear, trapping him in the Valley. Coordinating the movements of three independent forces appeared easy enough on the maps. Smashing Jackson would protect Harpers Ferry, save the Baltimore and Ohio Railroad, and quiet panicky Congressmen and citizens in Washington and Baltimore who feared the enemy's appearance among them at any moment. McClellan warned Lincoln that he was playing Jackson's game; that the move was a ploy to keep McDowell away from Richmond.[25] But the effort was wasted. The administration was hot on the trail of victory and the Army of the Potomac must wait until McDowell had captured Jackson.

McClellan now had three alternatives. He could forego the reinforcements and, ignoring Lincoln's injunction to cooperate with McDowell, transfer the army's base to the James. He could change his line of communications to the Fredericksburg and Richmond Railroad, approaching the city from the north. Or he could remain where he was until the crisis resulting from Jackson's activity had subsided.

The first alternative would leave insufficient force to hold Johnston's army east of Richmond, allowing it to concentrate in front of his intended movement up the James. McClellan had dismissed the second alternative before beginning the Peninsular campaign and the same considerations applied. This line was too exposed on the flanks and vulnerable to enemy raids. Moreover, the operations in the York River had strengthened his conviction that gunboats were valuable auxiliaries and that the enemy was afraid of them.[26] The northern approach would rule out naval support. The third alternative afforded the greatest flexibility. It would keep the Army of the Potomac in position to receive the promised reinforcements, while permitting a change of base at any time. Meanwhile, McClellan would secure his position behind strong entrenchments and press the enemy just enough to invite attack. If the Confederates waited too long to assume the offensive, his rifled guns would eventually come within shell range of the city.[27]

With these considerations in mind, and leaving his options open, McClellan continued to advance along the York River Railroad. There were admitted disadvantages to this approach. The most serious was the necessity for holding both banks of the Chickahominy in order to secure rail communications with White House, at least until the enemy could no longer threaten the army's right.

Critics have consistently exaggerated the degree of risk in McClellan's dispositions, however.[28] There was little actual danger of a serious defeat. While its bridges over the Chickahominy remained passable, the Federal army was not, of course, "divided" since all five corps could quickly concentrate on either side. Even without the bridges, the two corps south of the river and the railroad were capable, by themselves, of resisting the entire Confederate army. Keyes's IV Corps in its advanced position at Seven Pines, covering the railway and commanding the debouches from the Federal bridges below New Bridge with artillery, was deployed in three successive lines behind strong field works. Its left was anchored on the White Oak Swamp. In order to turn the right of this position, the enemy was required to penetrate into the angle between the railroad and the river over ground swept by Federal guns. A few miles in the rear, Heintzelman's III Corps held another series of two entrenched lines covering the approaches to Bottom's Bridge. Indeed, McClellan's position south of the Chickahominy was so strong that Johnston, never an advocate of futile assaults, declined attacking it—until political pressure and Davis' personal intervention left him no choice.[29]

The battle of Seven Pines–Fair Oaks vindicated Johnston's judgment. Although the Confederate assault was badly coordinated and begun too late in the day for decisive results, the Federals made an equal share of mistakes in handling the defense. Casey's division holding the first Union line, composed largely of raw troops led by inexperienced officers, broke in disorder leaving its arms on the field and surrendering before its supports arrived. Not understanding how to conduct a defense in depth, Keyes massed most of his corps—including the reserves—in the second line, failed to send them forward soon enough and, when compelled to fall back, held this line too long before retiring to his third position.[30] Heintzelman mistook the enemy offensive for a skirmish and was late coming to Keyes's assistance.[31] Nevertheless, while carrying only the first and part of the second line, the Confederates lost considerably more men than the Federals. The leading division of G.W. Smith's corps came on to the ground north of the railroad to attack Fair Oaks Station and was cut to pieces by Union shells, one of which struck General Johnston in the breast, inflicting a near-fatal wound.

Significantly, when Lee assumed command on 1 June, he did not renew the attack although the flooded Chickahominy still "divided" McClellan's army and only Sumner's II Corps had crossed the river to support Keyes and Heintzelman.[32] Instead, Lee pulled his army back toward Richmond, instructing the engineers to build entrenchments for resisting a Federal assault. In fact, it was the obvious impossibility of effecting anything against this "portion" of the line which induced Lee to attack Union communications north of the river.[33]

The effect of the battle on McClellan was simply to increase the strength of his defenses on both banks of the Chickahominy. He still hoped for the promised reinforcements and was therefore reluctant to change base prematurely. His sappers worked day and night building more bridges, field works, and gun emplacements. The object of all this activity was to permit *one* Federal corps to hold the entire line on either side of the river, thus setting four corps free to oppose another attack in force expected at any time.[34]

The result was not lost on his opponent. On 5 June, Lee summed up his predicament to President Davis, acknowledging that without a bold, almost desperate stroke, there was little hope of retaining Richmond:

> McClellan will make this a battle of posts. He will take position from position, under cover of his heavy guns and we cannot get at him without storming his works . . . . It will require 100,000 men to resist the regular siege of Richmond, which perhaps would only prolong not save it.[35]

Five days later he ordered Jackson reinforced; first, to smash Frémont in the Valley, then to "sweep down north of the Chickahominy, cut up McClellan's communications and rear, while I attack in front."[36]

While the final phase of the Peninsular campaign, the famous Seven Days Battles, has been generally recognized as a tactical defeat for the Confederate army, it is usually considered a strategic victory for the South. Subsequent events made it appear so. We have seen that, after the establishment of his base at White House and the Navy's repulse in the James River, McClellan kept his army along the upper Chickahominy for two reasons. First, only if this disposition was adopted would the government restore McDowell's corps, 40,000 strong, to his command. Second, it was the only means of preventing the Confederates from concentrating and constructing more formidable defenses on the south side of Richmond before the Federals were ready to assume the offensive on that front.

Both considerations presumed that the promised reinforcements, or at least a cooperating force acting simultaneously on a different line against the same objective, would be provided. McClellan could not know in late May and early June that most of McDowell's corps would never be sent. When he began to suspect that the government's support for his operations was lukewarm and their promises unreliable, he confronted an imposing problem.[37] What would have been an easy and unopposed movement in mid-May had become, a month later, one of the most difficult military operations—a change of base in the face of the enemy.

The Federal army could not, of course, just abandon its entrenchments and march away with all its artillery and baggage to the James. It must move across the front of an alert and aggressive enemy whose fighting strength nearly equalled its own. McClellan could expect neither Johnston nor Lee to watch quietly while the Army of the Potomac sought the protection and aid of gunboats to begin a new and more dangerous campaign. To suppose, as many critics imply, that this might have been accomplished without a bloody battle is unrealistic. McClellan was required to engage Lee north of the Chickahominy to prevent the whole Confederate army falling on his flank as he marched to the James. And what better means were there for drawing most of Lee's army above the river than by deploying one corps alone in an apparently exposed position on that flank, with the army's communications a short distance in its rear? Not that McClellan especially wanted Lee to attack Porter; but since it could not be prevented, he intended to turn it to maximum advantage.[38]

From the Southern standpoint, Major General J.E.B. Stuart's celebrated cavalry "raid" around the Union army on 13–14 June was ill-advised. Granted, McClellan's dispositions were so effectively screened that Lee needed a reconnaissance to determine the size of the Federal force north of the river and the location of its wagon route from the White House depot. But Stuart might have obtained the information less conspicuously and without fully revealing the intended point of attack. McClellan at once prepared to change base, shifting all except V Corps south of the Chickahominy. Porter's troops, which included the regulars aided by a large proportion of the army's best artillery, held a very strong advanced position behind Beaver Dam Creek, a line so well fortified by nature and industry that Johnston had refused to even contemplate an attack upon it in May. Fifth Corps was expected to blunt the edge of the Confederate onslaught and cover the army's withdrawal.[39]

The naval forces in the James River were notified of the impending move and the Army quartermasters began shipping the large accumulation of stores in the Pamunkey depots to Haxall's landing above City Point. All of the roads and bridges between the Chickahominy and the James through and east of White Oak Swamp had been previously reconnoitered and mapped, and communications were maintained with Rodgers' flotilla. Union gunboats were prepared to ascend the Chickahominy as high as Jones's bridge to support the army should it prove necessary to march down the Peninsula before turning toward the James.[40] As characteristic of McClellan's operations, every detail was prepared in advance and every contingency provided for.

Lee's attack of 25–27 June on Porter's corps was well planned and capably executed, his perfectionist critics notwithstanding, but it was a desperate expedient affording little opportunity for a decisive victory. Like most battles of last resort, it accomplished about as much as Lee could reasonably have expected, although of course he had hoped for more. At great cost, he succeeded in hurrying the Army of the Potomac into a position it intended assuming in any case, a position more potentially dangerous to the Confederacy than its previous line. That the Federal government would fail to exploit this favorable position, that it would, on the contrary, refuse McClellan the means for making up his losses and resuming the offensive, was a stroke of luck for the Confederates.[41]

Still, the bloody and disappointing offensive had driven the Federals from the suburbs of Richmond and, for this reason, both the Army of Northern Virginia and the people of Richmond considered it a great victory. But for how long? Although McClellan's army was diminished by battle casualties and sickness, it had got away with all of its ordnance and baggage intact, and had successfully transferred its huge stores depot to the new base.[42] The Confederate army under Lee had not,

Federal gunboats in action at Malvern Hill. When the Army of
the Potomac reached the James River on 1-2 July 1862, Rodgers's
flotilla covered its flanks and commanded the approaches from
Richmond. Its shells caused many casualties to Confederate forces
attempting to assault this position. (*Library of Congress*)

in fact, gained the initiative. On the 2nd of July, when the
Army of the Potomac withdrew to its new base at Harrison's
Landing after the battle of Malvern Hill, the initiative remained with McClellan and the cooperating U.S. fleet. With
a detachment thrown onto the right bank of the James, a combined attack on Chaffin's and Drewry's Bluffs, and a movement
in force by the Union squadron up the river, the brilliant
results which McClellan had envisaged in March might have
been attained, after all, in August.

The Union Navy was anxious enough to cooperate. Whizzing shells, crunching armor, and decks running blood had
made combined operations enthusiasts of Rodgers and his officers, despite Fox's comfortable assertion that unaided ships
could still destroy forts. Even Goldsborough, while he continued
balking at orders from Army quartermasters and complained
that McClellan did not respect the Navy's independent status,
strongly argued the case for a combined move on Richmond.[43]

The James River flotilla had gradually assumed fleet proportions. Besides the two ironclads, the *Monitor* and *Galena*,
it comprised fifteen gunboats and other vessels. Goldsborough's
duties as blockade squadron commander prevented his full

attention to affairs in the river. Besides, Welles was disgusted with his previous inaction and wanted a more aggressive senior officer for the combined operations. Consequently, Commodore Charles Wilkes, whose action in precipitating the *Trent* affair had made him something of a national hero, was appointed, and the James River Squadron was increased to twenty-three vessels. He was ordered to keep open the Army's communications below Harrison's Landing, protect all transports and supply ships, and cooperate fully with McClellan in offensive movements. To ensure that Goldsborough's dilatory habits did not again interfere with combined plans, Wilkes was instructed to report direct to the Navy Department.[44]

Wilkes found his command unprepared for its duties. Ships were undermanned, boilers and machinery on many of the vessels had broken down, and there were insufficient rations. Everything, he told Welles, was disorganized. If the department intended to breathe new spirit into the James River operations, it had clearly chosen the right man. Welles found himself immediately bombarded with requests for reinforcements, equipment, and stores. On 9 July, Wilkes ordered "scout canoes" from the constructor at the New York Navy yard. These craft, covered with light iron sheets to protect the men from sharpshooters, would allow him to pass through the barrier and explore the river above Drewry's Bluff. The squadron also required more shallow-draft gunboats to guard the flank "as the army moves toward Richmond."[45]

Despite the setbacks, it looked as though McClellan's strategy was about to terminate in a decisive offensive. By mid-July, the Army of the Potomac in its camp at Harrison's Landing would be rested, refitted, and reinforced. The administration did not, as was afterwards claimed, consider McClellan's movement to a new line of operations a strategic defeat. On the contrary, both Lincoln and Stanton now believed the fall of Richmond almost certain. Informed that the army's advance guard (IV Corps) had reached the James on 30 June, Lincoln remarked that, so far, McClellan had "effected everything in such exact accordance with his plan, contingently announced to us before the battle began, that we feel justified to hope that he has not failed since."[46] The same day, Stanton wrote Wool:

McClellan has moved his whole force across the Chickahominy and rests on James River, being supported by our
gun boats. The position is favorable, and looks more like
taking Richmond than any time before.[47]

Stanton's optimism went beyond McClellan's. With 100,000
men recruited by the state governors in addition to the 50,000
already promised, the Army of the Potomac would not only
take Richmond, but end the war. McClellan assured the administration that 50,000 men sent at once "will enable me to
assume the offensive."[48] Burnside's corps had been ordered
into the James and the government could send another 10,000
from the Department of Virginia. McCall's division of Mc-
Dowell's corps had joined the army before the Seven Days
battles. This left a balance of 25,000 to be obtained elsewhere.
Lincoln asked Halleck to send this number of infantry from
Corinth, and Stanton assured McClellan on 1 July that they
would join the Army of the Potomac in two weeks.[49]

There seemed little the Confederates could do to break up
the combination against them, or to drive the combined enemy
force from its threatening position. Along the Chickahominy,
Davis and Lee thought that a vigorous, well-planned assault
might turn the tide. But an offensive against the entrenched
Federal camp at Harrison's Landing would be suicide. The
position, carefully selected by McClellan and Rodgers, was a
flat plain along the river bank with flanking creeks on both
sides. Gunboats stationed off the mouths of the creeks swept
its approaches. On the land front facing the enemy, the Army's
powerful reserve artillery was massed along a rise commanding broken ground from which all vegetation had been removed.[50]

In short, the position was even stronger than the one at
Malvern Hill against which Lee had broken so many brigades
in hopeless assaults. McClellan's combination of the strategic
offense and the tactical defense—a technique the Germans
would employ with such astonishing success less than ten
years later—had forced the Confederate army to sustain losses
it could not afford.[51] A few more battles like Malvern Hill
would make an attack on Richmond unnecessary. Having

thoroughly examined the position at Harrison's Landing, Lee wrote Davis:

> The great obstacle to operations here is the presence of the enemy's gunboats which protect our approaches to him & should we even force him from his positions on his land front, would prevent us from reaping any of the fruits of victory & expose our men to great destruction.

The Confederate army must withdraw into Richmond, refit, and prepare to resist McClellan's new offensive.[52] If the Federal army and fleet were allowed to remain on the upper James continuously building up manpower and materiel, however, it was only a question of time before Richmond must fall. Faced with this dilemma, Lee could only delay a decision with the hope that the accidents of war would alter the strategic situation in his favor. He did not have to wait long.

Lincoln's brief career as Army "chief of staff" had produced one of the sorriest fiascos of the war. Not only had his great strategic combination to trap the swift-footed Jackson in the Shenandoah Valley resulted in the successive defeat of Banks's corps, Frémont's corps, and Shields' division of McDowell's corps, but lack of attention to supply and transport had reduced these units to a ragged and demoralized condition.[53] The ridiculous spectacle of three major generals quarrelling among themselves while the enemy left their front to fall on McClellan along the Chickahominy convinced the president that the evils both of armchair strategy and a divided command could only be remedied by a timely reorganization. Since he was still determined to hold a covering force before Washington to guard against more of Jackson's "raids," Lincoln decided to unite the three corps of McDowell, Banks, and Frémont under a single army command. To prevent further jealousy, Major General John Pope, a favorite of the Joint Committee because of his reputation as a "fighter," was brought from the West to take charge of the new Army of Virginia.[54]

The promised reinforcements for the Army of the Potomac were not affected under the new arrangement, and McClellan had reason to expect that Pope's consolidated force might cooperate very effectively with his projected attack on Richmond. Indeed, Pope wrote McClellan on 4 July urging a joint offensive. McClellan's enthusiasm immediately cooled, however, when he learned that Pope's army was not at liberty to move as its commander chose and might be called away at any moment to defend Washington. He had just emerged from an exhausting and disappointing campaign in which all of his plans were disrupted because the means to implement them were removed from his control. There was no guarantee that another promising strategic combination would not share the same fate. The recent alarmist response to Jackson's movements made such a prospect almost certain. No, McClellan would stay clear of Pope and rely on his own means and that of the fleet.[55]

But this was not so easily done. Pope at first saw nothing incompatible about his duty to cover Washington and his determination to take the offensive. He intended to march boldly to the north bank of the James and attack Richmond from the west. The administration quickly disabused him of this notion. Although his ardor to fight instead of maneuver was considered admirable, he was required to fight while defending Washington, not while attacking Richmond. Deprived of the strategic initiative, Pope became worried that the Confederates would plan his destruction and fall upon him before McClellan was ready to move on Richmond. He soon concluded that his only safety lay in one of two expedients. Either the Army of the Potomac must be withdrawn from the James River and placed in position to support the Army of Virginia directly or McClellan must be required to attack, prepared or not, the moment Pope felt himself in danger.[56]

Lincoln would not be responsible for another amateurish blunder. Suppose Pope got nervous and thought the main Confederate force was about to strike him when it was just another *ruse de guerre*? A peremptory order forcing McClellan out of his works prematurely might expose the Army of the Potomac to destruction if the Confederate army remained in strength on the James. On the other hand, ordering McClellan's army back to Washington before any danger to Pope justified such a move would cancel the attack on Richmond. Only a military man was qualified to decide if the offensive should be given up.[57]

Besides McClellan, General Halleck was the only Federal officer capable of exercising the chief command. In early July, Lincoln sent his friend, Governor William Sprague of Rhode Island, to persuade Halleck to come to Washington. The general refused, understandably preferring a field command that had won him distinction to a staff job in which he would likely run afoul of the politicians and be blamed for their mistakes. But the president was desperate and, after consulting General Scott at West Point, ordered Halleck to accept the post for the good of the country.[58]

Lincoln visited McClellan at Harrison's Landing on the 8th. While impressed by the Army, the fleet arrangements, and the general confidence in the projected offensive, he was unwilling to approve a forward movement unless Halleck authorized it. Two developments had already begun to darken the prospects for successful operations on the James River line. The first was a division of opinion among McClellan's senior officers concerning the number of reinforcements required. Heintzelman thought the army sufficiently strong without reinforcement; Keyes advised a minimum of one hundred thousand, while Barnard did not consider a successful offensive possible unless three hundred thousand more men were provided. Such diverse opinion further confused the government and promoted dissension within the army command.[59]

The second adverse factor was the growing threat to the army's communications. As early as 30 June, Rodgers had warned that the Confederates were reestablishing their batteries opposite Jamestown Island and that sharpshooters and guerrilla bands infested both banks, harrassing the supply vessels. During the month following, this situation grew steadily worse and Wilkes was required to detach more and more gunboats for escort duty. Welles tried to solve the problem by bringing Captain David D. Porter's mortar flotilla, recently employed in unsuccessful operations against Vicksburg, into the James to reduce the shore batteries. But the mortars did not reach Hampton Roads until 1 August at which time Wilkes discovered them useless for immediate work. Their beds were worn out and half of the crews were down with fever.[60]

Other difficulties plagued the James River Squadron. Because the sailors Wilkes had requested from the department in early July were not sent, he was forced to fill up his crews with McClellan's soldiers, none of whom had any training in seamanship and, in fact, caused more trouble than they were worth. The first shipment of "scout canoes" brought forth a series of angry dispatches from Wilkes to the Navy Department and the constructor at the New York yard. Instead of the small light canoes ordered, Wilkes received large rowboats heavily plated with boiler iron. The first of these ponderous craft launched into the Roads turned over and sank like a stone, at which point Wilkes would have nothing more to do with them.[61]

McClellan was not especially worried about his communications. During July he built up a huge stores depot at Westover Landing in case the Army was required to operate with its communications cut. Of greater concern was the number of reinforcements he could expect from the government. Without knowing the size of the force at his disposal, he could not devise a realistic operations plan.[62] It was upon this rock that the whole campaign foundered.

Lincoln's Army reorganization, however necessary, had suspended Federal movements for three weeks. Still more time was required for Halleck to confer with Pope and McClellan, and make the decision regarding the future line of advance. One thing was certain. Whatever move was decided upon in Virginia, no Union troops would be brought from the West. The capture of Richmond was secondary, in Lincoln's mind, to the invasion of east Tennessee. Strategic priorities were determined by the president, who naturally decided them for political rather than military reasons. The Union men constituting the majority in east Tennessee still called upon the Federal government to save them from the secessionists and Lincoln insisted that the western army, after the fall of Corinth, must march on Chattanooga.[63]

The president's June 30th request for reinforcements from the West had brought an abrupt reply from Halleck that, if these were sent, the Chattanooga expedition must be abandoned. Halleck further explained that his army was already too small to guard the long rail line into west Tennessee, and the

Mississippi valley. A detachment of 25,000 men for McClellan would lose Arkansas and west Tennessee to the Union. Such loss of territory, he concluded, would change the pro-Union sentiment in Tennessee and Kentucky and these states would go over to the Confederacy. Faced with this alarming prospect, the president would not order the reinforcements, although still urging Halleck to send them. Instead, General Hunter's command of 10,000 was withdrawn from the neighborhood of Charleston.[64]

Except for the new recruits beginning to fill the Washington camps who were not yet fit for the field, no other troops were available for McClellan's operations. Thus the government's overly optimistic promise of fifty thousand reinforcements was, by the second week in July, reduced to twenty thousand. If McClellan agreed to resume the offensive with this number of additional men, he would be allowed to do so. If not, the Army of the Potomac would be withdrawn from the James River and united with Pope's force before Washington.[65]

Although General Halleck was, as previously noted, something of a fanatic on the subjects of military concentration and unified command and did not appreciate the value of combined operations, he was reluctant to assume responsibility for aborting a promising campaign. Acceding to the chief command in the midst of an impending crisis and understanding nothing as yet of the situation in Virginia, he was unwilling to overrule the field commanders. He would only indicate the means available and leave the decision to McClellan; or at least he *supposed* McClellan would decide the question. Arriving at Harrison's Landing on 25 July, Halleck discovered that McClellan now planned a move across the James to cut enemy communications south of Richmond. Without a greatly superior force, McClellan thought a direct attack on the city would fail since the Confederates had been given ample time for perfecting its defenses. Reconnaissance and intelligence revealed only a token force and no fixed defenses around Petersburg, and the Navy could assist the projected movement by ascending the Appomattox River. Halleck indicated that this plan was unacceptable to the government because it would put the Army of the Potomac out of position to support Pope and would require too much time, allowing the Confederates to defeat the Army of Virginia or attack Washington before turning to oppose McClellan.[66]

There were just two acceptable alternatives. McClellan either had to attack Richmond along the James River line with the 20,000 available reinforcements, or join Pope's army to cover Washington. To McClellan's suggestion that troops be brought from the West, Halleck replied that, having just come from there, he knew that this was impossible without abandoning the Chattanooga project, which Lincoln was unwilling to cancel.[67]

McClellan was at first inclined to give up the offensive and return to Washington, especially since Halleck had promised him command of the combined armies.[68] He suspected, however, that the administration would interpret the army's withdrawal as an admission of defeat and remove him from command altogether, despite Halleck's intentions. There was already talk that Burnside, recently called to Washington for a Cabinet conference, had been offered command of the Army of the Potomac.[69] On Halleck's advice, McClellan consulted his corps commanders individually. All except Keyes favored proceeding with the offensive on the government's terms.[70]

Halleck returned to Washington on the 26th supposing the matter settled only to find a telegram from McClellan, again requesting reinforcements from the West and stating that he was not confident of victory unless a larger force was provided. Since this was clearly impossible and, anyway, Halleck was worried about the enemy's aggressive behavior on the lower James, he ordered the Army of the Potomac back to Washington.[71]

The loudest protest came from the Navy. Wilkes, who had not previously suggested any plan, was now certain that the combined force could take Richmond and urged Welles to dissuade Lincoln from withdrawing the Army. There was no question that within a very short time the fleet, supported by the troops, could take Drewry's and Chaffin's Bluffs, remove the obstructions, and enter the city. Ignoring the squadron's problems and its lack of preparation, Wilkes also neglected to mention the fact that the Confederate ironclad *Richmond* was nearly ready to descend the river; but Welles had not forgotten

it. Another "Hampton Roads" would be too much for the secretary and the country. Although the squadron was permitted
to remain in the James to cover the Army's withdrawal, Wilkes
was instructed to act strictly on the defensive and give up all
thought of going to Richmond with or without troops.[72] On
28 August, after the whole army had safely marched down
the Peninsula to embark at Fort Monroe and Yorktown, the
last naval vessel dropped down river to Newport News. Thus
the great combined movement, begun with such promise of a
rapid and decisive victory, came to an inglorious end.

Despite the lack of dramatic results, no Civil War campaign
better demonstrates the superior advantages of water communications than the Peninsular operations. Having used the
water highways of the York and the James to great logistic
and strategic advantage for holding their position at Yorktown
and saving their materiel from Norfolk, the Southerners
watched helplessly while the Federals employed these same
routes to shift their base from the Pamunkey to the James.
There was an important difference, however. Possessing an
inferior navy, the Confederacy was compelled to use this element defensively while the Union could employ it as an offensive force.

On the operational level, Franklin's assault division presaged
a revolution in amphibious tactics. But because it was the
product of Army engineers who ignored the Navy except in
matters of general fire support, and because all of the Army
of the Potomac's "specialists" were either disgraced in one way
or another in later conventional operations (or in the case of
McClellan's engineers, occupied for the next three years bridging streams, repairing railways, and corduroying roads), this
important development was not perceived at the time and was
eventually lost in the obscure annals of a painful campaign.[73]
Alexander's methods were, therefore, not taken up and refined
into any kind of combined operations doctrine. Following its
withdrawal from the Peninsula, the Army moved into the
fields and mountains of northern Virginia and Maryland while
the Navy, fascinated with the ironclad warship, did not return
to combined operations, except to a limited extent in the West,
for another year. By then, techniques for troop landings and
fire support had to be relearned by the slow and costly process

of trial and error. Nothing quite so sophisticated as Franklin's assault force was ever again achieved during the Civil War.

On the command level, McClellan demonstrated a knowledge of how to employ naval forces that is rarely encountered in an Army officer. A vessel represented more than an extremely mobile form of heavy artillery. It was also valuable for reconnaissance and transport, like the cavalry horse, enabling his troops to move with prior knowledge of the "terrain" further and faster than the enemy. Certainly he employed the fleet as a fourth arm, wherever possible, in combination with the traditional three. Had McClellan commanded Rodgers' flotilla as Johnston commanded the combined Confederate land and naval forces in eastern Virginia, or had Goldsborough pushed the flotilla up the James immediately after Yorktown fell, as McClellan had requested, the Navy would have taken Richmond just as Farragut took New Orleans. By the time Goldsborough was ready to cooperate with the Army, McClellan had lost his freedom of movement.

The Federal government's almost total failure to comprehend the most elementary principles of war, or to trust generals who did understand them, consistently ruined the soundest plans and disrupted the most careful arrangements. Washington's amateur strategists, suspicious of the professional military mind, blundered into the business of war with the usual overconfidence of ignorance. That they did not intentionally ruin McClellan's operations, as is frequently claimed, made no difference in the result.

Although the Cabinet's apprehension for Washington was understandable, the withdrawal of I Corps at the outset of the campaign deprived McClellan of his entire mobile striking force, while their action in demoting him from general-in-chief of the Army to a field command prevented him from coordinating the movements of other Federal armies with those of the main force or obtaining reinforcements from less active theaters of war. Consequently, the Confederates were able to withdraw most of their troops from the Carolinas and hold the West with a minimum force. The Navy's fear of the *Virginia*, inflamed by administrative overreaction, distracted Flag Officer Goldsborough at a time when his personal intervention in the York River might have proved decisive. Lincoln's incredible vacillation regarding McDowell's corps paralyzed the Army of the Potomac along the Chickahominy. Confused strategic priorities and continued indecision about approving McClellan's James River offensive allowed the South to recover its confidence, strengthen its defenses, and seize the strategic initiative. Outgeneraled and defeated in every battle, the Confederate army won the campaign by default.

McClellan had built his grand strategic design around interservice cooperation. Capture of important seaport towns and their rail connections was the vital first stage in his plan to paralyze the Confederacy. That the Navy had its own, and different, reasons for taking coastal cities was unimportant since the purposes of both services were furthered by attacking the same object. From the moment McClellan was deprived of the chief command, the Union had no strategic plan for defeating the Confederacy. Each department commander was permitted to define his own objectives and all competed for the necessary resources.

The Navy, whose aid McClellan had actively solicited and used, when available, to maximum advantage, was allowed to pursue an independent strategy while the Army commanders, lacking McClellan's foresight and flexibility of method, agreed with the Lincoln administration that wars were only won by slugging it out on the battlefield. The failure of the Peninsular campaign signalled both the demise of Federal grand strategy and the breakdown of combined operations planning.

7

REPERCUSSIONS IN THE WEST

ALL HISTORICAL ACCOUNTS of Federal operations to open the Mississippi River acknowledge the importance of Union naval supremacy. Unquestionably, the campaign could not have succeeded, or even been attempted, without some reliance on water communications. But to what extent the Union Army and Navy achieved that consistent degree of harmony essential for efficient combined operations is a question rarely examined.

Interservice conflict, although the most obvious, is not the only nontechnical difficulty that can plague a large scale waterborne offensive. All of the common intraservice problems also exist; indeed, they multiply as the number of independent command units increases. Where the operations plan has been carefully considered, understood, and agreed to by all of the responsible commanders in advance, this friction may be substantially reduced—submerged by the imperative to work out the grand design—or at least limited to matters of detail. Where there is no grand design, where the object is obscure, where as many plans flourish as there are heads to conceive them, efficient execution is impossible. Victory, if attained, must depend upon something other than skill; upon overwhelming numbers of men and materiel perhaps, or on enemy blunders, or the fortunes of war.

We have seen the destructive effect of McClellan's removal from the chief command on the Atlantic coast expeditions. Although with the aid of the Navy, Burnside in North Carolina and Sherman in South Carolina had seized vital bases from which to launch further offensives, the Federal government's fear for Washington and McClellan's Peninsular campaign absorbed the resources needed for exploitation. Repeated command changes in the Federal Department of the South further ensured that no very active campaign against Charleston would be undertaken during the remainder of 1862.

In the West, McClellan's demotion had more dramatic repercussions. Halleck's appointment to overall command brought about a shift in military objectives, resulting in a huge concentration of force on the line of the Tennessee River at the expense of operations already under way to open the Mississippi and "liberate" east Tennessee. Even though Butler's troops, detailed for combined attacks on New Orleans, Vicksburg, and Mobile, were not subject to Halleck's authority, this expedition was equally compromised by the command change.

The "triumvirate" of Lincoln, Stanton, and the Joint Committee, having fired the general-in-chief and finding itself charged with operational responsibility, discovered that it was easier to criticize McClellan than to fill his shoes. It was all very well to state that the purpose of Federal forces in the West was to open the Mississippi and occupy east Tennessee, but such a statement was far from a plan of operations. Indeed, no one in the Lincoln administration was equipped by education or experience to formulate a strategic plan. However much the government questioned, or historians may argue, the merits of McClellan's grand design, it was surely better than no plan at all.

Unable to issue military directives, the Federal government was forced to rely upon a method then common among the world's armies, although fast becoming obsolete. Informed of the general war aims of the administration, the field commanders were expected to make suitable military plans and assume entire responsibility for any movements within their departments. In theory, such a decentralized system might have worked in the 1860's; warfare was not as complex or as tightly geared to material requirements as it later became. In practice, however, this formula had no chance because it was not consistently applied. While Union field commanders were allowed, or rather required, to make their own plans and were certainly held accountable for the results, they were not free from interference in operational questions. On the contrary, the president, the secretary of War, the secretary of the Navy, and through them, the secretaries of State and Treasury, the quartermaster general, the Congress, the press, and the Northern business community all acted as advisors to the generals and admirals; and when, in their view, it was necessary, they asserted their authority over the armed forces. As a result, military plans had to be formulated initially, or altered in process of execution, to accommodate the divergent, vacillating, and sometimes incompatible notions of various government officials.

Given this state of affairs, it is not surprising that the demotion of General McClellan produced an immediate fragmentation of the Union war effort. The vacuum left by the collapse of his strategic plan was never filled. When evaluating combined operations after March 1862, it is improper to speak of a Federal war plan; we can only discuss Butler's intentions, Halleck's intentions, Grant's intentions, Banks's intentions, etc.

The naval forces were no more cohesive, only smaller and consequently subject to somewhat less confusion of purpose. Besides, the Navy Department had more continuity within the command hierarchy; squadron commanders were changed less often than army commanders and the secretary and his assistants served for the entire war. The government allowed Welles a much freer hand than his War Department counterpart, possibly because, while everyone gets about on land and may therefore feel comfortable playing general, the sea is a foreign element to most men. But if the government interfered less often with the Navy Department and the department less often with naval operations, such interference when it did occur produced profound consequences.

Strategically, the history of western combined operations may be divided into three phases: the capture of New Orleans and its aftermath, the 1862 campaign to open the Mississippi, and the capture of Vicksburg. Other peripheral operations contemplated or carried out in this theater were less important and are considered only in relation to some aspect of the main effort.[1]

Although McClellan's grand strategy died with its architect's demotion, its ghost lingered on. In the absence of an alternate plan, General Butler and Flag Officer Farragut received no new orders from Washington, nor did the government release them from their old instructions. The expedition was still expected to reduce the forts below New Orleans, occupy the city, seize the railroad junction at Jackson and attack Mobile.[2] However, McClellan's promise of substantial reinforcements, on which the plans for the follow-up to the capture of New Orleans had been based, was ignored. Butler and Farragut were expected to attain all of the above objects with the same means judged adequate for the initial attack. No account was taken of the need to garrison the forts or occupy New Orleans. Although there were enough ships for offensive purposes, the Navy Department likewise failed to anticipate or provide the requisite number or proper type of vessels needed to patrol the Mississippi River and its tributaries.

It is unnecessary to describe the Federal attack on New Orleans in April 1862. The details of the fleet action are found in every naval history and most general histories of the Civil War. But few naval chroniclers and even fewer Army historians have troubled to point out that the capture of New Orleans was a combined operation and that the city probably would not have fallen to an unsupported naval attack. Despite Porter's exaggerated claims, the many thousands of mortar shells which his flotilla hurled against Fort Jackson's masonry did almost no damage. Farragut's decision, fully concurred in by his Army associate, to run past the forts without silencing them was a calculated risk based upon the certainty that Butler's troops could, and did, land in the rear of Fort St. Philip and isolate Fort Jackson from the city.[3]

Without the Army's cooperation, Farragut's position after passing the batteries would have been precarious. Finding a city empty of both military targets and supplies, surrounded by a hostile population with the enemy still in his rear, Farragut could have remained but a short time in New Orleans before returning down river to reduce the forts.[4] It is possible, but by no means certain, that they would have succumbed to systematic naval bombardment without at least a threatened attack on their land fronts. The engineer reports of unsubstantial damage to Fort Jackson by naval gunfire lead us to suspect that the Southerners could have held out indefinitely against any number of the strongest warships brought against them.[5] Although Porter and other naval officers denied to the end of

New Orleans and Defenses

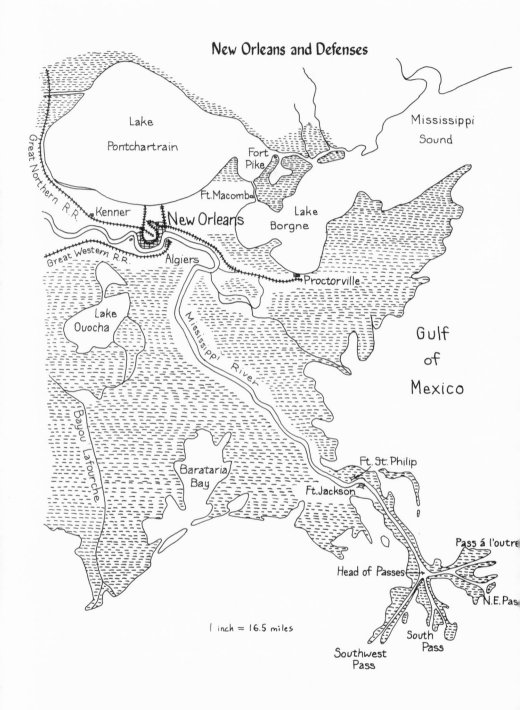

Mississippi Sound

Lake Pontchartrain

Great Northern R.R.

Fort Pike

Ft. Macomb

Kenner

New Orleans

Lake Borgne

Great Western R.R.

Algiers

Proctorville

Lake Ouocha

Gulf of Mexico

Mississippi River

Bayou Lafourche

Barataria Bay

Ft. St. Philip

Ft. Jackson

Pass á l'outre

Head of Passes

N.E. Pass

1 inch = 16.5 miles

Southwest Pass

South Pass

their lives that the troops played any important role in taking
the forts and the city, the Army's presence made their eventual
capture certain.

Farragut's decision to leave the forts behind, though only
for a short time, had one important result. While the warships
threatened to destroy New Orleans by gunfire and thus has-
tened its surrender to the U.S. Navy on 25 April, they could
not occupy the city. During the week between Farragut's appearance and the arrival of Butler's troops on 1 May, the Confederates removed almost everything of military value, including all of the rolling stock on the railroads, and most of the
river vessels. They even managed to dismantle and bring away
their armaments factories along with the machinery for making iron plates for their gunboats.[6] Had the forts been taken
first in accordance with the original plan, the Army and Navy
would have arrived off the city together and the opportunity to
destroy or capture all of the enemy's equipment and stores
would probably not have been lost.

Without the material saved from New Orleans, the Confederates would have been hard-pressed to fortify any point
on the river above the city or to arm local militia for its defense. On 12 May, when Confederate Brigadier General Martin
L. Smith assumed command at Vicksburg, there were only
three batteries in position. Without the rolling stock and water
transportation removed from New Orleans the Southerners
could not have strengthened these defenses in time to prevent
being overrun by the more mobile Federals. Even so, General
Smith was poorly prepared for the expected onslaught. By 18
May, when the Union gunboats arrived before Vicksburg, only
three more water batteries and some bombproofs had been
finished.[7]

The worried Confederates would have been surprised—and
greatly relieved—had they known the grossly inadequate size
of the Union expeditionary force and its lack of definite plans.
Despite his confidential instructions of 20 January from the
secretary of the Navy to push up river immediately after New
Orleans fell, take Memphis from the rear, and link up with
Foote's flotilla, Farragut intended to proceed at once against
the forts at the entrance to Mobile Bay. Since the capture of
Mobile was also included in his orders and in Butler's instruc-

tions from General McClellan, he did not expect to be accused of disobeying the government if he went there.[8]

This decision seems to have been made, in any case, by elimination. Because of very high water in the Mississippi at that season and the consequent danger of running aground, Farragut did not wish to operate above Baton Rouge.[9] Butler therefore tried to modify his plan for moving against Jackson. On 29 April he wrote Stanton that he now proposed "to persuade the Flag Officer to pass up the River as far as the mouth of Red River if possible, so as to cut off their [the enemy's] supplies and make there a landing and demonstration in the rear as a diversion in favor of General Buell [Halleck]." As for Mobile, Butler thought it could wait.[10]

It will be observed that, at this time, neither the Federal army nor naval commander intended an attack or even a demonstration against Vicksburg. Because of the lawless character of the inhabitants, Butler was obliged to keep a large proportion of his 18,000-man army in New Orleans. He also left two thousand troops to prepare the combined attack on Mobile. After providing a garrison for Baton Rouge, occupied as an advanced base on 8 May, Butler could spare only eighteen hundred men under Brigadier General Thomas Williams for further movements.[11]

Farragut's force was also inadequate for an up-river offensive. Yet, despite his intention to attack Mobile and his orders for Porter to begin bombarding the Mobile forts with the mortar flotilla in anticipation of the fleet's arrival, he could not entirely disregard his instructions about Memphis. An added incentive for sending at least part of his squadron in that direction was recently received information that the Confederates were building an ironclad at that place.[12]

Consequently, after the Union occupation of Baton Rouge, Farragut sent up a flying squadron under Commander Samuel P. Lee to make contact with the upper flotilla. It was intended that General Williams' detachment accompany the four gunboats to capture any river batteries uncovered en route to Memphis; but the Army was short of transport, Butler having expected to capture the enemy vessels which the Navy had allowed to escape from New Orleans. Williams was thus compelled to remain in Baton Rouge for a week after Lee departed up river.[13]

Farragut apparently intended—although his orders were vague—that Lee only carry out a reconnaissance of the river until the soldiers joined him. But Lee, attempting to discover if there were any batteries, threw a few shots into Vicksburg, alerting the enemy to the possibility of attack. When Williams arrived below the town on the 17th, it was therefore decided best to move quickly before the Confederates could further strengthen the defenses. Hoping that the mere sight of Federal forces would create panic, as had recently happened at the lower river towns, Williams and Lee foolishly demanded the surrender of the garrison. General Smith—his batteries situated, unlike those at Baton Rouge and Natchez, on the top of a 200-foot ridge—naturally declined, and the Federal commanders were left wondering what to do next. They had made no plans for an assault, or even a landing anywhere in the vicinity.[14]

Learning that the surrender of Vicksburg had been demanded and refused, although he disapproved of Lee's conduct, Farragut thought the Navy's honor was at stake. Despite the danger of grounding and against the advice of his fleet captain who pointed out that the warships could not reach such elevated batteries and that they must approach in line ahead only able to make three knots against the rapid current, Farragut decided to take all of his ships against Vicksburg. Perhaps an enemy not frightened by a few puny gunboats would surrender at the sight of the powerful fleet which had captured New Orleans. In case this gesture failed, the town could be taken by combined operations. Recognizing that Williams' eighteen hundred men might not be sufficient for this latter contingency, Farragut asked Butler for a larger force.[15]

But no more troops were then available without giving up the Mobile operation, which Farragut was unwilling to do. Commander Porter was already off this bay, bombarding Forts Morgan and Gaines with his mortars. His overly sanguine reports suggested that the Confederates would surrender these works as soon as any Union troops appeared. Butler thereupon attempted to get men from elsewhere. Using McClellan's authorization of 23 February, he called upon Brigadier General J.M. Brennan, commanding an inactive district at Key West, Florida. But because Butler could not command the reinforcements and McClellan no longer had the authority to do so, Brennan refused, stating that he momentarily expected an attack on his garrison in Pensacola.[16]

Without reinforcements, Williams would not agree to any direct attack on the Vicksburg defenses. Finally persuaded that an assault had no prospect of success and might end in disaster, Farragut nevertheless could not remain idle; nor could he forget the Confederate ironclads reported at Memphis. One such vessel loose in the river could sink all of his wooden ships and maybe even retake New Orleans. If Williams could land some of his guns on the neck of land opposite Vicksburg, maybe the fleet could run above the town and reach Memphis anyway.[17]

On 24 May the three Union frigates, eight gunboats, and fifteen hundred soldiers conducted a joint reconnaissance of the area around Vicksburg. The result was completely discouraging. Because the west bank opposite Vicksburg was under water, the troops would have to disembark at Warrenton on the east bank, eight miles below. This site was commanded by enemy batteries on the high ground to the north which the ships' guns could not silence. Still unwilling to give up, Farragut called for opinions from his captains, hoping they would agree to at least attempt to cover a landing; but only three of the younger officers approved. The seven seniors were opposed, suggesting instead that a landing might be possible up the Big Black River or Bayou Pierre below Grand Gulf.[18]

Twelve miles up the Big Black was a large railroad bridge carrying the Jackson road into Vicksburg. If Williams and Farragut could no nothing else, they thought they might at least demolish this structure thereby indirectly aiding Halleck's advance on Corinth. The expedition thereupon dropped down to the mouth of the Big Black on the 29th only to discover it closed by an 11-gun battery. Deserters described another heavy battery at the railroad bridge above. As for Bayou Pierre, the pilots reported the water too shallow for the Union vessels.[19]

Disgusted with having exhausted his command to no purpose, Williams returned to Baton Rouge. Butler had failed to procure any reinforcements, and Farragut, depressed and frustrated, planned to take up blockading in the Gulf of Mexico. Anything else, he explained to Welles, was impossible. Without troops, it was senseless to bombard Mobile; nor could he remain in the river. Williams' men were broken down by the climate and on half rations. The squadron was almost out of coal. The ships were in bad condition, the crews clamoring to go home. Worst of all, the river was falling; if he did not leave soon, the fleet would be stranded until next spring. "The elements of destruction to the Navy in this river", he complained, "are beyond anything I have ever encountered, and if the same destruction continues the whole Navy will be destroyed in twelve months."[20]

With the retirement of Farragut's squadron to the Gulf at the end of May 1862, the New Orleans campaign may be said to have ended. The follow-up phase to which McClellan had attached so much importance in his instructions and to which the men on the spot paid so little attention was so badly conducted that it actually benefitted the enemy. Not only was the port of New Orleans, previously almost closed by the Union blockade, suddenly opened to the trade of the world, first unofficially by General Butler, then officially by President Lincoln, but the Confederates were released from the liability of attempting to defend an indefensible city and forced to concentrate their meager resources in men and guns at points better situated to close the river.[21] Had the Federal expedition moved up river in force immediately after the fall of New Orleans, without allowing the enemy time to recover from the initial confusion of defeat, the entire Mississippi would have been in Union control by the summer of 1862. Even the alternative of going against Mobile, contained in McClellan's plan and in the government's instructions, if carried out quickly and in adequate force, would have taken full advantage of the surprise and shock effects which are the greatest assets of amphibious war.[22]

Instead, the Federals attempted to do both while preparing properly for neither and, in the event, accomplished nothing. Although Butler and Farragut were not responsible for the command change which prevented them from acquiring the reinforcements considered essential to the success of their original program, they might have more wisely used the means at hand. If, in their judgment, 8,000 soldiers—the maximum available for operations in Butler's department—were insufficient to take Vicksburg, surely it would have been more prudent to let it alone altogether until a larger force could be assembled, instead of hurling empty threats at the garrison—threats which, aside from hastening defensive preparations, only improved morale all over the South while intensifying impatience in the North.

Obviously, it is easier to see lost opportunities in retrospect. Farragut and Butler could not have known that the best chance for the Union to open the Mississippi in 1862 had been thrown away. They did not know, for instance, that there were barely two Confederate regiments at Vicksburg prior to 20 May; that when Williams' force and Farragut's whole squadron appeared to bombard the place on the 26th, there were but 2,600 of all arms to man the batteries and guard the 20-mile-long line covering the approach via the Yazoo River above the town. The only reinforcements available to General Smith were 1,200 green militiamen at Camp Moore 80 miles north of New Orleans. Indeed, General Lovell, commanding the department, was so pessimistic about resisting a Federal combined attack that he told Beauregard on 25 May that he would have to abandon all of the river towns to hold the vital rail link at Jackson. Smith stated in his report that the ten days following 26 May were critical because his defenses were incomplete and his troops and officers new to the service. In his opinion, even an inferior Union force could have easily taken the place.[23]

If Butler and Farragut did not know the enemy's true situation at Vicksburg, however, it was abundantly clear by the end of May that no *ad hoc* operation in regimental strength was likely to succeed. Their inclination was to join Porter for a combined attack on Mobile.[24] But they had not counted upon the understandable ignorance of the authorities in Washington.

Having received no reports since the capture of New Orleans and learning that Porter's flotilla was anchored off Mobile, Welles jumped to the conclusion that Farragut had disobeyed orders. In a scathing letter received in New Orleans on 2 June, Fox reprimanded Porter for "a most serious blunder, in persuading the flag officer to go at Mobile instead of obeying his instructions to go up the Mississippi River." The government was alarmed, said Fox, by the prospect that the Confederate ironclads reported at Memphis might sink the upper flotilla, forcing Halleck to give up Cairo and even St. Louis.[25]

Similar alarmist dispatches had reached Farragut on his return to New Orleans on 28 May. Disregarding the fact that messages from Washington could not reach the Gulf ports by regular sea mail in less than two weeks, Fox suggested on 12 May that Farragut arrive in Memphis "within the next few days" to cut off the escape of Beauregard's army from Corinth.[26] Farragut might have ignored instructions which were obviously inappropriate when received, but two days later he got a peremptory order from the department dated 16 May, which Fox had rushed out by special dispatch boat, instructing him to ascend the Mississippi at once. Three days later came an explanatory letter from Fox to the effect that his supposedly unauthorized withdrawal from the river, which the Cabinet had read about in the newspapers, had deranged all of the government's plans. The president had promised Foote and Halleck that the fleet would appear any moment in the enemy's rear at Memphis, said Fox, and Farragut must rectify his error at once because the Army was counting on his cooperation.[27]

Despite a conviction that nothing further could be accomplished in the river that season, Farragut felt that his duty required him to obey a definite order, however impractical. Realizing that they would probably not arrive in time to affect the contest for Corinth or Memphis, however, Farragut and Butler planned to attempt a landing near Vicksburg and an attack upon the town as a diversion in favor of Halleck's operations.[28]

This expedition was somewhat better prepared than the first. Because ships' cannon could not reach the elevated batteries at Vicksburg, and because Porter's bombardment at Mobile was disapproved by the Navy Department, Butler persuaded Porter to bring his mortar boats up river with the expedition. High-angle fire might reduce the town to ashes if an assault failed. This time, Williams was given all of Butler's disposable force—five thousand men—and instructed, if he could find no suitable landing on the east bank, to dig a canal through the neck opposite Vicksburg so Federal shipping might bypass the batteries.[29]

Although better organized, this expedition was similarly unsuccessful. The defenses were now too strong for a direct assault with the number of men in Williams' command, the canal project was a failure, and the climate in June was even more unhealthy for Northern soldiers than in May. Despite Porter's reports to the contrary, the mortar bombardment was a waste of ammunition. While a few fires were set, and the citizens were at first frightened of this unfamiliar menace, they soon observed that the shells were comparatively harmless and went about their business as usual. The soldiers in the bombproof batteries were not even momentarily intimidated.[30]

By 25 June, Farragut and Williams reluctantly concluded that the place could not be reduced by bombardment and that a much larger infantry force was required to turn the defenses from the land side. Since Butler had no more troops, the reinforcements must come from Halleck. It was not unreasonable for Farragut to suppose that this officer would gladly support operations against Vicksburg. After all, he had made the expedition in the first place, and against his judgment, to assist the general's offensive against Corinth. Only five thousand soldiers were required, a detachment Halleck's large army would hardly notice.[31]

Consequently, in order to communicate with the general by way of the upper flotilla and destroy the enemy ironclads reportedly being built in the Yazoo, Farragut's squadron passed the Vicksburg batteries on the morning of 28 June. Through some misunderstanding of orders, the USS *Brooklyn* and two gunboats failed to get by, but the rest of the vessels, only slightly damaged, anchored safely in the river above the town.[32] Farragut immediately dispatched a boat to Memphis with the following message for Halleck requesting reinforcements for Williams, or cooperation of his army against Vicksburg:

> My orders, general, are to clear the river. This I find impossible without your assistance. Can you aid me in this matter to carry out the peremptory order of the President?[33]

The issue of the 1862 campaign to open the Mississippi was

now in the hands of the Federal army commander in the West.

One of the greatest virtues of McClellan's strategic plan was that it did not envisage, nor did its success depend upon, co-operation among commands. Each army with its attendant squadron was to be sufficiently strong to take its designated objectives independently. The only coordination would occur at the top, in the person of the general-in-chief who ensured that each piece fit securely into the grand design. McClellan attempted to substitute this novel strategic method for the accepted Jominian maxim of physical concentration of force— no longer practicable because of the huge size of the Federal Army, the fixed nature of its communications, and the vast extent of the theater of war—while avoiding that often fatal evil of multiple commands, failure to cooperate at the right time.

His experience with Halleck and Buell during the Nashville campaign demonstrates his wisdom on this point. McClellan himself had neither desired nor calculated upon cooperation between these two generals. It was Lincoln who, during McClellan's illness, had initiated and insisted upon their coop-eration. The friction resulting from professional jealousy, incompatible command styles, and confusion of purposes might have wrecked the initial campaign in the West had not McClellan, aided by a large measure of enemy stupidity, finally intervened to save the situation. All other movements re-mained independent, with separate objectives, until McClellan's removal from the chief command.

For the Mississippi River expeditions, this strategic au-tonomy was especially important. As already explained, Butler and Farragut, after seizing New Orleans as a base, were to be heavily reinforced from the Army of the Potomac to enable them to take Mobile and Jackson. Meanwhile, Halleck's army and the upper flotilla were to project themselves down the Mississippi upon Memphis and upon Decatur via the Tennes-see. Until these forces joined, if subsequent developments re-quired, there was no need for cooperation, except between land and naval components of the same expedition; thus, there would be less opportunity for misunderstanding, petty quarrels over rank and jurisdiction, and other destructive elements to develop. By forcing McClellan to go after Richmond, however, the government tied up the strategic reserve from which the general-in-chief intended to reinforce Burnside, Halleck, and Butler; by taking away his authority over the whole army, they further ensured that most of these columns would be too weak to exploit their initial success without cooperation from other commands.

General Halleck had also witnessed at first hand the perils of cooperation; but his solution was different from McClellan's. Having at last secured control over Buell's army and over Major General Samuel R. Curtis' force in Missouri, he fell back upon his textbook principle of physical concentration of force. With the Army moving in one huge mass upon a single point with one commander, no misunderstanding was possible.[34]

The point selected was Corinth, Mississippi where the Memphis and Charleston Railroad crossed the Mobile and Ohio. According to his own (and Jomini's) precepts, this objective was near the center of the new enemy front extending from Knoxville curving southwest along the Memphis and Charleston through Decatur and Corinth and north again to Columbus on the Mississippi, and through Missouri south of St. Louis. Moreover, the available Federal line of operations—the Tennessee River—was perpendicular to this front, whereas an advance toward Chattanooga would expose the Union right, and a move on Decatur would place the Federal line of operations parallel to the Confederate front.[35]

The only other alternative was to go down the Mississippi against Memphis, also near the center of the enemy front. But Memphis was a river town; its approaches above were guarded by a series of fortified shore positions—Columbus, Island Number 10, Fort Pillow, and Fort Randolph—and a Confederate squadron had been rushed from New Orleans to support these defenses. The Navy's performance at Forts Henry and Donelson had been less than inspiring, and Foote had shown so little confidence after these engagements in the squadron's ability to effect anything against shore batteries that he had refused Halleck's repeated requests to bombard the fortifications at Columbus. After the enemy abandoned these works in early March, Foote expressed an even greater reluctance to approach the works at Island Number 10, declaring openly that his vessels were entirely useless in a direct attack.[36]

With these considerations in mind, Halleck effected a massive concentration on the Tennessee River to push the Confederates out of Corinth. Aside from the strategic value of the place itself, there is some evidence to suggest that he expected to fight a decisive battle with the western Confederate army now rapidly concentrating at Corinth under Generals A.S. Johnston and Beauregard.[37]

Although from his own point of view, Halleck's decision was entirely sound and one could argue that he was not as yet responsible for any department except his own, the government might have been justified in supposing that the foremost American expert on military strategy, whom Scott had recommended for the chief command and whose theoretical work was a West Point text, would give at least momentary thought to the war as a whole. But if Halleck was aware of Butler's expedition, of Farragut's instructions to push up the river and take Memphis in the rear, or of Lincoln's continued determination to send an army into east Tennessee, he took no account of them when formulating his strategic plan for the West.

Four days after the Army of the Ohio came under his authority, Halleck ordered Buell to bring his whole command to Savannah on the Tennessee River, except for a small force under Brigadier General Ormsby Mitchel which Buell had previously dispatched as an advance guard down the railroad from Nashville toward Stevenson. Two divisions of Grant's old command, now called the Army of the Tennessee, meanwhile established a depot camp higher up this river at Pittsburg Landing. For three weeks this force, cooperating with the wooden gunboats of Foote's squadron, occupied itself with burning bridges, carrying off cotton, and conducting reconnaissances in the direction of Corinth.

All of this preliminary activity alerted the Confederates to the intended point of attack. Since the Federals had not broken the Memphis and Charleston or the Mobile and Ohio, Johnston used these lines to consolidate the remnants of his field army and his scattered outpost garrisons at Corinth. Anticipating Halleck's intentions, he fell by surprise upon the Army of the Tennessee, still separated from Buell's force, in its camp around Shiloh Church (near Pittsburg Landing) on 7 April.

The ensuing two-day engagement—one of the most famous

of the war—although a strategic victory for the North, unnerved General Halleck. Losing whatever small confidence he
previously had in Grant, he determined to take the field himself for the "decisive" campaign against Corinth. Moreover, the
near disaster to Grant's army still further solidified his conviction that all United States forces under his control must be
assembled in one place.[38]

Consequently, on 15 April, Major General John Pope was
ordered to bring his 20,000-man command, called the Army
of the Mississippi, around into the Tennessee. Pope had been
engaged with Foote's ironclads and mortar boats in operations
to open the Mississippi between Cairo and Memphis. Despite
Halleck's decision to concentrate against Corinth, this force
had remained on the Mississippi for three reasons. First, the
mortar flotilla, a pet project of the president and built at great
expense to the War Department, could not be used on the
Tennessee; nor was Foote anxious to employ his river ironclads in a treacherous unpredictable waterway infested on
both shores by "guerrillas." Although Foote was reluctant to
bombard forts, the broad expanse of the Mississippi was a
more inviting refuge for the fleet.[39] Second, Curtis' army could
not be withdrawn from Missouri without risking the loss of
that state. So, in accordance with Halleck's theory of concentration, Curtis could affect the result at Corinth only by attacking some point on the Mississippi. Third, Pope's column in
cooperation with Curtis could force the enemy to abandon the
river defenses above Memphis in order to concentrate before
Corinth where Halleck hoped to smash him in a decisive
battle.[40]

Shiloh changed his mind. It now looked as though a general
engagement, even against inferior numbers, might not result
in a Federal victory, especially if it occurred away from the
river. In spite of his contempt for the Navy, Halleck had concluded that only the Union gunboats *Tyler* and *Lexington* had
kept Grant's army from being destroyed before Buell arrived.
He no longer wanted the enemy to assemble more force at
Corinth and, in fact, altered his whole grand tactical plan. The
advance on Corinth would now be methodical, protected by entrenchments every foot of the way. To guard against another
surprise, large detachments must cover both flanks and look

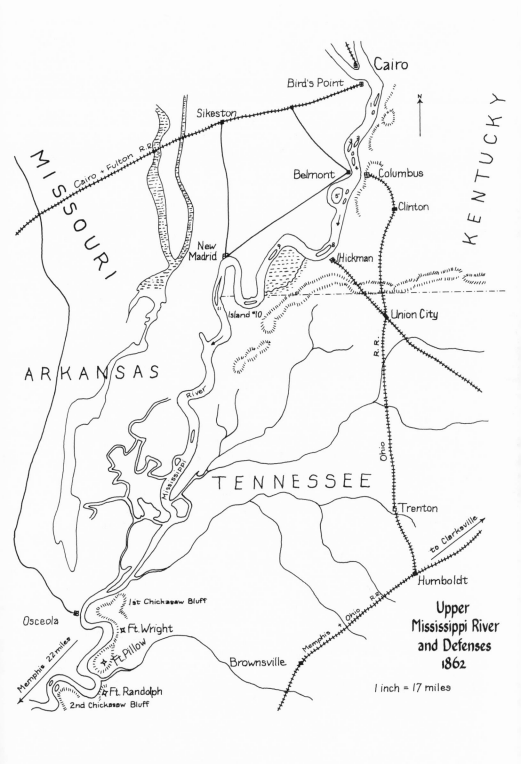

Cairo

Bird's Point

MISSOURI

Sikeston

Cairo + Fulton R.R.

Belmont

Columbus

Clinton

KENTUCKY

New Madrid

Hickman

Island "10

Union City

ARKANSAS

River

R.R.

Ohio

TENNESSEE

Mississippi

Trenton

to Clarksville

Humboldt

1st Chickasaw Bluff

Osceola

Ft. Wright

Ft. Pillow

Brownsville

Memphis + Ohio R.R.

Memphis 22 miles

Ft. Randolph

2nd Chickasaw Bluff

Upper
Mississippi River
and Defenses
1862

1 inch = 17 miles

well to the front and rear. Because this method of proceeding required an even larger force, Pope's army was withdrawn from the Mississippi.[41]

The order arrived at an inopportune time. After Foote's half-hearted two-week mortar bombardment of the strong enemy works at Island Number 10, Pope succeeded in flanking the position via the Missouri shore, isolating and capturing the garrison on 8 April. In assisting the land forces, Foote discovered that his river ironclads, so vulnerable at anchor in the daytime, could, in an unobstructed channel, run past formidable shore batteries at night with little or no damage.[42] This discovery should have made the next series of fortifications, Forts Pillow and Randolph, appear less forbidding. But, although Pope was anxious to push on against Memphis, Foote was still obsessed with the powerlessness of his squadron and relied upon the Army to open the way for his advance. Suddenly, most of the troops were gone. One brigade remained, but this small force could accomplish little. For three weeks its commander attempted to persuade Foote to attack Fort Pillow, or at least run vessels by, and to find a route for the troops into the rear of the works. Both efforts failed.[43]

Foote had been unwell since he was wounded at Fort Donelson, and this final challenge was too much. On 9 May he turned over the Mississippi Squadron to his second-in-command, Captain Charles H. Davis. Davis, it will be recalled, was an early combined operations enthusiast, secretary of the Blockade Board, and Du Pont's fleet captain during the attack on the Port Royal forts. Possessed of an intellectual temperament, unlike his man-of-action predecessor, he was not easily alarmed or frustrated.

Mississippi Squadron at Mound City (*Library of Congress*)

His intention to move down river against Memphis was strengthened by enemy action. The day after Davis assumed command, the Confederate River Defense Fleet—eight light vessels under Captain J.E. Montgomery—made a spirited attack on the Union mortar flotilla and its attendant gunboats then bombarding from its station at Plum Point above Fort Pillow. Caught by surprise, two Federal vessels, the *Cincinnati* and *Mound City*, were sunk by ramming and several others were damaged. Unable to approach the mortar rafts which were anchored in shallow water, Montgomery withdrew, having sustained no losses.[44]

This engagement was sudden and unexpected. Up until this time, the Federal river navy had encountered only fortifications. The new enemy was considered a greater threat, and a greater challenge for sailors. But Montgomery had been extremely lucky, for his vessels were not really gunboats, although they carried a few medium cannon. While faster than the Union boats, their speed would not help them much in an engagement upstream against vessels already in motion. Comparatively deep draft, bad steering, and lack of protection added further handicaps to their greatly inferior armament. Once Davis had passed the shore batteries, these fragile craft were the Confederacy's only hope for saving Memphis. The city itself, sprawling over low ground, was indefensible.

Davis proceeded systematically, bombarding the works while preparing his ships for their encounter with the Confederate flotilla. It was not necessary, however, to reduce the shore batteries. On 4 June, five days after Halleck's army entered Corinth, the Confederates evacuated Forts Pillow and Randolph and prepared to get out of Memphis. The ensuing fleet engagement before Memphis on the 6th was an anticlimax. Hopelessly outclassed, Montgomery's little fleet went down one by one in a "last ditch" defense. Only the CSS *General Van Dorn* escaped to New Orleans.[45]

After the fall of Memphis, one strongpoint remained in Confederate hands to close the Mississippi to Federal shipping —Vicksburg. Despite its geographical situation, with batteries atop 200-foot bluffs commanding a great horseshoe bend in the river, this place was not yet the fortress it later became. Less than five thousand troops were stationed there and the defenses

Rear Admiral David Glasgow
Farragut (*National Archives*)

Charles H. Davis; shown here
as a rear admiral.
(*National Archives*)

were all on the water side.[46] Opening into the Mississippi just
a few miles to the north, the Yazoo River, as yet weakly fortified, formed a convenient highway into the rear of the town.

On 1 July Davis' squadron appeared above Vicksburg, meeting Flag Officer Farragut whose wooden fleet had passed the
batteries on 28 June. One more combined operation would
free the river forever and inflict a terrible blow on the Confederacy.[47] But the hero of New Orleans was not to have the
satisfaction of taking Vicksburg. Halleck refused to send any
troops.

While the Mississippi Squadron moved slowly down the
river toward Memphis, Halleck's one hundred and twenty
thousand soldiers dug their way into Corinth. Beauregard, in
command of the western Confederate army after Johnston's
death at Shiloh, was himself too expert an engineer to risk
an assault on entrenched lines. Outnumbered two to one and
seeing that his position was hopeless, he nevertheless succeeded in holding the town until the last possible moment.
Suspecting nothing, the Federals were almost on top of the
parapets and preparing their decisive assault before they dis-

covered that the Confederates had gone. Entering Corinth on 30 May, Halleck found no troops, no supplies—nothing except a few charred storehouses and derailed freight cars on the edge of town. Beauregard's entire force with almost all of its materiel had escaped south to Tupelo on the railroad to Mobile. Although he sent first Buell's army and then Pope's in pursuit, Halleck was unable to catch the enemy; so he settled down in Corinth to consolidate his new position.[48]

Something odd appears to have happened to General Halleck during this campaign. Always an efficient officer, if somewhat rigid and doctrinaire, his head full of plans for great strategic combinations, he suddenly seemed absent-minded and stupid. To Lincoln's demand that he detach Buell's army to resume its advance toward Chattanooga—a clear violation of Halleck's most sacred principle—he offered not the slightest objection. In fact, he sent Buell off along the Memphis and Charleston with orders to repair it as he advanced, instead of allowing Buell to resume his old line via Nashville and Stevenson, thus abandoning another firm principle about choosing a line of operation perpendicular to the enemy front.[49]

When Memphis fell, Sherman was sent with a detachment to garrison the place. When Curtis, pressed back toward the Mississippi by the enemy advance in Arkansas, appealed for assistance, Halleck promised him large reinforcements, again violating his rule of concentration. To General Grant, placed in command of the Army of the Tennessee and charged with the defense of Corinth, he gave no instructions whatever, other than perfunctory orders to fortify the town and repair the railroad to Columbus.[50]

This strange behavior, inconsistent with his previous intentions and actions, is difficult to explain.[51] It is as though Halleck had only one idea since taking up his command at St. Louis—to break the enemy line in the West and seize Corinth. Having accomplished by great energy and planning his *ideé fixe*, he did not know what to do next. The logical step, according to his former reasoning, would have been to move on Jackson punching another hole through the Confederate center. But if Halleck thought about that possibility at all—and there is no evidence that he did—he would probably have considered it too dangerous. With the Confederates still in possession of

Cumberland Gap, Chattanooga on the right, and northern Arkansas on the left, a Union army at Jackson would have been at the apex of a huge salient; and because that army would be concentrated, no Federal forces would have been available to prevent the enemy from pinching off the salient, trapping Halleck's army in a pocket deep in enemy territory with no communications.[52]

Whatever his thoughts may have been, however, as he sat amid the gloomy trenches of his recent, somehow empty triumph, none of them have come down to us. We can only catch an impression of his state of mind from his orders and dispatches. These project a depressing picture of confusion, inaction, and despair.

By the time Farragut's request for troops to take Vicksburg reached Halleck on 3 July, the military situation had already begun to deteriorate. After the fall of Corinth and Memphis, the Southerners anticipated an immediate move on Jackson from the north in conjunction with a landing at some unguarded point along the lower Mississippi to seize the railroad from Jackson to New Orleans, at that time watched by only 5,000 soldiers. When the Federals failed to continue the offensive, General Braxton Bragg, having superseded Beauregard in command of the Confederate army in the West, decided that it was safe to leave slightly under half of his available force (32,000) evenly distributed at Vicksburg and Tupelo and, with his remaining 35,000, advance against Buell's communications in middle Tennessee.[53]

Halleck's absurd order for Buell to repair the Memphis and Charleston all the way to Chattanooga, and to use this line of communication, gave the initiative in middle and east Tennessee over to the enemy. To make matters worse, General Mitchel, moving down the Nashville road via Decatur and Stevenson with 7,000 men, had, without authority from either Buell or Halleck, attempted a coup de main against Chattanooga on 7 June. Unable to cross the river, Mitchel bombarded the town with twenty small rifled cannon established on the west bank. Having damaged the distant buildings, the Union troops assaulted the Confederate outposts and were thoroughly repulsed, quickly withdrawing the following day over the Cumberland Mountains into middle Tennessee. For good measure, some of Mitchel's cavalry demolished the large railway trestle over the Tennessee at Decatur, thus impeding Buell's progress for another three weeks.[54]

This foolish display, carried out before Buell's army even left Corinth, not only warned the Confederates of an impending attack on Chattanooga, but isolated another Union detachment under Brigadier General George W. Morgan who, on Buell's order of three months before, finally seized the Cumberland Gap northeast of Knoxville on 19 June. To keep Bragg from using this golden opportunity to eat up unsupported Union detachments, Halleck was required to reinforce Buell with half of Grant's command under Major General William Rosecrans.[55]

As though his hands were not full enough with the situation east of Corinth, Halleck allowed himself to become enmeshed in a "wild goose chase" west of the Mississippi. Curtis had run into trouble in north Arkansas, which his small army had invaded in an effort to recruit soldiers for the United States. The defending forces under Major General T.C. Hindman had pushed him back behind the White River, while a larger Confederate army under Major General Sterling Price was threatening to cut him off from his base.[56]

Stanton considered the recruiting efforts in Arkansas valuable propaganda for the Union and on 8 June suggested that Halleck ask Flag Officer Davis to send a few gunboats up this river to open a new supply route for Curtis. That the request did not come through the secretary of the Navy illustrates the confused command arrangements on the Mississippi at that time. Fox, it will be recalled, had been pushing for transfer of the Mississippi Squadron to the Navy Department since December 1861 when Foote opposed the change. Now that Davis was in charge, Fox again urged the government to agree to the transfer. But although the squadron commander had never reported to the War Department, Stanton insisted not only that it remain technically under his control, but that it be placed directly under Halleck for operational purposes.[57]

While this dispute was still unsettled, another jurisdictional dispute arose in connection with the Ram Fleet. This flotilla of wooden vessels had been proposed and fitted out at Pittsburg and St. Louis by Charles Ellet, Jr., a civil engineer, and his relatives, who had been impressed by the ramming of the USS *Cumberland* by the *Virginia* in March. Hiring a crew of riverboat adventurers and a contingent of army "marines," the Ellets had obtained commissions from Stanton and orders to "clear the Mississippi" of the enemy. Their anomalous position vis-à-vis both the Navy and the Army department commanders—that is, being directly under the secretary of War —was further exacerbated by their extremely aggressive disposition. Always anxious for excitement, their minds fertile with dangerous expedients, the Ellets would cooperate only on their own terms.[58]

Pressed for gunboats of suitable draft, Davis asked Charles Ellet to send his vessels up the White River to support Curtis. Had he agreed, Halleck's soldiers would not have become involved. But Ellet refused. He was bitter because the Navy had declined turning over one of the prizes captured by his flagship at Memphis. Therefore, on 14 June Davis sent several of his own vessels on reconnaissance and discovered a raft of heavy timber with which the Confederates had obstructed the lower White River. This convinced Davis that he must make a combined operation.[59]

The ensuing expedition was a fiasco. The only troops at hand were the two regiments of Pope's army which had accompanied the fleet to Memphis. Having removed the obstructions and steamed eighty miles up river, the expedition encountered a fort at St. Charles. Although the work was weakly defended against a land attack, it held out long enough to fire a 64-pound rifled shot through the steam drum of the Union ironclad *Mound City*, killing and scalding half of the crew and disabling the vessel. Shocked, Davis refused to go any further.[60]

By this time, however, Curtis had appealed by messenger directly to Halleck. Unfortunately for the Union, Grant was in a position to help him. On 21 June Halleck had sent Grant to take command of Sherman's corps at Memphis. Although Stanton passed on to Halleck a suggestion from Butler that this force might cut off Vicksburg from the rear in conjunction with the Navy on the river, Halleck paid no attention, instead reminding Grant that his main duty was to guard against raids on the railroads.[61] But he could not ignore Curtis, who represented his plight as desperate and whose defeat would open Missouri to invasion.

Reinforced by one of Grant's brigades and having secured Davis's reluctant approval, the combined expedition again set out up White River. This time, it reached a point one mile below Clarendon where the river was found full of dead trees and too shallow for the gunboats. Troops and vessels were constantly fired upon by guerrilla parties and it was rumored that the Confederates had a powerful battery at Devall's Bluff further up river guarded by ten thousand troops. Besides, they had discovered no Union sentiment in the region. All things considered, it was thought best to leave Curtis to his own devices and return to Memphis.[62]

Halleck would not give up that easily. Some of his old spirit had returned, and if the general was nothing else, he was determined. Curtis had to be supported if it took every vessel and every man of Grant's command. Luckily, before this large force could be fitted out, the remainder of Curtis' army (5000 men) appeared on the Mississippi at Helena, a little ragged but otherwise unhurt, having marched across country ahead of an enemy force which was insufficient to risk a serious attack.[63]

A more ill-conceived and fruitless affair could not have been contrived than this combined foray into the Arkansas wilds; nor could it have occurred at a worse time. The opportunity to take Vicksburg in a short, sharp campaign was rapidly passing away. By 16 July, when the gunboats were again free to descend the Mississippi, General Price's Confederate army had crossed over to the east bank below Helena and was in position either to reinforce Vicksburg or to join Major General Earl Van Dorn, commanding southern forces in Mississippi, in an offensive against Halleck's scattered army.[64] Throughout the month of July, the Union Navy Department appealed for troops to the War Department, which in turn appealed to General Halleck. They always met with the same reply; none were available. All troops had to be held at Memphis or Corinth to reinforce Curtis and Buell.[65]

In fact, the opportunity was gone. Feeling useless just sitting in the river above Vicksburg, Farragut soon became restless for more profitable employment. Experience had proved that no glory awaited the Navy at Vicksburg. He had been willing to bombard the batteries again as a diversion for the Army; but the Army did not seem especially anxious to have the place, and neither did the government, since they would not order Halleck to cooperate. On 8 July, Farragut suggested reviving the Mobile expedition. A week later, Welles authorized him to withdraw his squadron from the Mississippi to prepare for this enterprise, turning over to Flag Officer Davis all responsibility for keeping the river open above Vicksburg.[66]

Halleck's refusal to cooperate and his complaint that someone was interfering with his command by suggesting operations against Vicksburg also disgusted General Butler. On 16 July he ordered Williams to withdraw his force to Baton Rouge, reminding him sardonically that he was "in the geographical department of General Halleck."[67] The secretary of War did nothing to retrieve the situation; on the contrary, he further muddied the waters by referring to Butler a suggestion from Secretary of State Seward that he get up an expedition to seize Brownsville, on the Texas coast.[68] Of course, Stanton neglected to consult the secretary of the Navy about this project and Welles, in turn, had not bothered to inform Stanton about the Navy's plans for Mobile. Both were to be combined operations.

All immediate alternatives to Vicksburg that Farragut and Butler might have arranged between themselves were disrupted by the enemy. Farragut's primary reason for passing above the Vicksburg batteries, it will be remembered, was to destroy the Confederate ironclads building up the Yazoo River. The most dangerous was the CSS *Arkansas*, a heavily armed and plated ram which Captain Isaac N. Brown had removed half-finished from Memphis just before the town fell into Union hands.

As the result of a daring reconnaissance carried out on 26 June by Alfred Ellet, now commanding the Ram Fleet since the death of his brother Charles on the 21st, Farragut learned that only one four-gun battery covering a timber barricade 65 miles up river stood in his way.[69] On 13 July, having waited ten days for Halleck to change his mind about sending troops from Memphis, Farragut ordered his fleet captain,

Commander Henry H. Bell, to take an expedition up the Yazoo to destroy the *Arkansas*. A contingent of Williams' soldiers would accompany the vessels along with the Ram Fleet whose "marines" were expected to assist in removing the obstructions and capturing any land batteries encountered. However, the Yazoo was found to be too shallow for Farragut's warships and Davis was persuaded to send two gunboats, the *Carondolet* and *Tyler*, to assist in exploring the river before the combined movement.[70]

But the Federals had delayed too long. The *Arkansas* was ready and Brown was anxious to bring her down the Mississippi to cooperate with Major J.C. Breckinridge's division, then preparing an attack on Baton Rouge. The Confederates hoped to take her all the way to New Orleans to help recapture the city and raise the blockade at Mobile. By coincidence, as Brown descended the Yazoo in the *Arkansas* on the 15th, the two Federal gunboats and the *Queen of the West* were moving upstream. The Union boats were unprepared and unequal to a contest with the more powerful enemy. Having disabled and run aground the ironclad *Carondolet*, the *Arkansas* pursued

The CSS *Arkansas* running through the Union squadrons above Vicksburg, 15 July 1862.

the faster wooden vessels out of the Yazoo and into the Mississippi. Taken by surprise, their ships at anchor with fires low,
Farragut and Davis managed to get off only a few shots before
seeing the *Arkansas* anchor under the batteries at Vicksburg,
having passed through two Federal fleets.[71]

Despite Confederate expectations, the *Arkansas* was not a
serious threat to Union control of the river. Her miserable
engines could barely move her against the current, and her
steering was defective. Nevertheless, the psychological impact
of her spectacular maiden voyage was tremendous. Farragut
was mortified. Shore batteries were one thing—the fleet was
not expected to operate on land—but a lone enemy warship
defying the U.S. Navy was another. Although Brown had sustained severe damage in his unexpected tour de force and
showed no disposition to move, Farragut was obsessed with
the Confederate ship. If the *Arkansas* would not come out and
fight, he would destroy her under the guns of Vicksburg.[72]

Davis considered such impetuous action dangerous and
unnecessary. The enemy ironclad was a nuisance and an embarrassment perhaps, but surely not worth risking the Union's
command of the river, or any of the large wooden ships so
urgently needed for the Gulf blockade. Now that the U.S.
Navy was on guard, the *Arkansas* could not come out without
being destroyed. This calm, logical advice took some of the
wind out of Farragut's sails. Still, he was unwilling to go down
the river without attempting something. After a personal conference, Davis promised to send the ironclad *Essex* from the
upper flotilla plus some ships for covering fire. The *Queen of
the West* would cooperate by ramming the *Arkansas*, while
Farragut, whose squadron had passed below the city on the
15th, would send the USS *Sumter* to bombard the lower batteries.[73]

The attack was made on the 22nd. Considering the character
of the individuals involved in this joint adventure, perhaps it
is not surprising that it failed. We have already described
Alfred Ellet—impatient, fearless, and rash. The *Essex*'s captain was Commander William D. Porter, the ambitious brother
of the still more ambitious David Porter; like his brother, he
was irritable, flamboyant, and less than honest. Nothing went
according to plan. In his ardor to be the only hero, Porter did not

wait for the *Queen of the West*, but charged upon the *Arkansas* which raked *Essex* fore and aft, causing her to ground for almost an hour under the batteries. After Porter had finally managed to withdraw his battered ship downstream, the *Queen* appeared, only to meet a similar reception. While Ellet fruitlessly bumped at the enemy's iron hide, the *Arkansas* let go a terrific broadside which set the wooden ram on fire and killed her pilot. Scarcely had the *Queen*'s crew doused the blaze when the ship was struck by a shower of plunging shot which perforated the deck; at this point Ellet too called off the attack and escaped up river. Meanwhile, Lieutenant Commander S. Ledyard Phelps in Davis' flagship the *Benton*, attempting to take a position to silence the upper shore batteries, found that he could not approach close enough for his fire to be effective. The *Sumter* apparently never received the order, and in any case failed to appear.

The only result of this farcical engagement was a flurry of recriminations. Porter excused his failure by blaming everybody else, including both flag officers. He also refused to acknowledge that the *Queen of the West* participated in the action. For his part, Ellet called Porter a coward, claiming that the *Essex* had run from the *Arkansas* after firing a few rounds. He further complained that neither Davis nor Farragut gave the support they had promised. Phelps blamed Farragut's inaction for his inability to get the *Benton* in position to silence the batteries. Finally, Davis charged Porter with lying and with calumniating his commanding officer.[74]

Farragut, who never indulged in this kind of backbiting himself, had no stomach for it in others. Moreover, the attack clearly demonstrated how foolish it would have been to risk his whole squadron under the batteries. Three days later, he ordered the fleet to New Orleans, leaving the *Sumter* to support Williams' troops and patrol the Mississippi between Vicksburg and the Red River. The gunboats *Kineo* and *Katahdin*, unfit for sea duty, would remain at Baton Rouge. All other vessels, he told Welles, would be distributed among the blockade stations or taken to Pensacola, where he planned to establish a naval depot. If Butler could spare troops, he would prepare a combined attack on Mobile.[75]

After a summer of exposure to the pestilential fevers of the

Mississippi River swamps, however, the soldiers were in no condition to undertake further offensive operations. By 23 July, only eight hundred of Williams' men were fit for duty; the rest had died or were sick with malaria. Nor was the general prepared to leave a skeleton force, as requested by Davis, to keep open naval communications above Vicksburg. "For this object of opening the river," he wrote Davis, "a small land force I have found to be only an embarrassment, fit only to excite expectation and fit only to disappoint expectation."[76]

In the event, the Federals were compelled to retire all the way back to New Orleans. Butler had hoped to maintain his depot at Baton Rouge until he had raised sufficient Negro regiments in his department to renew the river offensive. But the crumbling Federal situation in the West during June and July had given the Confederates an opportunity. On 5 August Breckinridge's division fell upon Baton Rouge. Although the *Kineo* and *Katahdin* prevented the Southerners from occupying the town, Williams' troops were badly cut up and the general himself killed. Butler then decided that it was unwise to isolate small forces in advanced positions, especially since his chief engineer, Lieutenant (later Brigadier General) Godfrey Weitzel, assured him that Baton Rouge was indefensible from the water side and could be easily retaken by the Federals anytime they wished, since they commanded the river.[77] Consequently, on 21 August the remnants of Williams' command, having removed its stores and burned the warehouses, withdrew to New Orleans.

The attack on Baton Rouge solved Farragut's most immediate problem. On returning to New Orleans, he had found a peremptory order from Welles, dated some weeks earlier, to destroy the *Arkansas* at whatever cost. Thankful that he had not received this order while still below Vicksburg, he was even more relieved to learn that no heroic measures were necessary.[78] In attempting to cooperate with Breckinridge by sinking the two wooden gunboats protecting Williams' lines, the *Arkansas*'s faulty engines had broken down several times en route from Vicksburg. A few miles above Baton Rouge, her steering gear jammed and she grounded just as the Federal gunboats and the *Essex*, which Farragut had sent up from New Orleans to assist in covering the troops, discovered her.

Seeing that their situation was hopeless and since they were only able to fire the bow pivot guns at their antagonists, the *Arkansas*'s crew swam ashore and escaped into the woods after destroying the vessel.[79]

Farragut could at last turn his back on the thankless task of "opening" the Mississippi. There were no more troops to protect, no more river posts to guard, no more ironclads to destroy. If Butler could still find a few troops somewhere to occupy the Mobile forts, the Navy would drive the enemy out; if not, Farragut—who finally received his rear admiral's commission on 12 August—would attend to the long-neglected Gulf blockade. In any case, he had obeyed his orders as far as Vicksburg was concerned. Without the Army, nothing more could be done.[80]

For his part, Davis was not inclined to remain alone above Vicksburg after both Williams and Farragut had disappeared down river. The Mississippi between Helena and Vicksburg was infested with "guerrillas," and because half of his vessels were undergoing repairs, he was unable to convoy supplies. Besides, General Curtis at Helena, who still thought himself threatened by an overwhelming force, was loudly appealing for naval protection.[81] On 29 July, therefore, the Mississippi Squadron steamed back up river, leaving the Confederates in control of both banks for more than five hundred miles.

Ultimately, the 1862 summer campaign in the West was worse than a failure. By the end of August the Confederate grip on the Mississippi was firmer than ever. The Federal threat focused attention on Vicksburg resulting in a strengthening of its defenses. Union activity around the Yazoo alerted the enemy to their danger from this direction also, and spurred them to build works strong enough to resist a large-scale combined attack.

Although Union troops and vessels sustained few battle casualties, they fell victim to the inevitable attrition of continuous service in a bad climate. Men and ships were worn out, and their commanders were exhausted, frustrated, and discouraged. Tying up Federal forces in an uncoordinated campaign on the Mississippi permitted the enemy to seize the initiative elsewhere. While Farragut's vessels stood idle and impotent above Vicksburg, waiting for troops that never came, blockade runners brought vital stores into Mobile and Galveston. Commerce raiders roamed the Gulf and the Caribbean, sinking United States merchant ships and driving up marine insurance rates, to the anger and impatience of the Northern business community.[82]

On land, the situation at the end of August was even worse. The dispersion of the main Union army in the West after the siege of Corinth, and Halleck's failure to devise any further strategic plan, gave the Confederacy its only real chance to win the war. Everywhere the Federals suddenly found themselves on the defensive despite their navy's command of the rivers and coastal waters. On the Mississippi, Butler's troops were confined to the environs of New Orleans. Curtis' force, driven from central Arkansas, huddled on the river bank at Helena under the guns of Davis' flotilla. Grant, having abandoned the Memphis and Charleston railroad east of Corinth on Halleck's orders, was isolated in Memphis, his water communications with Cairo interrupted by roving bands of Confederate sharpshooters and field guns which had infiltrated along the upper Mississippi and the Tennessee. Southern forces in Missouri and middle Tennessee threatened Cairo and Paducah, while General Van Dorn planned operations against Corinth and Columbus, and General Price prepared to recover Nashville.[83]

Further east, Buell's advance bogged down because he lacked supplies and sufficient troops to guard his long line of communications. On 20 August Confederate General Edmund Kirby Smith, moving out from Knoxville, gained the rear of the Union detachment at Cumberland Gap and destroyed its supply train; this forced Morgan's men to disperse into the mountains to reach safety on the Ohio River.[84] Leaving Price to threaten Nashville, Bragg outmaneuvered Buell and, invading Kentucky from east Tennessee, menaced Cincinnati and Louisville. In Virginia, the Northern government's withdrawal of McClellan's army from the James River led to Pope's defeat at Manassas and Lee's invasion of Maryland.

These Confederate offensives were not isolated events caused by local circumstances, nor were they accidents. They were the result, both direct and indirect, of the collapse of McClellan's strategic plan and the failure of his successors to use the offensive power of combined operations intelligently. "We do not forget," wrote Fox to Farragut in July 1863, "that you and Davis met at Vicksburg a year ago and that five thousand troops which I vainly asked of Halleck . . . were denied and a years fighting on the flank of that river is the consequence."[85]

Beyond the cost in men and money was the issue of the war itself. That the Southerners did not fully exploit their unique opportunity for a decisive victory in September 1862, with the Northern elections just two months away and Britain and France on the verge of recognizing the Confederacy, was no thanks to General Halleck or his superiors in Washington. Not only did they refuse reinforcements to follow up Butler and Farragut's victory at New Orleans as outlined in the initial plan, but their utter failure to provide the leadership essential to any joint or combined operation was nearly fatal to the Union.

OPENING THE MISSISSIPPI

THE BAD EFFECTS of the collapse of McClellan's plan in the West were not limited to the spring and summer of 1862. Indeed, the divergence of purposes that characterized the follow-up to the capture of New Orleans, Memphis, and Corinth grew steadily worse throughout the autumn and winter of 1862 as Union forces fumbled for a formula to conquer the South.

Not recognizing that the fundamental cause for their failure to seize Mobile, capture Vicksburg, or exploit the victory at Corinth was the absence of a comprehensive combined strategy, the Federal high command supposed that the western offensive had ground to a halt because of insufficient means. More soldiers, more ships, more expeditions, and "better" commanders would put everything right. No attempt was made to direct these forces to the attainment of any one particular object; nor were they given more than vague instructions to cooperate with one another. The result was almost unbelievable confusion.

Admiral Farragut received no new orders from the Navy Department for several months. After withdrawing most of his squadron from the river in July, he turned his attention to tightening the long-neglected Gulf coast blockade. But Mobile festered like a thorn in his side. In August he established fleet headquarters at Pensacola, Florida, which had been evacuated by the Confederates after the fall of Memphis. From this spacious anchorage he kept a close watch on the forts at the entrance to Mobile Bay only thirty miles away. Although he could not see his most dangerous antagonists—the ironclads reportedly being built in the city—he knew that Confederate

Admiral Franklin Buchanan, his associate in the old Navy and the *Virginia's* first captain, would seize the initiative against the frail Union blockaders as soon as the ships were ready. Even Farragut's natural optimism could not erase the recent painful memory of his encounter with the *Arkansas*. No doubt the superior numbers and speed of the Federal squadron would triumph over Buchanan in the end; but the department, spurred by public opinion, was prone to panic in the short run. The enemy squadron must not be allowed to come out of Mobile Bay—if for no other reason, so that it could be more easily destroyed.[1]

Another stimulus motivated the Union admiral—inactivity. Although he was convinced of the merits of blockade, Farragut's was not a blockading temperament. Nor was he a good administrator; necessary attention to such routine details as repair, crew replacement, and fleet logistics made him restless and depressed. He had been sent out, he thought, to engage the enemy in battle; his orders were to take places of importance —New Orleans, Mobile, Vicksburg, Galveston. Yet only the opening phase of the campaign had been a success. Spurred by his initiative during the summer, the Confederates had turned Vicksburg into one of the strongest fortresses in North America. The defenses at Mobile were growing daily under the eyes of his squadron. Galveston—indeed, the whole Texas coast—remained in enemy hands and blockade-running through Matamoros on the Rio Grande had never been more profitable.[2]

The prospect for operations in the Gulf and the Mississippi had changed markedly since the previous December. The original plan had been based on Army cooperation; permanent results at New Orleans had depended absolutely upon this cooperation, while operations at Vicksburg had failed for lack of it. And now, Mobile could not be attempted without troops. Not many soldiers were required and they were not expected to do very much; but they had to be there to garrison the forts if the Navy could drive the enemy out by bombardment, to take them in the rear if the bombardment failed and, above all, to guard the fleet's communications with the Gulf once Federal vessels had entered the Bay.[3]

For reasons unknown to Farragut, however, General Butler

had lost interest in Mobile. The admiral's occasional applications for troops were answered by courteous letters agreeing in principle that the place should be taken as soon as possible. But no soldiers arrived. From a reply to his application for Army cooperation in October, he learned that most of Butler's movable force, under General Weitzel, was engaged in operations to clean out the LaFourche country west of the Mississippi opposite New Orleans.[4]

There were two main objects for this campaign, neither of them military. Although Butler told Farragut that its purpose was to drive away small enemy concentrations threatening the city and destroy their source of supply, the real attraction for Butler was the country itself. Since his arrival, New Orleans had been plagued by crowds of Negro refugees who had to be subsisted on Army stores. Providing for these people was a growing burden on the Quartermaster Department and the Treasury. It finally occurred to Butler that the only permanent solution was to get the Negroes to provide for themselves. This meant settling them on land taken from the enemy. The LaFourche district was ideal for the purpose. One of the richest regions of Louisiana, it was close enough to New Orleans to serve as a buffer zone between the city and Confederate forces in Texas.[5]

Another inducement was the large quantity of sugar produced and stored there. In Union hands, this valuable commodity would not only pay the cost of resettling the Negroes on the vacated land but would leave a handsome profit for the Quartermaster Department, for Butler's brother who was speculating in cotton under Army auspices, and for the general himself.[6] Compared with this lucrative enterprise, Mobile was not very attractive.

As time passed and no troops arrived at Pensacola, Farragut grew more and more impatient. In August, he would not consider going it alone with the fleet; by October, he wondered if a naval coup de main, even at the cost of most of his ships, might not be better than doing nothing. The sentiment gradually crept into his letters and reports to Welles and Fox. Finally, they advised him not to go off half-cocked against Mobile at the risk of the blockade and informed him that Major General Nathaniel Banks was preparing an expedition of New England and New York troops to take Mobile and Galveston and to clean up the lower Mississippi.[7]

Indeed, the Lincoln administration had been uneasy about Butler's activities for some time. Secretary of State Seward, in particular, was dissatisfied with the general. New Orleans was full of foreigners and foreign consuls who did not appreciate Butler's modus operandi. Instead of allowing all parties equal access to the profitable trade in cotton, sugar, and other Southern resources in exchange for finished goods, the general favored his own countrymen; thus Northerners made fortunes in this trade while European agents made little and their people at home suffered for want of cotton to supply their mills. Nor was Butler content with discrimination in practice. His Yankee patriotism would not allow him even to treat these worthy gentlemen with respect, since they represented interests antagonistic to American prosperity. His social and business relations with them were rude, peremptory, and harsh. By the fall of 1862, Seward's best diplomatic posture could no longer stem the tide of foreign complaints and protests against "Beast" Butler's military rule. He had to be replaced.[8]

But Butler's policies and the man himself were popular in the North, not only with the business community, but with the average citizen who tended to view foreign governments and their people (who often competed with them for jobs) with suspicion. His favoritism for Americans kept New England factories open, and trade through the port of New York helped offset the rising public debt and the wartime squeeze on commodity prices. His removal must not seem like repudiation by an ungrateful administration. The solution was to send out another expedition commanded by another Massachusetts politician and composed of those elements most likely to disapprove of Butler's dismissal. Military necessity could then justify the change; the officer who had raised the expedition, General Banks, would naturally supersede Butler in command of the department when he arrived at New Orleans.[9]

Banks's instructions from the government were no clearer than those given to previous expeditions, and in one respect they were worse. Whereas Sherman and Du Pont suffered from the lack of specific objectives at the outset, Banks was confronted with a plethora of military targets with no distinction made as to their importance. He would presumably not try to take Port Hudson, Mobile, and points on the Texas coast simultaneously, but nothing in his instructions indicated otherwise; nor was it mentioned that the sequence in which they were attempted might influence the result. Banks was left to decide these important strategic questions for himself.[10]

Butler was not the only source of government dissatisfaction. The deterioriating military situation in Tennessee and north Mississippi worried the president. We have seen that Halleck's refusal to detach troops from Corinth for a combined attack on Vicksburg in June allowed the Confederates to transfer most of their western army to Chattanooga for an offensive into Kentucky. Failure to take Mobile in accordance with McClellan's plan left Bragg free to use the rail junction at this city to move his army quickly and arrive in Chattanooga before the Federals divined his intentions.

Halleck's summons to Washington to become general-in-chief in mid-July did little to improve the situation. His promotion left Grant in charge of a truncated western department including the Armies of the Mississippi and the Tennessee. Characteristically, Halleck left no orders except the defensive command to guard the railroads leading into Corinth. There was not a written instruction, nor apparently a verbal order, about Vicksburg or cooperation with the Navy on the Mississippi.

The government at this time shared Halleck's rather low opinion of Grant both as a department administrator and a field commander. Except for Forts Henry and Donelson which, thanks to Fox, were credited to the Navy, Grant's record did not look promising. His repulse at Belmont was not forgotten, nor had Halleck, for all his protestations to the contrary, really forgiven him for following Buell to Nashville in February against orders. During the Corinth campaign, Grant was denied field command, acting as a superfluous second-in-command.[11]

Lincoln's dissatisfaction with Grant increased at the end of summer when Major General John A. McClernand appeared in Washington. A former Congressman from Lincoln's home state of Illinois, McClernand was nursing a grudge against Grant. He thought he had received insufficient credit for his part in the Donelson operation in which he had commanded one of Grant's divisions. He also blamed Grant for reducing his command at Corinth from a full corps to the divisional reserve, although the assignment had been determined solely by Halleck, who intensely disliked political generals and limited their scope of action as much as possible.

Personal motives aside, McClernand's political sense told him that the voters in Illinois and other northwestern states were disgusted with the slow progress of the war and especially with the government's seeming lack of urgency about opening the Mississippi. He warned the president that another winter must not pass before this great highway was again open to commerce. The railroads to eastern seaports were inadequate to carry western bulk produce, and spiralling freight rates were bankrupting the West.[12] With a congressional election looming in November, the voter's demands clearly would not wait upon more favorable military developments. If existing Northern armies were unavailable, the westerners might cheerfully enlist for an expedition specifically designed to take Vicksburg.

Lincoln was enthusiastic. It did not really matter where the soldiers came from; the North needed larger field armies. Since the Navy could not help Buell against Chattanooga anyway, it might as well support a different army operating down the Mississippi from Cairo. And so still another expedition was organized primarily for political reasons. Following the now familiar pattern, McClernand, having raised the army, was appointed to command it.[13]

The Navy attempted to prepare for its role in the new campaign. Large orders for double- and single-turretted ironclad gunboats, steamers, towboats, and other river craft were placed with the contractors at St. Louis and Pittsburgh. A special amphibious raiding force called the Mississippi Marine Brigade was organized around the Ram Fleet, commanded by the indomitable Alfred Ellet. This unit comprised eight hundred troops equipped with their own transports, cavalry, and mobile artillery. The unit was specifically designed to keep open the navigation of the Mississippi and its tributaries during the campaign by dispersing roving bands of Confederate artillerists and sharpshooters (wrongly called "guerrillas") and

Major General John A.
McClernand
(*Library of Congress*)

Major General William T.
Sherman
(*National Archives*)

breaking up their camps. Captain David D. Porter, promoted to acting rear admiral, replaced the more cautious but intellectually superior Flag Officer Davis as chief of the Mississippi Squadron which was finally transferred from the War Department to the Navy Department. Porter, who disliked West Pointers because of their supposed facility for stealing the glory from the sailors, was anxious to cooperate with McClernand.[14]

Before leaving for the West in early October, McClernand met Porter in Washington and worked out a rough plan. Under cover of a large gunboat squadron which was expected to silence any batteries the expedition might encounter, 60,000 troops would ascend the Yazoo River above Vicksburg, land at Drumgould's Bluff, and march on Jackson, Mississippi in conjunction with Banks's expedition which would open the railroad from New Orleans to that point.[15] McClernand's emphasis on seizing the rail junction at Jackson as the primary object, instead of first opening the Mississippi to Northern commerce by a direct attack on Vicksburg, is reminiscent of McClellan's grand strategy. Indeed, McClernand recommended

that Lincoln adopt much the same overall plan for defeating
the Confederacy. Local political considerations were important but should not be allowed to dilute or preclude a concerted invasion of the South:

> Experience has proven that a border warfare will not serve
> to extinguish the rebellion, and that the dispersion of our
> troops along exterior lines must continue to invite guerrilla
> raids and attacks by the enemy in overwhelming numbers.
> Five hundred thousand armed rebels now in the field, and
> inspired by confidence, cannot be conquered by such mode
> of warfare. It must and can only be done by destroying the
> enemy's railroad communications, cutting him off from his
> sources of supplies, and by invasion war and interior at-
> tacks upon his vital points.[16]

No sooner had Lincoln approved McClernand's plan, however, than Grant and Halleck began maneuvering to circum-
vent the politician-general. Learning in mid-October that Porter was at Cairo, Grant and his senior divisional commander,
Major General William T. Sherman, hurried north to confer
with the new admiral. Here Grant first heard of McClernand's
expedition and that the general was even then in Springfield
enrolling troops. There was no time to lose; Sherman would
have to take 40,000 men directly against Vicksburg by water
before McClernand was ready.[17] This was a large order. The
boats which the Navy Department had contracted for in September would not be ready for several months.

As though the situation was not confusing enough, Halleck's
thinking was at cross-purposes. His contempt for non-profes-
sionals like McClernand far outweighed his bad opinion of
Grant. On 10 and 11 November, he called Grant's attention to
Vicksburg, remarking that the administration still considered
the place important, although he, Halleck, did not care especially about it, and told Grant he could do what he liked with
his army. Despite his added assurance that all troops, including
McClernand's, operating in Grant's department would come
under his authority, Halleck implied that if Grant did not take
Vicksburg quickly, someone else would.[18]

However, Grant's proposed operations threatened to compromise what Halleck regarded as a more important object; the

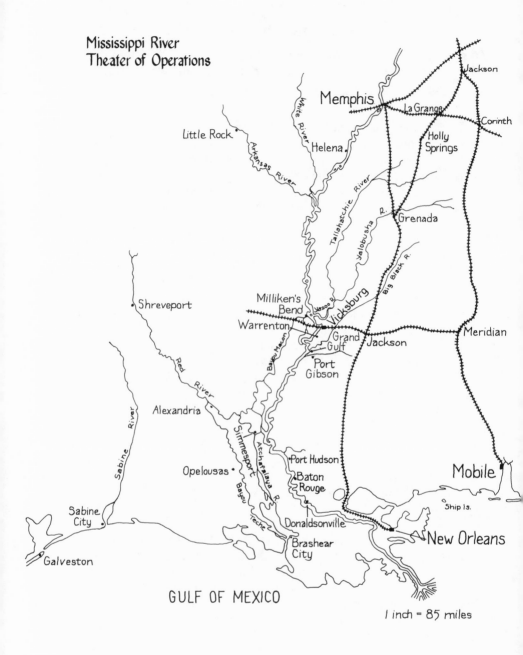

Mississippi River
Theater of Operations

Jackson

Memphis
La Grange
Corinth

Little Rock
Helena
Holly
Springs

White River

Arkansas River

Tallahatchie River

Yalobusha R.

Grenada

Big Black R.

Shreveport
Milliken's
Bend
Vicksburg
Warrenton
Grand
Gulf
Jackson
Meridian
Port
Gibson

Bayou Macon

Red River

Sabine River

Alexandria

Simmesport

Atchafalaya R.

Opelousas
Port Hudson
Baton
Rouge

Bayou Teche

Mobile

Sabine
City
Donaldsonville
Ship Is.

Galveston
Brashear
City
New Orleans

GULF OF MEXICO

1 inch = 85 miles

occupation of Arkansas and Missouri. The general-in-chief's curious preoccupation with the geographical area of his old St. Louis department persisted until the end of the war. He was truly a "Western" general—so far west that the center of his strategic thought bore no relation to the heart of the enemy's power. Located at the periphery of the Confederacy, Arkansas and Missouri were poor frontier regions of bad roads and scattered farms, producing nothing essential to either side. Yet Halleck's excessive concern with this region was shared by the president—not because Lincoln preferred operations in Arkansas and Missouri, but because, to his unmilitary mind, a blow anywhere seemed bound to hurt the enemy.

Halleck's myopia regarding his old department produced some unfortunate results. We have already seen the pernicious effect of his decision to reinforce General Curtis instead of sending the troops to cooperate with Farragut against Vicksburg in June. In August he ordered Curtis to take the Arkansas capital, Little Rock, in cooperation with Davis's flotilla. To Curtis' objection that the Mississippi River, including Vicksburg, had to be taken before he could operate in Arkansas and Missouri, Halleck replied that a different expedition was being sent against Vicksburg and that Curtis should go to Little Rock anyway.[19] Grant's September plan for employing Curtis' force on the Mississippi was intended to prevent it being ordered off in the opposite direction while the enemy was left free to concentrate against his own army on the Yazoo. By the time Grant saw Porter and learned of McClernand's expedition, Curtis had sent half of his command at Helena back to Missouri. Grant was thereupon required to detach a large corps under Sherman to operate against Vicksburg by the river line if the place was to be taken quickly.[20]

Grant's new plan was also designed to cover Corinth, against which the Confederates appeared to be massing a large force. While Sherman and Porter threatened Vicksburg from the water, Grant's other two corps (60,000 men) would push down the Mississippi Central Raidroad through Holly Springs to Grenada. He expected to encounter the western Confederate army, then concentrated under Lieutenant General John C. Pemberton at Jackson, Mississippi before reaching his objective. Once this army was defeated, the Confederates would

evacuate Vicksburg. In any case, the place would fall easily
to an attack from the rear.[21]

This was the proper line of advance for Grant's army and,
with adequate attention to his communications, he would undoubtedly have driven the enemy from Vicksburg without a
tedious eight-month campaign and an expensive siege. The
move looked even more promising when, on 3 November,
Halleck again changed his mind about Arkansas, ordering
Curtis to return to Helena for a cooperative expedition across
the Mississippi on Grenada. Sherman's corps, no longer needed
on the river, was at once added to the main army for the overland movement.[22]

The main advance got off to a good start. On 29 November
Grant's army occupied Holly Springs. By 1 December it had
reached the Tallahatchie, the first of several river lines between Grand Junction (on the Memphis and Charleston Railroad) and Jackson; this forced Pemberton to withdraw south
of the Yalobusha. But progress beyond the Yalobusha would
not be easy, even if the Confederate army continued to retire
without a battle. This region of Mississippi was poor and
another river line—the Big Black—lay between Grant and his
final objective. The enemy cavalry was very active and the
Union advance depended upon one 180-mile-long single-track
railroad. Anticipating logistical problems, Grant decided to
play it safe by reviving the original plan for opening an alternate line of supply via the Yazoo River, especially since Curtis'
expedition had sustained a repulse before reaching Grenada.
Admiral Porter was anxious to destroy the Confederate ironclads building up the Yazoo, so a combined operation in that
direction would have enthusiastic naval support. Consequently,
General Sherman with a corps-strength force was again detached and ordered to proceed down the Mississippi from
Memphis, ascend the Yazoo, and unite with Grant's army on
the railroad where it crossed the Big Black. No direct assault
on Vicksburg or its water defenses was intended or prepared
for.[23]

While it must be acknowledged that Grant was sometimes
careless about his communications, the detachment of Sherman's corps weakened the main army to a degree which

invited counterattack. On 19 December, the same day the Yazoo expedition embarked at Memphis, Major General Nathan B. Forrest's Confederate cavalry division struck the Mississippi Central around Jackson, Tennessee, tearing up the track for sixty miles north toward Columbus, Kentucky. The following day, General Van Dorn, having circled around Grant's left with another large cavalry force, fell upon the main Federal advanced depot at Holly Springs, capturing the 1500-man garrison and burning millions of dollars worth of vital stores. Grant was thus compelled to retire to La Grange on the Memphis and Charleston road. After receiving the engineer reports of severe damage to the line from Columbus which estimated several weeks for repairs, he decided to give up the land movement altogether. Besides, he had learned from Halleck on the 18th that McClernand was finally ready to leave Illinois.[24]

The general-in-chief had done his best to keep McClernand away from Vicksburg. All of the troops assembled at Springfield with their transports had been sent down river and absorbed by Sherman's corps. Several times in early December the puzzled McClernand wired Halleck explaining that he had not received orders for his expedition. He got no reply. On the 17th he complained to Stanton and was told that the government assumed Halleck had issued the appropriate order some time before. He also wired the president direct. Lincoln was furious and compelled Halleck to send McClernand's authorization the following day. Halleck did not do what the president had in mind, however. Instead of giving McClernand charge of the river expedition as Lincoln had intended, Halleck permitted him to command only in Grant's absence. And because he would be operating in Grant's department, McClernand in any case had to obey Grant's orders. To dilute McClernand's authority further, the general-in-chief directed that Grant's army be officially divided into four corps with Sherman in command of the best units of his old corps, leaving McClernand with scarcely 20,000 green troops.[25]

The Yazoo River expedition ran into trouble before it had fairly begun. On 12 December, anticipating Sherman's arrival, Admiral Porter sent four ironclads plus the *Queen of the West* on a reconnaissance up that river. This force was unpleasantly surprised by the thoroughness of the enemy preparations.

Just above Vicksburg where the Mississippi swings sharply south and the high ridge upon which the town is built extends away from the river to the northeast paralleling the lower Yazoo, the Confederates had emplaced heavy batteries affording flank protection for the main fortress and closing the Yazoo to the Federal Navy. The most formidable guns—8- and 10-inch seacoast cannon and 7-inch rifles—were clustered in separate redoubts upon two prominent hills, called Drumgould's (or Synder's) and Haynes's Bluffs, about twenty miles from the river mouth. Vessels proceeding upstream must approach these bluffs head on, exposing themselves to a raking crossfire. Moreover, the configuration of the river prevented the ships from shooting at long range while, at close quarters, their guns could not be elevated enough to bear on the batteries.[26]

The Federal squadron made little progress. Booms and heavy rafts obstructed the narrow channel. Armed guerrillas at-

USS *Cairo* (*Library of Congress*)

tempted to board the vessels and sharpshooters picked off the pilots. The new ironclad USS *Cairo* ran upon a mine and sank. Shocked, Porter withdrew the remaining ships.[27]

It will be recalled that neither Grant nor Sherman envisaged a frontal attack on any of the river defenses, relying on Porter's overconfident assertion that the Navy could land troops somewhere in their rear. Now, in view of what had happened to the squadron, embarking Sherman's force high up on the east bank according to plan was clearly impossible unless the channel could be kept clear of mines and other obstacles; and the mines could only be removed if the batteries were silenced. Since the Navy could not accomplish this by bombardment, the Army had to take them by assault.

Sherman should have called off the whole operation, especially after inspecting the Yazoo defenses on the 26th. The ground between the river and the ridge was almost impassable. Numerous small bayous and creeks intersecting boggy ground restricted attacking infantry to two or three narrow approach corridors, the debouches of which were enfiladed by rifle pits and commanded in front by heavy cannon.[28] But the stubborn general would not give up. That evening he disembarked his corps, now swollen to the size of a small army, below the batteries.

Preparations for an attack were already under way when he learned on the 25th that McClernand had left Cairo on his way down to take command of the expedition. In his memoirs, Sherman denied any knowledge of McClernand before that general actually arrived in the Yazoo on 1 January; he further insisted that his sole motive for attacking such strong defenses with so little preparation was his ignorance of Grant's withdrawal north of the Tallahatchie. But it seems hardly possible that he did not know about the disaster at Holly Springs. Although the telegraph to Memphis was cut, Brigadier General T.A. Davies, commanding the Federal post at Columbus, had that information on the 20th and would surely have considered it important enough to alert Sherman by dispatch boat. Some message to this effect probably came down on the same vessel which brought the news about McClernand.[29] In any case, it is quite clear that the imminent prospect of being

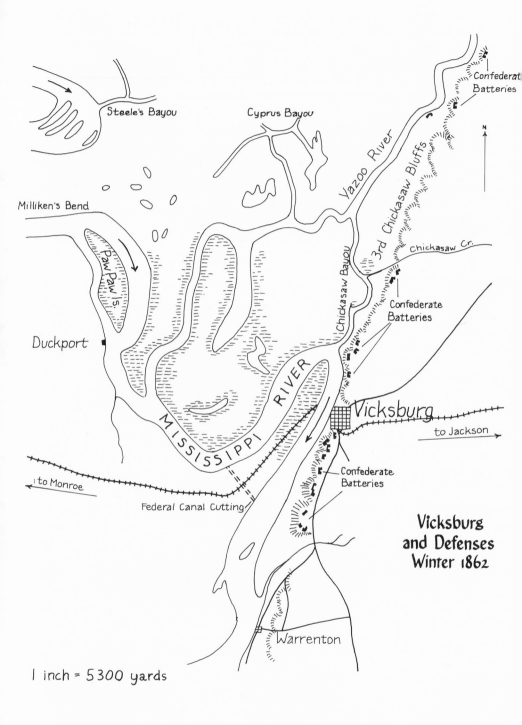

Steele's Bayou

Cyprus Bayou

Confederate Batteries

Yazoo River

Milliken's Bend

Paw Paw Is.

3rd Chickasaw Bluffs

Chicasaw Cr.

Chickasaw Bayou

Confederate Batteries

Duckport

N

Vicksburg

M I S S I S S I P P I   R I V E R

to Jackson

to Monroe

Federal Canal Cutting

Confederate Batteries

Vicksburg
and Defenses
Winter 1862

Warrenton

1 inch = 5300 yards

superseded was the catalyst for Sherman's final decision to assault on the 29th.

The Navy was restricted to a minor role, consisting of a "demonstration" against the batteries on Drumgould's and Haynes's Bluffs. Porter warned Sherman in advance that the ships could not hit anything on the ridge; he would not even order them to approach within range of the enemy's heavy guns for fear of losing his whole squadron.[30]

Sherman's costly and abortive frontal assault on the Yazoo batteries below Drumgould's Bluff has been meticulously examined by historians attempting to discover why it failed. Actually, there was no chance whatever for success. Despite the fact—generally thought to prove the possibility of victory —that a few men entered one of the Confederate works, the Federals could not have held it for an hour, clinging to the crest of the ridge, surrounded by the enemy, and facing large reinforcements arriving at Vicksburg by rail.[31] Because of the elevation, the Navy could provide no fire support at this point, and the nature of the ground confined the Union Army's own light artillery to the banks of the Yazoo.

It was a miserable affair altogether. Sherman's desperate bid for the glory of capturing the "Gibraltar of the West," which cost over a thousand Union casualties, only demonstrated what should have been apparent before the assault— that Vicksburg would not fall to combined operations on its northern flank.[32] When McClernand took over on 2 January, he wisely ordered the troops withdrawn to Milliken's Bend on the Mississippi. Whatever plan the new commander may have had in mind, however, was nullified by Grant's decision to employ his whole army on the river and to direct operations personally.[33]

Much has been written about Grant's "brilliant" strategic insight during the final Vicksburg campaign. Historians, although pointing out the time and effort the general wasted trying to get into the Yazoo above the batteries via the rivers and bayous to the north, claim that Porter and Grant had all along jointly intended to adopt the "correct" strategy of landing the army below the city to operate up the Big Black. Such eulogizing is extravagant as well as factually wrong. The idea of operating without communications is often described as a conception of genius, instead of the unenviable result of impulsiveness and lack of administrative skill. According to some military analysts, the whole campaign was a model of combined operations for its time.[34]

Most of these claims are nonsense. Grant had no real strategic plan for the movement which led to the siege, let alone a combined plan. Nor did anyone in the Union Navy, including Admiral Porter, formulate such a plan. If not exactly an accident, the campaign just seemed to develop in reaction to momentary contingencies and difficulties of detail. In fact, one might describe the capture of Vicksburg as the final process in a "chain reaction" of which the participants were hardly aware, and over which they exercised almost no control.

The deteriorating situation in the Gulf of Mexico caused by a series of naval "disasters" during December and January set the chain in motion. Almost from the beginning of operations on the Mississippi, the Gulf squadron had been spread too thin. Occupation of Pensacola, and of Galveston and Sabine Pass on the Texas coast in the fall, increased the danger of a setback at some point.

On the first day of the new year, Confederate General Magruder, now commanding at Houston, appeared off Galveston Island with a small cotton-clad fleet armed with field pieces and manned by infantry. Taking the Federals by surprise, he captured the island's garrison and two ships along with the naval force commander, driving away the other Federal vessels on the station and temporarily raising the blockade. Meanwhile, the Confederate raider #290 (CSS *Alabama*) ran through the Union squadron at Mobile, steamed down to Galveston, and sank the USS *Hatteras*. Another dangerous raider, the *Florida*, also escaped from this port.[35] These disasters alarmed every Federal post on the Gulf. Farragut, still at New Orleans, received frantic requests for reinforcements from Pensacola and Ship Island, along with alarmist reports that the enemy was about to descend on both naval stations. The blockading officer at Mobile, threatened with a court of inquiry, told Farragut that his crews were deficient and his ships worn out; thus, Mobile must be attacked at once.[36]

The admiral was more concerned about Texas. Magruder's "horse marines" had humiliated the Navy; "Our disaster at

Galveston," he wrote in his diary, "has thrown us back and done more injury to the Navy than all the events of the war." Galveston and Sabine Pass had to be recaptured immediately to stop the raiders and redeem the fleet's honor. Farragut attempted to go to Texas himself, but his flagship grounded on the Mississippi River bar, so the discouraged admiral returned to New Orleans.[37]

Even more frustrating was the Army's vacillation. Bound by non-specific orders to "cooperate" with Banks, Farragut could not discover just what the general intended to do, or when he intended to do it. This was not because Banks was especially secretive, but because he was not sure himself. He was receiving mixed signals; Lincoln's instructions were to operate on the Texas coast, while Halleck thought he should take Port Hudson; then again, maybe the crisis in Texas was more important. Anyway, Banks had to make his own decisions.[38]

On 17 January Farragut suggested that in view of the deteriorating naval situation outside of the river, the Army might take Port Hudson without fleet support, an idea which Banks rejected. Actually, Banks had already decided to avoid a direct attack on Port Hudson. Since the 1862 summer offensive, the Southerners had turned this town, also situated on high bluffs on the east bank of the Mississippi, into a miniature Vicksburg. Heavy batteries here were designed to prevent the passage of Federal warships and transports, thus keeping open Confederate water communications with Vicksburg via the Red River and the Mississippi above the town.[39]

In view of recent enemy aggression in the Gulf, Banks was worried about losing New Orleans. To guard against an attack from Texas, he sent General Weitzel in mid-January up Bayou Teche to clear out the lower Louisiana country west of the Mississippi. As a result of this movement, Weitzel conceived the idea of bypassing the Port Hudson batteries. Using Berwick Bay instead of New Orleans as a base, a combined force should push north along the Atchafalaya River and Bayou Teche into the Red River. Because the Confederate water supply route from west of the Mississippi to Vicksburg and Port Hudson crossed this line, he thought that Union control of the Atchafalaya and the Red would render both strongpoints "a cipher" to the Confederacy.[40]

Banks liked this plan; it avoided a head-on collision with strong works and seemed to serve two purposes at once. Having reduced Port Hudson to a "cipher," he could use the Atchafalaya and the Red River country as staging areas for his projected advance into Texas. This would please both Lincoln and Halleck.[41]

Since naval support was essential for the push to the Red River, Farragut was consulted about the plan. While anxious to proceed with any combined operation immediately so he could return to look after affairs in the Gulf, the admiral foresaw serious problems overcoming the enemy batteries recently erected on the Atchafalaya and adjacent bayous. His shallow-draft boats—the only vessels which could navigate these waterways—were deficient in firepower. Consequently, Farragut proposed sending an ironclad from Porter's squadron above Vicksburg into the Red River to take these defenses in reverse.[42]

This feature overcomplicated the plan because it involved cooperation from the upper flotilla not under Farragut's command. And most of Porter's vessels were fully occupied in trying to find a route into the Yazoo for Grant's army. Nevertheless, expecting Porter to comply with the request for an ironclad, Banks and Farragut decided to proceed with the movement.

By the time the request reached Porter, one of his vessels was already below Vicksburg. Colonel C. R. Ellet, Alfred Ellet's intrepid nephew commanding the *Queen of the West*, was spoiling for a fight. Spotting the steamer CSS *City of Vicksburg* at anchor under the batteries, he ran down through a hail of shells on 2 February. Having damaged his unprepared victim, Ellet continued on into the Red River, burning several small cargo boats and capturing large supplies of hogs, corn, and salt en route to Port Hudson.

Finding his coal exhausted, he returned up river, anchoring just above the Warrenton batteries opposite Vicksburg on the 8th. There he learned of Farragut's request for assistance to Banks, and that Porter was sending the new ironclad USS *Indianola*, Captain George Brown, in support. Too impatient to wait for Brown, Ellet at once steamed down to the Atchafalaya, landed his marines, and destroyed several camps. On the

14th, while collecting cotton in Red River, the *Queen* ran aground, could not be got off, and was abandoned to the Confederates, who put a crew aboard her and towed her off the shoal.[43]

Meanwhile, the *Indianola* had passed the Vicksburg batteries on the 13th. Because of the great difficulty getting coal into this section of the river, the ironclad was towing two coal barges to enable Brown to remain for a month on blockade at the mouth of the Red River. However, on the 24th, he returned upstream to communicate with Porter and unload some captured cotton. Just below the Warrenton batteries, he was set upon by the *Queen of the West*, now in enemy hands, and her consorts, the fast Confederate armed steamers *Beatty* and *William H. Webb*. Failing either to cut loose the barges or to head downstream, the *Indianola* was quickly rendered *hors de combat*; she was rammed, received a few shots through her unarmored stern, and was run upon the west bank and surrendered, to be destroyed by the Southerners the following day.[44]

Thus, within three weeks of the start of the upriver offensive, the U.S. Navy had again lost control of the stretch of water between Vicksburg and Port Hudson, and the enemy's Red River communications were open. The capture of the *Queen* and the *Indianola* greatly distressed Secretary Welles. Aside from the bad publicity, he agreed that Farragut's presence was urgently needed in the Gulf to shore up the blockade and to prevent more depredations by Confederate commerce raiders. Porter had to send down other ironclads to replace *Indianola*.[45]

But the question of running other vessels below Vicksburg had wide implications which neither Farragut nor the Navy Department appreciated. Porter was aware of the risk when he sent down the *Indianola*, unsupported by other ironclads. In fact, he could send no more boats without taking his whole squadron below Vicksburg permanently where it could not be maintained unless the Army opened communications via the west bank, bypassing the batteries. The *Indianola* was the only vessel in Porter's command that could make more than two knots against the current. Crawling upstream, the others would be sitting targets for the Confederate guns at Grand

Gulf and Warrenton. And even though barges could sometimes be towed through the canal which the Army had finally opened across the neck opposite Vicksburg, the gunboats must still ascend above Warrenton for coal.[46]

The Army might have solved this problem by operating below the town, taking the batteries by combined assault; but this involved a complete change of plan to a new line that Grant was not yet prepared to adopt. He was still determined to get into the Yazoo through the back door or, failing this, to replay Sherman's direct attack on the Yazoo batteries with a larger force. The breakup of his depot at Holly Springs made the general more cautious about his supplies. Army communications north of Vicksburg were easy and secure; south of the town, they would be difficult or impossible to establish, and hard to keep secure. Nor could the Army's heavy artillery with sufficient ammunition be brought below for use against the city should a siege prove necessary. No, such a change of base was a maneuver of desperation, and Grant would have none of it.

Nor was the admiral especially anxious to risk further defeat. Even before the vessels were lost, he was reluctant to consider any proposal for operating below Vicksburg.[47] On the 6th Assistant Secretary Fox had urged Porter to dig a more practical canal which would enable his squadron and Grant's army to go down and capture Port Hudson. If Vicksburg could not be taken except by siege, Porter had better let it alone. "The country can not stand it [a siege] at home or abroad," he remarked; "The President is of my opinion, that you better cut through farther back [upstream] and do it at once."[48]

The next day, Porter outlined the Navy's problem at Vicksburg to Welles. The city's fortifications were unlike other Confederate defenses encountered by Federal gunboats thus far in the war. There were no low-lying water batteries. Instead, all the river guns had been placed back from the water on top of the ridge to deliver plunging fire which even ironclads could not withstand. Such defenses would only fall to a large army investing the place from the land side. True, the Navy could destroy the city itself by mortar bombardment, but its defenses would remain intact. As for descending the river, it was too hazardous at that time. "My main object," he ex-

as in his judgment may seem best — but
I expect all to go by, who are able, and I think
the best protection against the enemy's fire,
is a well directed fire from our own Guns,
Shell and Shrapnel at a distance, and
Grape when within 4 or 500 Yards —

D. G. Farragut
Rear Admiral

Diagram of Port Hudson

Facsimile page of Farragut's operation order, March 1863, for
the passage of Port Hudson.

plained, "is to meet with no defeats, and I shall undertake nothing where there is no chance of success. A defeat of the Navy on this river would be considered a calamity."[49] Now that the calamity had actually occurred, Porter was even less willing to risk his remaining ships.

Porter's refusal to send any ironclads below Vicksburg prompted Farragut to take the initiative in this direction himself. Although still impatient to return to the Gulf, the admiral was becoming more alarmed about Union morale on the river. The recent reverses and false enemy reports of their strength, he told Fox, had produced a conviction of defeat. Something must be done to recover the initiative. Since the Navy could not cooperate with Banks until heavily armed vessels could get into the Red River, Farragut asked the general's support in running his squadron past Port Hudson. Once above, the first object would be to reduce the batteries at Warrenton which were shooting up Federal supply ships. Then, after cleaning out the Mississippi between Vicksburg and Port Hudson, his squadron would join Banks's army for operations on the Red.[50]

To distract enemy attention from the ships during the run-by, the troops were to land on the eastern shore just south of the town. Although Banks claimed that only a demonstration in favor of the Navy—a kind of reverse combined operation—was planned or prepared for, he missed a fleeting opportunity to take the town by coup de main. Reconnaissance parties had discovered an unguarded road leading from a good beach, itself undefended and screened from enemy view, to a point just eight miles distant in the left rear of the Confederate works. Even without Weitzel's force which was left on the Atchafalaya, the Federals had 15,000 men for the land attack, facing a garrison of six thousand. The general did not know the enemy's weakness, however, supposing from deserters' reports that there were 30,000 in the town.[51]

On 14 March the Union soldiers landed and occupied several points on the road without opposition. Here they remained that night when Farragut's squadron attempted to pass the batteries; their inactivity failed even to constitute a diversion.

Ignoring the supine troops, the Confederates made an all-out effort to stop the ships. The glare of bonfires projected by huge metal reflectors into the water, diffused amid clouds of gunsmoke, confounded the Union pilots trying to negotiate the treacherous bend in the river directly beneath the heaviest batteries. The flagship *Hartford*, in the van lashed to a wooden sidewheel gunboat, managed to get past with minor damage. After the Confederates found the range, the others were not so lucky. The USS *Richmond*, with another gunboat attached, was shot through the steam pipe causing the ship to lose way and fall back down the river. The gunboat *Monongahela* grounded on a shoal for twenty-five minutes; attempts to back her out overheated the forward engine and she too lost way in the current, drifting out of action. The final ship in line, the USS *Mississippi*, stuck fast on this same shoal while rounding the turn beneath the upper batteries, and was set on fire by her crew.[52]

Next morning, the admiral found himself alone above the batteries with the flagship and one gunboat. This situation called for a reversion to the old plan. Porter was again urged to send down some ironclads; again he refused. Somewhat disheartened by his losing contest with the Port Hudson batteries and by Porter's failure to cooperate, Farragut decided to go up to Vicksburg himself.

On the 22nd he sent Grant a message informing him that the Confederates were strengthening the Warrenton fort and suggesting that he send down some troops "to make a little expedition over that way to destroy it." Although Grant accepted the offer of naval assistance and agreed to send two regiments, he specified that the troops must return to their camp opposite Vicksburg after destroying these works.[53] Grant still had no intention of moving any part of his army permanently below Vicksburg. By the 22nd it had become obvious that the outflanking moves through the bayous had failed. In his mind, there was only one recourse—a full scale assault on Haynes's Bluff. He expected to lose a large percentage of his 60,000-man army but felt he had no choice other than to give up the campaign altogether, which, in view of political pressure, was unthinkable.[54]

Admiral Porter did not like this idea. Grant would doubtless ask for naval support for his *grand melée* in the Yazoo. The prospect of getting shot up for a second time by an enemy whom he could not damage was unappealing. Instead, the Army should return to its old line, marching 150,000 men from Memphis via Grenada on Jackson. Meanwhile, Farragut could cut off supplies to Vicksburg by the river. Porter did not envisage any role for himself in such operations. "As to any harm the gunboats can do Vicksburg," he wrote Welles confidentially on the 26th, "it is not to be taken into consideration at all. The batteries at that place could destroy four times the number we have here and not receive any damage in return."[55]

Thus far, although there was no coordination, there had been little friction among the various commands on the Mississippi. While the two armies with their cooperating squadrons remained separated by the enemy, no quarrels could develop. When Farragut appeared below Warrenton, however, and attempted to cooperate with Grant, the touchy Porter was displeased, especially since Farragut was his senior and had already earned a national reputation by capturing New Orleans. As in the case of McClernand, professional jealousy won out over military sense.

A minor incident was enough to touch off an argument, causing Farragut to cancel the planned attack on Warrenton and return down river. In view of impending operations below, the admiral was even more anxious to get vessels from Porter. His request came to the attention of General Ellet who was, as usual, ready for any dangerous enterprise. Deciding to run the rams *Lancaster* and *Switzerland* past the Vicksburg batteries to join Farragut, Ellet asked Captain Henry Walke, commanding the upper squadron in Porter's absence, for a gunboat to support the movement. Walke indignantly refused. Ellet had no right to make such a decision or ask for vessels. The naval officers disliked these upstart engineers with their civilian crews and their independent attitude. Nor could Ellet himself forget that, until very recently, his marine brigade had been under the War Department. In fact, he had never officially reported to Admiral Porter and still corresponded directly with the secretary of War.[56]

Determined to act in any case, Ellet ignored these petty protestations and sent the rams by themselves on the 25th. Since the danger of running aground was greater than the chance of being sunk, the vessels passed the batteries in full daylight. The *Lancaster* did not make it. A shell through the steam drum was followed by a large plunging shot which crushed in the stern, cracking the hull, and the old boat sank almost immediately. Although the *Switzerland* received a shot through the boiler, stopping her engines, she drifted down to join Farragut below Warrenton.

Walke was not slow in reporting the incident to Porter who was disgusted with Ellet for his rashness and presumption, and angry with Farragut for interfering with his command. The result was a paper controversy that was never entirely resolved so far as Ellet and Porter were concerned, and which produced a small furor and some bitterness between the War and Navy Departments.[57] Farragut was prepared to take the blame for the sake of getting on with the war, but the fuss induced him to abandon the proposed combined assault on Warrenton in favor of operations with Banks in the Red, suggesting to Porter that this river should constitute the boundary between their respective commands.[58]

Despite Farragut's withdrawal, and because the Yazoo expeditions had failed, Grant thought the operations at Warrenton and Grand Gulf should be carried out. But first, he wanted another look at the Yazoo batteries. Success here would crack the defenses open in the shortest time. Slogging through seemingly endless swamps was demoralizing to the men, and they were beginning to lose confidence in their officers. The government was impatient with army moves to outflank Vicksburg, and the Navy Department was pressing Farragut to return his squadron to the Gulf.[59]

A reconnaissance settled the matter. On 1 April Grant, Sherman, and Porter steamed up the Yazoo aboard the new United States broadside ironclad *Tuscumbia*. It was not an entirely pleasant trip. Although the ship approached within range, the Haynes' Bluff batteries remained silent. Hoping to provoke a response, the *Tuscumbia* opened on the works. Five shots had been fired when the starboard gun deck collapsed. Disgusted, Porter withdrew from the river. [60]

But the generals had seen enough. As a result of the reconnaissance, Grant was "satisfied that an attack upon Haynes' Bluff would be attended with immense sacrifice of life, if not with defeat." Instead, a detachment would proceed from Mil-

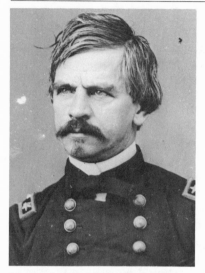 

Major General Nathaniel P.   Rear Admiral David D. Porter
Banks (*Library of Congress*)   (*Library of Congress*)

liken's Bend to hold New Carthage prior to the transfer of one
corps to this point to dispose of the batteries at Grand Gulf in
cooperation with the Navy. After opening a supply route
through the bayous paralleling the west bank, Grant would
concentrate the whole army below.[61]

Porter was at last compelled to agree. On the 6th he received
imperative instructions from the Navy Department to go down
river and relieve Farragut, who was ordered to get up an expedition against Mobile. Welles was very worried about the
Confederate ironclads building at that port. After Du Pont's attack on Charleston, expected to come off any day, the monitors
would be sent to the Gulf and Farragut must be ready to use
them against the Mobile forts at once.[62] Fox was afraid that
Buchanan, anticipating the U.S. Navy, might run out and sink
the blockaders. This would look terrible in the newspapers.
"The people will have nothing but success," he warned Porter,
"and they are right."[63]

No one was especially happy with the new line of operations. Porter wrote Fox confidentially on the 25th: "I am
quite depressed with this adventure, which you know never

met with my approval—still urged by the Army on one side, the President's wishes and hints of the Secretary that it was most necessary, I had to come." Sherman considered it far too risky, doubted that a supply route through tortuous bayous and over mud roads was practicable for a large army, and thought Grant should resume the old land approach through Grenada and Jackson.[64]

Nor was Grant certain what he intended doing once the Army was below Vicksburg. Because the vessels were ordered to go, the troops went also since they could accomplish nothing above without the squadron. Porter thought they might assault Grand Gulf and, using this as a base, attack the southern end of the Vicksburg defenses, only 45 miles distant by a good road. Grant rejected this suggestion because it would place his army between two enemy strongpoints. He preferred, after occupying Grand Gulf, to send McClernand's corps with the squadron to join Banks in reducing Port Hudson, after which Banks's force would unite with Grant's against Vicksburg.[65]

General Banks was not informed about this change in plan. One very important obstacle to concerted action between separate commands on the Mississippi was the difficulty of communication. Because there was no telegraph to New Orleans, the government could only contact Banks and Farragut by sea or via the Memphis wire from Cairo, using couriers to bring messages down river through enemy country. It took at least two weeks for Banks and Grant to receive each other's messages unless dispatch boats were available, which reduced the time to two or three days. According to the last information received through Farragut (dated 23 March but not delivered until 10 April), Grant intended to send 20,000 men via Lake Providence and Bayou Macon to join him in the Red River.[66] In order to prepare properly for such a large-scale offensive against Port Hudson, Banks was required to undertake some seemingly unrelated preliminary expeditions, which were actually essential to the main movement.

Federal occupation of New Orleans and the various probing expeditions up the Mississippi had not really "opened" the river; these movements had, in fact, only alerted the enemy to the possibility of closing navigation altogether to anything except warships. By April 1863 no Union store vessels or transports could use the Mississippi between New Orleans and Port Hudson without convoy, nor could they run above the Port Hudson batteries. Especially critical was the coal supply. Heavy barges towed against the current were favorite targets for enemy "guerillas." Without coal, the Navy in mid-river was practically immobilized. While most of the vessels could burn wood in an emergency, this sooty material soon fouled and damaged the engines.[67]

This vital problem might have been solved, in Banks's opinion, by opening a different supply route, from New Orleans down the Atchafalaya and the Red bypassing Port Hudson and the lower Mississippi. We have previously mentioned Weitzel's expedition in that direction during the late winter. This force was again set in motion on 11 April, and by the 23rd, had gained possession of the Red River mouth and the Atchafalaya.[68]

Having progressed so well and conquered so much territory, however, Banks forgot that he was conducting a preliminary operation. Pressing Grant for the promised reinforcements, he suddenly talked about expelling the enemy from the whole of Louisiana, and announced that he was marching on Alexandria up the Red River in the opposite direction from Port Hudson. "It is of the utmost importance," he wrote Grant,

Porter's squadron passing Vicksburg, 16 April 1863.

"that you should send a force to the Red River immediately to co-operate with the Army and Navy now here. We have the Atchafalaya and the mouth of the Red River. An addition to my force now will give us the whole country west of the Mississippi." Vicksburg and Port Hudson were unimportant; they would fall automatically once their supplies from the west were cut off.[69]

From a desire to do something important Banks had, of course, confused cause and effect. The fall of Vicksburg and Port Hudson would mean, as events proved, that the Confederates would lose Louisiana—not the other way around. Shutting off supplies by the river hardly weakened Vicksburg, since almost all of its stores came in by rail from the east. Port Hudson was a better target for blockade, but even this place was supplied, with difficulty, by wagons from the New Orleans and Jackson road. In fact, the place most injured by shutting off the Red River traffic was the city of New Orleans, already in Union hands. Nevertheless, Banks was off and his expedition had Farragut's enthusiastic support. The admiral wanted some of the vessels Porter had sent below Vicksburg on 16 April; Banks thought he should come in person with his whole squadron. To Farragut's surprise, Porter was amenable to this suggestion. He had not accomplished very much in the Mississippi, and the prospect of capturing a few forts as trophies for the Navy raised his spirits.[70]

The combined assault on the Grand Gulf fortifications had gone awry through Porter's own misjudgment. Porter assured General McClernand, commanding the assault force, that his naval guns could destroy or at least silence any batteries they could hit prior to the landing; but he later found it to be impossible. After reconnoitering the works on 22 April, McClernand suggested that, instead of assaulting Grand Gulf, he should move his corps 25 miles down the west bank to a point opposite the mouth of Bayou Pierre, embark on the gunboats, and ascend this waterway to the railroad bridge, turning the position by the left. Until the defenses fell, the soldiers could subsist off the country.[71]

Grant was at first unwilling to leave the Grand Gulf fortifications in his rear. He was worried that his tenuous supply line from Milliken's Bend would be broken, especially in case of a reverse. Responding to a drop of the water level in the Mississippi, Bayou Macon and its tributaries were drying up. Unless Grand Gulf could be taken immediately, it might prove impossible to take at all. Accordingly, Grant persuaded the already overconfident admiral to attempt a close bombardment, enabling McClernand to gain a beachhead on the low ground in front of the works, in preparation for a full-scale assault.[72] Given his prior experience in the Yazoo, Porter should have known better.

The Navy attacked on the 29th. For six hours, seven gunboats engaged the upper battery at incredibly short range—at times as close as 50 yards—firing almost three thousand rounds of 9- and 11-inch explosive and shrapnel shell. This was the heaviest Union naval bombardment thus far in the war. Amazed at the result, Porter thought it "remarkable that we did not disable his [the enemy's] guns, but though we knocked the parapets pretty much to pieces, the guns were apparently uninjured." While the defenders lost only fourteen wounded, and the Federals eighteen, the vessels were badly cut up. The plating on the ill-starred *Tuscumbia*, closest to the enemy, was too thin to withstand plunging 100-pound shot at such range; much of the casemate armor was knocked off, and the ship riddled. The USS *Benton* was disabled. Although no vessels were sunk, all were extensively damaged.[73]

Another three-day operation above Vicksburg (29 April— 1 May) further revealed the Navy's powerlessness against well-constructed shore batteries. As a demonstration in favor of the attack on Grand Gulf, Sherman and Lieutenant Commander K.R. Breese, with seven gunboats, three mortar rafts, and ten regiments on transports, steamed up the Yazoo. Landing, the soldiers marched up the levee toward Haynes's Bluff while Breese bombarded the forts. The Confederates, again ignoring the troops, who made no serious attack, concentrated on the vessels. The ironclad USS *Choctaw*, struck fifty-three times, was forced to retire out of range; the others wisely remained well below the batteries. The whole affair was an impressive display that accomplished nothing.[74]

The failure of the combined attack on Grand Gulf induced Grant to adopt McClernand's suggestion for outflanking the position.[75] Leaving Sherman's corps to build supply roads

parallel to the falling bayous, he marched the rest of his army
(two corps) to a point three miles below Grand Gulf, using
the gunboats which had run past to land troops on the east
bank. His subsequent movements are well known. After maneuvering the Confederates out of Port Gibson and Grand
Gulf on 1 and 3 May, he proceeded up the Big Black and,
"cutting loose from his communications," fell upon Jackson,
compelling General Joseph Johnston's small force to evacuate
this vital point on the 14th, and shutting up Pemberton's army
in Vicksburg, where it surrendered on 4 July.

Standard accounts of this final phase of the Vicksburg campaign imply that the results were inevitable, so that we are
perhaps surprised that no one conceived this "brilliant" plan
in the first place. But even the operations which led to the
siege were not thought out in advance. Like all other moves
on the Mississippi after the collapse of McClellan's plan, they
were improvised to suit local conditions at the moment. Only
in retrospect, and from the results, can we trace the lines of
connection that *appear* to form an integrated whole.

Grant did not, of course, cut loose from his communications
intentionally—he was not that incapable—nor is it technically
true that he had no supply line after leaving the river, even
though his wagon transport proved inadequate for the size of
his force and he was required to forage somewhat off the
country.[76] Finding himself below Vicksburg, his security de-
pendent upon a naval force which could not go up again until
the city fell, unable to reduce the Grand Gulf batteries by
direct attack, he was compelled to outflank them in order to
protect his shaky communications along the west bank. He
must either do this or go down to the Red River where his
army could be supplied via the Atchafalaya. Porter fully
grasped the frightening finality of the decision to go below.
"The portion of the squadron now here," he wrote Welles on
24 April, "can not ever return above Vicksburg until that place
is taken."[77]

In fact, right up until the occupation of Port Gibson, Grant
was inclined to favor cooperation with Banks and the Navy
against Port Hudson. The move to Jackson was impulsive,
undertaken for no particular strategic purpose except a desire
to fight the enemy army wherever it could be found. In reply to

Banks's inquiry received on 10 May as to why the reinforcements did not join him as promised, Grant explained that he had intended to send them, but "meeting the enemy . . . as I did, south of Port Gibson, I followed him to the Big Black, and could not afford to retrace my steps."[78]

Having "burned his bridges," Grant felt it was imperative that the army reach the Yazoo to gain a broad, safe line of supply. His wagon route west of the river was not fully established and might never become practicable for bulk stores. In any case, it was vulnerable to attack.[79] That the Confederates chose to attempt a countermove against Banks's communications instead of his was a stroke of good fortune.

On 12 May Banks received Grant's message that his army was moving up the Big Black and could spare no men for the attack on Port Hudson. Grant, on the contrary, now urged Banks to join him, or at least send reinforcements. Pleading insufficient transport, Banks rejected this suggestion, even though his initial instructions had authorized him to command the whole if the two armies operated together in either department. In view of Halleck's previous machinations against political generals, perhaps Banks was wise to stay away from Vicksburg. Anyway, the capture of Shreveport would give Lincoln the victory so badly needed to shore up sagging morale in the North.[80]

By the 19th even the general-in-chief could not persuade him that Vicksburg was more important. Having discovered that Grant had moved to Jackson and Banks to Alexandria, in opposite directions away from the Mississippi, Halleck told Banks that he did not approve. These "eccentric" operations would both fail. Unless all Federal forces were concentrated east of the river against Vicksburg, Grant would be defeated. No help from the Navy should be looked for, because their river gunboats were useless against land batteries. "I have strongly urged the Navy Department to send the monitors to the Mississippi River," he complained, "but I am answered that they can do nothing against Vicksburg and Port Hudson."[81]

Halleck's admonition about "eccentric" operations, repeated with greater force on the 23rd, might have carried more weight had he not succumbed to the same temptation himself. It seemed that only the general-in-chief's pet projects were exempt from the strategic requirement to concentrate against one objective at a time. On 18 May Halleck informed the naval officer commanding at Cairo that an expedition would be sent up the Arkansas River, and demanded cooperation. Fortunately, this project was postponed until Vicksburg was taken.[82] In any case, Banks, who had been confounded in his intention to seize Shreveport by a sudden drop in the Red River above Alexandria which immobilized Porter's cooperating flotilla, finally contented himself with reducing Port Hudson. Finding, like Grant at Vicksburg, that assaulting strong works only produced large casualties and that the Navy's firepower was insufficient to soften up the defenses, he was also required to take his objective by siege. Unlike Grant, he was pressed for time.

The great delay in deciding upon definite operational plans very nearly allowed the Confederates to strike a blow which might have changed the course of the war. On 20 May General Kirby Smith, now commanding the Trans-Mississippi Department, ordered Major General Richard Taylor, commanding Southern forces in Louisiana and Arkansas, to break up Grant's unprotected communications from Milliken's Bend to New Carthage. Discovering that Grant had shifted his main supply line to the Yazoo—opened by the junction of Sherman's Corps and the naval forces at Drumgould's Bluff on the 18th—Taylor determined to stop Banks's offensive against Port Hudson.[83]

Repossessing all of the Red River so recently conquered and abandoned by the Federals, the Confederates moved up the Atchafalaya. By 3 June they had captured Brashear City, and appeared at Simmesport above Port Hudson. The Union Navy quickly felt their presence; no coal now reached the lower squadron except for small quantities Porter could spare, floated down past the "guerrilla" camp opposite Bayou Sara.[84] Lieutenant George Perkins, assigned to patrol the lower Mississippi, described the situation in a disconsolate letter to his family on the 4th. "The rebels," he lamented, "are now doing pretty much as they please everywhere. They come and go freely, in and out of New Orleans, and all our affairs are in a confused and disorganized state."[85]

Taylor did not stop at Brashear City. He and Kirby Smith planned to recapture New Orleans. Although the Confederate force was very small (about 3,000 men in two columns), the Federals had left the city nearly empty of soldiers to bring the maximum strength against Port Hudson, and the heavily secessionist population was anxious to expel the invaders. With the city in Southern hands, Smith could send reinforcements from Texas to hold it.[86]

On 28 June, the Confederates attacked Donaldsonville, only sixty miles above New Orleans, but their force was too small and was temporarily driven off by a Union gunboat. The occupation of this place would have completely broken Banks's communications, compelling him to raise the siege of Port Hudson or else lose New Orleans. By the time Taylor had assembled a larger force, however, and renewed the attack on 12 July, Vicksburg and Port Hudson had surrendered. Before commencing the two-day engagement, Taylor knew his chance was gone. Even if he took the place—now reinforced from above—and New Orleans, he wrote Smith, it could not be held with the river open to the Federals from Cairo. The movement was begun too late.[87]

Although successful in the end, at least insofar as taking Vicksburg and Port Hudson, the second Mississippi River campaign was plagued by the same problems, writ large, which characterized the first. The various combined operations undertaken in this theater were not tied to any particular strategic plan, or integrated with one another. Peripheral political and economic considerations were again allowed to interfere with military aims.

One of the worst problems—too many independent commanders, both naval and military—was compounded by the personal peculiarities and prejudices of the individuals involved. Halleck's opinion regarding the uselessness of the Navy, and thus of combined operations, was only one of these prejudices. His preoccupation with a secondary theater of war, Arkansas and Missouri, was another.

More destructive to Federal strategic planning was his concept of the function of the general-in-chief. Whereas McClellan had adopted a modern approach, taking upon himself in the absence of an Army chief of staff the responsibility for strategic plans and their implementation, Halleck contented himself with the role of "adjutant," simply reporting the government's inconsistent and often contradictory proposals to the field commanders, rarely expressing his own view as to the best course of action, never fixing priorities; in fact, he exercised no leadership whatever. His one effort to direct any aspect of military operations—the sabotaging of General McClernand—resulted only in stopping Grant's promising fall offensive against Jackson and in Sherman's costly repulse in the Yazoo. Halleck would not go near the Navy Department and was thus entirely ignorant of their plans.

For his part, Welles seemed unable to fix naval priorities with any greater precision; he either issued no orders, or gave contradictory instructions to his squadron commanders, and was susceptible to improvised schemes. Buffeted by the contrary winds of popular opinion and political pressure, the secretary and, to an even greater extent, the assistant secretary, expected the admirals to do everything at once—enforce the coastal blockade, occupy the Texas ports, protect New Orleans, patrol the Mississippi, "blockade" Vicksburg, destroy the enemy ironclads in Mobile Bay, and capture the commerce-raiders—all the while cooperating with the Army in any and every project it might decide to undertake. It was almost impossible to follow any combined plan through to its conclusion when the vessels and their commanders were always wanted somewhere else.

Lincoln and the Cabinet did not fill this leadership vacuum. They had learned little, after all, from the failure of the Peninsular campaign and the early movements toward east Tennessee; but the little they had learned was worse than nothing. Having proved themselves bad strategists, they were no longer willing to risk the country's censure for their decisions. Instead, a constant stream of their "advice," "suggestions," and "recommendations" poured out of Washington through the hand of the general-in-chief or the mouths of special administration envoys like Adjutant General Lorenzo Thomas and Assistant War Secretary Charles Dana who appeared at New Orleans or in Grant's camp to further "impress" the fighting generals with the government's views. Such interference was not necessarily bad; in fact, it might have produced good results given the absence of any other leadership. But the advice itself was inconsistent, and when the chips were down, Lincoln and Stanton refused to enforce their ideas with orders, falling back upon the ineffective and sometimes harmful device of nagging, prodding, criticizing, and threatening the generals.

While the chaotic condition of the high command certainly made victorious operations much more difficult for the Union field commanders, it does not entirely explain their lack of efficiency. It did not, for example, prevent Grant and Banks from cooperating on their own, or Porter, Ellet, and Farragut; or the two services from cooperating more effectively with one another. Perhaps the Navy, with its unpredictable materiel, could not silence shore batteries, nor could the Army take strong works without naval gunfire support; but had these men put aside their professional touchiness to plan their joint operations in advance, had they adopted any consistent strategic scheme rather than allowing momentary considerations to lead them into situations for which they were unprepared, these facts could have been taken into account and different plans based on actual capabilities and known resources might have been devised. Coal is a case in point. No one, it seems, bothered to think very much about this requirement until the vessels found themselves immobilized for lack of it, or both services were forced to undertake complicated and dangerous movements to obtain it. The same can be said for various lines of communication.

For combined operations, already more difficult to control than operations by an army or navy alone, the absence of careful study, of preliminary planning, of sustained and intelligent cooperation and, above all, of a clear idea of the object to be attained by joint effort, has often proved fatal. The Federal offensive on the Mississippi and the Gulf after the collapse of McClellan's plan, taken as a whole, is probably one of the worst examples of combined operations strategy in the history of war. That the enemy's tremendous relative weakness, especially on the water, allowed it to succeed anyway should not alter this judgment.

PART THREE

The Evolution of Combined Tactics

9

CHARLESTON: THE NAVAL ATTACK

WITH THE COLLAPSE of the last vestiges of McClellan's
strategic plan—the Peninsular campaign and Federal
combined operations on the Mississippi in the summer of 1862
—Union grand strategy had come full circle. The elevation of
General Halleck to the chief command of the armies of the
United States practically ensured that, except for the capture
of Vicksburg, all subsequent major offensives were conducted
by the land forces.

Halleck's role as general-in-chief has never been properly
understood. Historians have all more or less agreed with Secretary Welles's assessment that, in this office, Halleck "plans
nothing, suggests nothing, is good for nothing."[1] While this
judgment may be correct, it ignores the peculiar political
framework in which Halleck operated. If he made no plans,
or if he never revealed some secret plan which he might have
implemented under a different form of government, there may
have been a reason for his reticence. He had perhaps learned
from McClellan's experience.

In any case, he did not allow himself to become a target
for the Northern politicians by directing the war from Washington; nor did he formulate any overall strategic scheme for
which the government, the Congress, the Joint Committee, or
the newspapers could have held him to account. Instead, as
was previously pointed out, responsibility for operational planning was diffused among the various Union field commanders
far from the seat of government. As well as protecting his
own skin, this system enabled Halleck, by transmitting the
administration's instructions in his own terms, to exercise

more influence over military operations than he could have by a head-on collision with the politicians.

Such a diffuse command system, whatever its purpose, could not accommodate the further complexity of large, strategically oriented combined operations. Moreover, Halleck's experience with Foote in the West had left him with a bad opinion both of the Navy's capability against land defenses and of its willingness to cooperate fully in implementing Army plans.

The Federal Navy Department was equally anxious to abandon combined operations, but not to resurrect the Anaconda strategy. Unlike in the summer of 1861, the Navy was no longer content with a secondary operational role. The early victories at Hatteras, Port Royal, Fort Henry, Memphis, and New Orleans had enormously enhanced the fleet's public image. In fact, it appeared to Fox, and other enthusiasts like David Porter, that the Navy had won the only significant victories thus far in the war.

Emphasizing the moral effect of reducing fortifications produced an important consequence. By limiting the object of U.S. naval forces to the simple attainment of victory, and thus rendering all potential points of attack approximately equal in strategic value, attention became focused upon the tactical problems and possibilities of amphibious operations. For the rest of the war, technical problems preoccupied the Navy, ultimately giving rise to more "modern" and effective combined tactics.

Welles and Fox did not embrace combined tactics willingly, however. They thought they had learned an important lesson from the early naval engagements with Confederate coast and river defenses. Despite Farragut's view that a military force was always necessary to reduce shore batteries, Porter's conviction that the New Orleans campaign was a purely naval triumph confirmed their belief that operations with the fleet alone almost always succeeded, while those requiring cooperation with the Army almost always failed.[2]

This remarkable proposition did not appear absurd in the autumn of 1862; indeed, most of the facts seemed to support such a conclusion. Fort Henry, and the works at Hatteras and Port Royal, did fall to naval bombardment without Army assistance. But in its enthusiasm for the fleet as a destroyer of fortifications, the department did not pause to consider the circumstances which had permitted these early victories.

The peculiar geography of the southern coast and the overwhelming reliance of most Southern states upon water highways induced the Confederacy to adopt a peripheral system of coast defense during the first year of the war. To close the mouths of large rivers which were navigable for long distances upstream, works were situated on the outer approaches, usually marshy islands or low, narrow peninsulas. Not only were such defenses easily outflanked, but the low open ground favored the fleet's heavy-caliber, flat-trajectory fire. So disadvantageous, indeed, was this system to the Southerners that it may seem strange that they did not begin to adopt interior defensive lines before December 1861. This latter alternative, however, meant abandoning the outer approaches and closing the Confederacy to foreign munitions upon which, in 1861, its war effort depended. Only the defeats at Hatteras, Port Royal, and Roanoke Island convinced the Southerners that defenses easily seized were worse than no defenses at all, since their armament was wasted, the garrisons were liable to capture along with the works, and the very existence of weak defenses invited attack. Their bad situation was compounded by the miserable armament in these fortifications. Many guns were useless or dangerous because they were supplied with the wrong ammunition, the artillerists were inexperienced, and the garrisons of local militia or foreigners were badly disciplined and likely to panic at the first shot or run away when their escape route was threatened.[3]

The initial campaign on the western waters found the Confederates at a similar disadvantage. There was no high ground along the lower Tennessee or the Mississippi between Columbus and Fort Pillow. Fort Henry was partly flooded during the naval attack. The works at Island Number 10 and the mainland opposite were admirably constructed and well armed; but the whole position was almost surrounded by water, allowing it to be easily turned and the defenders trapped by the interruption of their fragile communications. Memphis was indefensible against warships, as was New Orleans.[4]

But while the Federal Navy Department was overly opti-

mistic about the fleet's ability to reduce fortifications regardless of specific conditions, it could not fail to note that elevated
batteries were far more dangerous antagonists. Foote's repulse
at Donelson might be explained away by the closeness of the
range and narrowness of the channel; and Farragut's losing
contest with the Port Hudson batteries accounted for by the
vulnerability of wooden ships to plunging shellfire. Rodgers'
engagement with the Drewry's Bluff battery was more difficult
to interpret. Although the *Galena*'s light plating had been
riddled, the *Monitor* had sustained no damage. On the other
hand, the turretted ironclad had failed to injure the fort. It
was logical to suppose that the stalemate was caused by the
Monitor's inability to elevate her guns to bear on the battery
at close range and that, since the fort had hit the ship without
effect, the result would have been more favorable against a
battery sited on lower ground.[5]

Not that Fox or Welles gave much thought to the *Monitor*'s
offensive capability. Indeed, unlike professional sailors such as
Rodgers and Du Pont, they focused exclusively on her seeming invulnerability. The Drewry's Bluff engagement therefore
reaffirmed the Navy Department's decision to adopt the monitor as the standard ship type of the fleet. Added advantages
of this design, in Welles's mind, were its fast delivery time—
three to six months—and its very low cost. The first of about
a dozen vessels ordered after the battle in Hampton Roads, the
USS *Passaic*, was completed on 30 August 1862. Another
larger and much more heavily armed experimental vessel, the
USS *New Ironsides*, an armored frigate launched at Philadelphia on 11 May, was available to support the monitor squadron.[6]

Fox had been fascinated with the supposed invincibility of
the *Monitor* since her fight with the *Virginia* in March, and
had even then proposed using her to capture Charleston or
Wilmington. The failure of the Peninsular campaign did not
dampen his enthusiasm; on the contrary, he now regarded
these projects as necessary to restore the Navy's damaged
reputation. Consequently, in early November 1862, he urged
Goldsborough's successor, Rear Admiral Samuel P. Lee, who
had been complaining that it was impossible to blockade the

various channels with his small force of antiquated ships, to attempt a naval coup against Wilmington.[7]

Lee, a solid and sensible officer, insisted upon first reducing the forts on the outer approaches. He insisted that this required substantial infantry support. Although Halleck was predictably uninterested in any coast expedition, the admiral managed to make some arrangements for a combined operation on his own with the new commander of the North Carolina Department, Major General John G. Foster. Instead of an assault from the water side, Foster intended to make a land expedition toward Goldsborough, cutting the railroads and driving off the small enemy detachments reported at that place. His force would then emerge in the rear of Wilmington, establishing contact with the fleet via New Topsail Inlet.[8] Thus the operation would be conjunct only as to timing.

Meanwhile, the Navy Department was cooking up a grander scheme. Fox had proposed a naval descent on Charleston—the "cradle of the Confederacy"—to Admiral Du Pont during the late spring and summer.[9] At that time, Du Pont, who was greatly affected by Rodgers' recent repulse at Fort Darling, displayed no interest in the enterprise. In fact, he consistently maintained that Charleston could be taken only by combined operations—more specifically, by a landing on James Island from the Federal base in the Stono River. Although such an operation, attempted by a small force from General Hunter's department in June, sustained a decisive defeat, the admiral rightly blamed the army commander, Major General Henry Benham, a hopeless bumbler whom General Rosecrans had earlier expelled from the West Virginia department, threatening to court-martial him for incompetence. Relying on the views of his special confidant, Captain Percival Drayton, who commanded the gunboat squadron during Benham's operation, Du Pont insisted that the Stono was the only proper line of advance against Charleston. All that was required for a successful combined operation was a different troop commander.[10]

Apparently by coincidence, but more likely through the influence of Du Pont's powerful friends in Congress, Hunter was replaced in early September by a favorite of the Joint Committee, the same General Ormsby Mitchel who had attempted the foolish descent on Chattanooga in June. In his new department Mitchel actually proved an able officer. He had barely arrived at Port Royal when he presented Du Pont with a plan for combined operations on James Island which was just what the admiral had in mind.[11] Fox was not at all pleased with this development, however, believing there must be no attack on Charleston until the monitors were ready for their grand descent upon the city from the harbor side. These vessels would be finished in October; meanwhile, the admiral must not compromise the blockade. Wooden ships were too vulnerable, he told Du Pont, adding that he had recently refused Farragut's request to attack the Mobile forts without ironclads.[12]

Although Du Pont appeared willing to cancel the operation, even telling Fox that he was right, since Drayton's experience in the Stono showed the gunboats useless in covering landings on James Island, the implication of Fox's unusual caution was obvious. The department was going to insist upon an unsupported naval attack.[13] It was now the admiral's turn to issue a strong warning. Reminding Fox that there was no similarity between a city situated on a river bank, like New Orleans, and one at the head of a cul-de-sac, he urged the department not to "go off half-cocked about Charleston." Any operation there must be studied carefully and thoroughly prepared—not because Charleston was of any military importance, but because failure would have disastrous political repercussions at home and abroad.[14]

But Du Pont's best logic was so much waste paper. Charleston was Fox's obsession, the first city to declare for the "rebels," the "hot-bed of secession" whose batteries had defied his attempt to relieve Fort Sumter in April 1861. Beyond personal motives, his keen eye still on the newspapers, Fox saw this place as the ultimate propaganda prize for the U.S. Navy. The Army, under Halleck, had decided to go its own way strategically, leaving the Navy to take places less important to the general-in-chief than Chattanooga, Richmond, or even Shreveport. Thus it was up to the Navy Department to prove its worth to the Congress and the nation by attaining a spectacular psychological victory. Charleston under the guns of Federal warships would serve this purpose better than anything else.[15]

In October, Du Pont was summoned to confer with naval officials in Washington. Fox had cleverly arranged the admiral's itinerary to include a tour of the New York shipyard and the Naval Ordnance Bureau. Impressed by the *Passaic's* heavy plating—six inches on the sides, eleven on the turret—and even more by Captain John A. Dahlgren's new 15-inch naval cannon, adapted from the Army's Rodman smoothbore to fit in the new monitor turrets, Du Pont was willing to consider Fox's proposition about Charleston.[16]

Nevertheless, his reservations were substantial. What worried him most was the same consideration which had made him hesitant to attack Port Royal a year earlier. Then, his fleet had possessed overwhelming superiority over the fortifications, in both volume and rate of fire; yet he still had doubted the efficacy of an unsupported cannonade right up until the forts surrendered. It was common doctrine to sailors of the old Navy that, because of the many factors producing inaccuracy in naval bombardment, a fleet needed a fire superiority of fifteen guns to silence each gun in a shore battery. And the ships must maintain a rapid rate of fire to spoil the enemy's aim, exhaust his gunners, and prevent repair to the works. Du Pont did not know to what extent the new heavier Dahlgren cannon could compensate for their small number and slow rate of fire, but he was not anxious to be the first to find out.[17]

No matter how much the assistant secretary downplayed the risk, citing Du Pont's own triumph at Port Royal, Farragut's defiance of the New Orleans defenses, and the department's contempt for all types of fortifications, the admiral would not commit himself to Fox's enterprise. In view of Du Pont's preference to have troops around, just in case something went wrong, or to occupy the forts if he should succeed in penetrating the harbor, Fox got Stanton to agree that General Hunter would be returned to Port Royal with ten or fifteen thousand soldiers, although Du Pont was to understand that the Navy was expected to take the city. Halleck raised no objection since the troops he intended to send were raw recruits not needed, or wanted, for duty with the main armies; but the Navy had to recognize that this operation was of no consequence to the Army and that Hunter could not be reinforced.[18]

Halleck's casual attitude and the promise of a few thousand untrained troops without operations orders were still insufficient to convert the wary admiral. So Welles employed the ultimate weapon. He hinted none too subtly to Du Pont that the president's favorite, the same Captain Dahlgren, Chief of Naval Ordnance, who developed the naval cannon, had recently pleaded with Welles for an operational command to win his promotion to Rear Admiral. Moreover, Dahlgren, a proved expert on the new technology, being confident that a fleet of monitors could effect a coup against Charleston, had actually volunteered for the assignment.[19]

This was too much pressure even for the easygoing Du Pont. Reluctantly, he agreed to Fox's plan. After all, something more satisfactory might yet be arranged with the local army commander. On his return to Port Royal, finding General Mitchel eager for an active campaign, he asked that the ten thousand soldiers promised by Stanton be sent out immediately, not necessarily for a combined operation, he assured the Navy Department, but to guard against a reported Confederate plan to retake Beaufort and other points on the South Atlantic coast. Furthermore, having got wind of the Wilmington project which would likely tie up the new ironclads for several months, he informed Welles that the Confederates were building ironclads at Charleston which would raise the blockade and capture his base at Port Royal unless the *Ironsides* and *Passaic* were attached to his squadron at once.[20]

A letter from Drayton written from the New York shipyard on 8 November further worried the admiral. After inspecting the new monitors, Drayton was convinced that the fleet could enter the harbor only if the Army first seized the outer approaches, since the channel obstructions between Fort Sumter and Sullivan's Island could not be removed under fire even with the newly devised apparatus for blowing them up with torpedoes. The Army's active assistance was therefore indispensable.[21] Unfortunately, Mitchel, so keen to undertake combined operations on his own responsibility to aid Du Pont, had succumbed to yellow fever on 30 October.

By December a conviction of certain defeat was setting in. Du Pont began referring to Charleston as "stronger than Sevastopol" and to the projected naval engagement as an "experiment." But he dared not express his fears more explicitly to the department; otherwise, he might find himself ousted by an upstart captain of ordnance. At best, the ironclads needed to sustain the blockade would be given to Admiral Lee or sent to Farragut. Caught in this dilemma, Du Pont simply asked Fox for more monitors, naturally giving the department a false impression that the admiral was confident of victory if enough ships were provided—when in fact he was fundamentally opposed to the *method* of attack. Regrettably, the department was allowed to retain this illusion right up until the repulse of his squadron four months later.[22]

Events elsewhere nearly got Du Pont off the hook. Foster's expedition against Wilmington went awry. The expedition toward Goldsborough from 11 to 17 December ran into greater opposition than expected, convincing the general that a land offensive against Wilmington was impracticable. Having secured reinforcements from Norfolk and permission from Stanton and Halleck, he then arranged with Admiral Lee to attack the fortifications below the city by water, assembling an army corps with its stores at New Berne in late December where he waited for the expected naval force.[23]

However, the monitors upon which Lee had counted to silence the forts met with a series of accidents. The *Passaic*'s machinery broke down en route to Hampton Roads and she had to return to the Washington navy yard for major repairs. On the last day of the year the *Monitor* sank in heavy seas during her passage to New Berne. This was too much for Admiral Lee who, by this time, entertained serious reservations about the enterprise anyway. Reconnaissances during November and December had confirmed the presence of extensive shoals off the mouth of the Cape Fear which might prevent the ships from passing over the bar and would certainly restrict their bombardment of the strong defenses on the outer approaches to comparatively long range. Since Foster would not agree to assault the works without heavy naval gunfire support, the Navy Department postponed the operation and decided to send the monitors against Charleston first.[24]

Unable to make progress against Wilmington, Foster now suggested that his corps join General Hunter for the attack on Charleston. Because this move would justify the expense of

Assistant Secretary of the Navy   Major General David Hunter
Gustavus V. Fox   (*National Archives*)

preparing his expedition, Stanton and Lincoln readily approved. For Halleck, it was a welcome solution to the problem
of finding the ten thousand infantry reinforcements promised
Fox and Du Pont.[25]

Hunter was delighted. Another of Lincoln's political friends,
he was not a professional soldier (although educated at West
Point) and had never commanded troops in battle. Foster was
not only an experienced line officer, but was thoroughly familiar with Charleston harbor, having supervised construction
of its prewar defenses and having acted as General Robert
Anderson's engineer during the Confederate attack on Fort
Sumter in 1861. His troops, unlike Hunter's own motley crowd,
were well-disciplined veterans led by competent regular officers. Furthermore, Foster had an operations plan which he
was confident would succeed and which did not depend on the
Navy's ability to reduce the forts by bombardment alone. This
last consideration was especially important to Hunter as well
as Du Pont. Despite Halleck's opinion, Hunter had never liked
the Navy's Department's idea that the soldiers should be mere
spectators or auxiliaries of the fleet.[26]

On Hunter's invitation and with Halleck's verbal authoriza-

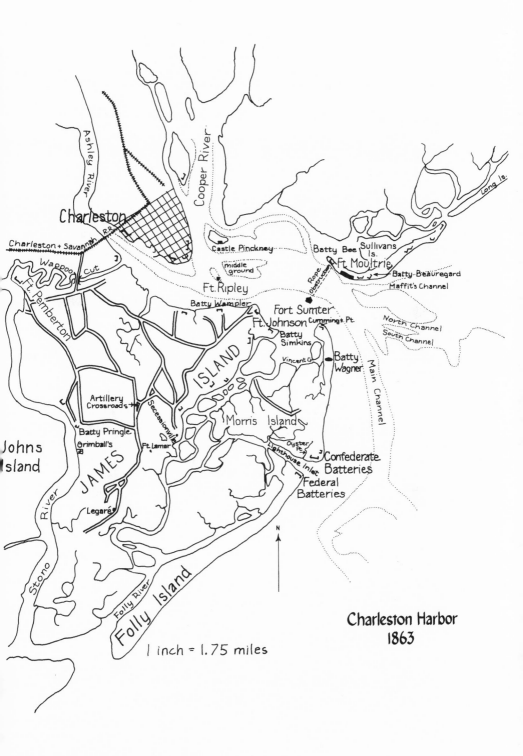

Charleston

Ashley River

Charleston + Savannah R.R.

Wappoo Cut

Ft. Pemberton

Cooper River

Castle Pinckney

middle ground

Ft. Ripley

Batty Wampler

Batty Bee

Sullivans Is.

Ft. Moultrie

Batty Beauregard

Maffit's Channel

Rope Obstruction

Fort Sumter

Ft. Johnson

Cummings Pt.

North Channel

South Channel

Batty Simkins

Vincent G.

Batty Wagner

Main Channel

ISLAND

Artillery Crossroads

Secessionville

Batty Pringle

Grimball's

Ft. Lamar

Morris Island

Oyster Pt.

Lighthouse Inlet

Confederate Batteries

Federal Batteries

Johns Island

JAMES

Legaré

Stono River

Folly River

Folly Island

Long Is.

N

Charleston Harbor
1863

1 inch = 1.75 miles

tion, Foster embarked his corps at New Berne, arriving off Port Royal on 1 February 1863. After reporting briefly to Hunter, the general, his chief of staff, and his senior divisional commander, Brigadier General Henry M. Naglee, went aboard the flagship to discuss the plan of operations. Foster proposed that, while Hunter's X Corps remained in reserve, his own troops (XVIII Corps) under Naglee would land on the southern tip of Morris Island under cover of the light-draft gunboats. Meanwhile, the monitor squadron with the flagship *New Ironsides* would silence Fort Sumter in preparation for an infantry assault on Battery Wagner, a strong sand fort on the northern end of the island. Siege artillery could then be emplaced on Morris Island within range to reduce Sumter, after which the Navy would run into the harbor.[27]

The naval officers showed little enthusiasm for this plan. They doubted that the gunboats could provide enough fire to overcome the beach defenses or protect a Federal base on Morris Island. Having examined the position himself on the 7th, Foster agreed. During another conference with Du Pont later that day, he suggested that the *Ironsides* or a couple of monitors supply the necessary fire support for the landing, a proposition the admiral refused. In Du Pont's opinion, the monitors could not anchor in the shallow water off Morris Island without drifting on shore while the *Ironsides*'s deep draft prevented her from approaching close enough to fire with accuracy upon either the enemy's batteries or his troop concentrations. Although Du Pont was anxious for a combined operation to relieve him from the department's pressure to capture Charleston with the fleet alone, Foster could not demand the impossible. If, as the Navy suggested, the Army landed on James Island from the Stono, it could have all the fire support it could possibly require, since the river channel was deep enough even for the flagship.

It was Foster's turn to object. Granted, the Navy might put the soldiers on the western shore of James Island and protect them there; but what then? They could not advance. This island was much larger than Morris, the ground intersected by marshes and small creeks, none of them navigable. Numerous clumps of trees would restrict the direct fire of the vessels. And once out of range, the Army would have no artillery support except for a few field pieces it could carry along. The enemy, on the other hand, could quickly mass and deploy a very large force on this island which was easily accessible to both the city of Charleston and the railroad from Savannah. The forts on the island's eastern, or harbor, shore were reported to be very strong. Even if the Army could defeat the enemy infantry and approach these works from the land side, the fleet had to enter the harbor to bombard them in front, a tactic unlikely to succeed until the outer forts were reduced.[28]

USS *New Ironsides*

The whole idea was impractical from the viewpoint of both services. Foster's troops huddled on the James Island beaches under cover of the fleet would have been no use whatever to Du Pont in his effort to crash through the channel between Forts Sumter and Moultrie. He could not even have withdrawn the squadron from the Stono without withdrawing the Army also.

Foster thought the problem with his original plan could be solved by emplacing some heavy rifled guns on the northern end of Folly Island just south of Morris across a narrow inlet. These would enable him to silence the beach defenses on the latter island without naval fire support. He therefore returned to Fort Monroe for the necessary ordnance. Moreover, in view of the problems revealed during his discussions with the Navy, he wished to consult personally with the Washington authorities.[29]

Arriving in the capital on the 15th, he met with Fox, Halleck, Stanton, Welles, and Lincoln. Du Pont, he reported, would not cooperate with the Army in operations on Morris Island and was reluctant to attack Charleston with the Navy alone. If the government wanted the place, the forts would have to be taken by siege. Although Lincoln and Stanton were almost frantic for action at Charleston, they were unalterably opposed to a siege for all of the usual reasons: it would take too long, cost too much, damage the administration with the press, discourage the public, encourage foreign intervention, and so forth. After reminding everyone that Charleston was of no military importance and that he had no interest in the project, Halleck reminded Foster that the troops were not expected to do anything; they were only sent at Fox's request to satisfy Du Pont. Fox then assured Lincoln and Halleck that the Navy Department never intended a combined operation either. Du Pont knew what was expected of him and had agreed in October to force the harbor with the fleet alone. Nothing had changed, said Fox; the monitors were invulnerable, and no batteries could stop them.[30]

While Foster was discussing high policy in Washington, something occurred in the Department of the South that rendered these discussions academic. Of all similar incidents that plagued combined operations during the Civil War, this was one of the most unfortunate, and certainly the most absurd.

The root of the trouble was Halleck's customary failure to define command responsibility, leaving this important detail to be worked out among the men on the spot. This procedure was risky because it assumed a compatibility of personality and command style among the men involved. Having invited Foster to Charleston to compensate for his own military incapacity, Hunter soon resented that officer's conspicuous ability and energy.[31] And like many volunteer generals conscious of their inferior status, he was overly concerned with the niceties of military regulations and the small prerogatives of rank.

No sooner had the boat carrying Foster steamed out of Port Royal on 10 February than Hunter's aide appeared at General Naglee's headquarters demanding that he and Foster's other divisional commander report the strength of their units to Hunter's adjutant general. This request was refused. Foster must have suspected something brewing behind his back, for before leaving he had instructed Naglee, commanding XVIII Corps in his absence, to resist any move to incorporate his force into X Corps. These instructions placed Naglee in an untenable position. If he submitted to Hunter's order, he would be tacitly admitting that Foster's troops were part of Hunter's command in violation of orders from his superior. If, on the other hand, he obeyed Foster's instructions, he could be considered insubordinate for ignoring an order of the senior department commander. In an attempt to avoid a showdown and on Foster's prior assurance from Halleck that the North Carolina detachment would remain independent, Naglee explained the situation in a personal interview with Hunter who he thought agreed to recognize the autonomy of XVIII Corps.[32]

But the vitriolic department commander, incensed by what he regarded as Naglee's presumption and insulting defiance of regulations, issued an order the following day incorporating the North Carolina troops into X Corps. Further, he dismissed all of Foster's staff, ordered them out of the department and threatened to arrest the general himself if he returned. He further explained to Halleck that Naglee was undermining his authority and demoralizing his men by communicating with Hunter direct instead of through his adjutant. The general-in-chief's reply further confused the issue. Halleck would not allow XVIII Corps broken up or its staff dismissed. While Foster's officers had to obey Hunter's operational orders as long as they remained in his department, they were not to be considered part of his command for administrative purposes. The ridiculous order threatening Foster with arrest must be revoked at once. If Naglee was insubordinate, said Halleck, Hunter should remove him.[33]

This dispatch alarmed Hunter. With the amphibious operations at Charleston about to begin, or so Hunter thought, he could not afford to lose his only competent field commander. Besides, no one on his own staff knew the operations plan and Foster's staff had already gone, taking most of the maps and papers with them. In a panic, he told Halleck on 17 February that he had been wrong to blame Naglee for the unfortunate misunderstanding. This officer had simply obeyed the misguided directions of his superior; thus only Foster should be reprimanded. Furthermore, Naglee was a first-rate troop commander, indispensable to the success of the projected operations. Wearily, Halleck replied that Hunter could retain or dismiss Naglee as he pleased.[34]

By the time this last message reached Hunter, General Foster had decided not to return to Charleston. When he left Washington early on the 16th, he was already displeased with the government's petty wrangling and the general-in-chief's indifference. While waiting in Baltimore for the boat to Fort Monroe, he was overtaken by Halleck's adjutant who filled him in on Hunter's machinations and handed him a copy of the orders dismissing Naglee and the XVIII Corps staff. Shocked and angry, Foster declared that he could no longer work with Hunter and was returning to North Carolina, suggesting that Halleck send Burnside to Charleston in his place.[35]

If Foster expected sympathy from the general-in-chief, he was cruelly disappointed. While Halleck did not entirely approve of Hunter's actions and had instructed him to rescind the order breaking up XVIII Corps which could only be authorized by the president, Foster and Naglee had to understand that, as department commander and Foster's senior, Hunter had every right to insist that his orders be obeyed, and could remove or expel from his department any officer who questioned or defied his authority. Whether or not Foster went back to Charleston was entirely up to him.

Disgusted with this legalistic mumbo-jumbo, Foster returned to New Berne where the Confederates were threatening to take the offensive in the absence of XVIII Corps, only to discover that Halleck had reassigned the North Carolina department to its old commander, General Burnside.[36] Nor did he recover his two best divisions which remained permanently in the Department of the South.

With Foster out of the way, Hunter thought his troubles were over. He could use the XVIII Corps and Foster's best general to support Du Pont without having to share the honor of the expected victory. But his failure to win General Naglee's confidence, already strained by the dispute with Foster, was his undoing. Instead of consulting with Naglee, who was now responsible for commanding all of the assault forces, Hunter left the arrangements entirely in the hands of his own chief of staff, Brigadier General Trueman Seymour.[37]

Not that Seymour failed to devise a good plan; in fact, his was the most promising combined plan ever proposed against the Charleston defenses. Instead of landing on Morris Island, XVIII Corps would land on Long Island on the other side of the harbor entrance, just north of Sullivan's Island. If Fort Sumter did not fall to naval bombardment, this corps would cross to Sullivan's Island, driving the enemy into Fort Moultrie, which would then be taken in conjunction with the fleet. Meanwhile, X Corps would create a diversion on James or Morris Island to prevent enemy reinforcements from reaching Sullivan's in time to stop the Federal assault.[38]

When Naglee finally heard about the new plan, he was furious. For several weeks he had bided his time expecting Foster to straighten out the command quarrel with the Washington authorities and return to take charge of operations. In a confidential letter to Foster on 3 March, he graphically described the rampant confusion and ineptitude in Hunter's department. No one knew who was to command what, he had no corps staff, nor did he know the tactical plan. The dismissal of Foster's staff had caused a hopeless muddle in the quartermaster department so that the North Carolina divisions had no transport. Such gross incompetence, said Naglee, was more than he could stand and would surely produce a disaster.[39]

That same day Hunter falsely advised Halleck that the Army was ready any time the Navy was. There was just one problem; Naglee continued to complain instead of getting on with the preparations. Hunter was convinced that these "delaying tactics" were part of a plot to wreck his operations, and thus get even with him for his alleged mistreatment of Foster. Halleck had to consolidate the two corps in his department at once and appoint a good brigadier *senior* to Naglee to command the whole expedition. Before Halleck could reply, Naglee lodged another protest with Hunter's adjutant, this time about the inadequate allocation of supplies to XVIII Corps. Finally, Naglee was relieved on the 5th.[40]

The biggest loser in this whole miserable affair was Admiral Du Pont. Since Hunter was unable to obtain a replacement for Naglee and could not himself command a corps in battle, the Navy was left to capture Charleston by its own efforts with no active assistance from the Army.[41]

Du Pont could not understand why the government seemed in such a hurry to have Charleston. Given sufficient time, the Army might resolve its administrative problems, the monitors could be tested and strengthened if necessary, and the whole operation thoroughly studied and prepared.[42] He was never told, nor was it his business to know, the administration's fundamental reason for insisting upon an immediate attack.

As already pointed out, the winter of 1862–63 was the darkest period in the war for the Union. On the coast and inland waters, no progress had been made since the capture of Memphis the previous summer, despite several expensive expeditions fitted out that fall for operations in the Gulf and Mississippi. Meanwhile, the Confederates had recovered Galveston. The situation on land looked equally dismal. Although the Southern forces invading Kentucky and Maryland had been pushed back and contained, they were not conquered; nor had Federal armies taken any place of importance since Halleck's occupation of Corinth. The gloom resulting from Burnside's disaster at Fredericksburg in December was only slightly lifted by Rosecrans's costly and indecisive victory over Bragg's army in middle Tennessee.

As the winter wore on and there were no more reports of Union successes, criticism of the government mounted alarmingly. Public disaffection was bad enough—the fall congressional elections clearly indicated a swing away from the Republicans. But in January the government was assailed from a more dangerous quarter. On the 29th, the New York *Tribune* warned that, unless the war ended in three months, the United States would be bankrupt. The Treasury had been forced to ask the New York financial houses for another large loan; this one for $300 million to fund the war debt. While the bankers agreed to the loan, it was conditional upon the government's promise that it would be the last. If such promise could not be given, the *Tribune* urged the president to negotiate with the Confederacy. The New York *World* was even more pessimistic. Subduing the South was impossible; the government should sue for peace at once, regardless of the decision on the loan.[43]

These dire rumblings naturally threw the president and Cabinet into a panic. Northen forces must score an immediate success *somewhere* or the war would be lost. Vainly Lincoln and Stanton urged Rosecrans to move on Chattanooga, the Army of the Potomac to attack Lee, Grant to take Vicksburg; but Halleck assured both men that the Army was doing its best and he could not ask more. Farragut could do nothing on the Mississippi without the Army, or against Mobile without ironclads.[44]

Well, what about Du Pont? In October, Lincoln recalled, Fox had guaranteed a quick victory at Charleston without the Army, and Du Pont already had more ironclads than originally promised. What was Du Pont waiting for? The admiral's repeated warnings about the ugly foreign and domestic repercussions of a defeat at Charleston would be meaningless if the whole Union war effort collapsed before the attack was made. Du Pont must be compelled to realize that he must act immediately, whatever the prospect of victory.

Welles's confidential dispatch to Du Pont on the 31st did not reflect the government's panic, nor did it refer to the financial crisis. Relying as usual on implication rather than plain speaking, the secretary gave the admiral what amounted to two alternatives. "If, after careful examination," Du Pont should "deem the number of ironclads insufficient to render the capture of that port [Charleston] reasonably certain," he could cancel the operation. While not explicitly stating what would become of the monitors in this case, his reference to a possible offensive against Mobile left Du Pont in no doubt they would be sent immediately to Farragut. If, on the other hand, he should consider a naval attack practicable, it must be carried out at once. No more monitors would be ready for six months, so the admiral must not wait for a larger force. As to the reason for such haste, Welles simply explained that the large number of wooden vessels then blockading off Southern seaports were needed to chase commerce raiders in the

West Indies, "making the capture of Charleston and Mobile imperative."[45]

By the time this dispatch reached Port Royal, two local events had emphasized the need for Federal offensive action at Charleston. On 30 January the South Carolina regular artillery ambushed the U.S. gunboat *Isaac Smith* on station in the Stono River. This fast vessel, armed with eleven pieces of the latest rifled ordnance, was captured intact and swiftly converted to a blockade runner.[46] Under cover of a dense fog the following morning, the two Confederate harbor ironclads *Chicora* and *Palmetto State* launched a spirited surprise attack on the Union squadron patrolling outside the bar. Although only two wooden blockaders sustained sufficient damage to strike their colors, five of their consorts were iron-hulled ships purchased from civilian firms. Aware that a single large shot below the water line would quickly send them to the bottom, their captains wisely withdrew toward Beaufort. The unseaworthy Confederate ships could not follow up their advantage, and Beauregard's subsequent claim of having raised the Charleston blockade according to international regulations was clearly not true. Nonetheless, the incident gave Du Pont a nasty shock. What had happened to Renshaw at Galveston might happen to him. More than ever, the monitors were needed to protect the frail blockaders. But to keep them, the admiral must agree to the naval offensive or Welles would send them to the Gulf.[47]

The pressure of enemy aggression against the blockaders, increased by yet another reminder of the government's desire that Farragut should have all of the monitors, caused Du Pont to try an "experiment" on a smaller scale than Charleston. Perhaps a practical demonstration would convince the department that it badly overestimated the Navy's power to reduce fortifications.

To understand the decrease in the U.S. fleet's fire capability brought about by adopting the monitor design, a brief description of these ships is necessary. The *Passaic*-class monitor was a small vessel with an 11-foot draft. Her low-floating light iron hull supported an overhanging wooden raft shielded on the sides by six inches of rolled iron plates. A pair of large smoothbore muzzle-loading cannon were mounted in a more heavily armored circular iron turret, which revolved on a center shaft along a brass track at its outer edge. A pilot house made of 9-inch-thick solid iron bars, large enough to accommodate only three men, was perched on top of the turret. With a clean bottom and in a moderate current, the vessel averaged only six knots.[48]

Her main defect as an offensive weapon against forts was her armament. Because the original *Monitor* had been built to combat other armored ships—either those of the Confederacy or, in case of foreign intervention, those of Britain and France—rapidity and volume of fire were sacrificed to attain larger caliber. For crushing iron plates, the size of individual projectiles was more important than the number of guns.[49] Nor, despite the experience with the *Virginia*, did the U.S. Navy yet regard rifles or breach-loaders as suitable for a fleet engagement at short range. The rifle's greater range and accuracy was attained at the expense of close-in striking power whereas the new breach-loaders, in addition to being considered unsafe at this time, would allow the inexperienced gunners aboard American vessels to shoot off their ammunition supply in a remarkably short time during the excitement of battle, leaving the ships at the mercy of their more deliberate and better-trained adversaries.[50]

Although the monitors were designed, therefore, to carry two 15-inch cast-iron guns, this very large ordnance was not available in sufficient quantities when the ships were finished. Consequently, each monitor (except for the USS *Patapsco*, which carried an 8-inch rifle in place of the smaller gun) mounted one 15- and one 11-inch Dahlgren cannon. These heavy guns, as noted, had a very slow rate of fire, the 15-inch requiring nearly ten minutes to load, aim, and shoot. A warning from the Naval Ordnance Bureau further reduced their effectiveness. Fearing that these experimental guns might explode in the close confines of a turret if fired with the full 50-pound powder charge, the bureau advised the monitor captains to use a 20-pound charge, thereby nullifying, even at short range, the greater initial velocity and impact of the heavier projectile.[51]

On 27 February, Du Pont sent Commander John Worden in the USS *Montauk*, the only monitor yet arrived at Port

Royal, to bombard Fort McAllister on the lower Ogeechee River near Savannah. Unlike earlier Confederate coast batteries, this was a solidly built earthwork mounting seven heavy guns and rifles in embrasure, manned by experienced artillerists. At a range of 600 yards, the *Montauk*, supported by three gunboats and a mortar raft, shelled the battery for four hours without effect. Although the injury to the ironclad from enemy fire amounted to a few superficial dents in the thin deck armor and the explosion of a mine close along her side produced only minor damage, Du Pont was greatly worried by the unfavorable result. For the moment he chose to ignore his doubt about the monitors' vulnerability, supposing that their defensive properties could be strengthened by adding more deck plates and engaging at longer range. Instead, his report stressed their offensive weakness.[52]

The bombardment of McAllister, he wrote Welles on the 28th, confirmed the lesson of Rodgers' attack on Fort Darling which the admiral had explained to Fox the previous October. "Whatever degree of impenetrability they might have," he told the secretary, "there was no corresponding quality of aggression or destructiveness as against forts, the slowness of fire giving full time for the gunners in the fort to take shelter in the bombproofs." Since the enemy's fire could not be smothered by a greater volume of fire from the ships, the channel obstructions barring the entrance to Charleston's inner harbor could not be removed. In short, the engagement had conclusively demonstrated that the department's idea for running by the forts was impracticable and "that in all such operations, to secure success, troops are necessary."[53]

Unfortunately, the die was already cast. Two days after dispatching the above appreciation, Du Pont was astonished to receive two confidential letters from Fox sent on the 16th and 20th in reaction to Foster's recent visit to Washington. Reflecting the Federal government's overconfidence and ignorance of technical problems, they contained probably the most extraordinary orders ever issued a squadron commander.

Du Pont must not worry about the fleet's fire capability, said Fox, since the department did not envisage a stand-up fight with the forts. He should simply run past the batteries in imitation of Farragut at New Orleans. So enamored was the theatrical Fox of this idea and of the monitors' invulnerability that he actually begged Du Pont not to spoil the magnificent occasion by opening on the forts at all, but "carrying your flag supreme and superb, defiant and disdainful, silent amid the 200 guns," steam up to the city docks and receive the surrender. Nor should the admiral consider combined operations; Halleck himself and his chief of staff, both expert engineers, had personally assured him that the enemy must evacuate all of the harbor defenses once the monitors passed Fort Sumter. With the victory headlines already before his mind's eye, Fox concluded: "The sublimity of such a silent attack is beyond all words to describe, and I beg of you not to let the Army spoil it."[54]

Snubbing an enemy into submission was such a novel tactical technique that Du Pont's first inclination was to laugh. But when he suddenly realized that Fox was deadly serious and that the government actually considered this ridiculous "program" practicable, his amusement turned to alarm. For almost a year he had repeatedly hinted to the department that their favorite mode of attack was impossible at Charleston. While Du Pont had been willing all along to try reducing the forts by bombardment as an "experiment," he was naturally appalled by the unreality of this latest instruction, assuring Fox that there could be no question of passing the batteries before they were silenced. Charleston harbor was, in his words, a "cul-de-sac" bristling with batteries. Even if he got past the outer forts, an army would be required to occupy them if the city failed to submit. Otherwise, without the necessary communications to remain inside, the fleet must pass them again on the way out, probably leaving several disabled monitors in enemy hands.[55]

All such arguments, however sound, were a waste of effort and only irritated the already impatient administration. Du Pont's tragedy was not a failure of military judgment, but an inability to perceive that when civilian officials are determined upon a course of action for political reasons, no amount of military logic will have the least influence.

Convinced that the project was foolhardy and hopeless, Du Pont should have resigned his command, or at least threatened to do so. An ultimatum might have shocked the department into sensibility. But the admiral was incapable of such an act. We have seen, in his fear of being superseded, his excessive concern for his public reputation, and his desire for promotion after the war, a certain lack of moral courage which contributed to his dilemma. Moreover, his personal fears and ambitions were inseparable from his sense of duty.

Like McClellan, and in contrast to officers like Farragut and Grant, Du Pont's concept of duty was very broad. It included not only the right but the responsibility to pass judgment on the decisions and acts of his civilian superiors; that is, to make as well as implement policy, despite his ignorance of the non-military factors that often restricted the government's freedom of choice. Indeed, the secret of Farragut's success, and of Grant's, may have resided in their narrower definition of professional responsibility. These men never questioned the wisdom of their instructions, assuming—sometimes wrongly —that the authorities knew what they were doing. Farragut, for instance, never asked himself whether Mobile was an important strategic objective, or Galveston, or Vicksburg, or whether its capture was worth the cost in men or ships. If the government said to take it, it was his sole duty to make the best attempt with the means at hand.

Du Pont, on the other hand, could never limit his judgment to tactical questions or the simple obedience of orders. He was perhaps too well educated and cosmopolitan. Every order, every decision, involved an enormous complex of ramifications, an agony of reflection and analysis. So with his decision to remain in command. Should he resign, some less capable officer— Dahlgren probably—unfamiliar with the squadron and with the theater of operations would be forced to make the attempt. If the fleet was sunk or captured, if his younger protégés, the ironclad captains, were killed or ruined, he would feel responsible. By directing the attack himself, if one had to be made, he might at least avoid a disaster instead of a repulse.[56]

Despite his suspicion that the administration's decision to have Charleston at any price might be unalterable, the admiral tried one more argument. Although Du Pont knew that Fox could not have received the report of Worden's engagement with Fort McAllister when he wrote his preposterous letter of instructions, even this report, which stressed the monitors' inferior fire capability, was unlikely to impress a man who insisted that two hundred guns could be silenced without firing a shot. Another demonstration, with a different emphasis, was required.

On 3 March, the day after receiving Fox's letter, Du Pont ordered another attack on Fort McAllister. Three recently arrived monitors, the *Passaic*, *Patapsco*, and *Nahant*, supported by three gunboats, shelled the fort for six hours at twice the range (1,200 yards) of the first bombardment, again inflicting no discernible injury. The monitor *Montauk* was present but fired only upon a Confederate blockade runner lying above the fort. This time, however, the long range allowed the Confederates to remain at their guns instead of being forced under cover of the bombproof.[57]

While damages to the ships were minor, Du Pont carefully detailed them in his report to Fox on 7 March. It was no longer just a question of the monitors' offensive weakness; this most recent contest disproved their supposed invulnerability. Of the four monitors involved, he told Fox, "two got aground, two had their concussion boxes injured, one had her XV in gun carriage injured, one was injured by a torpedo [mine], and one by a bomb shell—without taking a 7 gun fort." How much these injuries would be magnified during a contest with the more than seventy guns in Charleston's outer harbor defenses he left to the department's imagination, simply warning Fox that "part only of those vessels which go into the fight at Charleston will be efficient at the end of it."[58]

Bombardment of Ft. McAllister, 3 March 1863 (*Navy Department*)

This report was followed on the 19th by another letter to Fox complaining about the mechanical defects of the monitors and their armament, their poor steering qualities, and the propensity of their engines to break down. To his friends he was more candid. The monitors, he told James Biddle, were not only vulnerable; they were entirely "unfit for action." Attacking the Charleston forts with these inferior vessels and their unreliable batteries was an invitation to disaster. As for combined operations, nothing could be done. The Army ought long ago to have landed on James Island where it could have destroyed all of the harbor forts. It was now too late; the enemy commanded the landing sites and the whole island was covered with earthworks.[59]

Du Pont's brief reference to the Army, which he carefully excluded from his reports to Washington, reflects his bitterness at being unable to secure any active cooperation from Hunter's command. We have already described the jurisdictional dispute which led to the permanent departure of General Foster, the dismissal of General Naglee, and the collapse of the Sullivan's Island plan. On 7 March, after explaining that his disposable force—12,250 men—was too small for a serious offensive against a Confederate army grossly overestimated in excess of sixty-five thousand, he informed Halleck that he intended to limit Army activity to taking possession of any forts captured by the Navy. This reversion to a passive role was not what Hunter wanted, nor was it his fault. "For the record," Halleck should remember that Foster had fouled up his plans. He even blamed Foster for the Confederate fortifications recently erected on Morris Island, claiming that this officer had conducted his reconnaissances in full view of the enemy, warning them of an impending attack.[60]

Having received no reassurance or, indeed, any reply from the general-in-chief, Hunter wrote again on the 23rd. Conveniently forgetting that he had invited Foster and Naglee to Charleston in the first place and had welcomed the reinforcements, he accused the administration of forcing upon him the ten thousand North Carolina troops, along with their insubordinate and "pro-slavery" officers. "And how," he whined, "can you hold me wholly responsible for the conduct of generals in whom I have no confidence, when every act of the authorities in Washington has tended to disorganize and demoralize my command?"[61]

Du Pont also embarked upon a vigorous campaign to cover his tracks. On 1 April, after telling his close friend and strongest supporter in Congress, Henry Winter Davis, that the Navy Department had got up the attack on Charleston merely to satisfy "a morbid appetite on the part of the public," he informed Davis that he was sending him a copy of his service record, and another to his wife, "in case anything should ever come up making reference desirable."[62] On the 4th, having heard that Halleck told Lincoln that Du Pont doubted the success of the naval attack, the admiral wrote his wife that he was glad Halleck had said this so that the president would not expect victory, "for no attempt can be more problematical." Seeing Hunter again that day confirmed his impression that the Army would do nothing, while the newspaper reporters there expected the general to make an attack and would blame Hunter for not supporting the Navy. All of this information, he concluded, should be placed in his private files, "for these operations and the capture of Charleston, or what is more probable the *failure* of its capture, will be a matter of historical discussion."[63]

Thus, two weeks before the first attack on Charleston, we find the responsible Army commander behaving as though the battle had already been fought and lost, and the responsible naval commander justifying his failure in advance of his defeat, preparing records for his defense at a court of inquiry, and attempting to excuse his intended course of action in the eyes of history. In their anxiety to save themselves from censure, Du Pont and Hunter forgot about the enemy and were therefore unable to make a realistic assessment of his capabilities. The engagement itself was the mere acting out of a scenario written and interpreted in advance. Whether or not Du Pont's military judgment was correct—and it is by no means conclusive that an aggressive commander, say Farragut, could not have forced the harbor, though at considerable cost—his determination to run no risk and his prior conviction of defeat made victory impossible.

Charleston's harbor defenses were certainly formidable, especially against direct attack by warships armed with an in-

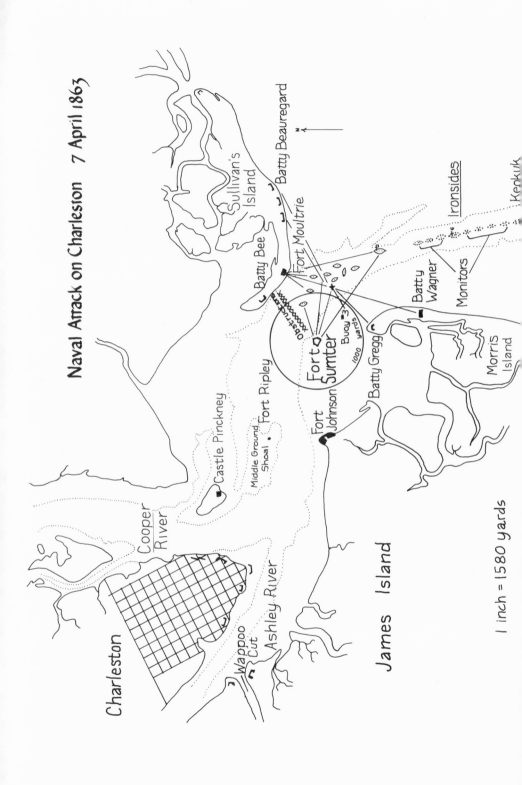

Naval Attack on Charleston 7 April 1863

Charleston

Cooper River

Castle Pinckney

Middle Ground Shoal

Fort Ripley

Wappoo Cut

Ashley River

James Island

1 inch = 1580 yards

Sullivan's Island

Batty Beauregard

Fort Moultrie

Batty Bee

OBSTRUCTIONS

Fort Sumter

Buoy #3

1000 yards

Fort Johnson

Batty Gregg

Batty Wagner

Ironsides

Monitors

Morris Island

Keokuk

N

ferior number of slow-firing guns. In arranging their batteries the Confederate engineers, under the skillful eyes of General Beauregard and Brigadier General Roswell S. Ripley commanding the Charleston district, took maximum advantage of the peculiarly favorable configuration of the harbor to construct a complex of defenses consisting of three interlocking "circles of fire," extending from the perimeter at Morris and Sullivan's Island to well beyond the city.[64]

In April 1863 the outer circle—comprising Battery Beauregard and Fort Moultrie on Sullivan's Island, Fort Sumter, a two-tiered brick casemated fort on an artificial island flanking the main channel, and Batteries Gregg and Wagner on Morris Island—was by far the strongest, the others being incomplete and weakly armed. For a distance of 2,000 yards the fire of seventy-six heavy guns from four directions could be poured in upon the main ship channel, the only approach to the inner harbor for vessels drawing more than eight feet of water. About 1,200 yards in front of the rope obstructions extending between Sumter's northeast angle and Fort Moultrie, the fire of these two main forts converged at a point marked by a red buoy, called by the Confederates Number 3. In preparation for the expected naval assault, most of the guns in both forts were placed and preregistered to fire upon this point.[65] Thus the Federal squadron had to pass through a "wall of fire" to reach the obstructions or even to come within optimum range (under 1,000 yards) for bombarding the works with their large smoothbore cannon.

For his part, Du Pont took every precaution to avoid injury to his ships. His published battle orders—which were never altered—specify that the whole squadron was to steam up the channel and take up bombardment stations off Sumter's northwest face, thereby requiring the ships to pass by Fort Moultrie and through the obstructions.[66] But a council of war the day before the engagement judged these orders impracticable and agreed unofficially to substantial modifications in the tactical plan.

First, Commander Thomas Turner, the *Ironsides*'s captain, refused to expose his ship to the concentrated fire of the forts at close range, pointing out that the flagship was a huge target compared with the monitors, and her unarmored ends were especially vulnerable to rifled shot. In fact, Turner would have preferred, and Du Pont actually considered, leaving her out of action altogether; but the admiral rejected this idea because, as he wrote his wife that day, it would make a bad impression upon the public and the Navy Department since this ship had half of the fleet's total firepower, "and if disaster came upon the other half, it would be said the Ironsides would have saved the others and was much stronger than I represented." So while Turner was compelled to include her in the line of battle, he was assured that he would not be required to expose her unduly by closing the range to under a thousand yards.[67]

Another difficulty concerned the obstructions. All of the monitor captains had previously refused to carry into battle a cumbersome bow raft armed with a torpedo, another Ericsson invention which the department had sent down with complete confidence that the device would blow a hole in the obstructions large enough for the fleet to pass through. They had, perhaps rightly, concluded that this raft, attached by long chains to a monitor bow, might well flip up exploding its charge with devastating effect against its host instead of the enemy barrier; or that a lucky Confederate shell might set it off prematurely with similar results.[68]

Nevertheless, Commander John Rodgers had agreed to carry the raft without the torpedo on the lead monitor *Weehawken*, thinking that the weight of the platform alone might break part of the rope network comprising the obstructions. Recent experiments with this device, however, had convinced Rodgers that it might make his ship unmanageable and act as a battering ram against her bow. Although still willing to carry the thing if Du Pont wished, he correctly predicted that he would be forced to cast it loose before proceeding very far up the channel.[69] Since the obstructions could not be removed and the *Ironsides*'s captain would not attempt to pass between Sumter and Moultrie in any case, the plan for anchoring off Sumter's northwest face obviously had to be abandoned.

What to do instead was never really decided. Du Pont seems to have had a vague notion of inflicting some damage on Sumter's east and northeast faces, possibly silencing or dismounting a few guns. At any rate, his only definite verbal instructions were that the ships should remain in motion, as at Port Royal to spoil the enemy's aim, fire as fast as the limitations of their armament allowed, and aim at the fort's barbette batteries whose plunging fire was most dangerous to the monitors' thin deck armor.[70] Beyond a further decision to go in on the ebb tide, instead of the flood, so any disabled monitors would be carried out of the harbor, Du Pont apparently intended to improvise as the battle developed.[71] One thing is certain. He did not intend to press the attack at the cost of any of his ships and was better prepared to retreat than advance.

Despite these precautions and modifications in plan, the admiral's contest with Fort Sumter on 7 April was brief and still more one-sided than he had anticipated. During an engagement lasting barely two hours, the iron-hulled, lightly armored ship USS *Keokuk* (not a monitor) was fatally perforated by ninety shot and shell.[72] Five of the seven monitors sustained extensive damage. Struck mostly near the base of the turrets by plunging shot from Sumter's barbette batteries or on the port stoppers, their guns were rendered useless. Smoke from the incessant cannonade blinded those in the pilot house attempting to keep clear of shoal water, and loose hardware cut down the gunners.[73] Only one monitor, the *Nahant*, and the *Keokuk* passed within 1,200 yards of Sumter—that is, beyond Buoy Number 3—and this was accidental. At the insistence of the flag pilot, the advance had been delayed so that, when these last two vessels ran into the Confederate "wall of fire" which had caused the preceding monitors to turn away after damage to their armament, the flood tide had set in full and they were unable to avoid a closer approach to the forts. The *Nahant*, carried within 1100 yards of Sumter, was at once struck by thirty-six heavy projectiles.[74]

The *Keokuk*'s unfortunate captain, the aggressive Commander A.C. Rhind, finding that his own inferior vessel had drifted to a point about 900 yards from the fort and within 300 yards of the obstructions, put up a gallant fight; but by the time the ship could be turned around in the tideway she was shot full of holes and retired from action in a sinking condition. The *Ironsides* became so unmanageable that she was forced to anchor at approximately 2,000 yards' range to avoid running aground. She might have been brought somewhat closer in to cover the monitors if her captain, who was familiar with the ship's peculiarities, had been present in the pilot house. But because there was only room for three men—the admiral, the fleet captain, and the pilot—Turner had been sent below to take charge of the gun deck, an error which may have cost Du Pont more than he realized. Because of the difficulty maneuvering, the flagship shot off only one broadside during the fight, meanwhile being struck by ninety-three enemy projectiles.[75]

The disparity of fire was tremendous. Fort Sumter alone expended over 2,000 rounds, while the Federal squadron got off only 139 shots.[76] The fort's shooting was remarkably accurate against such small targets, especially from the 7-inch Brooke rifles on the barbette tier.[77]

Ironically, Du Pont never got close enough to observe the impact of the fleet's fire on Sumter's walls. The brick ramparts were only five feet thick, and several heavy shots passed completely through the east wall near the lower casemates. The Federals might have accomplished more had they aimed exclusively at this level. Trying to dismount the barbette guns caused more than half of the shots to pass over the work. Judging by the effect of several projectiles striking near the base of the wall which loosened the masonry in all directions, the repeated concussion from 15-inch shot fired at low elevation might have brought down the entire face.[78] An English observer aboard a blockade runner waiting to escape from the harbor thought the damage to Sumter substantial considering the small number of rounds fired by the Federal warships and, in fact, concluded that the monitors were not so vulnerable as the Confederates had supposed and that brick forts could not withstand prolonged bombardment by 15-inch guns.[79]

The admiral saw only the injury to his squadron, however, and in his mind that was enough. His judgment had been proved correct; the physical evidence was before his eyes and before the eyes of the newspaper reporters who would tell the world that no number of frail monitors could stand up to such powerful shore batteries. Surely "Captain Fox" and the other officials in Washington, including "Old Brains" Halleck, must finally acknowledge what he had known and insisted upon from the beginning—that only a large-scale combined operation could take Charleston.

10

MORRIS ISLAND OPERATIONS

ALTHOUGH DU PONT failed to reduce Fort Sumter, he succeeded in his main object. The repulse of his squadron before Charleston convinced the Navy Department that military strategy, even when its aims are purely political, must be founded on tactical capability.[1]

In view of the admiral's known prejudice against monitor-type vessels, his report by itself would have carried little weight. But the department could not ignore the joint report of the monitor captains, unanimously condemning these vessels for assault purposes. The opinion of Commander John Rodgers, a "modern" technically minded officer who had previously expressed great confidence that the monitors could destroy masonry works, was decisive.[2] While the president ordered Du Pont to keep his squadron inside the Charleston bar to prevent Beauregard from releasing troops to oppose General Hooker's intended offensive against the Confederate army in Virginia, and Welles halfheartedly encouraged Du Pont to renew the naval engagement, by the end of April 1863 the Navy Department had clearly changed its mind about combined operations. Army cooperation, although difficult to obtain and not really welcomed, now appeared to Welles and Fox an essential component of future coast expeditions.[3]

The nature and extent of interservice cooperation required was still to be determined, however. That tactical integration of defensive systems would demand tactical integration of the assault force was by no means obvious. Nor did the Confederates themselves at first perceive that Charleston's fortifications represented a new and much stronger harbor defense system.[4]

We have previously described the character and situation

of early Southern coast defenses. All were isolated works. That many of them fell to naval bombardment alone does not alter the fact that they were entirely exposed to attack from the land side and could have been easily taken by infantry assault unless an army could be supplied to defend them. Their guns, unlike those in regular land fortresses and field works, had not been placed to interdict ground. Nor were their approaches commanded by the fire of other forts.

At Charleston, a fortuitous event had introduced the Confederates to a system which turned the unfavorable southern coast topography into an asset. The first bombardment of the war had been directed against Fort Sumter, then in Union hands, by Confederate land batteries disposed in a circle to produce a converging fire. These batteries were not only in position, therefore, to support Sumter against an attempt to force the harbor, but Sumter's guns covered the surrounding batteries and bore on their approaches.[5] Batteries Wagner, Gregg, Bee, and Beauregard, and Forts Moultrie and Johnson on Morris, Sullivan's, and James Islands became, in effect, outworks of the main fort. The defenders found the flat open terrain ideal for the employment of wide sweeping fire, while the engineers became so expert in building strong parapets and bombproofs and revetting low brick walls with sod and wet cotton bales that even the huge shells of the Federal fleet fired at close range failed to injure their works. This mutually supporting fortified system disconcerted the Union Army and Navy, proving almost impregnable to combined attack.[6]

The decision to resume operations against Charleston came from the president himself. Although Welles was now pessimistic about the Navy's chances against the forts and would have preferred sending the ironclads to Farragut for an attack on Mobile, he was willing to concede that, from a political standpoint, Charleston might be more important. Redeeming the Navy's honor was only one consideration.[7]

Increasing disaffection among New York and New England shippers, which coincided with the financial crisis, was the most pressing worry for the Lincoln administration throughout the spring and summer of 1863. Overreacting to the threat of Confederate commerce destroyers, American marine insurance underwriters, by May, were charging eight to ten times their prewar rates, precipitating the notorious "flight from the flag" which ruined the United States shipping industry for the next half century. Among those most injured were the government's biggest creditors.[8]

The U.S. Navy was unprepared for a sudden shift in strategy; by mid-1863, it had lost its operational flexibility. During the preceding year, almost all of the department's energy and funds had gone into building and fitting out monitors and river ironclads. If the capability of these vessels against shore batteries was still somewhat in doubt, their uselessness in any other offensive role was a certainty.[9] Barely able to remain afloat under tow on the open sea, the monitors could not even blockade except from protected stations inside harbors and inlets—let alone pursue the enemy's swift ocean cruisers. Nor could they serve as escorts for valuable Northern cargo like the California gold shipments. Only by detaching oceangoing ships from the blockade could the raiders be eliminated, and only by taking the South's remaining seaports, or at least occupying their harbors, could the blockaders be released for this duty. Since Charleston and Wilmington, the ports most difficult to close by outside blockade, tied up the most vessels, their capture was given the highest priority.[10]

We have observed that, although Welles and Fox had hoped to secure these places by naval coup, assuring the president that Army cooperation was neither wanted nor required, this mode of attack had failed. Ironically, General Halleck, having rejected a McClellan-type strategy based on combined operations in favor of "continental" offensives, now found himself under great pressure from Lincoln and Welles to provide the infantry support necessary to implement a separate "naval" strategy against the Confederacy. Because this requirement not only violated his sacrosanct principle of concentration but threatened to derange the plans of those commanding the main Union armies, the general-in-chief, for the only time in the war, openly opposed the president.

Renewing the attack upon Charleston was, in his opinion, bad strategy; and bad strategy, because it always failed, was bad policy. The whole of Hunter's force, the monitor squadron —everything on the South Atlantic coast except the blockaders and small garrisons for Port Royal and Beaufort—should be sent up the Mississippi, if not to assist Grant at Vicksburg, then to join General Banks for an expedition into northwest Louisiana and Texas. Occupying the coast would not shorten the war, he argued. Only by seizing the enemy's resources, which Halleck still strangely supposed were centered somewhere in the trans-Mississippi, could Union forces compel the Confederate States to surrender.[11]

Lincoln might have used his authority as supreme commander to overrule the general-in-chief. But this was not his style. Besides, he had called Halleck to replace McClellan in order to avoid both a clash of wills and responsibility for issuing direct orders to the Army, orders which might either offend their professional sensibilities or produce another debacle like the Valley campaign of 1862. Instead, he convinced the general to approve further operations against Charleston.

The method of persuasion was clever and effective. In mid-May several influential New York friends of the administration contacted Quincy A. Gillmore, General Sherman's former chief engineer in the Department of the South, now a brigadier, suggesting that the War Department might welcome a technical officer, experienced in knocking down forts and familiar with the South Carolina coast, to replace Hunter in the Charleston command, and offered to recommend him to Secretary Stanton. On the 23rd, Gillmore wrote General Cullum asking him to remind Halleck of his plan, submitted to McClellan in February 1862, for destroying Fort Sumter with rifled siege artillery and to urge the practicability of such an enterprise to fulfill the Navy's requirement for Army cooperation at Charleston.[12]

A letter from Hunter received a few days later furnished Lincoln an excuse to replace him. In the overblown style characteristic of his correspondence, Hunter railed against Du Pont for his lack of initiative and begged to be "relieved" from his orders to "cooperate with the Navy." Freed from the admiral's shackles, he would carry the war to the enemy's heart, invade South Carolina and Georgia and, pillaging for his supplies and arming the slaves with old muskets and pikes, would lay waste the country in all directions, winning the war single-handed before the end of summer.[13] Lincoln's horrified reaction to this bombastic proposition was mild compared with that of the general-in-chief, who had long suspected that all political generals were a little crazy.

General Gillmore now appeared in Washington carrying his detailed plan for reducing the Charleston defenses. Brisk and efficient, his remarks brief and to the point, his whole manner inspired confidence. Here was a fellow engineer whom Halleck could trust to do the job without fuss, follow orders, and avoid wild schemes, and who offered an uncomplicated plan that Halleck could understand. The operation was simple, said Gillmore. If the Navy could put the Army within a mile and one-half of Fort Sumter, he guaranteed to knock the fort to pieces as he had Pulaski. With Sumter gone, the monitors could enter the harbor and demand the surrender of the city.[14]

The Navy Department was immediately won over; Fox, in particular, was enchanted with the plan. Charleston would fall to the Navy after all; the monitors and the department's judgment would be vindicated. Of course Du Pont must go. The admiral continued to reject operations on Morris or Sullivan's Islands. Despite repeated urging from Welles, the only offensive proposal he had submitted to the department since the defeat of his squadron on 7 April involved an indirect approach to the city via the Edisto River or Bull's Bay north of the harbor. Since neither approach could place the Army's siege batteries in position to destroy the harbor fortifications, these suggestions were unacceptable.[15]

Having finally secured Halleck's approval for combined operations against Charleston, the government acted quickly. On 12 June 1863, General Gillmore was appointed to command the Department of the South with the understanding that his limited task was to destroy Fort Sumter for the Navy and that he should neither request, nor expect, reinforcements.[16] As his naval counterpart Welles chose another technical expert, Captain Dahlgren, who at last received his promotion to rear admiral for the assignment. Dahlgren had never commanded a ship, nor Gillmore infantry, but this fact was thought to be of no importance.

The prerequisite for levelling Fort Sumter was the occupation of Morris Island, a long low sand island, the northern half of which was within shell range of Sumter. Batteries Wagner and Gregg, earthen outworks of Sumter, protected this part of the island from seaborne attack. The only deterrent to a landing on the southern tip of Morris Island, however, was a line of one-gun batteries emplaced among the sand hills commanding the beach. These were beyond the range of Battery Wagner's artillery.

The first stage in what Gillmore termed the combined "program" for cracking Charleston's defenses called for the establishment of a beachhead on the southern end of Morris Island, followed by the capture of Wagner. Having secured a base of operations, the second stage would comprise the erection of breaching batteries on Cummings Point and the destruction of Fort Sumter. In the final stage, the fleet, using the monitors to keep down Fort Moultrie's fire, would remove the channel obstructions and run into the harbor.[17]

Since the first two stages of the operations plan were mainly an Army responsibility, General Gillmore selected the point of attack. Everyone, including Gillmore, recognized that James Island was the key to the Charleston harbor defense system. Confederate General Beauregard, expecting an attack in this quarter, had stationed most of his troops there.[18] Union control of the Stono River apparently enabled a force to land by surprise anywhere on the island's long western shore.

In fact, extensive marshes along, or immediately behind, the shore line made James Island accessible from the Stono at only two points. On the extreme right of the Confederate line, near Wappoo Cut, the practicable landing site was commanded by a very strong earthwork, Fort Pemberton. A bend in the river and its narrowness at this point would not allow Federal gunboats to bring effective fire against this work to silence it. A landing near Legaré's plantation at the left of the western line, on the other hand, looked deceptively easy. A good road led from this site over firm ground to a point called Artillery Crossroads, the occupation of which would turn the Stono defenses and threaten the rear of the enemy works fronting the harbor.[19]

But the road was commanded in flank from the direction of Secessionville. Impassable swamps restricted the approach to the town on that side to a narrow neck of land debouching in front of another earthwork, Fort Lamar. As earlier noted, a Federal division under General Benham had attempted an assault upon this work in the summer of 1862 when it was weakly manned. Its decisive repulse demonstrated to Gillmore the futility of mass infantry attacks on a narrow front without adequate covering fire. Field pieces were useless for silencing heavy guns, even where the ground permitted their deployment in large numbers, and siege batteries could not be erected within range of the fort unless its fire could be kept down by other means. The two Federal gunboats engaged in the 1862 operation, forced to employ indirect fire at extreme range, were worse than useless. Their shells failed to injure the well-protected garrison, falling mostly among the attackers on the open ground in front of the work.[20] In short, Gillmore could not bring a sufficient volume of fire to bear on the enemy defenses on James Island. In order to use the fleet's fire to maximum effect, he chose to attack on Morris Island.

In an effort to contract, and thereby strengthen, their extensive fortified line, the Confederates had abandoned Folly Island which lay just south of Morris across narrow Lighthouse Inlet. Under cover of darkness and thick woods, Gillmore emplaced forty-seven heavy guns on the northern tip of Folly Island to command the sand hills above the landing site. The original purpose of these batteries was apparently not to soften up the defenses or protect the assault force, but to cover its withdrawal in case of a repulse.[21] Gillmore's sudden lack of confidence was the result of consultations with Admiral Du Pont concerning the details of the proposed landing.

Du Pont still refused to risk the ironclads in support of an assault on the Morris Island defenses. He had not changed his view that a station inside the bar was unsafe in all but the calmest weather for the unseaworthy monitors whose bad steering qualities were likely to get them aground off Morris Island beach where they would fall into Confederate hands and be used to break the blockade.[22] Besides, Du Pont had been relieved as of 3 June and was reluctant to commit his successor to any definite arrangement with the Army.[23]

But the best season for operations in that climate was rapidly passing and it was apparent to Gillmore that his activity would soon alert the Confederates to their danger. Since it was imperative to move at once and since the fleet could not secure its lodgment on Morris Island, the Army must rely instead on surprise and celerity of movement. Only a night assault could capture the enemy beach defenses without artillery support.[24]

Fortunately, this expedient was not attempted. A night attack under ideal conditions with the best troops is an uncertain enterprise. Gillmore's force—a motley collection of Negro regiments, raw recruits, and veterans of a year's garrison duty in coastal outposts—was yet to become an army. Even in broad daylight, they frequently shot at their own men, panicked under fire, and were useless without their officers. Landing such a mob on the enemy's shore from small boats at night would have proved an almost certain disaster. Nor could they have surprised the alert Confederates who had long anticipated an attack and now knew where, when, and in what strength the blow would fall. If Morris Island was weakly held, it was not due to inadequate information, but to inadequate means. The security of James Island was Beauregard's first concern. The second was guarding Sullivan's Island. Morris Island's defenses received last priority since a Federal lodgment there was considered least dangerous, and Battery Wagner was relied upon to keep the enemy beyond breaching range of Fort Sumter.[25]

Still, Beauregard might have expected the batteries at the southern end of Morris Island to delay the Federal assault force long enough to permit the transfer of troops from James and Sullivan's Island for a counterattack. The heavy guns were carefully masked among the sand hills and supported by a well-disciplined regiment and a company of sharpshooters.[26] The ease with which the Federals overran these defenses was due entirely to intelligent planning and skillful coordination of the combined attack.

While Gillmore reluctantly pushed forward his preparations to land without naval fire support, his urgent appeals for Halleck to press the Navy Department into immediate cooperation brought results. At the end of June, Welles instructed Du Pont to draw up a more realistic combined plan and the night attack was cancelled. The revised scheme called for a joint preparatory bombardment from Folly Island and several monitors and gunboats in Lighthouse Inlet, after which the troops would hit the beach and carry the defenses by storm.[27]

General Pierre G. T. Beauregard
(*Library of Congress*)

Rear Admiral John A. Dahlgren
(*National Archives*)

When Admiral Dahlgren arrived to take command of the fleet at Charleston on 4 July, he was not satisfied with the arrangements. It seemed too easy for the Confederates to wait out the bombardment, then reman the guns and open on the unprotected assault boats, or to reinforce the works with troops landed at Cummings Point or from Battery Wagner. Unlike his distinguished predecessor of the "old Navy," Dahlgren favored experimenting with new weapons and techniques. An inventor, rather than a sailor, his faith in the value of technology caused him to appreciate the advantages and minimize the defects of the monitors. These vessels were ideal for close infantry support and laying down interdicting fire. Their shallow draft allowed them to approach near shore while the turrets permitted a wide arc of fire without constantly changing station.[28]

Consequently, the final plan was more sophisticated than previous combined operations and involved all available means. The assault division was divided into two groups; one brigade supported by howitzer launches to land at Oyster Point, and another slightly larger brigade to cross directly from Folly Island beach under cover of the gunboats stationed in Light-

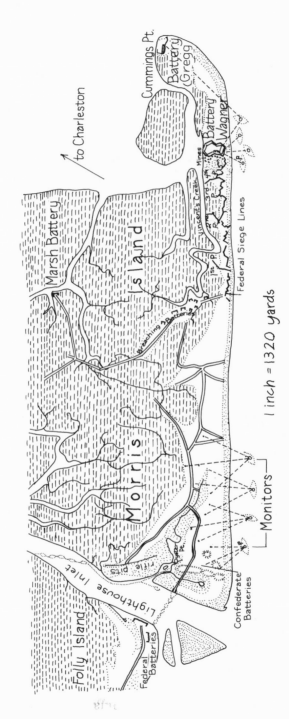

Operations on Morris Island   July–September 1863

1 inch = 1320 yards

to Charleston

Cummings Pt.
Battery (Gregg)
Battery Wagner
Mines
Vincent's Creek
Federal Siege Lines
Marsh Battery
Island
Breaching Batteries
Morris
Lighthouse Inlet
Folly Island
Federal Batteries
Rifle Pits
Confederate Batteries
Monitors

house Inlet.[29] While Gillmore's batteries pounded the defenses in front, the monitor squadron, lying off the eastern shore of Morris Island, would isolate the enemy's detached works from Battery Wagner and take them in enfilade and reverse. For the first time, an American amphibious force would land under fire and nothing was left to chance. Dahlgren's orders were unusually detailed. The monitors were to shoot only grape and canister, exploding the projectiles just above the heads of the gun crews or on the ground surface, dispersing their fire over a wide area. The gunboats were to use carefully aimed fire with both shell and canister. Army signalmen were stationed in the lead boat, with the detachment to land behind the batteries at Oyster Point, aboard the flagship, and at Gillmore's headquarters on Folly Island.[30]

The joint bombardment opened at dawn on 10 July. By eight o'clock the Confederate guns were silenced and the leading brigade, waiting in Folly Island Creek since midnight, landed at Oyster Point. The Confederate infantry, consisting of one volunteer regiment, responded quickly and prevented the Federals from advancing into the rear of the batteries. This attack, designed as a holding operation, accomplished its purpose. The remaining Union brigade—three regiments and a battery—had meanwhile crossed the inlet from Folly Island beach at low tide, taking shelter under the high north bank of the inlet until the enemy artillery was silenced.[31] On signal from the flagship, the Federal bombardment shifted to the ground north of the batteries, and the troops rushed in among the sand hills, capturing the Confederate guns and outflanking their supports who retired into Battery Wagner under a heavy fire from the fleet. By 9:30 the Union army occupied the southern two-thirds of the island and the ironclads were pounding Wagner's sea face.[32]

The rapid collapse of the beach defense encouraged Gillmore to believe that Wagner would fall to an immediate assault. But he had made no preparations for this and his men were tired and strung out all over the island. Having spent the remainder of the 10th resting and reorganizing, the Federal infantry attempted to storm the work at dawn the following morning without fire support. It was the attackers who were taken by surprise.[33]

Battery Wagner, an enclosed earthwork measuring approximately six hundred by three hundred feet, extended completely across Morris Island, three-quarters of a mile south of Cummings Point. In July 1863 it was armed with one 10-inch columbiad and one 32-pounder smoothbore on the sea face, plus two 8-inch naval guns, and eight guns and howitzers of smaller caliber firing through embrasures on the land face. The bombproof behind the sea face could accommodate 900 men. A sand ridge 250 yards south of the battery furnished good cover for sharpshooters and a wide ditch filled with seawater protected its front. Battery Gregg, a small earthwork mounting one 10-inch columbiad and a 9-inch naval gun bearing on the channel, was manned by an artillery detachment.

United States Coast Survey maps in Gillmore's possession revealed that, at a point about 200 yards in front of Battery Wagner, Morris Island narrowed to 100 yards. But the maps, prepared in 1858, were no longer accurate. By 1863 the sea marsh had nearly cut through the island; thus the first assault brigade found itself squeezed into a front of barely 25 yards. Although a few hearty souls braved Wagner's withering shrap-

Federal assault on Battery Wagner, 18 July 1863 (*Navy Department*)

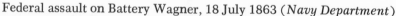

nel fire to reach the ditch, their supports were inevitably far
behind. The attack quickly dissolved and the survivors withdrew without organization and badly demoralized.[34]

A preliminary bombardment was therefore arranged with
the fleet in preparation for a second assault. The huge 15-inch
shells of the monitors and *Ironsides*'s powerful broadside kept
Wagner's gunners in the bombproof while the Army's rifled
siege guns were emplaced along the land front. On 18 July
the Federals opened a terrific bombardment. For eleven hours,
Battery Wagner was pounded with nine thousand heavy shot
and shell. A cloud of loose quartz sand was hurled from the
parapet and traverses high into the air, only to fall back to
its original position. The fort had remained almost silent
throughout the bombardment and Gillmore supposed that, if
the garrison survived, it was at least demoralized. The fleet
thereupon ceased fire and, at dusk, the assault force sprang
forward. Emerging unharmed from the bombproof, Wagner's
defenders discovered their guns equally uninjured. The attackers again met a hail of grape, canister, and rifle balls and
were driven back with great slaughter.[35]

It was apparent at this point that different tactics were
required to take Battery Wagner. Neither the length of the
preparatory bombardment nor the weight of metal striking the
target seemed to produce the least effect upon the fort's capacity to resist assault. Although the work could not be demolished nor its guns disabled, it could be neutralized by a
continuous smothering bombardment. To avoid hitting their
own men, however, the Federals had to stop firing just before
the assault, allowing the enemy to reman his guns. A covered
approach to within 50 yards of the parapet could be achieved
only by constructing siege lines.

Accordingly, on 19 July, Gillmore converted his line of batteries into a first parallel about 1500 yards in front of Wagner.
Because Morris Island at this point was less than 300 yards
wide and all of this space was required for infantry trenches,
the Union artillerists built additional gun emplacements in
the swamp on the left flank of the approaches. The right was
protected by the fleet.[36]

At first the Federals made rapid progress and, by 8 August,
had opened their third parallel only 500 yards from the fort.

But here the advance was stopped. More destructive than Wagner's fire were the shells from Fort Sumter's barbette guns, fired over Batteries Gregg and Wagner, which fell almost vertically into the trenches. This feature of the defense had not been anticipated and produced a change in the original "program." Since his rifled guns were useless against Wagner anyway, Gillmore decided to demolish Sumter at long range before driving the Confederates from Morris Island. Indeed, unless Sumter's barbette batteries were silenced, Wagner could probably hold out indefinitely, compelling a Federal evacuation of the island because of sickness and attrition.[37]

Admiral Dahlgren was immediately informed of the new plan and asked to employ his monitors against Sumter's east face, and the *Ironsides* against Wagner to prevent interference with the breaching batteries. Although the admiral preferred a combined assault on Wagner, offering to land an army regiment in rear of the fort while the main body attacked in front, Gillmore considered his force too weak to divide and would agree to another assault attempt only if the fleet furnished a column of sailors and Marines. Since Dahlgren's crews were already understrength, the request for sailors was refused.[38]

Nor was it found possible to use Marines. At the admiral's suggestion, Welles had assembled and equipped a battalion of 400 Marines whose special assignment was to land and isolate Battery Wagner from the north. On 7 August, the day after the Marines arrived at Charleston, Dahlgren issued instructions for an amphibious assault to be carried out on the night of the 16th in cooperation with a frontal attack by the Army in brigade strength. This operation had an excellent chance of success. The Confederates were unaware of the Federal plan and had no defenses in the rear of the fort.[39]

However, the Marines were totally unprepared for any kind of fighting, let alone a night landing and assault. Most of the battalion were raw recruits that had never been under fire. Their commander complained that nine days were insufficient to train the men who, though brave as individuals, were not used to acting in concert. It was impossible, he maintained, to conduct boat drill in the hot sun; the nights were too dark, and the twilight too short. Many men were sick and insubordinate; the remainder, unaccustomed to living ashore, could not even

Major General Quincy A. Gillmore and staff at Morris Island, S.C., 1863 (*Library of Congress*)

cook for themselves. Reluctantly, Dahlgren called off the operation on 16 August. Having exhausted other possibilities, he promptly approved the joint bombardment.[40]

Gillmore found Fort Sumter a more rewarding target than Battery Wagner. In a massive precision bombardment lasting fifteen days, the masonry of Sumter's gorge wall was systematically knocked to pieces. Struck in front and in reverse, the rest of the barbette tier and upper casemates soon fell into rubble. When Gillmore stopped firing, only a small section of the northeast wall remained standing and only one gun, in the western face, was serviceable.[41]

The second phase of the combined program had been successfully completed, but the fleet was not yet free to remove the obstructions and run into the harbor. Battery Wagner remained defiant and Dahlgren's assistance was still required to take it. If the destruction of Fort Sumter had appreciably diminished the enemy's fire onto Wagner's approaches, allowing the Federals to push their siege lines to within 150 yards of the work, progress beyond this point seemed impossible. A thick minefield protecting the ground in front of the ditch caused many casualties and demoralized the men. Wagner's fire, previously kept to a tolerable level by cohorn mortars, the fleet, and the enemy's need to conserve ammunition, now fell with full fury on the head of the sap. Work parties in the trenches unearthed the bodies of Union soldiers killed in the two assault attempts. These added to the noxious effect of an already unhealthy climate to swell the sick list.[42]

It then occurred to Gillmore that the troops might take heart if Wagner could be kept silenced. He therefore brought forward his mortars and again asked Dahlgren to bombard the sea face of the work, especially at night. Meanwhile, the rifled guns attempted, unsuccessfully, to penetrate Wagner's bombproof. Another idea arranged with Dahlgren was that the Navy should complete the investment of Morris Island with a line of picket boats. A calcium light placed at the left of the second parallel threw a circle of illumination over Battery Gregg allowing the boats patrolling just outside the circle to interrupt enemy vessels landing supplies or reinforcements at Cummings Point. Although bad weather often interfered with these arrangements and the Confederates were able to rotate the garrisons every four or five days, the light plus the continuous bombardment prevented Wagner's defenders from repairing damages.[43] After 23 August, it was only a question of time before Wagner fell.

But time was important. Beauregard's one purpose for expending lives in defense of Morris Island after Fort Sumter was silenced was to gain time to strengthen his inner line of works. Throughout the bombardment and during the two weeks preceding the evacuation of Batteries Wagner and Gregg on 7 September, the Confederates systematically removed and transported all of Sumter's dismounted, but still serviceable heavy guns, with their ammunition and appliances, to James Island, Fort Moultrie (Sullivan's Island), and the city of Charleston.[44] Thus, by the time Dahlgren was ready to begin the final phase of the combined operations plan, the inner defenses were more formidable than the outer "circle of fire" which had so severely damaged Du Pont's ironclads in April.

Other problems worried the admiral. For two months, the monitors had been almost continuously engaged in support of operations ashore. Having designed and tested their armament himself, Dahlgren knew that the large shell guns, particularly the 15-inchers, were quickly expended in action. Only a few 11-inch replacements were available at Port Royal. Even with new batteries, the ships themselves would remain in poor condition. The enemy's shot, while it failed to penetrate the side armor, had bent many of the plates, loosened the turret packing, and sheared off dozens of nuts and bolts. Lying close inshore during often foul weather had strained the monitor hulls, especially beneath their armored overhang, causing some of them to leak badly. Although the great strain on the crews and their need for relief had been recognized by the Navy Department in July and a few replacements were sent in August, the problem of sickness and exhaustion was chronic in the fleet.[45]

As early as 21 August, Dahlgren warned the Army command that its constant calls for fire support might so expend the ironclads' offensive power that they could not carry out the final stage of the operation. Having attempted on several occasions to neutralize Wagner's fire with the land batteries alone, however, Gillmore had quickly discovered that the enemy was not only able to stop all work on the approaches but to dismount the siege guns.[46] Without the fleet's fire, indirectly applied against Wagner, Fort Sumter could not have been reduced nor the troops maintained on Morris Island for even a day. The one factor determining Beauregard's decision to reject an attack in force to drive the Federals from the island— the only expedient which might have saved Sumter—was the Federal Navy.[47]

Ironically, the very success against Sumter and Wagner of Gillmore and Dahlgren's well-planned and executed combined operation, made possible by a degree of enthusiastic cooperation unusual in any campaign, was largely responsible for the eventual breakdown of harmonious command relations and the consequent failure of the overall plan. While Sumter's destruction was certainly a masterpiece in the long-range employment of direct fire against permanent works, its timing had important repercussions. Had it been possible to take Wagner first, the subsequent levelling of Sumter followed immediately by a naval attack would probably have opened the channel while the fleet might still hope to overwhelm or run by the inner defenses.

But the obstructions still stood in the way. Dahlgren's information concerning their character was obtained wholly from the questionable accounts of enemy deserters and carefully fostered Confederate rumors that the entire channel between Fort Sumter and Sullivan's Island, as well as most of the inner harbor, was full of mines.[48] Since Du Pont had never intended to run into the harbor without reducing Sumter and none of his vessels had approached within 300 yards of the barrier, his reports minimized its importance. Sumter's artillery, especially the barbette guns whose plunging fire was most destructive to the monitors, was seen as the primary obstacle for the fleet. After the fort's batteries had been destroyed or removed, therefore, the Navy anticipated no difficulty in taking up the obstructions, since the monitors could prevent the Sullivan's Island batteries from interfering with Federal work parties. In fact, both Dahlgren and Gillmore expected the Confederates to abandon Sumter once it had been rendered useless for mounting heavy artillery.[49] That it could close the harbor equally well as an infantry post was an unpleasant surprise.

On 7 September, upon discovering that the Confederates had evacuated Morris Island, Dahlgren summoned Sumter's garrison to surrender the ruined work. After consulting General Beauregard, the post commander replied that "Admiral Dahlgren must take it and hold it if he can."[50] The following night a force of 500 Union sailors and Marines attempted to land from small boats and occupy the fort. The attack was doomed before it began.

In April the Confederates had recovered a code book from the wreck of the USS *Keokuk*, and were thus able to read the signals exchanged between the Union flagship and Army headquarters. Dahlgren and Gillmore often discussed their plans through this medium and apparently never suspected that the thoroughness of the enemy's preparations was related to this valuable source of information. Having intercepted the admiral's signal on the afternoon of the 8th, the Confederate gunners in Fort Moultrie, Batteries Bee and Beauregard, and the James Island works fixed their ranges and trained their guns on Sumter's sea approaches. Riflemen from Charleston reinforced the small garrison, and the ironclad CSS *Chicora* took up a position to enfilade the threatened landing points.[51]

The first division of boats had barely pulled ashore under Sumter's northeast face when all of the enemy batteries opened on the supporting divisions. The effect was so sudden and overwhelming that the men whose craft remained afloat, panicked in confusion, colliding with one another and with those in the rear. Isolated on shore, their boats destroyed, the advance party was greeted by a hail of bullets and chunks of masonry were thrown upon their heads from the ramparts. Although the survivors found some protection at the base of the wall, they soon realized that their situation was hopeless and surrendered, while the remnants of the expedition beat a hasty retreat to their vessels, out of range of the enemy's guns. The whole adventure, which resulted in few Union casualties but 125 men taken prisoner, was over in an hour.[52]

Gillmore's soldiers, assembled at Cummings Point, remained frustrated observers during the unequal contest. Strangely enough, the general had made independent plans to launch a similar expedition that same night. Informed in the afternoon of Dahlgren's intentions, in reply to his request for some landing boats, Gillmore very sensibly suggested a combined expedition under a single command. Although he did not specify an Army officer, the man he had selected to command the troops was a brigadier general and outranked, in equivalent terms, Lieutenant Commander E.P. Williams who was assigned to lead the naval attack. Dahlgren insisted that he would accept the Army's "aid" only if the combined force was commanded by a naval officer.[53]

Gillmore was astonished. While the Navy apparently considered anything having to do with boats its peculiar responsibility, he really could not see that sailors were better qualified for storming forts than soldiers. He reminded the admiral that the object of the campaign was more important than professional pride and that their success thus far was due to a selfless spirit of cooperation. He did not offer to place his men under naval command, however. The most that could be arranged was a set of signals to prevent the two expeditions from running into each other.[54] In the event, Gillmore considered the risk of collision too great and held his troops ready in their boats off Cummings Point to exploit any success gained by the Navy. Its decisive repulse convinced him that a second attempt would meet a similar fate, and the Army returned to its captured works with the intention of assuming the defensive.

Although it was by no means clear in September 1863, neither the Federal fleet nor Army would advance any closer to Charleston until the Southerners evacuated the harbor in February 1865. The boat attack produced the first sign of trouble between the respective commanders. Over the next several months, the rift grew wider. Circumstance was a more important determinant than the character or intelligence of either man.

Frustrated by his inability to remove the channel obstructions and prevent the Confederates from continuously strengthening their second defensive line, his men exhausted by sickness and overwork, his ships and their guns in poor condition, Admiral Dahlgren saw the chance for victory steadily slipping away. He must have remembered how, in the fall of 1862, he had begged Secretary Welles to give him Du Pont's command. He, the inexperienced fleet commander, the object of resentment among line officers because he was the president's favorite and had won his promotion in the laboratory instead of in battle, had promised to win for the Navy the honor of capturing the "cradle of the Confederacy." And he, Du Pont's most ardent critic just six months before, perhaps reflected on the fate of the old veteran, whose reputation and accomplishments were among the highest in the service, now cast upon the shelf and embittered toward the government he had so faithfully served. Could Dahlgren, indeed, accomplish more than Du Pont?

That the fault was not his, nor Gillmore's, was small consolation for the failure. If the general could do little to aid the fleet, he might at least have understood its problems. But now that Gillmore had occupied Morris Island and destroyed Fort Sumter, as he had assured General Halleck he could do, he seemed to consider his work finished. The rest was up to the Navy and, since Halleck had never thought Charleston—or the fleet—of any importance, he was satisfied with the campaign as a great feat of engineering and it was unlikely that he would press Gillmore into undertaking further combined operations or send an army large enough to attack the inner defenses.[55]

For his part, General Gillmore saw no further use for his services at Charleston and was anxious for more active employment. Halleck would send no reinforcements. Dahlgren would accept no advice from the Army and could not seem to face reality. He insisted that the obstructions could not be removed from open boats unless the Confederate riflemen were driven out of Sumter's ruins or the place occupied by Federal soldiers, claiming that ships could not approach the rope barrier without fouling their propellers.[56]

While Gillmore could shell the rubble as often as requested, his artillery on Morris Island would not drive out the enemy's well-protected sharpshooters. Nor did Dahlgren seem to understand that Sumter, ringed on three sides (most importantly on its channel faces) by Confederate batteries, was untenable for Federal troops if it could be captured. When Gillmore offered—generously, he thought—on 27 September to remove the obstructions himself in lieu of expending more ammunition in fruitless bombardments, Dahlgren was greatly offended. He reminded the general that the capture of Morris Island and the destruction of Sumter, for which the Army took full credit in the press, would have been impossible without the fleet, remarking that, if the Navy no longer functioned efficiently, it was the Army's fault. The obstructions were a naval responsibility and Gillmore should not presume to interfere except on request.[57]

Further consultation was useless. While a subsequent combined operation might have failed to take the city in any case, such a complete breakdown in command relations made it impossible. By October, the Army and Navy were moving in different directions and making wholly independent plans. Gillmore wrote Halleck suggesting that most of his troops be organized into an army corps and employed in some more promising theater of war. On 20 November, he sent Major General Alfred Terry to Washington to propose an expedition against Wilmington.[58] This first suggestion was not carried out until May 1864, when Gillmore's force, as the X Corps, was assigned to General Butler's Army of the James for its move on Richmond. In the interval, the troops undertook nothing more ambitious than outpost skirmishing. General Foster, who succeeded Gillmore, attempted several minor descents on James Island and another boat landing at Sumter with the army detachment left at Charleston, but his force was too small and was everywhere repulsed.[59] By 1864 the Confederates had further strengthened the inner defenses with dozens of earthen batteries placed to support one another, and had filled the whole harbor with mines.

Admiral Dahlgren meanwhile pressed his earlier requests for new and more powerful monitors, a fast steamer for ramming the obstructions, and self-propelled submersible craft for cutting the ropes and exploding the mines. In truth, Dahlgren, despite his claims to the contrary, preferred leaving the obstructions in place until he felt prepared to pass the inner batteries. The Navy Department still overestimated the defensive properties of the monitors and, judging by Du Pont's experience, would expect him to go in once the channel was open. While Dahlgren was willing to take the risk rather than give up the objective altogether, he had no illusion that the fleet could reach Charleston without heavy cost. Estimating the probable loss in sunk and severely damaged vessels at close to fifty percent, he informed Welles that he must have at least ten new or recently repaired and strengthened monitors before going in.[60]

Dahlgren was right to suppose that the secretary wanted him to attempt another naval attack in spite of such adverse odds. At Welles's insistence, a council of war was held aboard the flagship on 22 October 1863. Present were the admiral, the seven ironclad captains, the fleet captain, and two staff officers. After a six-hour discussion, the four junior officers voted to attack at once with the seven available monitors; the six seniors agreed with Dahlgren that the attack should be postponed until December when the new ironclads were expected to arrive.[61]

Unfortunately, the Federal Navy's ironclad building program had encountered a variety of difficulties. Having temporarily suspended construction of heavy monitors in favor of a new and untested shallow-draft type which proved a complete failure, the department next tied up the yards with ambitious contracts for several powerful seagoing ironclads as a response to intelligence that the Confederacy had ordered vessels of similar design from European firms. To make things worse, the plans were not carefully examined by competent naval architects, so that many changes delayed completion of the ships; contract irregularities also greatly increased costs and further slowed production.[62] Meanwhile, the hero of New Orleans, Admiral Farragut, was becoming understandably impatient to receive the monitors he had requested since mid-1862 for his projected attack on Mobile.

The result was that the additional monitors promised Dahlgren for December, when finally completed in the spring and summer of 1864, were sent to the Gulf. Although the department assured the admiral that he could have the next batch, they had still not arrived on 17 February 1865 when Charleston, threatened in the rear by Sherman's army, was abandoned to the Federals. By that time, the Confederacy was collapsing and the "victory" was unimportant.

Given the Union government's lack of strategic sense, it is tempting to dismiss the Charleston campaign as futile from the beginning. Du Pont certainly thought so, as did Halleck. Even Welles, despite his public optimism and reluctance to let the object go once the naval attack had failed, seriously doubted that the city itself could be taken. But such a judgment ignores the real alternatives available within the restricted operational framework imposed upon the field commanders from above. While the combined force was limited to attacking Charleston from the harbor side, it was not required to proceed by way of Morris Island. The Federals might have revived General Seymour's plan for landing on Sullivan's Island, which formed the northern arm of the outer harbor. The capture of the Sullivan's Island batteries, followed by the destruction of Fort Sumter, would have opened the channel without risk to the fleet. Although the records are silent regarding this alternative, Coast Survey charts reveal extensive shoals off the eastern end of the island, the only practicable landing point, which might have prevented the fleet from closing to effective range. Two other factors—the lack of a nearby Federal base north of the harbor, or a protected anchorage for the ships—may have made this approach unattractive. Still, something might have been attempted in this direction, or at least considered.

If topography prevented the Federals from concentrating enough guns against the James Island defenses, their maximum firepower was equally insufficient to reduce Wagner. That the work eventually fell to a siege does not prove the wisdom of pressing the attack at this point, because the cost of fulfilling the prerequisite for the main operation was so high that nothing further could be done. Although these technical experts, having no experience in field command, perhaps lacked the ability to adapt quickly to unforeseen developments, this alone is not sufficient to account for their failure.

One of the most striking features of the campaign is Dahlgren's and Gillmore's repeated confusion when the military situation did not develop as they expected. The rapid success of the initial landing so surprised Gillmore that he was unprepared to exploit the momentary opportunity to overrun Battery Wagner. He was surprised that the fleet bombardment of 10 July did not permit his troops to walk into the work on the 11th. He was surprised again by the disastrous failure of the second assault. Neither he nor Dahlgren anticipated the need for constant fleet support for the troops or the siege batteries, even though the Morris Island approach was initially selected with this consideration in mind. Both commanders were disconcerted when the Confederates did not surrender Fort Sumter on 7 September. What neither those involved, nor subsequent Civil War analysts, fully appreciated was that the Federal attack on Charleston was a new kind of combined operation and that past assumptions about the uses and requirements for such operations were inappropriate.

Prior to the Charleston campaign, combined expeditions were used to threaten some weak point on the enemy's coast or to secure a base for invading the country. Since the vital element was surprise, elaborate preparations were dangerous because the design might be discovered and dispositions made to defeat it. Minimum cooperation was required between services. The troops usually landed unopposed on some remote beach and the vessels were needed to guard against the sudden appearance of a hostile fleet, or for some other strictly naval duty. Such fleet support as might become necessary during the operation was arranged on an ad hoc basis and, since the enemy was taken unprepared, generally sufficed to ensure success. If strong resistance or difficult problems arose, the troops simply reembarked to repeat the performance somewhere else.

At Charleston, the attackers confronted an entirely different situation. The harbor's organic defensive system was the strongest in North America, designed and commanded by the South's best military engineer. A combined force which deliberately set about attacking the enemy at his strongest point, where no surprise was possible, violated the existing "rules" for amphibious warfare. Inevitably, both services found the old casual methods inadequate.

Neither the Federal commanders nor the Lincoln administration can be blamed, of course, for not anticipating the complex problems and demands of a novel situation, which could only be discovered through the costly and discouraging process of trial and error. Nor could Dahlgren and Gillmore have perceived, in their determination to wrest Morris Island from a tenacious enemy, that their imaginative expedients would eventually bring about their defeat. In fact, had the government supplied the additional means required, the defenses of James Island, Sullivan's Island, and the inner harbor would have succumbed to the techniques used against Battery Wagner.

But Charleston's greatest significance does not lie in what the Federals might have accomplished had the object been considered worth the price, or even what was actually achieved, but rather in what it should have revealed about the character and requirements of future combined operations. A fundamental lesson might have been derived from the campaign— the need for a combined assault doctrine upon which to base good operational plans. Although Gillmore and Dahlgren's primitive operations "program" was undoubtedly better than none and "stage one" would probably have failed on the old "ad hoc" principle, the scheme was too rigid and sketchy. It did not allow for wastage in men and equipment. There was no timetable for successive stages and no prior calculation of the necessary logistical support. The problem of removing the obstructions was not well considered in advance, so the means were not available when wanted. Better planning and prior discussion of contingencies and alternative solutions could have prevented most of the frustration leading to the decisive rupture of command relations.

Nevertheless, an important tactical lesson did emerge from the Charleston experience. The Federals demonstrated that the key to a successful amphibious assault against a strong enemy position was the systematic employment of continuous and overwhelming fire, attained through judicious dispositions involving all arms as a unified whole, and constant communication between the ships and the forces ashore. This lesson was imperfectly learned, however, as evidenced by the abortive first attack on Fort Fisher.

THE FIRST ATTACK ON FORT FISHER

T HE PACE of the war slowed considerably in the fall and winter of 1863. Federal failure to follow up the hard-fought victory over Lee's army at Gettysburg and the long siege of Vicksburg seemed to produce a mental torpor exceeding even the physical exhaustion of the armies. Freeing Chattanooga from the grip of Confederate forces under General Bragg in November, although a welcome relief after a tedious and difficult campaign, generated surprisingly little enthusiasm in the North.

On the coast, nothing of great importance occurred for eight months after the capture of Battery Wagner. This was not the fault of the Union field commanders. Many had come to recognize the enormous difficulty of subduing the vast Confederacy by land, and the operational potential of Northern sea power. Frustrated by the futile and expensive shelling of defiant rubbish piles in Charleston harbor and the dubious satisfaction of burning that city's churches and hospitals by long-range bombardment, General Gillmore wanted to try a combined operation against Wilmington. Although the Navy was especially anxious to close this pipeline of foreign trade, the War Department was not interested. General Seymour, chief of staff in the Federal Department of the South, wrote Congressional friends urging that the administration change the grand strategy of the war and proposing that the whole force at Charleston move inland from Port Royal on Branchville or Savannah. What good was naval supremacy, he argued, or the possession of fine harbors, if Union armies did not use them to invade and conquer the South? Even the Joint Committee suggested seizing strategic points within the Confed-

eracy from Union coastal bases.[1] Nothing came of these proposals either.

In the West, Generals Banks and Grant, having finally met
after the fall of Port Hudson, discovered that they agreed
upon the next objective—a large-scale attack on Mobile. Working together and in cooperation with Farragut's West Gulf
Squadron, they would descend upon this city by land and
water, following up its capture by operations against Montgomery in conjunction with a drive by General Sherman's
army on Atlanta. Important results were expected from this
campaign, not the least of which was to unite the energy of
all of the major military and naval forces west of the Alleghenies in a common object.[2]

But Grant and Banks underestimated both the power and
the obstinacy of the general-in-chief. While Halleck remained
in charge, there were no large-scale coast operations. Halleck
never lost either his prejudice against amphibious warfare or
his preoccupation with the trans-Mississippi, and he was an
exceedingly clever man. Skillfully concealing the real power
of his office under the pretext of being a mere servant of the
president and secretary of War, he continued to direct the war
according to his own strategic ideas.

Having eliminated McClernand during the Vicksburg campaign, Halleck soon got rid of Banks, another "political" general and combined operations enthusiast. In August, after
having dangled before Lincoln and the Cabinet the enticing
prospect of confiscating cotton and holding Federally spon-
sored local elections in Arkansas, Louisiana, and Texas, Halleck
informed Banks that his plan to take Mobile was unacceptable
to the government, which insisted instead upon an immediate
expedition into Texas. His hand was strengthened by the
alarm of Secretary of State Seward over French activities in
Mexico. Solely for "political reasons," explained Halleck, Union
forces must occupy some point in Texas at once.[3]

Banks did not fall in readily with the general-in-chief's design. Finding the water in the Atchafalaya and the Red too
shallow at that season for operations toward Shreveport, as
suggested by Halleck, he arranged with the Navy to seize some
point on the Texas coast to satisfy the administration.[4] Having

failed in two attempts to land at Sabine Pass from which base he intended moving against Houston, his forces descended by surprise upon Brazos Santiago in late October, occupying this harbor and the border town of Brownsville, Texas through which the Confederacy had conducted most of its trade with Mexico.

When Halleck heard about this activity, he was furious. Banks had no instructions to operate on the coast; he had gone on another "wild goose chase," and had divided his forces in violation of military principles, exposing New Orleans to attack and leaving General Steele's army in Arkansas with no support against a possible enemy invasion from north Louisiana and Texas. The true and only line for Banks was the Red River. From Shreveport he could advance into Texas while securing this river as a safe boundary and supply line for Steele. Banks's perfectly sound argument—that the water level in the Red was at best unpredictable for cooperating vessels as he had discovered that summer, and that an overland march of such a distance through the wilderness was impossible and likely to end badly—left Halleck unmoved.[5] Nor would he even reply to further suggestions about Mobile.

Banks was a hard man to convince. A politician himself, he was not averse to disagreeing with the politicians in Washington, especially since he was toying with the idea of running against Lincoln for president in 1864. He was, however, an "amateur" general, unsure of his own military capacity, and easily intimidated by professionals. That was Halleck's trump card. After arguing fruitlessly with Banks throughout much of the winter, he played it. Enlisting the aid of his only friend in the Army, General W.T. Sherman, and of Admiral Porter who was already counting the prize money he could collect from captured cotton, Halleck informed Banks that the best professional opinion indicated that the Red was his proper line of advance into Texas. To this stick, the general-in-chief added a carrot. Sherman and Porter were ready to cooperate with Banks, as was General Steele.[6] Halleck neglected to mention until later that Banks had to arrange this cooperation for himself. Thinking he had no choice, and unwilling to disagree with two West Point generals and an admiral, who had been

craftily informed by Halleck that the whole movement was
Banks's idea and his preferred line of operation, Banks at last
agreed to make the attempt.[7]

The details and result of the unfortunate Red River campaign during the spring of 1864 are well known. It was an old
story for Federal operations devised by Halleck; Banks had
been right, and everything went wrong. The detachment from
Sherman's army was called away in the middle of the operation by General Grant. Steele, pleading that his force was
inadequate even to defend himself and that he was busy holding local elections, refused to cooperate until compelled by
government order; and then his assistance was too little and
too late. The water in the river failed to rise, so Porter's
squadron, which had wasted a good deal of time rounding up
cotton, became grounded above Alexandria and was nearly
lost. Naturally Banks, the amateur, was blamed for this
blunder.[8]

Halleck might have found some consolation in getting rid
of Banks even though the campaign failed. But he had gone
too far in approving the Red River venture at the expense of
the much more important Mobile project. Although neither
Grant nor the administration recognized Halleck as the architect of this misfortune, by shifting the blame onto the field
commanders and continuing to plead that he was only the
president's "chief of staff" with no authority or will of his own,
he convinced Congress and the Cabinet that such a weak, irre-
sponsible man was unfit for the chief command. Grant, whose
own plan in the West had been wrecked along with Banks's
reputation, was promoted to Lieutenant General and called
to command all the armies of the United States.[9]

The demotion of General Halleck should have signalled a
fundamental change in Federal operations planning, a renewed appreciation and use of conjunct movements, an end
to the wasteful, self-defeating policy of marching back and
forth through the interior to points which could not be held,
or of again and again fighting Confederate armies that could
not be captured unless shut up and besieged. Grant's experience in the West had matured his judgment, enlarged his
perspective, and brought him to the same conclusions Mc-
Clellan had earlier reached by study and reflection. Indeed,

the plan he had in mind for 1864 was almost a replica of McClellan's grand strategy for 1862.

Months before his promotion—probably in early December 1863, right after his occupation of Chattanooga—Grant had delineated this plan on a recent Colton's Guide Map of the United States. Upon his appointment to the chief command in March, he sent a copy to General Sherman indicating that it was the scheme to be followed for the spring offensive. Fed-

Lieutenant General Ulysses S. Grant at City Point, Virginia, 1864 (*National Archives*)

erally held territory, including coastal bridgeheads, were outlined in red pencil. From these, blue lines indicating proposed
lines of operation terminating in blue circles representing objective points, extended from Sabine City to Shreveport; from
Chattanooga and Savannah to Atlanta, and from this point to
Montgomery and Mobile; from New Berne to Raleigh; from
Knoxville, across the crest of the mountains through Lynchburg; and from the head of the York River along the railroad
to Richmond. The reader will readily perceive, in the light of
what actually happened in 1864, that the most interesting
features of this scheme were its reliance on coastal bases,
especially for operations against Atlanta, and on the York
River line for moving the Army of the Potomac upon Richmond.[10] Significantly, only one of these movements—Sherman's Atlanta campaign—was actually carried out in 1864,
and this was wholly land-based.

Most historical accounts assume that, after three long, frustrating, and costly years of war, the Lincoln administration
finally recognized the importance of unity of command, and
allowed its last general-in-chief an entirely free hand. They
also assume that, for reasons of taste or temperament or some
other cause peculiar to himself, Grant chose to pursue a
strategy of "attrition," or "annihilation" against the Confederacy. This is not so. We have seen that the main object of
the plan he intended to implement was to seize the enemy's
internal communications from the secure base of Federal sea
power, not to destroy the Confederate armies in the field, or
use them up, or make war on civilians, or any other "total
war" motive usually attributed to the general.

But like McClellan, Pope, and Burnside before him, Grant
quickly discovered that the government's fear of "uncovering"
Washington to Lee's army was still to be the primary determinant of Federal military strategy in the East. Nor were the
politicians, in this instance, solely to blame for Grant's decision to reject the York River approach to Richmond and
abandon the other water-based movements comprising his
initial plan. Although Halleck had lost the appearance of
power—a consideration of no importance to him anyway—he
had retained most of its substance.[11] As he had earlier controlled the movements of the armies by playing off the presi-

dent and secretary of War against the field commanders, he now sought to manipulate them as chief of staff through General Grant.

Two factors worked in his favor. The first was Grant's admiration of and deference to his old commanding officer. Practically uneducated in the history and theory of war despite his years at West Point, Grant was impressed by Halleck's erudition and self-assurance. A good general by instinct rather than calculation, he was unable to explain why his strategic ideas were better than Halleck's and therefore never entirely sure that they were. The other factor was the long-standing friendship between Halleck and Sherman. Extremely ambitious and, like Halleck, willing to control from behind the scenes, Sherman had, by his outstanding organizational skill, his great energy, and his absolute loyalty, made himself Grant's right-hand man, his trusted confidant and advisor. It was Sherman who suggested that his friend Halleck be retained as chief of staff; further, that Grant take the field personally, either with the Army of the Potomac or in the West, leaving Halleck, whose outstanding intellectual ability better qualified him for the job, to manage affairs for the Army in Washington. After all, he told his gullible chief, Grant was too honest and unassuming to withstand the cunning machinations of unprincipled politicians—they would destroy him.[12] Grant, who sometimes listened too closely to the persuasive and eloquent Sherman, and who was modest enough to admit his own shortcomings, was easily convinced. He promptly left Washington with Meade's army, and Halleck remained. And so did Halleck's prejudices.

Moving the Army of the Potomac against Richmond by way of the York River involved naval cooperation, and we have observed many times that Halleck had no use for combined operations. Although General Butler, again commanding an army at Fort Monroe, got Grant's permission to conduct a waterborne diversion against the Confederate capital by way of the James—a movement Halleck considered wasteful and pointless—all of the other coast-based operations envisaged by Grant in late 1863 were cancelled.[13]

Following another of Halleck's dicta, the two principal Union armies remained "concentrated" and moved frontally in huge masses upon Richmond and Atlanta, like Halleck's own grand advance upon Corinth in 1862. Playing upon the administration's almost hysterical fear of the resourceful Lee, Halleck "agreed" with the Cabinet that Washington must be "covered" by Grant's army as it moved south against Richmond, with its line of operation, in good Jominian fashion, perpendicular to its base. As he had explained to McClellan during the Antietam campaign, the idea was not, as the stupid politicians supposed, that the army should defend Washington; but that the city and its fortifications, once lost, could not defend the army which, cut off from its base, would be destroyed.[14] Halleck's disregard of sea power made it impossible for him to perceive that this element permitted strategic flexibility. If driven from Washington, the Army of the Potomac could as easily have based itself upon Baltimore, or Philadelphia, or Norfolk, or any point on the southern coast. Continental-minded to the end, his was the strategy that prevailed until 1865.

Sherman was content with it. No great strategist himself, he willingly followed where the enemy led. It was only after failing to come to grips with "Joe" Johnston's army and finding himself triumphant but stranded in the empty city of Atlanta, with his rail communications broken and his army in danger of starving, that Sherman began to question Halleck's continental strategy.[15] Even then, he appreciated only the logistical advantage of seacoast bases while ignoring their operational potential.

Although the general-in-chief was unhappy with the final plan, he saw no alternative. Not one to question the orders of superiors, Grant did his best to move on Richmond as the president and his chief of staff wished. He may have realized prior to the event that only such enormous casualties as those sustained in his frontal offensive against Lee north of Richmond during May and early June would convince the administration to approve some other approach. But it is certain that the government, even then, only partly removed Grant's strategic shackles.

It was all right for Grant to besiege Petersburg because, in an emergency—such as actually happened in July when Confederate General Jubal Early attempted a bold raid on Washington—part of his army could be brought by sea in time to defend the capital. Should he move further south, however, to New Berne or Wilmington—a move Grant had seriously considered before opening the spring campaign—this could not be done.[16] The politicians were still unwilling to risk even a temporary occupation of the capital, supposing that the moral effect would dangerously strengthen the Northern peace party in an election year.[17] Unable to move from the Petersburg lines or to take them by assault, Grant was compelled to employ the Army of the Potomac as a holding force to fix Lee in position, hoping that Sherman's army or events elsewhere would break the military deadlock.

The strategic realities of the Army's 1864 campaign have been discussed at length because of their relation to combined attacks upon Mobile and Wilmington and, specifically, to the tactical methods employed in the first Fort Fisher operation. Because the capture of Mobile city—as a follow-up to the seizure of Mobile Bay for purposes of the blockade—was, along with the rest of Grant's projected coast operations, dropped from the final plan, a large infantry force was not made available to take the place until the final months of the war.[18] Fortunately for the Navy, the outer forts, like the early Confederate Atlantic coast defenses, were easily isolated by the fleet under Admiral Farragut and a small army detachment under Major General Gordon Granger in August. Serious structural weaknesses exposed the principal work, Fort Morgan, to reverse fire, and its magazines were poorly protected. No great expenditure of time or means was therefore required and no refinement of the tactics previously used against coastal fortifications emerged from these operations.[19]

It was otherwise at Wilmington. The infantry force allocated for this operation was too small to assault or besiege either Fort Caswell or Fort Fisher and the Navy found it impossible to get into the river to bombard these defenses from the rear. Problems encountered during the first expedition against Fort Fisher led, in the second attempt, to the development of more effective combined tactics than the ones employed against Battery Wagner.

Wilmington had been a thorn in the side of the Navy since early in the war. Almost impossible to blockade because of

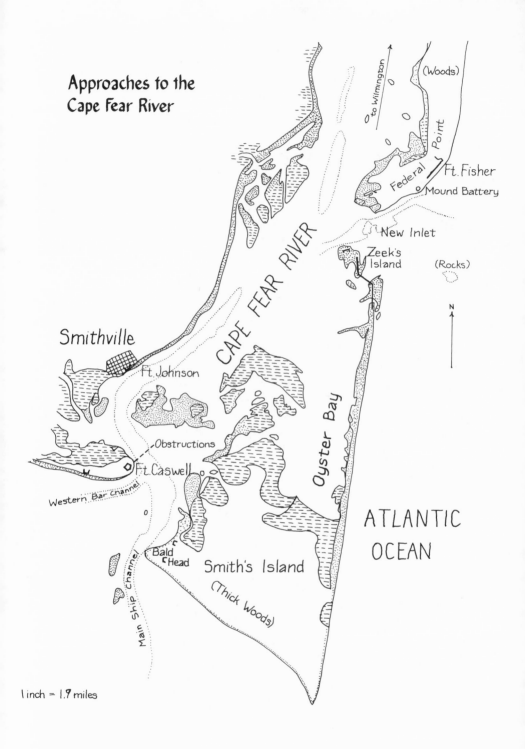

Approaches to the
Cape Fear River

(Woods)

to Wilmington

Federal Point

Ft. Fisher

Mound Battery

New Inlet

Zeek's Island

(Rocks)

N

Smithville

Ft. Johnson

CAPE FEAR RIVER

Oyster Bay

Obstructions

Ft. Caswell

Western Bar Channel

ATLANTIC
OCEAN

Main Ship Channel

Bald Head

Smith's Island

(Thick Woods)

1 inch = 1.7 miles

hydrographic conditions at the mouth of the Cape Fear River, it had grown through four years of war from a small, not-very-prosperous town into the primary entrepôt of foreign trade with the Confederacy. Blockade-running was not the town's only occupation. As larger ports were sealed off by Northern fleets and European governments became less willing to incur Washington's displeasure by harboring Southern vessels, the Confederate Navy Department turned Wilmington into a haven for commerce raiders.[20] This policy was adopted during the summer of 1864 over the loud protests of Major General W.H.C. Whiting, commanding the Wilmington defenses, and of General Lee, who feared that it would spur the Lincoln administration into an all-out effort to capture the place.[21] They were partly right.

The Union Navy Department did, indeed, react immediately and aggressively. Pressured by panicky New Englanders who lost over thirty vessels to the Wilmington-based raider CSS *Tallahassee* alone during the first two weeks in August, Secretary Welles appealed to Stanton and Lincoln for troops to assist the Navy in reducing the outer fortifications, thus sealing the harbor. The War Department referred him to General Grant who, though not explicitly refusing cooperation, saw no strategic purpose in it at that time and was very reluctant to detach the ten thousand veteran infantry asked for by the Navy. Halleck quickly stiffened the general's resolution. Having categorically refused a similar request for cooperation against Wilmington while still general-in-chief in January, he now assured Grant that he was quite right to withhold the troops. If he insisted upon senselessly besieging Petersburg instead of withdrawing his army north of Richmond once more, which Halleck still thought the wisest strategy, he must at least keep his force concentrated and in sufficient strength to threaten Lee constantly and confine him to his defenses. Otherwise, the crafty Confederate might again invade the north or fall upon Washington.[22]

Another reason for Grant's lack of enthusiasm for a joint expedition in the early fall was his disapproval of the War Department's choice to command the army contingent. At Fox's urging, General Gillmore submitted two plans for operations against Wilmington to Halleck and Grant on 6 September.

The first required five thousand infantry to occupy Smith's Island, allowing vessels to be stationed in the river above the defenses, closing the harbor without taking the forts. The second, requiring ten thousand troops and a large fleet, envisaged reducing Fort Fisher by the same combination of siege and naval bombardment he had employed at Charleston.[23]

The Navy favored the second plan. But Fox neglected to consult Grant, or Butler, in whose geographical Department of Virginia and North Carolina the expedition would take place. Gillmore's performance as one of Butler's corps commanders during the opening phase of the Richmond campaign in May was so bad that Butler had demanded his dismissal; and Grant, having lost, largely through Gillmore's incompetence, a chance to grab Petersburg while its defenses were weak, was equally reluctant to trust him with another assignment.[24]

The Navy encountered command problems of its own. Optimistically viewing Grant's noncommittal attitude as a willingness to approve the expedition if pressed, the department on 5 September appointed Farragut to relieve the conservative Admiral Lee in command of the North Atlantic Blockading Squadron with orders to prepare a naval descent upon Wilmington for 1 October. The Army, he was told, would probably provide a small force. To Welles's surprise and Fox's chagrin, their star performer wanted no part of this particular project. Aside from his quite legitimate plea of physical exhaustion following the recent operations in Mobile Bay, Farragut thought it incredible, and unwise, that the department should not only remove Lee, whose thorough knowledge of the Wilmington approaches and defenses best suited him for the command, but that it expected him, a stranger to the squadron and in bad health, to organize a major expedition at such short notice. Besides, the prospects for success did not look good without the cooperation of a very large infantry force and Farragut did not wish to end his career with a repulse.[25]

Fox got the message at once. Wilmington was considered a nasty job, likely to end in defeat and humiliation for the Navy. Only one senior officer was young and brash enough to actually welcome the assignment—David Porter. And Fox could be certain, from Porter's long record of twisting the facts and baiting the Army, that whatever happened, the Navy would come out looking good. Moreover, his skill in organization was unsurpassed.

Taking up his command on 12 October, Porter discovered that the Navy Department had been too sanguine in its assumption that, once the naval preparations were under way, Grant would readily release the ten thousand troops judged necessary for the reduction of Fort Fisher. But then, Grant did not expect much from the proposed enterprise anyway. If Fisher or Wilmington could be seized by surprise with a small force, fine. The Navy would be happy and Wilmington would afford a base for raids upon the railroads supplying Lee's army.[26] Grant finally agreed on 6 December to send Butler, with 6,500 men from the Army of the James under General Weitzel, to assist the Navy against Fort Fisher. But it is clear, given the poor quality of the troops detailed, the small amount of field artillery, ammunition, and provisions taken, and the absence of any reference to siege equipment or reinforcements, that Grant, echoing Halleck's old line, would not allow this naval venture to become a major commitment which might compromise the operations of the two main armies.[27] His views were to change radically, but not before January 1865. The principal object, in Grant's words, was "to close the port of Wilmington." If Butler was unsuccessful in "effecting a landing" to surprise Fort Fisher, he was to return his detachment immediately to the James River lines. While the wording of these orders is ambiguous, their meaning, in the context of Grant's strategic priorities at the time, is not. Given the vitriolic and prolonged controversy and the confused accounts generated by the first Fort Fisher expedition, this point can not be overemphasized. The Army never expected more from this operation than might have been accomplished by coup de main and only agreed to it reluctantly under continuous pressure from the Navy Department.[28]

Before examining the attack in detail, another point should be clarified. Based on statements and reports made after the event, most accounts heavily stress the alleged bad personal relations between Porter and Butler as an explanation for their supposed reluctance to cooperate and their consequent failure to take Fisher. Aside from Porter's usual bombastic prophecies

Major General Benjamin F. Butler, Brigadier General Godfrey
Weitzel, and staff, at Bermuda Hundred, Virginia, 1864.

that the operation was easy and that, if the place was not
taken, it would be the Army's fault, there is no evidence of
bad feeling between the admiral and General Butler prior to
the attack.[29] On the contrary, they had much in common,
visited often socially, and collaborated closely on the powder
boat project. Both liked a good fight, and each considered the
other a very clever fellow. Even after the war, during their
most venomous exchanges in print, one detects a strong note
of grudging admiration. By contrast, Porter thought Grant a
weak, dull man, jealous because Butler could run intellectual
circles around him and control him.[30] Words aside, neither
the general nor the admiral acted, before the repulse, as one
would expect them to have acted had they disliked each other.
As for actual cooperation, nothing asked of either party was
refused by the other. If there was poor coordination between
the Army and the Navy, or if communications between them
appear unsatisfactory, a different cause than personal animos-
ity was responsible.

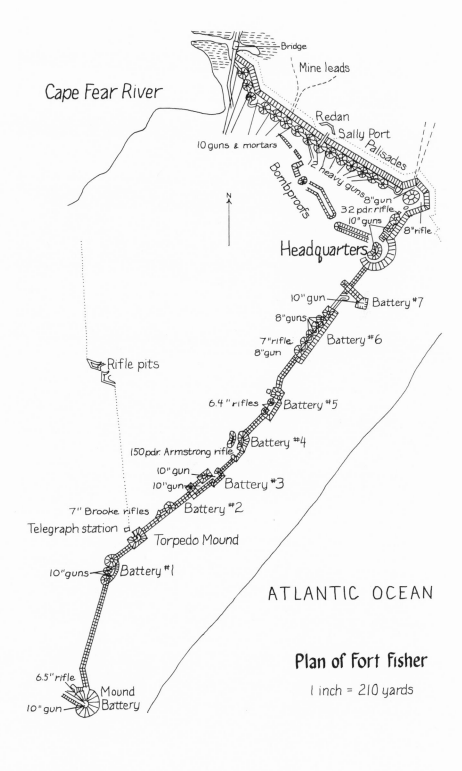

Bridge

Mine leads

Cape Fear River

Redan

Sally Port

Palisades

10 guns & mortars

2 heavy guns

8" gun

Bombproofs

32 pdr. rifle

10" guns

8" rifle

N

Headquarters

10" gun

Battery #7

8" guns

7" rifle

Battery #6

8" gun

Rifle pits

6.4" rifles

Battery #5

Battery #4

150 pdr. Armstrong rifle

10" gun

10" gun

Battery #3

7" Brooke rifles

Battery #2

Telegraph station

Torpedo Mound

10" guns

Battery #1

ATLANTIC OCEAN

Plan of Fisher

1 inch = 210 yards

6.5" rifle

Mound

10" gun

Battery

Fort Fisher, at the mouth of the Cape Fear River in North
Carolina, was regarded by both sides as the strongest earthwork ever built. Because Wilmington was thought to possess
no strategic value other than as an entrepôt, the Confederate
engineers had concentrated their resources in defense of the
outer approaches, leaving the inner line very weak.[31] Their
confidence that Fort Fisher was impregnable was justified. Its
680-yard-long land face, commencing 100 yards from the river
and joining the sea face in a bastion at the east angle, contained twenty-two heavy barbette guns and rifles mounted in
pairs, separated by massive bombproof traverses.

The sea face, approximately 1900 yards long, was composed of ten self-contained batteries mounting 24 rifled and
large smoothbore cannon, some of them in embrasure, connected by a heavy curtain and protected against enfilade by
merlons and huge traverses rising 15 feet above the parapet.
At the southern end of this face was a conical battery 43 feet
high, appropriately called the Mound, containing one 10-inch
columbiad and one 6.5-inch rifle bearing on the shoals at the
entrance to New Inlet. A mile farther south, at the extremity
of the peninsula called Federal Point (Confederate Point by
the Southerners) was a four-gun naval battery (Buchanan)
whose fire, crossed with that of another battery on Zeek's
Island, covered the channel and also bore out to sea. Well
masked along a low sand ridge, Fisher's parapet was 25 feet
thick, the exterior slope, firmly sodded with marsh grass, forming a 45-degree angle. There was no counterscarp and only a
shallow ditch in front of the land face; but a row of palisades
and an electrically controlled minefield guarded this approach.
Except for a line of rifle pits running on an acute angle from
just north of the Mound to the river, and extensive patches of
swampy ground, the work was open to the rear.[32]

At the time of the first attack, the garrison numbered about
1,400, a third of them junior reserves (under age 16) or
militia who had never seen action. Nearly a regiment of infantry was scattered outside the fort, in entrenchments along the
river, in two small earthen batteries several miles up the
beach, and at a place called Sugar Loaf Hill, six miles north
of Fisher opposite Masonborough Inlet on the river side of the
peninsula, which commanded the road to Wilmington. The

most vulnerable point in the fort was at the left of the land face where the Wilmington road crossed a bridge and entered into the rear of the work. This entrance was guarded by only a section of light field pieces. Between the road and the river, however, were several strongpoints which, if properly manned, could have proved dangerous to an assaulting infantry force.[33]

The Federal Navy planned to open the attack by blowing up an old steamer filled with gunpowder close to the beach off the fort's east angle. In fact, the plan for the whole expedition was, to a large extent, based upon the anticipated effect of this device.

There is some question how the project originated. While Grant, Porter, and many others claimed it was one of Butler's contraptions, the idea actually seems to have been conceived in the Navy Department in late October as a response to the Army's refusal to allocate the ten thousand troops requested in September. Nonetheless, Butler immediately took to the project with his usual enthusiasm, becoming a convert to the Wilmington expedition and eventually persuading Grant to approve it.

Of all the Northern generals, including even the ingenious McClellan, Butler was the most imaginative, the most fascinated by new technology. Himself the inventor of an unsuccessful rifled cannon, he was the first to use balloon reconnaissance, to purchase Gatling guns, to use wire entanglements to protect his lines, to employ signals for indirect artillery fire. His discriminaton was not always good, however. Many of his projects were impractical, even fantastic. Of his activities on the James during the siege of Petersburg, Meade's aide wrote that Butler "never is happy unless he has half a dozen contrivances on hand," and that he was "going to get a gun that would shoot seven miles and, taking direction by compass, burn the city of Richmond with shells of Greek fire. If that didn't do, he had an auger to bore a tunnel five feet in diameter, and he was going to bore to Richmond and suddenly pop up in somebody's basement . . . ."[34] The massive explosion of a Confederate clockwork bomb aboard a Federal ordnance boat at City Point in August, setting off a chain reaction that exploded nearby ammunition dumps and flattened many buildings (including Grant's headquarters), induced Butler to propose that he "blow up Charleston with a vessel loaded with a thousand tons of powder." The accidental detonation of two powder barges and several magazines near Woolwich, England in October also caught Butler's attention.[35]

Thus when Assistant Secretary Fox, the same innovator who had devised the stone-ships project earlier in the war, proposed the scheme to blow down Fort Fisher during a visit by the general to Washington in early November, Butler readily agreed to "cooperate." Admiral Porter, Butler's naval counterpart in his enthusiasm for novel ideas and gadgets and the person probably responsible for suggesting this particular project to Fox in the first place, agreed to supply a "shaky" steamer capable of carrying 300 tons of gunpowder.[36] The vessel selected was a decrepit 500-ton iron steamer, the *Louisiana*, then serving as a wharf boat in the North Carolina sounds. She was to be loaded with 150 tons of Navy powder and 150 tons of Army powder which Butler agreed to supply from Fort Monroe. The powder, tightly packed in the ship to ensure maximum bursting effect, would be overlaid with live shells and canisters of "Birney's liquid fire," a substance Butler had been experimenting with at his field headquarters on the James.[37]

But this project hit the first of many snags before it was fairly under way. Although the War Department was anxious to try the "experiment," later terming it "interesting and important" and sending a technical observer to report the details of the explosion, Stanton naturally sought the advice of the Army's chief engineer, General Richard Delafield. His report was discouraging. After thoroughly reviewing the history of such explosions, Delafield concluded "that the explosion of a vessel load of gunpowder at the nearest point it can approach Fort Caswell or Fort Fisher (estimated as 950 yards), can produce no useful result toward the reduction of these works," and advised against it. Stanton thereupon refused to authorize Butler to turn over the 150 tons of powder asked for by the Navy.[38]

Fox would not give up so easily. Armed with two more favorable reports from the Naval Ordnance Bureau, he arranged a meeting of experts on 23 November at the Washington home of Captain Henry A. Wise. Also present were three officers of the Army Ordnance Bureau (including General Dyer the bureau chief) and three naval ordnance officers, among them Lieutenant Commander W.N. Jeffers in charge of the Naval Ordnance Explosive Department who had reported most favorably on the project and to whom Fox had entrusted the technical arrangements. Since no engineers were invited, Fox was able, by ignoring the reservations of General Dyer, to get a consensus that 300 tons of powder exploded within 450 yards of Fort Fisher "would injure the earthworks to a very great extent, render the guns unserviceable for a time, and probably affect the garrison to such a degree as to deprive them of power to resist the passage of naval vessels by the forts and the carrying of these works by immediate assault."[39]

Three points about this joint opinion should be noticed: first, the quantity of powder estimated to be effective was 300 tons; second, the vessel had to be placed within 450 yards of the fort—that is, within 250 yards of the beach; and third, the purpose of the explosion was to silence the fort long enough for ships to pass into the Cape Fear River, after which the work could be taken by assault. In actuality, none of the conditions upon which this opinion was based were fulfilled. Indeed, from beginning to end, nothing connected with this powder boat went according to plan.

The Navy delayed and was unprepared when Grant gave the go-ahead for the Wilmington expedition on 2 December and indicated that he could spare only 5,000 troops, making the powder boat, in Porter's view, essential for success. The *Louisiana* had arrived at the Norfolk yard, but little had been done toward converting her, the commandant having refused to authorize any night work.[40] Through the exertions of Fox, who rushed down to supervise the work, the alterations were completed and the vessel ready to receive the powder on 10 December.

Grant pressed Butler, either to get the expedition off while Bragg—now commanding at Wilmington—was opposing Sherman in Georgia, or give it up. Butler had already assembled the troops with their stores and transports, and had delivered the Army's half of the powder that day.[41] The Navy's 150 tons was another matter. Although a sufficient amount was on hand in Norfolk and Captain Wise had, as early as 2 December, authorized its use "if there is great *urgency* for it," he regretted the loss of so much "good" powder, assuring Porter that he was arranging to have a large quantity of "second-class" powder sent down from northern yards. It would arrive, said Wise, in a week.[42]

Trying to operate on the cheap produced a comedy of errors which cost the Navy precious time and compromised the chances for a successful expedition. For getting the second-class powder to Norfolk, the department hired the second-rate steamer *George Shattuck* in Boston to pick it up at Portsmouth and New York. This vessel sailed promptly, by mistake, to Provincetown. On her return to Boston two days later, the ship's agent refused to accept the charter unless the government supplied an engineer and two firemen. Another steamer was hired, but the agent again changed his mind. The *George Shattuck* finally left Boston directly for New York on 8 December, a week after the original charter. Having loaded the powder, she was further delayed in New York until the 13th, waiting for coal. She at last reached Norfolk on the 17th where she was detained another day because of leaky boilers. She finally departed for Beaufort on the 19th, six days behind the *Louisiana*.[43]

Admiral Porter had meanwhile grown desperate. Grant and Butler insisted they could wait no longer for the powder boat and urged that the expedition sail without it. The admiral would not agree. The troops could not prevent Fort Fisher from sinking his ships; only the stunning effect of a large explosion could do this. It was better that the *Louisiana*, already loaded with 155 tons of Army and 25 tons of "good" Navy powder, should proceed at once to Beaufort where Porter would load on another 90 tons stored there. On this understanding, the *Louisiana* sailed under tow with the rest of the fleet on 13 December.[44]

Even with a much lighter load than intended, the voyage was a nightmare; the awkward old tub almost foundered. Someone had obviously miscalculated her cargo capacity. Having taken on another 35 tons of Navy powder at Beaufort —making a total of 215, instead of 300, tons and leaving a large air space forward—the *Louisiana* floated so low that Porter feared she would sink at the dock. Nor could she accommodate the additional weight of explosive and incendiary shells, the most destructive element of the whole device.[45]

The actual explosion of the *Louisiana* off Fort Fisher on the night of 23 December was an appropriate ending to a miserably managed affair. Porter had intended the detonation for the night of the 18th, but a storm came up, the vessel could not be brought inshore, and the Army transports, having reached the rendezvous off the mouth of the Cape Fear on the 15th during beautiful weather, had used up their coal and water waiting for the Navy to arrive with the *Louisiana*, forcing Butler to put into Beaufort, 75 miles away, to take on supplies and ride out a gale.[46]

Due to the uncertainty of the weather, Porter gave Commander Rhind, in charge of the powder boat, discretionary orders to blow her up, despite the absence of the Army, any time he could get near the fort. But the sea refused to cooperate. Finding the wind dying down on the 23rd, the admiral ordered the *Louisiana* blown up that night around midnight when the moon would be dark and the tide favorable.[47]

The original plan, it will be recalled, specified that the powder vessel be run up very close to, if not actually upon, the beach. On reflection Porter thought this too hazardous. He told Rhind not to run the *Louisiana* aground where she might break apart, but to rely on her flat bottom to settle itself upon the shoal. In fact, he thought it best that Rhind anchor her "a little way out" so that the enemy could not board her except by boat.[48]

In a conscientious effort to make absolutely certain all the powder would explode at the same instant, the Naval Ordnance Bureau had provided three alternate arrangements for touching it off: a set of clockwork mechanisms, candles cut to timed lengths, and a slow match. Each of these devices was attached to a lead of Gomez fuse spread at intervals throughout the packed powder, a new invention which was supposed to ignite instantaneously over a distance of 100 yards. For once, however, Porter's faith in technology deserted him. Suppose the clocks and fuses and other timed arrangements failed? Just in case, he told Rhind to be sure to start a large fire in the stern before leaving the ship.[49]

Rhind and his party found it very difficult to maneuver their awkward charge in close to the beach. The night was extremely dark and they could not see the fort. Becoming increasingly nervous and supposing himself, from the noise of breakers over a nearby shoal, to be about 300 yards off the beach—he was actually over 500 yards out—Rhind let go the stern anchor, set the clocks, lit the slow match and the candles, and started the fire. Noting that the *Louisiana* was dragging further offshore in the current, he let go the bow anchor and, fearful about getting far enough away, hurriedly left the ship to join Porter's fleet standing twelve miles off. During the almost two hours before the detonation, the *Louisiana* drifted another 400 yards, placing her at least 900 yards from the beach and 1100 yards from Fort Fisher.[50]

At 1:40 A.M. on the 24th, the Union sailors heard a series of low, dull explosions and felt a slight motion of the ships. That was all. The fire had worked before the timing devices could go off, so the powder in the *Louisiana* had not ignited simultaneously but in succession as the fire reached the various storage holds. Because the deck compartments were almost empty, there was no resistance to the weight of powder below; the whole mass blew straight up in the air. Eighty percent of the powder did not burn.[51]

Needless to say, nothing happened to Fort Fisher or anyone in it. So mild, indeed, was the *Louisiana*'s impact on the defenders that they never realized until after the war that they were the targets of this "interesting and important" experiment. Colonel William Lamb, commanding Fort Fisher, reported briefly to General Whiting the next day that a Union gunboat had run aground during the night and was blown up, vanishing without a trace—which he thought curious, but not significant.[52]

Despite the actual result, the powder-boat project had a greater effect than has been recognized. Not only did its elaborate and confused preparations delay the expedition until Bragg had returned to Wilmington and Lee had rushed a division from the Petersburg lines to augment the defense; its failure changed, at the last moment, the tactical plan for reducing Fort Fisher.

The explosion having failed to "wind up" the fort, Porter and Butler were left with several alternatives: to call off the attack;

to run the shallow-draft monitors into the river and, landing troops as Farragut and Granger did at Fort Morgan, wait for the isolated garrison to surrender; or to reduce Fisher by outside bombardment, after which the troops would land on the sea beach and take possession, or storm the damaged works if necessary. Given the public mood and the expense of the expedition, the first alternative was out of the question, at least so far as the Navy was concerned.

The second choice, the only mode of attack General Grant and the Navy Department throught practicable, was attended

Rear Admiral David D. Porter and his staff on the flagship *Malvern* before the first Fort Fisher expedition. On the left stand Lieutenant Commander William B. Cushing, Commander A. C. Rhind (rear), and Lieutenant Benjamin H. Porter, killed in the beach assault. Flanking Admiral Porter are Lieutenant Commander S. K. Breese (left), Fleet Captain and commander of the landing brigade, and Lieutenant Commander T. O. Selfridge who led the third division of the assault column. Before the ladder are Lieutenant S. W. Terry (left), Detail Officer, and Lieutenant S. W. Preston (right), Flag Lieutenant, who was killed in the beach attack. (*Library of Congress*)

by difficulties not appreciated in Washington.[53] Porter had, in fact, issued orders on the 17th for the light-draft monitors to run through New Inlet at night. In preparation, twelve men from the USS *Monticello*, landing in front of the Mound Battery early that morning, had dug up and cut the wires leading to some electric mines in the channel. But the perils of night navigation, amply demonstrated by the failure to get the *Louisiana* into position on the 18th and 19th, plus the impossibility of obtaining good pilots, caused the admiral to change his mind. By the 20th he had decided upon the third alternative.[54] He did not then suspect that this mode of attack was equally futile.

After almost four years of war, Admiral Porter was one of the few officers in the U.S. Navy who still supposed that a heavy fleet bombardment could destroy a strong fort. Although his experience on the Mississippi had left him no illusions about elevated batteries that naval guns could not reach, Fort Fisher looked like an easy target for direct fire. Nor did Du Pont's contest with Fort McAllister, or Dahlgren's with Battery Wagner, appear relevant to this situation. The monitors were unquestionably deficient in firepower. Porter's fleet, on the other hand, included a squadron of frigates whose tremendous rate and volume of fire he had witnessed during Farragut's passage of the New Orleans forts. More appropriate precedents seemed to be the Navy's reduction of Fort Hatteras and the Port Royal defenses early in the war. Since Porter had never commanded any of these large broadside vessels, he had yet to discover their limitations.

General Butler did not recognize them either. His experience with combined operations led him to view the Navy as the primary offensive force against shore batteries. While the fleet's role was active, that of the cooperating troops was passive; they were expected to take possession only after the Navy had forced the defenders to abandon or surrender the works.[55] These assumptions in the minds of the officers commanding the first Fort Fisher expedition must be taken into account; otherwise their plan of attack makes no sense.

Consequently, although Porter had sent an aide early in the evening of the 23rd to inform the Army that he would explode the powder boat that night and attack in the morning, he saw no reason to wait until Butler or his men arrived before commencing the bombardment. The time required to reduce the fort would, doubtless, allow the Army to get there from Beaufort. And the enemy should not be permitted to further strengthen the defenses.[56]

Deploying the fleet on the 24th took several hours so that the first division, which included the frigates, and the second division, composed of wooden gunboats, did not open fire until almost noon. The *Ironsides* and monitors, anchored close in (about half a mile) for direct fire against the land face, commenced an hour earlier. Porter had intended to position the wooden vessels one mile from the fort, but thinking the risk of damage too great at this range, ordered them further off. The first division was stationed to enfilade the land front, while the second concentrated its fire upon the Mound battery and the southern extension of the sea face. A squadron of older wooden ships was in reserve.[57]

For five hours, Fort Fisher was pounded with every specimen of projectile known to the Navy. Despite the admiral's orders that the vessels fire slowly and deliberately to avoid wasting ammunition, they did not do so. The range was too long and the guns in Fisher were well masked. Many smoothbore shells fell short. Several 100-pounder rifles on the gunboats, which had quickly silenced the Mound, fired too fast and exploded, making the crews in the other vessels reluctant to use these guns. Except for the large number of shots directed against the main flagstaff and the quarters, which were set ablaze, the bombardment was diffused over the works.[58]

Not a gun on the sea face was injured and only three on the land front were temporarily disabled by injury to their carriages. The fort fired very slowly, expending only 672 rounds to conserve shells since the fleet was too distant to hit with any accuracy. No bombproofs or magazines were damaged, and casualties to the artillerists, who were never driven from their guns, amounted to one fatality and 22 slightly wounded.[59]

Despite the defenders' impression that the Federal bombardment was faster and heavier on the 25th, more shells were probably fired on the 24th because the frigates were in action an hour longer. But the fleet stood farther out on the 24th, and many projectiles fell into the water, while a large number of rifled shots passed over in a wasteful attempt to cut down the flags on Fisher and the Mound.[60] Oddly, no record of the exact quantity of ammunition expended by the fleet on either day is available; it is possible to make a rough calculation, however. The USS *Colorado*, a 48-gun ship, fired 1,569 shells on the 24th (1,200 on the 25th); the *Minnesota* (47 guns) and *Wabash* (46) must have shot off nearly as many, making the probable expenditure for these three vessels alone in excess of 5,000 shells, or one and one-half times the amount of ammunition on hand in the fort. Considering that the fleet carried over six hundred guns, the Confederate estimate of 21,000 projectiles fired by the ships during the two-day bombardment seems about right.[61]

When he ordered the ships withdrawn around 5 P.M., Porter was not aware that the fort was undamaged. There was no wind that afternoon and huge clouds of thick smoke hung in the air, making it impossible to see the effect of the fire. Because the Confederates had almost stopped shooting after 3 o'clock, Porter presumed that the great weight of metal hurled against Fisher must have dismounted or injured every gun, and reported that the bombardment had "destroyed" the works, and "set them on fire"; that they were "blown up" and "demolished." The Navy did its job splendidly, he wrote Welles; the troops could now take possession.[62]

Part of the army arrived in the late afternoon. Due to bad weather and unreliable pilots, neither Porter's aide nor one of Butler's staff officers, also sent out on the 23rd to communicate with the fleet, got into Beaufort that night. Thus until almost noon on the 24th, the generals were unaware that the naval attack had begun. Some of the transports were still waiting for coal and water. Immediately ordering those that were ready to proceed to the rendezvous, Butler and Weitzel departed on a fast steamer at 2:30, arriving off Federal Point just in time to witness the end of the bombardment and the withdrawal of the fleet. The remaining Army vessels were left to follow from Beaufort as they finished refueling. Among the last to obtain coal was the ship carrying the landing craft.[63]

Running in close to the flagship, Butler hailed Porter, inviting him to come on board for a conference. Although Weitzel afterwards accused Porter of petulance and bad spirit for refusing to go to Butler who was his "senior," and Porter, in self-defense, claimed that a fall had rendered him incapable of leaving his flagship, the ensuing confusion was more likely the result of an unsatisfactory mode of communication. Each thought the other had agreed to a consultation aboard his own vessel. By the time it occurred to Butler that he must have misunderstood and that the admiral was not coming, it was too late to land any troops.[64]

Weitzel finally saw Porter that evening and arranged the plan of attack for the next day. The conference lasted two hours. Judging by the plan adopted, Weitzel must have doubted that Fort Fisher was "destroyed." This engineer, it will be recalled, had a similar disagreement with Porter during the New Orleans campaign concerning the mortar bombardment of Fort Jackson. At that time, the admiral also claimed to have "blown up" and demolished a strong fortification which, on Weitzel's examination, had proved scarcely injured as a defensive work. Weitzel undoubtedly pointed out during the conference, as he afterwards claimed, that there was a great difference between a fort which was "silent"—because its commander wisely chose not to waste his shells against the fleet but to save them for a possible assault—and one that had been "silenced," meaning its guns were no longer serviceable. Besides, even if the fleet had actually "silenced" Fisher that day, the enemy could replace or remount his artillery during the night, repair damages, and bring up reinforcements to prevent its occupation by Federal infantry. Nor could the generals be certain, in view of the many delays attending this expedition, that a large Confederate detachment from Lee's army was not waiting for them on the beach.[65]

In any case, Porter agreed to provide a gunboat squadron for beach fire support and to employ the rest of the fleet in another bombardment of Fisher. It would appear from Butler's request for the Navy to "silence the fort and keep it silenced" that he shared Porter's faith in the power of ships against fortifications, despite Weitzel's reservations.[66]

The problem of coordinating the bombardment with the

landing caused considerable delay in renewing the attack on the 25th. Although Weitzel informed Porter at 6:30 A.M. that he would be ready at eight and wanted an hour-and-a-half bombardment before landing, the steamer carrying the Army surfboats had not arrived from Beaufort. Chafing impatiently at the delay, Porter ordered the ironclad division to resume station, and at 10:30 the *Ironsides* reopened on the works closely followed by the monitors. Several unpleasant facts were at once apparent. The fort was very much "alive"; the range, as on the previous day, was too long for each shot to take effect; and the bombardment this day must be shorter because the huge expenditure on the 24th had seriously depleted the fleet's ammunition supply.[67]

While the ships were being maneuvered into closer position, Porter sent an aide to find out what the Army was doing and to inform the generals that the bombardment, commenced without further consultation, could be maintained for only a few hours. It was now past noon and the surfboats had still not appeared. Concluding that they could wait no longer, Butler and Weitzel told the aide that they would land a reconnaissance party followed by the bulk of Brigadier General Adelbert Ames's division. If conditions looked favorable, the rest of the soldiers—Brigadier General Charles J. Paine's division of United States Colored Troops—would disembark and assault the works under cover of the fleet. Porter would have to supply landing boats until the Army's own craft arrived.[68]

The unexpected call for Navy boats upset the admiral's calculations. He had at last realized that an outside bombardment alone would not sufficiently soften up Fort Fisher for a successful assault. After seeing to the placement of the first division, which reopened on the fort at 1:30 at a range of one mile, Porter moved to the left of the line and positioned the gunboats for a concentrated fire upon the Mound and the gun emplacements on the southern flank of the main work. His intention was to run the shallow-draft ironclads through New Inlet into the river to take the land face of Fisher in reverse and cover the right of the Army's lines.[69]

But the channel had first to be sounded. A boat party and several pilots under Lieutenant Commander W.B. Cushing, who had made several daring raids into the river during the summer and autumn, was dispatched for this purpose about two o'clock. Immediately it ran into trouble. Shifting sand around the rotting hulks of dozens of vessels wrecked on New Inlet bar had made the channel very narrow and tortuous. The covering squadron, almost out of ammunition, was required to slacken its fire to conserve the precious rifled shells so effective in silencing the Mound the previous day.[70]

Having waited until the boats were casting lines, the naval gunners in Battery Buchanan suddenly opened on the fragile craft now exposed to a cross-fire from the powerful battery of two 7-inch Brooke rifles in Fort Fisher and plunging fire from the Mound. One launch was smashed in two and sank. The flagship *Malvern*, which Porter had brought in close to the shoal so that he could judge the practicability of running into the river, was a wonderful target for the Confederate sailors manning the Brooke battery. Although one of their pieces had already burst on the third round, the other remained serviceable long enough to put a rifled bolt through the *Malvern*'s boiler, at which point this gun too exploded, and the Union admiral hauled off to a safer anchorage.[71]

Still Porter did not recall the boat party. The enemy's fire had slackened and the soundings were resumed. Then Porter's aide, who had searched over an hour for the flagship, arrived with the news that the Army was about to land and needed all of the available boats in the fleet, along with enough sailors to pull them ashore. Since the Army's request could not be refused without later charges of noncooperation, and besides, the idea of running into the river did not look promising, the admiral at once recalled the boats and sent them north to assist General Weitzel.[72] It was now 2:30.

The bombardment had been maintained at a furious rate for an hour, and already some of the smaller ships were out of shells. The admiral ordered the frigates to fire more slowly. This order could not be obeyed. The moment they fell silent, all of the heaviest batteries in the fort, including a beautiful and very accurate Armstrong 150-pounder breech-loading rifle in the center of the sea face which had not fired the day before, opened on the large wooden ships. Within minutes, both the *Colorado* and the *Minnesota* were hulled below the water line. Shot, shells, and 10-inch bolts crashed through the decks. Without orders the captains of these vessels opened their broadside batteries furiously for self-protection, and the other ships, not so seriously threatened, followed suit. At 4:15, Porter signalled the frigates to save their remaining ammunition for the expected assault and to withdraw out of range if necessary.[73]

Meanwhile, a reconnaissance force of 500 soldiers under Brevet Brigadier General N. Martin Curtis had landed and moved down the beach to a line of abandoned rifle pits 300 yards from the land face of the fort. Another 2,000 infantry—the rest of Ames's division—were put safely ashore, but remained near the landing place. The debarkation did not go smoothly. The soldiers had very little boat drill and were used to their own small craft instead of the larger Navy launches. Further delay resulted from the necessity to silence a two-gun battery a mile up the beach which had been annoying the boats as they left the transports. Toward 4:30 the wind came up and the sea, previously calm as a lake, began to swell.[74]

At three o'clock, General Weitzel and Colonel C.B. Comstock, another engineer serving on Grant's staff, went ashore. They found Curtis's men huddled in the rifle pits under a sniping fire from sharpshooters behind the palisades and an occasional round of shrapnel from one of Fisher's heavy guns. While Curtis seemed anxious to try an assault if reinforcements could be brought up promptly, Weitzel and Comstock took one look at the place and decided an attack would be suicide.[75]

The Navy's massive cannonade had done almost no damage. Seventeen guns on the land face were uninjured. Although breached in several places, the palisade remained a formidable obstacle which had to be cut down under fire before reaching the ditch. The parapet was not badly broken and the bombproofs were uninjured. Having no heavy artillery of its own and only a few light pieces, the Army had to rely upon the fleet to keep the garrison in the bombproofs. The time required to pass the obstacles and mount the parapet was sufficient for the defenders to reman the guns and line the works with riflemen. Weitzel had commanded troops, both attacking and defending, in similar circumstances too many times during the war to believe that the most determined assault could take such a strong fortified position.[76]

Agreeing that an assault was hopeless, the two engineers returned to the landing place around five, and were rowed out to the Army headquarters ship where they met General Butler. After hearing Weitzel's report and hardly believing that any fort could survive such a pounding, Butler ran the *Ben Deford* in to about 700 yards off the east angle to look for himself. This position afforded a very good view of the defenses and the beach approaches. He concluded not only that the work was indeed substantially uninjured, but that the approach did not permit wide enough deployment for the assault force to protect its right from enemy infantry massed around the left extremity of the land front and at entrenched strongpoints near the river.[77]

In Butler's view, there was no time to lose. It was getting late; the sea was becoming too rough to land the remaining force, and the fleet's fire had practically ceased. A decision to storm the works had to be made quickly or the expedition might end in disaster. Some Confederate soldiers captured in a battery north of the landing point had indicated that they belonged to the advanced brigade of Major General Robert F. Hoke's division sent from the Petersburg lines to reinforce Bragg. The rest of this division had reached Wilmington and were probably en route to Federal Point.[78] There was a good chance that Ames's division, if it failed in the assault, would be caught between two fires and captured despite the efforts of the Union gunboats to protect their lines. The naval gun crews could not see to shoot accurately at night.

Finding no assault practicable and perceiving that there was nothing to be gained by the troops remaining there, Butler had good grounds to order them withdrawn. The most important was the unpleasant fact that the fleet was almost out of ammunition. If the soldiers survived on the beach and in the rifle pits that night, the bombardment could not be resumed in the morning. Porter must take the ships into Beaufort. Meanwhile, the Army would have no fire support and could not even reembark to save itself without such cover.[79]

The decision was quickly made. There was no time for consultation with Porter even if Butler had wished to share the responsibility for what was bound to be an unpopular move. If the troops did not get off immediately, they would probably have to stay at whatever risk. Nor could supplies or field guns be got to them. Butler had faced a similar situation at Hatteras three years before when his men were stranded on the beach all night without supplies or protection. He had been lucky then, for the enemy had not attacked; but the general was unwilling to run the risk again unless there was some purpose in it.[80]

There was no opposition to his decision within the Army command. Comstock informed Butler that, in his expert judgment, the fort was as strong as before the bombardment, and Weitzel, in overall command of the infantry, refused to assault. The order thereupon went out to General Ames at 6 o'clock to withdraw his division and return to Fort Monroe as per Grant's instructions. Porter was notified and asked to supervise the reembarkation. He did not object. In fact, he neither offered any suggestions nor expressed any disapproval whatever at that time, assuring Butler that the Navy would see to his men so the general could return at once to his army on the James with an easy mind.[81]

Although Butler was severely criticized by Porter after his departure, it is difficult to quarrel with his decision not to assault the fort on the 25th and to withdraw the troops altogether. Even had Butler been inclined to interpret Grant's instructions as definitive orders for the soldiers to entrench and remain on the beach, and had it been possible to do so, it would not have been wise. Butler had no heavy guns and had been told that Grant could spare no more men for this expedition. Besides, there was no advantage to be gained. If a base for the siege of Fort Fisher was required, the Union Navy's absolute command of the sea would allow this beachhead to be seized again, whenever weather conditions allowed. The Confederate attack on his forward depot at Baton Rouge during the Mississippi River campaign had taught Butler this important amphibious lesson. Indeed, it was better for him to maintain no force at all in the vicinity until he was ready to resume the offensive. Instead of building up at the point of attack, the enemy, lulled into a false confidence in the security of his defenses, might have returned his reinforcements to Petersburg.

It can be seen that, aside from the many errors of detail in the planning and preparation of this expedition, the fundamental reason for its failure was a faulty tactical plan. Because their experience with the older type of combined operation had not been tempered by the sobering realities of the Federal attacks upon the Charleston forts, both Porter and Butler assigned the Navy a role it could not fulfill. Everything else—the poor coordination of the bombardment with Army movements, the neglect of adequate communication between services; and above all, the exhaustion of the fleet's ammunition which precluded an assault on intact defenses and compelled the withdrawal of the troops—followed almost inevitably from the wrong assumption that Fort Fisher could be reduced by an unsupported naval bombardment. Even the powder-boat project, so questionable in conception and mishandled in execution, was designed to facilitate the positioning of the ships for a massive cannonade.[82]

It was only after the fleet had expended over half of its ammunition without effect on the 24th, and after conferring with Weitzel, that Porter considered using these ships, either those outside or those that might have been run into the river, in a fire support role. By the time the Army had procured boats, landed some of the troops, and reconnoitered the defenses it was too late to improvise a new tactical plan. Forced to continue rapid firing to protect itself from serious injury by the fort's heavy armament, the fleet had shot off almost all of its remaining shells and the weather prevented the rest of the infantry from landing.

Had Ames's men taken the fort by some miracle, their position would hardly have been less precarious. The great delay in sending off the expedition, due both to the Navy's slipshod arrangements regarding the powder boat and to Grant's lack of strategic interest in Wilmington which denied the Navy a firm commitment as to timing and troop allocation, also precluded secrecy and afforded the Confederates ample time to bring up reinforcements.[83] Again, because this "naval" venture was, in late 1864, unrelated to the strategy adopted for the main armies, no simultaneous attack was made upon the Petersburg lines to prevent Lee from detaching a whole division for the defense of Wilmington. With the enemy holding the river, reinforcements could also have reached Hoke from

Fort Caswell and the other Confederate works on the right bank of the Cape Fear. Could 2,500 Federals, minus the expected large casualties sustained in a frontal assault, have held the fort against a counterattack by eight or ten thousand without constant fire support to interdict its approaches? Probably not.

To view the first attack on Fort Fisher as a total loss for the Union, however, would be misleading. Of those involved, only Butler and Weitzel—who as a reward for sound military judgment were sacrificed to allay the popular furor attending this repulse of Northern arms—did not profit from it. Porter's conversion alone was worth the cost of the expedition.

Although he continued to insist publicly and in his correspondence with the Navy Department that his ships had destroyed, or at least "silenced," Fort Fisher on the 25th and that it was only Butler's criminal and unaccountable neglect to occupy the work which robbed him of a decisive victory, he did not believe it. Much as Porter still wished to take the fort single-handed as a prize for the Navy, he now recognized that this was impossible.[84] Against such formidable defenses, the Army and the Navy could no longer be used separately or successively in the attack; they had to work together as a tactical team, or both would fail.

12

THE CAPTURE OF FORT FISHER

IRONICALLY, just as Butler decided to abandon the Fort Fisher expedition, General Grant was reassessing the strategic importance of Wilmington. By the end of December 1864, Sherman's entry into Savannah and the decisive defeat at Nashville of the western Confederate army under General John B. Hood, by Union forces under Major General George H. Thomas, had altered the military situation.

Throughout Sherman's retreat upon the sea coast, Grant had been extremely worried about his army which had left Atlanta on 16 November with worn-out animals and few supplies. Grant expected the Confederates to make an all-out effort to stop Sherman's progress through Georgia, either by detaching large forces from Lee or by destroying everything in its path. Although Sherman had been careful to demolish the railroad from Chattanooga, the city of Atlanta, and the railroads along his line of march, so that Hood could not attack him from the rear, the Federal government, prior to the battle of Nashville, feared that Hood might ignore Thomas and invade Kentucky, thus causing another alarm and loss of morale in the North.[1]

None of these possibilities materialized. Sherman encountered almost no opposition, being allowed to take all the supplies he could use from the rich heartland of Georgia, while Hood's army was shattered and dispersed on 16 December. However, Grant's relief as seeing Sherman safe on the coast, where his army was soon re-equipped from the abundant stores previously sent to Port Royal, was replaced by another concern. Contrary to his expectations, Lee had made no detachments except Hoke's division sent to Wilmington. Having spent six weary months trying to hold the Army of Northern Virginia in its entrenchments while the South was conquered by other Federal armies, Grant had finally realized that Lee intended to hold Richmond and Petersburg in strength regardless of the threat to distant points. To wind up the war quickly, he must either force Lee out of his lines and defeat him decisively in battle, or encircle him in them. However the Confederates might respond to the threat of investment, Grant needed a larger force. He therefore intended, once Savannah had been occupied, to bring Sherman's whole army of sixty thousand men by sea to reinforce the Army of the Potomac on the James.[2]

But Sherman had other plans. Encouraged and flattered by his friend Halleck, who termed his retreat from Atlanta the most "brilliant" strategic maneuver of the war, Sherman wanted to make another "raid" through the Carolinas, breaking the railroads south of Raleigh. This would, he assured Grant, certainly force Lee out of Petersburg, allowing the Army of the Potomac to fall on him from the rear. Besides, his men would be opposed to the transfer. The whole army, he told Halleck confidentially on 13 December, was "crazy to be turned loose in South Carolina," and it would not be wise to disappoint them.[3]

Faced with this challenge to his judgment, Grant backed down. He had long ago learned from Halleck that a supreme commander, ignorant of local conditions, should never insist upon a plan not recommended by the generals who must carry it out. Although Sherman assured Grant that he would, as a good subordinate, obey any order of his superior without complaint, he would not have "advised" the transfer, arguing that it would require too much time. He neglected to explain that his soldiers, with Halleck's blessing, intended to punish South Carolina for having started the war, knowing that Grant would disapprove of such motives. Instead, he confined his arguments to the strategic benefits to be attained by an overland march. These were admittedly a bit vague as yet, but Grant could be sure everything would come out right in the end.[4]

Grant was not at all sure anything would come out right. While bowing to Sherman's opinion buttressed by "advice" from Halleck, he did not really like their plan which seemed to involve unnecessary risk. What if the Confederates abandoned Charleston as they had evacuated Savannah? What if the remnants of Hood's army should somehow reach North Carolina despite the damage to the railroads? By marching up from the south, was not Sherman inviting, even compelling, the enemy to concentrate in his front? And what about supplies? Sherman would not find North Carolina as rich in provisions as Georgia. In Grant's view, his overconfident subordinate had been lucky to escape from Atlanta unmolested; yet this dangerous retreat was to be followed by an even more hazardous movement.[5]

Having reluctantly agreed to let Sherman do as he pleased, Grant was determined that he should not run out of stores. Wilmington was the obvious point through which to supply his army in North Carolina. The Cape Fear River was navigable to Fayetteville one hundred miles above Wilmington. This line plus the railway from New Berne to Goldsborough would prove sufficient.

By the end of December, therefore, Grant saw the capture of Wilmington in a different light. It now deserved top priority since the safety of Sherman's army depended on it. Moreover, because Halleck approved Sherman's plan, a renewal of the Wilmington expedition had his hearty support and, consequently, that of the government. Welles and Fox, whom Porter had bombarded with requests to renew the attack on Fort Fisher, were surprised and pleased to discover a changed attitude at Army headquarters. Grant assured Fox on 1 January that troops would be sent as soon as transportation was available.[6]

Grant's view as to the practicability of reducing Fort Fisher and the means required was much influenced by a letter from his old friend Commander Daniel Ammen of the USS *Mohican* which had reached him on 28 December. In Ammen's opinion, the plan of attack should be modelled upon the Morris Island operations. Although the bombardment of 24–25 December demonstrated that the Navy could "control the fire of the fort" as it had earlier neutralized that of Battery Wagner, it could not cause enough physical damage to permit a successful assault. Instead of repeating the bombardment–assault tactics which had already failed, the troops should disembark several

miles north of Fisher and entrench across the peninsula isolating the work by land, while the Navy passed its shallow-
draft vessels into the river at night. With its communications
cut, the fort would be useless to defend either the river or the
town and "would then serve the enemy no better purpose than
if it were miles away at sea." Having closed the port to
blockade runners, the Federals need only tighten the investment, wearing out the garrison by continuous bombardment
until it surrendered. Or, if it was found impossible to get
vessels into the river, the fort could be taken by siege. In any
case, an officer familiar with the Charleston operations should
be sent in command of the troops.[7]

Upon deciding to resume operations against Wilmington,
Grant therefore selected Major General Alfred H. Terry who
had commanded a division in the attack on Battery Wagner.
This time, there was no ambiguity about what the Army was
expected to do. Terry was to land and hold a position on
Federal Point. "If such a position can be obtained," advised
Grant, "the siege of Fort Fisher will not be abandoned until
its reduction is accomplished or another plan of campaign is
ordered from these headquarters." As for cooperating with
Porter, who might have a different plan in mind, Terry was
cautioned that, while he should be "guided" as far as possible
by the admiral's views, any operations plan agreed upon should
be put in writing to protect the Army from unjust recriminations should this attack also fail.[8]

The infantry force was composed of the same units as in
the first expedition, plus Terry's old brigade now commanded
by Brigadier General Joseph C. Abbott.[9] In addition, Grant provided a strong reserve, a feature conspicuously absent from
Butler's expedition. Now that Wilmington was considered an
important strategic point for the Army, no means were with-
held to ensure success. On 2 January, Major General Philip
Sheridan was instructed to send a division to Baltimore where
it would be embarked upon transports, ready to reinforce
Terry quickly if needed. The measure of Grant's interest in the
Wilmington project is his order that Sheridan, a general of
whom Grant had the highest opinion, should command these
reinforcements in person.[10]

Every detail of the arrangements for the second expedition

differed sharply from the first. In addition to several batteries of rifled field guns, the Army contingent was provided with a siege train and abundant ammunition, plus extra provisions, entrenching tools, calcium lights, signal equipment, and reserve coal for the transports. And just in case Sheridan's veterans proved insufficient reinforcement to secure Fort Fisher and Wilmington, an entire Federal corps—the XXIII, commanded by Major General John M. Schofield—was ordered transferred from Nashville to Baltimore by rail on the 9th.[11]

The naval preparations were also much more thorough. Determined to prove that the Navy had not been responsible for the failure of the first attack by making sure of the second, Admiral Porter would not find himself again embarrassed for want of essential supplies. Large stocks of coal and ammunition were shipped to Beaufort in advance of the Army's arrival.[12]

Thus when Terry's force reached Beaufort on 8 January, everything was ready. The whole expedition sailed for Federal Point four days later and, on the 13th, the troops disembarked on the sea beach five miles north of Fort Fisher. Since the plan agreed upon between Porter and Terry was to besiege the work if it could not be taken immediately by surprise, the initial landing site was selected with an eye to maintaining continuous supply for the forces ashore.

It was supposed, prior to the landings, that an arm of the sea called Masonborough Sound would protect this part of the beach from enemy attack and that the Sound itself could be used by the smaller vessels to land supplies and siege material during bad weather.[13] However, the Navy had neglected to explore this waterway prior to landing the troops. Terry discovered the sound too shallow to accommodate vessels or protect his beachhead from counterattack. He therefore moved his force two miles down the peninsula around five o'clock that afternoon, intending to establish a new line adjacent to a large pond shown on his maps as occupying one-third of the peninsula. The position would have given him a short defensive line in the direction of Wilmington, freeing some of Paine's regiments for operations against Fort Fisher.[14]

By the time this "pond" was found to be a sand flat, it was too dark for the ships to fire with accuracy and Terry learned, soon after landing, that Hoke's division had not been sent to oppose Sherman in South Carolina as Grant had supposed, but was still in the vicinity. The first requirement was to get a defensive line across the peninsula. Accordingly, Paine's division set off in the direction of the Cape Fear River which it reached around nine o'clock. It was now very dark and the fleet had withdrawn for the night except for several gunboats which maintained indirect fire into the woods to the north.[15]

During this time, the Federals were most vulnerable and it was by good fortune that no attack was made upon them. General Bragg had arrived at Sugar Loaf Hill that afternoon. Seeing that nothing could be done while the Union squadron maintained its covering bombardment, he ordered Hoke to assume a defensive position north of the landing point. Bragg's greatest worry was that the Federals might interpose between Hoke and Wilmington and, ignoring Fort Fisher, march straight upon the defenseless town, a move that would have been disastrous for the Confederates. After dark, he ordered cavalry patrols to discover Terry's whereabouts, but these remained too far north and were unsuccessful. Nor did Fisher's garrison detect the enemy's approach. The commandant, distracted by a six-hour bombardment by the Federal ironclads that day and expecting a repeat of the tactics employed in December, had called in his outposts before dark.[16]

General Paine had meanwhile located a good position on the river as an anchor for his left and, at 2 A.M. on the 14th, began to dig in on this line, extending breastworks covered by abattis completely across the peninsula, two miles north of the fort. By eight o'clock, when the Confederates finally located Terry's position, it was too strong to be overrun and the Union gunboats had resumed their inshore station. Still, the line was much longer (about a mile in extent) than Terry had supposed would be necessary, absorbing Paine's whole division plus Abbott's brigade. He was also required to land the field artillery to protect the left of this line from two Confederate gunboats which had appeared in the river.[17]

It will be recalled that the Union Army had envisaged a repeat of the tactics employed at Charleston. Consequently, on the 14th, Terry ordered the siege train disembarked early the next morning. However, Colonel Comstock, again accompanying the expedition as chief engineer and remembering the sudden change in weather and rough seas which had interfered with the December operations, doubted that enough ammunition could be supplied on a regular basis over the open beach to make a siege practicable.[18]

After reconnoitering Fisher that afternoon from the sand hills six hundred yards in advance of the land face, the commanding general agreed. The situation was explained to Porter, along with the opinion, shared by Terry, Comstock, and General Ames—whose division would again be responsible for offensive operations—that an assault adequately prepared and covered by the fleet might succeed. In any case, all agreed that to withdraw the Army again, without at least attempting to capture the fort, was unthinkable.[19]

The decision to risk an assault having been reached for want of a better alternative, Terry's greatest worry was the strength of his command. Since he could not withdraw any of Paine's troops from the lines confronting Hoke without inviting counterattack from the rear, Ames's three brigades (3,000 men) were the only forces available for the assault. In order to ensure sufficient momentum to carry the work at any point, these brigades had to be deployed in succession leaving a front of attack less than half the width of the land face, a circumstance that would probably lead to a bloody repulse.[20]

Admiral Porter had a ready solution. His experience against a river battery during the Mexican War had given him the idea for a combined assault. He had already suggested such an idea to Terry before the expedition left Beaufort, and had boasted to the Navy Department and to various subordinates that, if the Army failed in its "duty" this time, he would take Fisher himself with a detail from the fleet.[21]

Now was his opportunity and Porter eagerly seized it. While Terry's men struck the western half of the land front, two thousand sailors and Marines, deployed on their left and armed with pistols and cutlasses, would "board the fort" at the north face of the east bastion. Because the naval column was to wait until the Army assault was under way, Porter did not anticipate strong resistance, the Confederate infantry being fully engaged in repelling Terry's men allowing the sailors to get into the angle almost unopposed. Taken by surprise, the enemy might even surrender the fort at once to the Navy.[22]

In the admiral's eyes, the most hazardous time would come before the charge, while his men were getting into position. To permit an approach within two hundred yards—estimated to be the maximum distance the sailors could move across open ground with reasonable safety in a single rush—a battalion composed of the Marine guard from the various vessels of the squadron was detailed to cover an advance party of sailors with shovels to dig rifle pits and throw up breastworks. This accomplished, the Marines, who carried Sharps carbines instead of pistols, and a few landsmen among the ships' crews armed with muskets, were to shoot down enemy riflemen appearing on the parapet, pick off the gunners of any cannon that might remain active after the fleet bombardment, and follow the third (rear) line into the fort.[23] The north face of the east bastion was chosen as the naval column's objective for two reasons. First, the sailors could approach this point without exposing themselves to direct artillery fire from the guns on the sea face or sweeping fire up the beach from the Mound. Second, it allowed the Navy to maintain contact and facilitated communications with the Army on the right.[24]

General Ames's division planned to attack in echelon; the leading brigade (Curtis) was to align with its left opposite the center traverse and its right extended to just beyond the re-entrant angle of the west half-bastion. Curtis was to press forward his left, consisting of the 112th and 142nd New York regiments, striking the center traverse. Aside from the psychological attraction of this particular mound of earth over which floated the tattered but defiant flag of Fort Fisher, the large bombproof here opened to the outside, being guarded in front by a small redan mounting two field pieces.[25] Obviously, if part of the First Brigade could gain quick entry into the inside of the work through this sally-port, the chances of success for the rest of the brigade scaling the parapet would be greatly improved. The Second Brigade (Pennypacker) was to follow three hundred yards behind and somewhat to the right so as to overlap the road; while the Third Brigade (Bell) with its right on the river and its center on the road was to envelop the western end of the land face.[26]

The timing of both assaults was to be regulated by signals; at least one officer aboard each vessel of the squadron had previously been instructed in their use by an officer of the Army signal corps. To avoid a premature charge by the naval column, signal 2211, meaning "change direction of fire," was to be given by General Terry just as the Army began its charge. The flagship, hoisting signal 2211, would then blow its steam whistle to be echoed by all of the whistles in the fleet. As the vessels shifted their bombardment from the land to the sea face, the sailors would rise up from their rifle pits and rush pell-mell into the fort.[27]

Before parting for the night, Porter and Terry agreed that the assault would take place at two o'clock the next afternoon (15 January) following a bombardment of five hours by the ironclads and two hours by the entire fleet; this was expected to disable the nine serviceable guns remaining on the land face. During the night, each vessel of the ironclad and 1st Divisions fired for one hour in succession to prevent the enemy repairing damages or remounting his cannon.[28]

At 9 A.M. on the 15th, as the *Ironsides* reopened the direct bombardment of the works, the ships of the other divisions dispatched their boats to the flagship and were ordered in toward the beach, landing about three miles north of the fort and out of range of its guns. By noon, 1,600 sailors (including landsmen serving as coal-heavers) and 400 Marines under Captain L.L. Dawson were safely on shore, being formed at once into "divisions" by Fleet Captain K.R. Breese to whom the admiral had entrusted command of the naval assault.[29]

This part of the operation was efficiently managed. Lieutenant Samuel W. Preston with his "pioneer" detail covered by sixty Marines under Lieutenant Louis E. Fagan of the *Wabash* had already completed the first line of rifle pits about a mile from the fort. At 1 P.M. the whole body—three divisions of about five hundred sailors each—advanced to this line and lay down behind improvised breastworks.[30] Thus far the sailors had followed their intended course, their left advancing along the crest of the shelving beach 300 yards inland, their center in line with the north salient of the angle.

The Marine battalion (the Fourth "division") had meanwhile deployed further inland and somewhat in advance to bring

The bombardment of Fort Fisher, 15 January 1865.

more effective sniping fire against the enemy's uninjured 8-inch gun in the east bastion, which was annoying the sailors. They soon found excellent cover in some entrenchments which the Confederates had abandoned during the night, 600 yards from the fort. Here they also came across a half-company of the 142nd New York regiment forming up for the assault. However, the remainder of the regiment pouring into these trenches forced the Marines to seek cover elsewhere.[31]

It was now about 2:30, a half hour past the appointed time for the assault, and no signal had been received by the Navy from General Terry. For those prone in the sand with only revolvers—useless at that range—to protect themselves, the long wait was almost unbearable. Although an occasional shell from the fort exploded harmlessly several hundred yards in front, the Union bombardment kept up in full fury against the land face, the gunboat projectiles whizzing menacingly overhead. Some exploded prematurely, showering fragments of metal upon the closely packed seamen. Feeling uncomfortable on land to begin with, the sailors grew increasingly nervous with each passing minute and their officers, being subject to the same impulse, with difficulty restrained them from bolting toward the fort before receiving the signal.[32]

Fearing a disaster because of the restlessness of his men and, for some unaccountable reason, having no signal officer to communicate with Army headquarters, Commander Breese had gone off to consult with General Terry. As he returned around 2:45 with the information that the Army's assault was postponed until 3:00, he encountered Lieutenant Fagan with his company who told him that the Marines could find no cover on the right and were beginning to break up into small squads for lack of orders about where to station themselves during the assault.[33]

Breese ordered the Marine battalion down onto the sea beach whose shelving edge afforded good protection at low tide. Seeing the Marines filing across their front, some of the sailors decided this was a good idea and ran for the beach themselves, compelling Breese to move all of his men in that direction to keep his formations intact. Nevertheless, the "divisions" fragmented, with the officers gravitating to the front and the lowest ratings to the rear.[34]

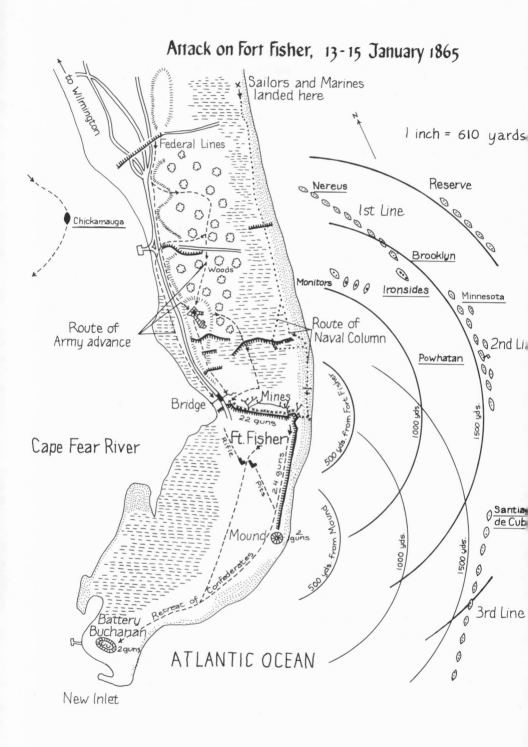

Attack on Fort Fisher, 13-15 January 1865

to Wilmington

× Sailors and Marines landed here

1 inch = 610 yards

Federal Lines

Chickamauga

Nereus

Reserve

1st Line

Brooklyn

Route of
Army advance

Woods

Monitors

Ironsides

Minnesota

Route of
Naval Column

Powhatan

2nd Li

1500 yds.

1000 yds.

500 yds. from Fort Fisher

Cape Fear River

Bridge

Mines

22 guns

Ft. Fisher

24 guns

21 guns

Rifle

Pits

Mound

2 guns

500 yds. from Mound

1000 yds.

1500 yds.

Santia
de Cub

Retreat of Confederates

3rd Line

Battery
Buchanan

2 guns

ATLANTIC OCEAN

New Inlet

Three o'clock came, and went. The fleet was still firing. Now about 600 yards from the fort, the naval column had begun to sort itself out. But the degree of order was only relative to the rampant confusion of a few moments before. The First Division with some of the other officers had moved forward, digging little holes in the sand for additional cover now that the column had been spotted by Confederate gunners on the sea face who threw shrapnel in their direction. Most of the Marines ended up with the Second Division, while the third and fourth "lines" merged into a compact mass. Remembering Admiral Porter's instructions not to charge until the Army went in, the fleet captain went to the top of the beach, and peered through the smoke toward the west looking for blue uniforms approaching the parapet. He saw none.[35]

The Army's advance toward Fisher was slower than expected. Most of the 14th had been consumed landing the light artillery and getting it into position to protect the left of General Paine's line, not only against a threatened attack by Hoke but against the Confederate gunboat *Chickamauga*. This vessel first appeared in the river on the afternoon of the 13th, delaying both the completion of Paine's entrenchments and the progress of Ames's division.[36]

As Curtis's men marched down the river road on the 14th, the *Chickamauga*, moving along the shore, dropped shells among them, forcing them under cover of the dense woods on the left. This unexpected change in the line of approach caused much confusion, especially among the regiments of the supporting brigades—some of which, losing all sense of direction, came out on the seacoast and had to countermarch. Others were still floundering about among the trees and the sand hills more than a mile from the fort on the morning of the 15th.

Although Curtis's brigade kept together fairly well in the advance, spending the night at a captured redoubt on a ridge 900 yards from the fort's northwest angle, its deployment and further progress were slower than Terry had anticipated. Coming off this ridge, the two left regiments found themselves in a swamp with no cover. Enemy sharpshooters appeared on the parapet and shells from three uninjured heavy cannon on the land face tore up the ground in front.[37]

General Ames decided that a series of entrenched lines was necessary to get his men into storming position on the left. Fortunately, the two New York regiments mentioned earlier came upon the abandoned Confederate advance line 600 yards from the fort about 1:30 in the afternoon. Approaching below the crest of the ridge near the river road, unseen by the defenders, Curtis's other three regiments had dug in about 300 yards from the northwest angle.[38] Meanwhile, Pennypacker and Bell, after collecting most of their stragglers in the woods, had regained the road, marching swiftly to Curtis's support. This time the Federals were ready for the *Chickamauga*. As she approached the shore, the U.S. gunboat *Nereus*, occupying the most northerly bombardment station in Line Number 1, opened on her across the peninsula with a 100-pounder rifle, and the Confederate ship beat a hasty retreat across the river, out of range.[39]

Thus the situation at the prearranged hour for the combined assault (2 P.M. on the 15th) was as follows: Curtis occupied an oblique line with his left 600 yards in front of the sally-port on the left and 300 yards from the northwest salient on the right. Pennypacker was entrenched across the road 300 yards in the rear, with Bell moving up between the river and the ridge. The sailors were lying behind their breastworks about a mile north of the fort and 300 yards in from the water, while the Marines were changing position from the right to the left front of the naval column to cover the charge on the east angle.

It will be observed that the main weight of the Federal Army was on the right, a situation not intended by General Terry, but brought about by the configuration of the ground. This deployment not only ensured loss of contact between the Army and the Navy in the assault, but made it necessary for Curtis's command to approach the fort more cautiously for lack of support on its left. Nonetheless, Terry was still determined that Curtis should strike the sally-port, this being considered the most vulnerable point of the work. An entrance here would allow direct access to the main bombproofs while cutting off the enemy in the eastern half of the land face, who would then be overwhelmed by the sailors.[40]

Therefore at 2:00 the commanding general ordered Ames

to begin a cautious advance, throwing forward his left and bringing his supporting forces more into line with his leading brigade. One hundred sharpshooters armed with repeating rifles moved by rushes and dug in 175 yards from the fort. The 112th and 142nd New York closed up by companies, finding cover among some small sand hillocks and finally lying down behind a low ridge fifty yards in rear of the sharpshooters. The Confederates reopened from their cannon in the center emplacement and the two 12-pounder smoothbores in the redan; but this fire was quickly silenced by the *Ironsides* and several gunboats of the first line which Porter, on request by signal from Army headquarters, had moved into position to enfilade the land face and the palisade line. Finally, at 3:25, Terry ordered General Ames to assault and sent signal 2211 to the flagship.[41]

Breese's men had remained inactive in their new position on the sea beach for twenty minutes. The huge shells of the *Ironsides*, now directed at the center traverse in support of the Army, still screamed overhead. The sailors had again grown restless, ready to charge in some direction at the least provocation. In front, Lieutenants Preston and Benjamin H. Porter edged down the beach and Commander Breese, himself unnerved by the long delay, had almost decided to order a charge without waiting for the Army.[42]

Suddenly the bombardment ceased. The effect on the naval column was instantaneous. With a loud cheer, the tars dashed forward, the officers waving their swords and challenging their men to keep up with them. During the few minutes required for the fleet to blow its whistles and redirect its fire to the Mound and the sea face, the leading seamen advanced over 300 yards. While some of the First Division stopped to catch their breath and others slipped and fell in the sand, the remainder pressed on. Since it was now impossible for them to strike the north face of the bastion, Lieutenant Porter, in the lead, headed for the palisade line between the fort and the sea intending to storm the south face instead. He never made it.[43]

As though the lifting of the Federal bombardment was not enough to alert the Confederates that an assault was imminent, the blare of dozens of steam whistles summoned all of the

The charge of the naval brigade at Fort Fisher

defending infantry out of the bombproofs. Quickly filling the angle and lining the parapet on both sides, the Southerners fired volleys into the defenseless naval column. Porter and Preston were immediately killed and other officers of the First Division severely wounded.[44]

Without their leaders, stunned by the ferocity of the enemy musketry, and confused by the obstacle in their front, the sailors bunched up behind the palisades, some lying down, some moving to the right. An officer and sixty men on the left charged around the end at the water's edge, only to stumble into the ditch and be struck in flank by a charge of grape from the 10-inch columbiad in Battery Number 7 on the sea face. Lieutenant Commander James Parker, the *Minnesota*'s executive officer, led two hundred men along the palisades to the right and, finding a small opening, attempted to charge up the steep slope of the *pan-coupé*, but was repulsed by a furious volley of rifle balls and shells from the Mound Battery, which was now shooting up the beach. Although Porter immediately directed the fire of his second and third lines of ships upon the Mound, the fleet was unable to silence Battery Number 7 or the 8-inch smoothbore in the bastion which, when not firing on Curtis' men, was swung around to discharge canister at the sailors.[45]

In any case, it was too late. The naval "column" had become a disorganized mob. They were already disposed to panic by their long wait before the assault; and upon seeing their comrades, trapped behind the palisades with no weapons to defend themselves, being picked off by enemy riflemen shooting down upon them from the crest of the parapet, and others lying wounded on the beach, the Second and Third Divisions dissolved, the officers and a few men rushing to the front, the rest to the rear. Observing their supports faltering, the sailors remaining at the palisade line could not be restrained. All but about eighty deserted their officers and joined in the rout. Commander Breese and officers of the Third Division tried several times to rally the men, correctly perceiving that more would be killed in retreating than in attempting to advance, but it was no use.[46]

Fortunately for those who survived this disastrous assault, the coolest head on the beach that day was Captain Dawson. Having received no orders from Breese and seeing that the utter demoralization of the sailors made success impossible, Dawson collected the bulk of his battalion—the rest of the Marines had gone in with the advance—and, pulling them back to the rifle pits, began firing to cover the retreat. While lying there, he was approached by General Terry's aide, who, upon learning of the repulse of the naval column, asked that he bring his command and any sailors he could collect to relieve General Abbott's brigade on the Army's northern line so that Abbott could reinforce Ames's division now fighting for possession of Fort Fisher. Since all of the seamen, except the badly wounded and the remnant left near the palisades who got safely away after dark, had by this time assembled near their boats, Dawson promptly replied to this request, arriving with five hundred men to relieve Abbott at 4:30.[47]

The Navy afterwards claimed—and this claim was substantiated by General Terry and the commander of the garrison, Colonel Lamb—that the futile and expensive assault of the seamen and Marines, by distracting the defenders at a critical moment, allowed the Federal infantry to gain a foothold in the fort thus leading to its eventual capture. Because the naval charge went in just *before* instead of just *after* the Army's, in violation of Porter's instructions, the Confederates mistook it for the main attack, massing nearly all of their available force in the east angle. By the time Lamb recognized his error, Curtis's brigade was already in possession of the three traverses in the northwest angle and could not be dislodged.[48]

This explanation is too simple, however. Much more can be credited to the Navy in the actual assault than the indirect effect of the repulse of a badly managed "boarding party." The preparatory bombardment was, of course, important. While not stated explicitly in the records, General Terry's experience at Charleston probably accounts to a large extent for the change in fire tactics employed during the second attack on Fort Fisher, although the systematic efficiency with which the fire plan was carried out was due entirely to the admiral's own skill in organizing his squadrons. Instead of the undirected fire diffused over the work which had proved useless in December, Porter employed aimed fire against the land face while the monitors and gunboats maintained a close-in bombardment for two days and nights.[49] This time there was no ammunition shortage in the fleet. Having ensured that a large stock was available at Beaufort, Porter used the older vessels of the reserve line to resupply the ironclads and gunboats at anchor during the night.[50] Before the assault, every gun on the land front was disabled, the palisades on the western half of this face demolished, and the mine leads cut.[51]

Still, the preliminary bombardment was not enough to ensure victory. Nor did the "distraction" of the garrison occasioned by Breese's attack secure more than a precarious toehold for the Federal Army in the fort. The Army's assault plan had, in fact, fared little better than the Navy's.

We have already observed the change in deployment which placed the greatest weight of the Union infantry opposite the left extremity instead of the left center of the work. As soon as Curtis began the final charge he realized that it would be impossible to get in through the sally-port, because his left regiments were being struck in flank by fire from the east bastion. Veering sharply to the right and passing along the front, the 112th and 142nd regiments, now intermixed with the other New York units in the brigade advancing on the run, struck the first gun emplacement, planting their flags on the adjacent traverse. Rushing down the road, Pennypacker's brigade split into two groups. The smaller, led by the general in person, attempted to pile in behind Curtis while the larger, encountering no opposition, passed along a covered way emerging in a field behind the fort. Although surprised, these latter units quickly dug in with shovels and tin plates to protect themselves from the fire of the Confederates, who had observed Curtis's flags and were hurrying toward the left of the land face.[52]

The Federal Army's point of entry into the fort made its task much more difficult than it would have been, had the original plan been followed. Instead of separating the defenders into fragments easily overwhelmed, the assailants confronted the whole body of the garrison (approximately 1,900 men) and were required to storm, one by one, every emplacement on the land front. The intermixing and bunching of their units in such a confined space and the gallantry of their officers—both Pennypacker and Curtis being badly wounded near the beginning of the action—placed them at a further disadvantage as the attack threatened to dissolve amid the smoke and confusion. Noting that his men were not getting forward and that the enemy was about to charge, General Ames sent in Bell's brigade which, scaling the parapet, took the third and fourth emplacements. But the Confederates, bounding over the fourth traverse, drove Bell's men back into the salient where they were soon opened upon by the columbiad in the east bastion and the reversed barbette batteries on the sea face.[53]

Unable to move forward and without room to retreat, success for the Federals would have ended there with the probable capture of the assault force had the fleet not come to its assistance with a renewal of the bombardment. The fire was not directed toward dismounting guns or tearing up the parapet as before. The fort's heavy traverses allowed the enemy to defend successive gun emplacements as separate works, massing men behind them for a counterattack.[54] Observing the Union soldiers losing ground, Porter perceived that the traverses could protect friend as well as foe. He therefore directed the fire of the *Ironsides*'s powerful battery, joined by that of the smaller gunboats with rifled pivot guns, into the emplacement just ahead of the soldiers. Caught in a hail of projectiles, the closely packed Southerners abandoned the emplacement to the Federals. Proceeding deliberately down the line of traverses, the barrage, followed closely by the infantry, drove the defenders out of the first eight emplacements after a stubborn three-hour fight.[55]

Arriving at the fort just as it was getting too dark for the ships to maintain the close support bombardment, Abbott's brigade—relieved from the right of Paine's line two hours earlier by the weary sailors and Marines of the naval assault party, and covered by Pennypacker's men in the field whom Lamb had been unable to dislodge by artillery fire—completed the capture of the work by storming the rear of the remaining emplacements and cutting off the sea angle.[56]

The Confederates could have done no more. There was no defense against this kind of coordinated combined attack except driving off the ships, which they were unable to do. So effective and pervasive was the fire of the Navy on this occasion that General Whiting, who had come to "share Lamb's fate" as he termed it, could not even bring up the reinforcements landed the previous night at Battery Buchanan because the fleet interdicted the entire ground between Federal Point and the Mound and shot up every Confederate steamer coming down the river with men and supplies.[57]

Finding half of the work in Federal hands, cut off from all outside aid, their commanders seriously wounded, the Confederates gave up the contest about 9:30 P.M. Those caught in the east bastion surrendered as the remainder, carrying their wounded officers, retreated toward the end of the peninsula, hoping to make a last stand there. But the Confederate sailors manning this work and the Mound battery, demoralized by the furious fire of the Union fleet that afternoon, had already concluded that the situation was hopeless. Leaving Fisher's exhausted garrison to take care of itself, they blew up the Mound guns, spiked those in Buchanan, and withdrew across the river in the only available boats. Whiting, Lamb, and over a thousand of their brave followers, without arms or any means of escape, surrendered in Battery Buchanan at 10:00 to Abbott's brigade and Blackman's regiment of U.S. Colored Troops.[58]

General Bragg was severely criticized at the time and in subsequent accounts of the action for not saving Fort Fisher— either by preventing a Federal landing altogether, or by a vigorous attack on Paine's lines while the assault was in progress. But this criticism takes no account of the actual circumstances during the engagement, or the responsibilities of the Confederate commander of the Wilmington Department.

Unlike Whiting, who was willing to sacrifice himself and every man in the vicinity to hold a work upon which he had spent years of skill and industry and of which he was justly proud, Bragg was required to weigh the risks and assess the strategic consequences.[59] Had Hoke been defeated in an all-out attack to relieve Fort Fisher, nothing would have stood between the Federals and the town; and Lee could spare no more detachments. While loss of the river defenses was a hard blow to the Confederacy, the loss of Wilmington would mean the end of the war.

Even if Fisher could have been saved by a diversionary attack on the 15th, it was obvious when the Federals returned after their repulse in December with a larger and better-organized force, that they were determined to take the place; so overwhelming was their superiority in material and manpower by January 1865 that they could afford any expense required to ensure victory. A repulse on the 15th would only have meant another attack on the 16th, or the 20th, or whenever Union reinforcements might arrive. Meanwhile, the Southerners would have used up the only troops available for the defense of Wilmington, now threatened not only by the combined force below but by Sherman's army, ready to march from Savannah upon its rear. Never a popular commander because he did not hesitate to make unpopular decisions when necessary, Bragg was right not to sacrifice Hoke's division in a vain attempt to relieve the fort.

Then too, the Confederate commander was justified in supposing that Fisher could withstand assault on its own.[60] Despite its defects—the most notable being the extraordinary amount of dead ground on the approaches, which the defenders might have remedied by levelling the sand hills and cutting down some of the trees—the fort was a remarkably strong defensive work for the period, as is demonstrated by the difficulties encountered by the assailants. Indeed, the Union infantry would have been repulsed, if not captured, had Admiral Porter not employed close support fire at the right moment, a technique which the Confederates could hardly have anticipated.

Moreover, all historical experience, and all Civil War experience, confirmed the principle that a strong, well-defended fortified position could not be taken by assault, combined or otherwise, unless first invested or isolated. Thus as late as 2:30 on the afternoon of the 15th, Bragg assured General Lee that the Federal effort would fail "at a heavy sacrifice" because the fort "is not invested and cannot be unless the fleet passes" into the river.[61] That an objective could be "invested" without physical encirclement—that is, by fire alone—would have occurred to no one on either side prior to the fall of Fort Fisher. Even then, Porter himself never perceived that this manner of employing gunfire, plus the close support in the assault—both new concepts improvised to meet the necessities of a particular situation—was the real key to the Union victory and would become, in the next century, the primary requirement for successful amphibious operations.

All kinds of fire were employed by the fleet during the three-day engagement and, at every stage, the Confederates found themselves unable to respond or their alternatives severely restricted.

It was one thing for Whiting to claim that Bragg should have prevented the Federal infantry from landing and consolidating its positions on the 13th—and another to have actually done so. Almost fifty vessels, including the heavy frigates, covered the landings and a whole squadron of gunboats threw indirect fire into the woods and the ground behind the beachhead and in front of the Federal lines at night. On several occasions during the 14th, Hoke's men tried to approach the Union positions and were driven off by this fire. Nor could the Confederate gunboat in the river prevent Ames's division approaching the fort along the road. Only part of the reinforcements—Hagood's brigade sent by Bragg to Fort Fisher on the 14th—could be landed at Battery Buchanan, the remaining transports being driven off or destroyed by vessels of Porter's third line.[62]

Contrary to his critics' charges, Bragg tried every expedient to save the fort. Frustrated in his attempt to reinforce or relieve the exhausted garrison on the 15th or to supply it with ammunition, and acting against his better judgment, he ordered an attack on the Federal lines at 4:00, just after the assault began. But Porter had anticipated this move for two days and was ready. As Hoke's skirmishers approached the Union entrenchments, the reserve squadron stationed close inshore opened a devastating fire upon them and rained shells upon the woods where the main units were forming up.[63]

The one piece of heavy artillery available to the Confederates on this front—a Whitworth rifle in a redoubt near the water on the left of their line—failed to drive off the ships, and was itself silenced within a few minutes by a smothering fire. Thus Bragg realized that pressing the attack would destroy Hoke's division without drawing off one Federal soldier from the assault on Fisher. He therefore ordered Hoke back to his lines, keeping up demonstrations on the river flank only to prevent any of Paine's troops from reinforcing Ames's division in the fort.[64] Nevertheless, Terry was able to withdraw Abbott's veteran brigade from the right of Paine's line, replacing it by a weak and demoralized collection of sailors and Marines, with complete confidence that the proximity of the Federal squadron precluded a successful enemy assault on that part of the line.

In his 1964 article, "The Fall of Fort Fisher," Jay Luvaas described the assault as "a model amphibious operation even by modern standards."[65] While this judgment may be somewhat extravagant, it is certainly true that the essential elements of modern combined operations, first employed to a limited extent against the defenses of Charleston, were present during the second Fort Fisher expedition. The fleet's fire was used to maximum advantage because the Union leaders had a sound appreciation of its capabilities prior to and during the assault; this meant greater tactical coordination between land and naval forces than had existed in previous amphibious operations. The whole expedition was, from the outset, much better equipped and prepared for unpredictable situations that arose, or might have arisen, during the campaign.

Despite what one might have expected, thorough advance planning and elaborate preparation did not limit operational flexibility. On the contrary, without it, such flexibility was impossible. Throughout the Civil War, armies and squadrons were rendered harmless to the enemy, stopped short of their objectives, or placed in hazardous positions because of poor preparation, bad equipment, or lack of foresight. The generals and admirals conducting these ad hoc operations, regardless of their initial intentions, quickly lost control of the situation allowing chance circumstances, local distractions, or enemy action to determine the course of their campaigns. Moreover, both services, frustrated by their inability to meet contingencies, tended to expect from each other a level of performance beyond their capability. It took the Navy years to recognize that infantry could not capture strong positions by assault without continuous fire support, while the Army failed to appreciate the limitations of seaborne artillery or the technical and logistical problems of maintaining an efficient naval force.

Union success at Fort Fisher was less the result of good cooperation between Porter and Terry—although, of course, this did no harm—than of superior organization. No more perfect harmony could have existed than that between Gillmore and Dalhgren during the Morris Island operations; yet the campaign as a whole was a failure. According to the plan of attack agreed upon for the first Fort Fisher expedition, Butler and Porter cooperated well enough, but both land and naval components were improperly organized, in addition to being badly prepared.

In the second attack, Porter used his outstanding organizational skill to full advantage. The composition of each squadron (or line) of the fleet was appropriate to the role envisaged for it. Each ship was assigned not only a bombardment station suitable to its armament, but specific targets upon which to fire at every stage of the action. The fire plan was altered, when necessary, by signals agreed upon before the engagement. No vessel was too old, too small, or too weak to perform some valuable service, such as supplying ammunition to the ironclads, bringing coal from Beaufort, towing damaged ships out of line, or carrying dispatches. The only disorganization in the Navy was that of the assault party.

The Army contingent was also well organized. Each unit knew its function and its position in the line of battle. Detailed written instructions were given to all commanders down to regimental level, and copies of these and subsequent Army orders were distributed among the fleet.[66] Without this high level of organization before the assault, which prevented the difficulties encountered during the approach, and the unexpected change in deployment, from producing hopeless confusion and demoralization, Terry's men would never have reached the parapet.

The strategic effect of the capture of Fort Fisher was even more important than Grant had anticipated. We have observed that his motive for operating against Wilmington was to open a safe line of supply to ensure that Sherman's army would not waste away during its march through North Carolina.

Bragg's decision to "sacrifice" the fort to save Wilmington, and Porter's estimate that 13,000 reinforcements were required to outflank the enemy's remaining defenses on the river approach to the town, induced Grant to send XXIII Corps, just arrived by rail from the West, to Fort Fisher on 9 February. General Schofield, placed in command of his own and Terry's troops (about 30,000 men) was instructed, after taking Wilmington, to open the river to Fayetteville, which Sherman expected to reach before the end of the month.[67]

The Federals were successful in forcing Bragg to evacuate Wilmington on the 21st—an outcome made inevitable by Whiting's failure to construct a strong inner line of permanent works prior to the fall of Fort Fisher. But Sherman's advance, delayed by bad roads and scarcity of forage in the country north of Columbia, South Carolina was still one hundred miles south of Fayetteville.[68] This was the situation Grant had most feared when reluctantly assenting to Sherman's plan in December. Unaware of the wretched state of the enemy's communications, Grant thought it likely that Bragg, having held Wilmington long enough for elements of Hood's army to arrive in North Carolina, would unite with these forces and with other Confederate units retreating from Charleston and Savannah. Further reinforced by detachments from Virginia, or possibly by Lee's whole army, the Confederates could fall on Sherman before he reached the Cape Fear. His degree of apprehension is reflected in his orders of 31 January that XXIII Corps cut loose from its communications if necessary to save Sherman's army.[69]

Such a drastic expedient proved unnecessary, however. The situation of the Confederates in February 1865 was not nearly so favorable as Grant supposed. Lee had, in fact, wasted the month given him by Bragg's delaying defense of Wilmington in pondering what to do. Although Davis had appointed Lee general-in-chief on 6 February, the Confederate forces in the Carolinas and the West remained scattered and without overall leadership, and they were left to withdraw as best they could before the superior Federal armies.[70] Perhaps the repeated failure of the Federals to follow up any of their coast operations by an immediate strong advance on some vital interior point had encouraged a belief that the forces which overpowered Fort Fisher would also disperse or remain idle on the coast.

In any case, the fall of Wilmington forced Lee to act. On 22 February, he appointed General Joseph Johnston to command all of the forces in the eastern Confederacy except the Army of Northern Virginia. Johnston was to concentrate every available man to oppose Sherman's advance into North Carolina. Lee further proposed a desperate plan for restoring the fortunes of the South. If the Army of Northern Virginia could unite with Johnston before Schofield joined Sherman and before the latter could be resupplied via the Cape Fear, there was a chance of defeating Sherman, then turning to attack Grant while the Army of the Potomac was reorganizing for a further advance south. A major repulse when the end seemed so close would have been a tremendous moral blow to the North and might have produced a negotiated peace instead of unconditional surrender.[71]

The success of this plan depended upon Johnston's ability to hold Fayetteville and close the Cape Fear above Wilmington. While the Army of Northern Virginia could, by heroic exertions of the quartermaster department, obtain enough food from southwestern Virginia and other supplies from U.S. Treasury agents through the recently reopened port of Norfolk, the critical item was ammunition.[72] In fact, it was this requirement, apart from the need to contain Grant's huge army, that had kept Lee in his lines for six months to the bewilderment of his opponent. The only place other than Richmond from which Lee could obtain small arms and ammunition was the arsenal at Fayetteville.[73] These two points were, therefore, the only available bases for the Army of Northern Virginia during the final campaign. As long as Fayetteville remained in Confederate hands, Lee could have given up Richmond and still kept his army intact as a fighting force.

But Lee's decision to unite all Southern forces came too late. Due to the broken-down condition of the railroads, his army was unable to accumulate the necessary supplies and transportation for a quick move into North Carolina.[74] And on this occasion, the Union high command did not forfeit the advantage of coastal bases.

The Federal movement on Fayetteville, Goldsborough, and Raleigh was a model of efficiency compared to previous combined operations. While the Navy transported millions of tons of stores, including railway equipment, along with a construction corps for rebuilding the roads from Moorehead City and Wilmington in anticipation of Schofield's advance, Union gunboats ascended the Neuse and cleared the mines and obstructions from the Cape Fear.[75]

Without reinforcements, Johnston's 15,000 men—all he could assemble to oppose both Sherman and Schofield—were hopelessly outnumbered. Although the advance of XXIII Corps up the Neuse was momentarily checked at Kinston, the secure river line of operation and the presence of Federal gunboats assured Schofield's eventual success. The Confederate forces under Bragg, sent to oppose Schofield at Kinston, retreated to Goldsborough on 10 March. The following day, Sherman's army entered Fayetteville and, on the 12th, the first Federal vessel reached that town from Wilmington.[76]

With the opening of the Cape Fear and the Neuse and the occupation of Fayetteville went the last hope for the Confederacy. Any number of Northern troops and supplies could now be thrown into North Carolina. Threatened with encirclement at Petersburg, Lee's only alternatives were to attempt an escape into the mountains where his army would have to disperse and resort to guerrilla warfare, or to capitulate. Reluctant to see the Southern cause, for which he and his army had fought so bravely against such odds for four years, reduced to the first alternative, Lee hesitated too long before abandoning his lines and was trapped by the Army of the Potomac at Appomattox Court House twenty miles east of Lynchburg, where he surrendered on 9 April. Johnston surrendered to Sherman at Durham Station, North Carolina on the 18th.

In spite of the disparity of forces during the final campaign, the war would have lasted much longer without the intelligent application of combined operations, both on the tactical and the strategic level. It is also evident that, had this form of warfare been employed as envisaged by McClellan in 1861, or by Grant in late 1863, the war would have ended much sooner. The final offensive itself might have been shortened by several months, with a considerable saving of lives and money, had Grant been permitted to move his army to the vicinity of Richmond by sea at the outset of the 1864 spring offensive (as McClellan had done in 1862) or to throw a corps or two against Wilmington to disrupt Lee's communications south of Richmond.

An almost universal assumption is that Sherman's march through Georgia and the Carolinas was of great strategic importance. Indeed, some analysts have claimed that, without this "brilliant" conception, Lee's army could have held out much longer against Grant. There is almost no evidence to support such a judgment. On the contrary, the weight of evidence leads to the opposite conclusion.

From a military point of view—that is, leaving aside Sherman's personal ambition—the famous march accomplished nothing that could not have been more quickly and cheaply attained by other means. Had this large force, which Grant called his "spare army" been brought to Baltimore after the Atlanta campaign to cooperate with the Navy in taking Wilmington and opening the Cape Fear, Lee would have been maneuvered out of Richmond in December 1864.

As for the destruction of vital resources, the senseless burning of Columbia and the demolition of a few hundred miles of railroads already too worn out to supply the Army of Northern Virginia does not compare with the seizure of the Fayetteville arsenal, which could have been more easily effected by a short expedition up the Cape Fear than an exhausting overland excursion from Atlanta. Operationally, Sherman's advance by the line of the Cape Fear in conjunction with the Navy would have separated the Confederate forces in Georgia and South Carolina from the main army in Virginia, instead of driving them back upon it, a situation Grant rightly regarded as a dangerous violation of sound military principles.[77]

Thus the capture of Fort Fisher and Wilmington represented an abandonment of the wasteful and ineffective continental strategy practiced by General Halleck with the approval of the Lincoln administration. Instead, a waterborne offensive was used; this approach not only took full advantage of superior Northern manpower and material resources, but it exploited the Union's command of the sea to bring about the rapid collapse of enemy resistance and the end of the war.

CONCLUSION

R EGRETTABLY, those who analyze policy and strategy seldom
examine the operational implementation of these ideas.
When they do, the gap between what was intended and what
was accomplished, or capable of being accomplished in the
particular circumstances surrounding an action, is explained
by blaming some hapless general or admiral—not for making
a bad decision in the light of the practical alternatives open to
him at the moment of decision, but for not conducting his
operations according to some principle of war or some tidy
scheme designed for ideal conditions.

Although we should, by all means, recognize bad judgment
when it occurs, we should not require that every general be
a Napoleon or every admiral a Nelson. Above all, let us not
expect any man to transcend difficulties beyond his influence.
If this study has frequently shown what was aimed at by
those in command of armies and squadrons and suggested
what might have been, it was only to throw a sharper light on
what actually was; to call attention to the *process* by which
ideas in war are so often transformed into something quite
different from what anyone intended. This transformation is
rarely the consequence of large policy decisions. It results more
often from some seemingly trivial, but crucial detail, or a
whole complex of action and reaction to solve some apparently
minor problem.

Civil War operations—combined and otherwise—provide
striking examples of "kingdoms lost for want of a nail." An
error in the ordnance department—the guns are useless and
the engagement lost. An oversight by the engineers—there are
no bridges and the army is paralyzed. A miscalculation by the

naval constructors, and the ships will not float or the gunports are too small—the Navy is powerless. Some clerk mislays a requisition—the fleet is immobilized for lack of coal, or the army for want of wagons, shoes, or forage. And so on. Since no one expects perfection at the operational level, this class of errors is usually dismissed as the "elements of chance" or the "accidents of war," as though all such occurrences are not only inevitable and unpredictable but require no explanation of their cause and effect. No attitude could be more misleading in the minds of those responsible for the conduct of war or the historians who interpret their decisions.

This study shows that, while perfection may be unattainable in any human activity, the closer an operation approached the ideal, the fewer "accidents" happened. The key to maintaining control of the situation was the extent to which a movement was thought out in advance and careful attention given to detailed planning, organization, and preparation. Failure to anticipate and provide for contingencies was characteristic of most Civil War combined operations.

A comparison of the Peninsular campaign and the first Fort Fisher expedition will demonstrate this point. Although McClellan never intended to besiege Yorktown, he recognized that unavoidable circumstances might force this alternative upon him. He therefore took along a siege train and so was able to reduce Yorktown when his preferred plans went awry. Butler and Porter, on the other hand, made no allowance for the failure of their tactical plan and were thus compelled to abandon their expedition. The wisdom of being prepared for any problem that might reasonably interfere with the attainment of an objective is even more dramatically illustrated by the Charleston experience. Both Gillmore and Dahlgren were meticulous technicians. They were so well equipped with guns, ammunition, coal, lights, signal equipment, and landing boats that they were able to improvise new tactical techniques to overcome defenses far stronger than anticipated. Only one contingency was unprovided for—the necessity of removing the channel obstructions under fire. Lack of attention to this single detail rendered all the rest of their preparations worthless.

One might argue that it is impossible to provide for every

eventuality. While true in the abstract, this proposition applies in practice only to genuine accidents of war; that is, to circumstances entirely unpredictable or over which the field commanders could exercise no control. Nothing went wrong with the Peninsular campaign that an action by McClellan could have prevented. Although this general could, and did, direct the movements of his own army and, by skillful maneuver, the responses of the enemy, he could control neither the actions of his government nor those of its Navy. Still, McClellan was far in advance of his contemporaries, not only with respect to strategic conceptions, but in his scientific and thoroughly professional approach to military problems at all levels.

This judgment is in no way a criticism of other generals, who doubtless did their best, or of the Navy, which was compelled to learn the requirements of modern war by trial and error. Nor should those sympathetic to the military be too hard on the Lincoln administration, despite the pernicious effect of government interference on operations. With a shaky mandate, under sustained pressure by special interest groups, sectional factions, Congress and the press, and facing the threat of foreign intervention, the president and Cabinet were naturally prone to view every unforeseen political development as a crisis amenable to relief only by precipitous military or naval action. Nor is it fair to blame civilian officials for being ignorant of the art of war and thus failing to foresee the likely result of changing strategic directions in the middle of a campaign, or of appointing too many commanders, or aiming at multiple and diverse objects.

If fault must be found with the politicians, let it be for the right reason; that is, for not restricting their activity to the definition of political goals while entrusting the responsibility for their military attainment to the generals and admirals. When some emergency arose (such as the numerous financial crises) which made some kind of immediate victory imperative, the commanders should have been consulted; not regarding the political situation, which was none of their business, but about the best line of military action. Whatever secondary operations required to reassure the public might then have been managed without disrupting existing plans or tying up resources needed to carry major offensives through to a decisive conclusion.

This procedure was not followed except to a limited extent after the November 1864 elections, when both foreign and domestic pressures subsided and the government's credit improved. Lincoln was fortunate in finding a general-in-chief like McClellan so early in the war—a man not only willing and capable of assuming full responsibility for military operations, but who recognized the importance of purely political objects and designed his strategic plans to accommodate such aims. The Northern administration threw away this advantage, supposing that what worked in the political arena would suffice for the battlefield; believing that enormous and ponderous organizations like armies and navies could be manipulated as easily as individuals, to suit the aspiration of the moment.

The politicians never understood that to be certain of success, even the stronger belligerent must be adequately prepared and reasonably well organized; that to know what organization and preparations are necessary, one must have a definite plan of campaign; and that a sound operational plan must accord with military as well as political reality. While Lincoln perceived, for example, both the political and the military importance of east Tennessee, he could never appreciate that it was harder to get there directly over the mountains or along the railroads than via the river lines. Nor did he ever understand that occupation of the coast and border regions, while of some political and economic benefit to the North, was a serious military liability, tying up forces that could have seized vital objectives, thus ending the war sooner and making such occupation either unnecessary or more easily accomplished.

Enough has been said about the importance of strategic planning. Of course, these observations apply to all forms of war. What is especially significant about the requirements of combined operations is not that they are different in kind, but in degree. Amphibious warfare is more complicated. The forces differ in tradition, experience and training, the material is more varied and specialized. Several independent commanders with distinctive operational styles, personalities, and prejudices must reconcile their differences to attain a common end. There are simply more opportunities for something to go wrong; more details to worry about, and more equipment which might be left behind, or sunk, or worn out. Weather conditions assume greater importance. Supply and maintenance problems are more diverse. Greater attention must therefore be focused upon the pre-engagement phase, because this stage usually determines the ultimate success or failure of the whole enterprise.

Before 1861, combined expeditions could be improvised. They frequently aimed at some weak or undefended sectors of the coast and involved no sophisticated equipment or complex tactical plan. Except in Europe, internal communications were too poor to make waterborne invasions practicable, so that no provisions for exploitation were required and the initial choice of objectives depended more on the ease with which they could be seized than on their strategic relation to interior points. Expeditions of this type were successful during the first year of the Civil War, but not thereafter. Once the Federals had decided to go against the strongest points in the enemy's defensive system and had developed weapons of a more intricate character and specialized capability, ad hoc expeditions were no longer effective. An improvised combined force could succeed tactically only if it struck some place of small strategic importance.

The American Civil War was a great "watershed" between the eighteenth and twentieth centuries with respect to amphibious warfare. During this conflict, in response to the challenges of new problems and conditions imposed by the technological revolution, combined operations evolved, at least in the United States, from their "maritime" to their "continental" form. Under McClellan, and later under Grant, what was once only an "indirect" extension of sea power onto the land had become a powerful instrument for projecting large armies directly into the enemy's heart.

NOTES

Abbreviations Used in the Notes

B & L   *Battles and Leaders of the Civil War.*
JCR   *Report of the Joint Committee on the Conduct of the War.* The year of publication of the various series is in parentheses.
ORA   *The War of the Rebellion: A Compilation of Official Records of the Union and Confederate Armies.* References are to Series I unless otherwise indicated.
ORN   *Official Records of the Union and Confederate Navies in the War of the Rebellion. All references are to Series I.*

CHAPTER 1

1. Scott to Seward, 3 Mar 1861, quoted in Marcus J. Wright, *General Scott* (New York, 1894) pp. 299–300.

2. Scott to McClellan, 3 May 1861. *ORA*, LI Pt. I, 369–70. The expedition was not practicable until fall due to the unhealthy summer climate in the Mississippi Valley and the low level of water in the river.

3. Scott to McClellan. *ORA*, LI, Pt. I, 387.

4. C. H. Davis to his wife, 22 May 1861, in C. H. Davis, *Life of Charles Henry Davis* (Boston, 1899) pp. 121–22; David Donald (ed.) *Inside Lincoln's Cabinet: The Civil War Diaries of Salmon P. Chase* (New York, 1954) pp. 11–13.

5. H. A. Du Pont, *Rear Admiral Samuel Francis Du Pont* (New York, 1926) pp. 105–06; Daniel Ammen, "Du Pont and the Port Royal Expedition", *B & L*, I, 671.

6. All of the board reports, except the second, are in *ORN*; reports Nos. 1, 3, and 4 in Vol. XII, 195–206, and No. 5 in XVI, 618–30. The second report (13 Jul 1861) is in *ORA*, LIII, 67–73. The first two reports also appear in *JCR* (1863) III, 316–22.

7. *ORN*, XII, 195–98.

8. *ORA*, LIII, 67–73.

9. *ORN*, XII, 198–201.

10. Welles to Du Pont, 3 Aug 1861. *ORN*, II, 207.

11. Testimony of Brig-Gen T. W. Sherman, 16 Apr 1862. *JCR* (1863) III, 292–94.

12. See Map 9. Testimony of Maj-Gen McDowell, 26 Dec 1861. *Ibid.*, I,

124. McDowell was appointed to command the Department of Northeastern Virginia on 28 May, less than two weeks after submitting this proposal.

13. William Starr Myers, *General George Brinton McClellan* (New York, 1934) pp. 183–86.

14. Testimony of Maj-Gen Butler, 15 Jan 1862. *JCR* (1863) III, 282. Welles to Stringham, 9 Aug 1861. *ORN*, VI, 69–70.

15. Special Orders #13, 25 Aug 1861. J. A. Marshall (copyrighter) *Private and Official Correspondence of Gen. Benjamin F. Butler*. 5 vols. (Norwood, Mass., 1917) I, 213–14; E. D. Townsend (AAG) to Wool (for Butler) 13 and 21 Aug 1861. *ORN*, VI, 82, 106.

16. Butler to Lt-Gen Scott, 16 Aug 1861. *Butler Correspondence*, I, 226; Lt. C. Churchill (AAG) to Butler, 25 Aug 1861. *ORA*, IV, 580.

17. John C. Barrett, *The Civil War in North* Carolina (Chapel Hill, N.C., 1963) pp. 33–34.

18. Reports of Maj-Gen Butler, 30 Aug 1861, Col Max Weber and Flag-Off Barron (CSN). *ORA*, IV, 581–83, 589, 592–94: Report of Flag-Off Stringham, 2 Sep 1861. *ORN*, VI, 120–23. Testimony of Maj-Gen Butler, 15 Jan 1862. *JCR* (1863) III, 284. Daniel Ammen, *The Atlantic Coast* (New York, 1883) pp. 168–70.

19. Captain Parker, CSN, observed that "if the attack on Hatteras had been made a few months later in the war, when our men had learned how little damage the fire of ships does to earthworks, the fort would not have fallen." William Harwar Parker, *Recollections of a Naval Officer* (New York, 1883) p. 213.

20. See Butler's letter to Chase dated 27 April 1863 expounding at length upon this theory. *Butler Correspondence*, III. 61–64.

21. Fox to Stringham, 1 Sep 1861. *ORN*, VI, 131. Report of Maj-Gen Butler, 30 Aug 1861. *ORA*, IV, 584–85.

22. Welles to Stringham, 17 Jul, 10 Aug, and 3 Sep 1861; New York Board of Underwriters to Welles, 12 Aug; H. Barney (Collector, Port of New York) to Chase, 9 Aug 1861. *ORN*, VI, 6–7, 71, 72–73, 76–77, 162–63.

23. Welles to Lincoln, 5 Aug; Welles to Stringham, 19 Aug 1861; Instructions from the secretary of the Navy re Blockade Regulations. *ORN*, VI, 53–56, 266–67.

24. John Niven, *Gideon Welles, Lincoln's Secretary of the Navy* (New York, 1973) p. 389; Presidential Proclamation, 16 Aug 1861. *ORN*, VI, 90–91; Howard P. Nash, Jr., *A Naval History of the Civil War* (New York, 1972) pp. 14–15.

25. Rowan to Welles, 3 Sep 1861. *ORN*, VI, 160–61. Hawkins to Wool, 7 and 11 Sep 1861. *ORA*, IV, 607–10.

26. Pres. Davis to Howell Cobb, 31 Aug; R. C. Gatlin (CSA) to Cooper (AG), 30 Aug 1861. *ORN*, VI, 137, 138. Hawkins to Wool, 19 Sep 1861. *ORA*, IV, 617–19.

27. Rowan to Stringham, 5 Sep; Rowan to Welles, 20 Sep 1861. *ORN*, VI, 172–73, 240–41. Hawkins to Wool, 21 Sep 1861. *ORA*, IV, 619–20.

28. Stringham to Fox, 13 Sep; Welles to Goldsborough, 18 Sep 1861. *ORN*, VI, 205–06, 233–34.

29. Du Pont to Mrs. Du Pont, 28 Nov 1861. John D. Hayes (ed.) *Samuel Francis Du Pont: A Selection from his Civil War Letters.* 3 vols. (Ithaca, N.Y., 1969) I, 262.

30. Welles to Goldsborough, 18 Sep 1861. *ORN*, VI, 233–34.

31. Frederick W. Seward, *Reminiscences of a War-Time Statesman and Diplomat* (New York, 1916) pp. 168–69.

32. Joseph E. Johnston, *Narrative of Military Operations* (Bloomington, Ind., 1959) pp. 76–77; Allen Tate, *Jefferson Davis: His Rise and Fall.* Reprint ed. (New York, 1969) pp. 107–08.

33. Welles to Stringham, 18 Sep; Second Report of the Blockade Board, 16 Jul 1861. *ORN*, VI, 231–32, XII, 198.

34. Du Pont had commanded a blockading squadron during the Mexican War and was considered an expert on the subject. Du Pont, *Admiral Du Pont*, p. 107.

35. Rowan to Chauncey, 26 Sep; Report of Cmdr Rowan, 5 Oct 1861. *ORN*, VI, 264–65, 275–76. Reports of Brig-Gen Mansfield, Brig-Gen Huger (CSA) 5 Oct 1861. *ORA*, IV, 595–97. See Map 5.

36. Stellwagen to Goldsborough, 2 Oct 1861. *ORN*, III, 279–80.

37. Wool to Scott, 24 Aug 1861. *ORA*, IV, 601–03; also VI, 171; *ORN*, XII, 208; Roy P. Basler (ed.) *The Collected Works of Abraham Lincoln.* 10 vols. (New Brunswick, N.J., 1953) IV, 528.

38. Wool to Scott, 6 and 11 Oct; Mansfield to Scott, 14 Oct 1861. *ORA*, IV, 621, 623–24, 626. Mansfield was an old soldier and Indian fighter who had served with General Scott in Mexico.

39. Du Pont to Mrs. Du Pont, 8 Sep and 17 Oct 1861. *Du Pont Letters*, I, 145–46, 171; Welles to Du Pont, 12 Oct 1861. *ORN*. XII, 214–15. Also see Du Pont to Welles, 6 Nov 1861. *Ibid.*, p. 259.

40. Testimony of Brig-Gen T. W. Sherman, 16 Apr 1862. *JCR* (1863) III, 292–93. Du Pont to Cmdr F. S. Haggerty and Lt I. B. Baxter, 26 Oct 1861. *ORN*, XII, 229–30.

41. Du Pont to Welles, 18 Sep and 6 Nov 1861. *ORN*, XII, 209, 259. Also see Welles's order to Col John Harris, Commandant U.S. Marine Corps, dated 19 Sep 1861. *Ibid.*

42. Jenkins to Du Pont, 9 Aug 1861. *Du Pont Letters*, I, 130–31; Du Pont to Fox, 25 Oct 1861. Robert Means Thompson (ed.), *Confidential Correspondence of Gustavus Vasa Fox, Assistant Secretary of the Navy, 1861–1865.* 2 vols. (New York, 1919) I, 59.

43. 29 Oct 1861. *Fox Correspondence*, I, 64. Emphasis in original.

44. Du Pont to Mrs. Du Pont, 30 Oct 1861. *Du Pont Letters*, I, 201.

45. United States National Archives (R.G. 23), A. D. Bache, Notes on the Coast of the United States, 1861, with charts, Sect. IV, South Carolina.

46. Samuel Jones (Maj-Gen, CSA), *The Siege of Charleston* (New York, 1911) pp. 51–53.

47. Report of Maj F. D. Lee, 4 Dec 1861. *ORN*, XII, 312–14.

48. Report of Lt J. S. Barnes, 9 Nov 1861. *ORN*, XII, 270. Du Pont, *Admiral Du Pont*, p. 122, note 1.

49. Report of Capt R. Saxton (QM) 9 Nov 1861. *ORA*, VI, 186. Du Pont to Mrs. Du Pont, 6 Nov 1861. *Du Pont Letters*, I, 221. Goldsborough to Fox, 8 Nov 1861. *ORN*, XII, 291–92. Before the expedition left Hampton Roads, General Wool complained to Secretary Cameron that Sherman's ships were not combat-loaded and that he had had to supply ammunition and large quantities of provisions while his troops stayed at Fort Monroe because their supplies were "stored at the bottom of his ships and could not be got at short of four days." "I will venture to assert," he added, "that a worse-managed expedition could not well have been contrived." 28 Oct 1861. *ORA*, VI, 184. For Sherman's instructions concerning combat loading, see his letter to Captain Saxton dated 27 Sep 1861. *Ibid.*, pp. 174–75.

50. Report of Brig-Gen Sherman, 8 Nov 1861. *ORN*, XII, 288–89. Du Pont to Mrs. Du Pont, 6 Nov 1861. *Du Pont Letters*, I, 221.

51. Report of Maj Reynolds (USMC), 8 Nov 1861; Ringgold to Welles, 6 Jan 1862. *ORN*, XII, 233–35, 239–43. Major J. G. Reynolds, commanding the Marine battalion persuaded Commander C. Ringgold of the *Sabine*, despite severe damage to his own ship, to take his men to Port Royal. They arrived just too late for the fight.

52. See Map 4.

53. Detailed report of Flag-Off Du Pont, 11 Nov 1861; Unofficial report of Cmdr P. Drayton. *ORN*, XII, 262–66, 272–74.

54. Report of Col J. A. Wagener (CSA), Capt. Josiah Bedon (CSA) and Col R. G. M. Dunovant (CSA). *ORA*, VI, 14–16, 20–21, 23–27.

55. Journal Letter #6, 5 Nov 1862. *Du Pont Letters*, II, 276; Ammen, *Atlantic Coast*, p. 23.

56. Report of Capt S. Elliott (cmdg Ft. Beauregard) 13 Nov 1861. *ORA*, VI, 27–29.

CHAPTER 2

1. Draft article on General Jomini (1870). McClellan Papers (Container #5). McClellan interviewed Jomini in Paris during an extended visit to Europe in 1869. There is no evidence that McClellan had read Clausewitz, but he was probably familiar with his ideas through friends in the Prussian army.

2. Their report was presented to Congress and published in three separate volumes. See reports of Capt G. B. McClellan (1857), Maj A. Mordecai (1859), and Maj R. Delafield. *U.S. Military Commission to Europe, 1855–56* (Washington, D.C., 1857–60).

3. McClellan's unusual linguistic fluency gave him access to information incomprehensible to most other Americans and facilitated his long-standing contact with military men in Europe.

4. "It can not be ignored that the construction of railroads has introduced a new and very important element into war, by the great facilities thus given for concentrating at particular positions large

masses of troops from remote sections, and by creating new strategic points and lines of operations." Memorandum to the president on military operations, 4 Aug 1861. *ORA*, V, 6–8.

5. While a cadet at West Point, McClellan belonged to the Napoleon Club. His special object of study and analysis was the Russian campaign.

6. Notebooks on observations in the Crimea, Sep 1855–Feb 1866. McClellan Papers (Container #12).

7. See Map 1.

8. Louis d'Orleans, Comte de Paris, *History of the Civil War in America*. 4 vols (Philadelphia, 1876–88) I, 474.

9. McClellan to T. Scott, 17 Oct 1861. McClellan Papers, A-28; Scott to Cameron, 4 Oct 1861, quoted in Wright, *General Scott*.

10. Memorandum to the secretary of War, 30 Oct 1861. McClellan Papers, A-29; Du Pont, Journal Letter #40, 10 Mar 1863. *Du Pont Letters*, II, 483. C. H. Davis to Mrs. Davis, 4 Sep 1861, quoted in *Charles Henry Davis*, 130. McClellan to Cameron, 6 Sep 1861, *ORA*, V, 585. S. Williams (AAG) to Burnside, 12 Sep; Gov W. Buckingham (Conn.) to Lincoln, 27 Sep 1861. *ORA* Ser. III, I, 500, 543. Testimony of Maj-Gen Burnside, 19 Mar 1863, *JCR* (1863), III, 333. There is some question whether Burnside's force was to be self-contained. See Robert W. Daly, "Burnside's Amphibious Division", *Marine Corps Gazette* (Dec 1951), pp. 30–37. Burnside himself seems to have thought of the "coast division" as a special commando-type unit, capable of landing unsupported at defenseless points and carrying out raids on the railroads, although it was never used for this purpose. Ambrose E. Burnside, "The Burnside Expedition", *B & L*, I, 660–69.

11. Bache, Notes on the Coast, Sect. III, 34.

12. McClellan's orders to Burnside, dated 7 Jan 1862, *ORA*, IX, 352–53.

13. *Fox Correspondence*, I, 206–10.

14. For particulars see *ORA*, IX, 73–191; *ORN*, VI, 549–600; Ammen, *Atlantic Coast*, pp. 176–83; Confederate States of America, Testimony taken by the Confederate Committee to investigate the Roanoke Island defeat, 3rd Ad. Sess., 1862; Edward A. Pollard, *The First Year of the War*, 2nd rev. ed. (New York, 1864) pp. 228–33.

15. Rush C. Hawkins (USV), "Early Coast Operations in North Carolina", *B & L*, I, 640–42; Parker, *Recollections*, pp. 237–40. Captain Parker, CSN, commanded the *Beaufort*. Barnard to McClellan, 15 Feb 1862. *ORA*, VI, 691.

16. For the defenseless condition of the Roanoke River and Weldon, see report of Brig-Gen R. C. Gatlin (CSA), 30 Jan 1862. *ORA*, IV, 577.

17. See McClellan to L. Thomas (AG) for Burnside, 13 Mar 1862. *ORA*, IX, 370–71. Thomas F. Edmonds (Lt-Col USV) "Operations in North Carolina, 1861–1862," *Military Historical Society of Massachusetts Papers*, IX (1912) 80–82.

18. Testimony of Brig-Gen T. W. Sherman, 16 Apr 1862. *JCR* (1863) III, 294–95.

19. Davis to Mrs. Davis, 2 Dec 1861. *Charles Henry Davis*, p. 193.

20. See Map 18. Journal Letter #14, 5 Dec 1861. *Du Pont Letters*, I, 272. Du Pont to Fox, 16 Dec 1861. *Fox Correspondence*, I, 79.

21. Testimony of Brig-Gen Sherman, 16 Apr 1862. *JCR* (1863) III, 295.

22. Hazard Stevens (Maj) "Military Operations in South Carolina in 1862", *Military Historical Society of Massachusetts Papers*, IX (1912) 142–227.

23. T. W. Sherman to Capt Saxton, 13 Sep 1861. *ORA*, VI, 171. Testimony of Capt R. Saxton (QM) 15 Apr 1862. *JCR* (1863) III, 323.

24. See Map 6.

25. James A. L. Fremantle, *The Fremantle Diary*, ed. by Walter Lord (Boston, 1954) pp. 140–41. Rbt May (Mayor of Augusta) to Gov Brown (Ga.), 11 Feb 1862. *ORA*, VI, 381. Jones, *Siege of Charleston*, pp. 71–72; Charles E. Cauthern, *South Carolina Goes to War, 1860–1865* (Chapel Hill, 1950) pp. 137–38.

26. Special Orders #206; J. P. Benjamin to Gov. J. Brown, 12 Nov 1861; Lee to Cooper (AG), 21 Nov 1861. *ORA*, VI, 309, 318, 327.

27. 8 Jan 1862. *Ibid.*, p. 367.

28. See Lee to Davis, 4 Aug 1862. *Lee's Dispatches, 1862–65*, ed. by Douglas Southall Freeman, new ed. by Grady McWhiney (New York, 1957) p. 205. Lee to Ripley, 19 Feb 1862. *ORA*, VI, 394. A. L. Long, "Seacoast Defences of South Carolina and Georgia", *Southern Historical Society Papers*, I (Feb 1876) pp. 103–07. General Long was Lee's chief of Artillery.

29. Lee to Gov Pickens (S.C.) 27 Dec 1861; Lt G. N. Rains (CS Eng) to Brig-Gen T. Jordan (COS) 10 Feb 1862. *ORA*, VI, 357; LIII, 282–83. Robert C. Black III, *The Railroads of the Confederacy* (Chapel Hill, 1952) pp. 161–62.

30. Gov Pickens to Pres Davis, 7 Jan 1862. *ORA*, VI, 366. Long, *op. cit.*, p. 105

31. See Map 7. T. Sherman to L. Thomas (AG) 15 and 17 Nov, and 4 Dec 1861. *ORA*, VI, 188, 189, 193. Sherman's Memorandum to War Dept. and McClellan in *JCR* (1863) III, 298–99. U.S. Dept. of Commerce. *Military and Naval Service of the United States Coast Survey, 1861–1865. Official Letters and Documents* (Washington, D.C., 1916) pp. 57–58.

32. Testimony of Brig-Gen Sherman, 17 Apr 1862. *JCR* (1863) III, 306–313.

33. Du Pont to Fox, 9 and 11 Nov 1861. *Fox Correspondence*, I, 67, 68–70. Davis to Mrs. Davis, 6 Dec 1861, in *Charles Henry Davis*, p. 197.

34. Sherman to McClellan, 26 Dec 1861. *ORA*, VI, 211–12. See Map 17.

35. Jones, *Siege of Charleston*, p. 144.

36. T. Sherman to McClellan, 27 Dec 1861. *ORA*, VI, 214. Gillmore to Sherman (confidential) 30 Dec 1861, enclosed in Du Pont to Fox, 4 Jan 1862. *Fox Correspondence*, I, 92–93.

37. *ORA*, VI, 214–16.

38. Testimony of Brig-Gen Sherman, 16 Apr 1862. *JCR* (1863) III, 299–309. Du Pont, *Admiral Du Pont*, pp. 148–49.

39. Daniel Ammen, *The Old Navy and the New* (Philadelphia, 1891) p. 359; Sherman to Maj-Gen D. Hunter, 31 Mar 1862. *ORA*, VI, 257.

40. *ORA*, VI, 22. He later learned that his steamers and rowboats had been seized en route from New York by Burnside's expedition. *JCR* (1863) III, 302.

41. Fox to Du Pont and reply, 4 and 11 Jan 1862. *Fox Correspondence*, I, 100–01.

42. McClellan to Sherman, 12 Feb 1862. *ORA*, VI, 224.

43. McClellan to Sherman, 14 Feb 1862. *Ibid.*, p. 225.

44. Sherman to Maj-Gen D. Hunter, 31 Mar 1862. *Ibid.*, p. 257. For a good account of the bombardment, see Walter J. Buttgenbach, "Coast Defense in the Civil War—Fort Pulaski, Georgia," *Journal U.S. Artillery*, Vol. 40 (Jul–Nov 1913) pp. 205–15.

45. Benjamin To Lee, 18 and 24 Feb 1862. *ORA*, VI, 390, 398. Jones, *Siege of Charleston*, pp. 78–79, 121–24.

46. Du Pont to Wm Whetten, 28 Dec 1861. *Du Pont Letters*, V, 292–93. Testimony of Brig-Gen Sherman, 16 Apr 1862. *JCR* (1863) III, 306.

47. Cameron to Butler, 10 and 12 Sep 1861. *ORA*, VI, 677. Testimony of Maj-Gen Butler, 15 Jan 1862. *JCR* (1863) III, 288.

48. Benjamin F. Butler, *Butler's Book* (Boston, 1892) pp. 321–22.

49. Robert S. Holtzman, *Stormy Ben Butler* (New York, 1954) p. 58.

50. See Treasury Department Regulations. *JCR* (1863) III, 558–620.

51. Richard S. West, Jr., *Lincoln's Scapegoat General: A Life of Benjamin F. Butler, 1818–1893* (Boston, 1965) pp. 104–05, 127. Melvin Thomas Copeland, *The Cotton Manufacturing Industry of the United States* (Cambridge, Mass., 1923) pp. 14–15.

52. Phelps to Thomas (AG) 3 Feb 1862. *ORA*, VI, 679–80. Phelps thought both New Orleans and Mobile unsuitable for large vessels.

53. McClellan to Stanton, 25 Jan 1862. *Ibid.*, p. 677. See Map 1.

54. Richard S. West, Jr., *The Second Admiral: A Life of David Dixon Porter, 1813–1891* (New York, 1937) p. 65. Had he observed the English bombardment of Cronstadt in the Baltic, he would have reached the opposite conclusion regarding the effect of mortar shells on masonry.

55. See memorandum from the Union Defense Committee of Chicago to President Lincoln dated 1 Oct 1861, warning of serious disaffection in the West unless the Mississippi was opened to trade that winter. *ORA*, Ser. III, Vol. I, 549–50. Benjamin P. Thomas and Harold M. Hyman, *Stanton: The Life and Times of Lincoln's Secretary of War* (New York, 1962) p. 265.

56. See Map 14.

57. Barnard to Colburn (AAG) 7 Feb 1862. *ORA*, VI, 684. West, *Porter*, pp. 114–16. John Randolph Spears, *David G. Farragut* (Philadelphia, 1905) pp. 170–73.

58. Spears, *Farragut*, pp. 175–76.

59. Barnard to Colburn (AAG); Barnard to McClellan, 7 Feb 1862. *ORA*, VI, 684–85.

60. *Ibid.*, pp. 694–95.

61. *ORN*, XVIII, 5. Spears, *Farragut*, p. 176.

CHAPTER 3

ORA references in this chapter are to Volume VII unless otherwise indicated; *ORN* references to Volume XXII.

1. See Map 1.

2. George Edgar Turner, *Victory Rode the Rails: The Strategic Place of Railroads in the Civil War* (Indianapolis and New York, 1953) p. 118.

3. As a reward for their loyalty Lincoln paid special attention to their views, as did the U.S. Congress. Johnson became a power on the Joint Committee.

4. See memorial to the General Assembly of the State of Tennessee, 20 Jun 1861. *ORA*, LII, Pt. I, 178–79.

5. 27 Apr 1861. *Ibid.*, pp. 338–39; Memorandum of 27 July 1861. *Lincoln Works*, IV, 457–58. McClellan to Scott, 27 Apr 1861. *ORA*, LI, Pt. I, 338–39.

6. *ORA*, V, 42–45.

7. Lincoln's Memorandum, Sep 1861. *ORA*, LII, Pt. I, 191. Comte de Paris, *Civil War in America*, I, 391–94. Nelson's experience was typical of numerous Federal expeditions sent into this area. A large force could not be supplied and a small force was usually eluded, ambushed, or otherwise compelled to withdraw having accomplished nothing permanent.

8. William Tecumseh Sherman, not to be confused with Brigadier General Thomas West Sherman, commanding at Port Royal, South Carolina.

9. Sherman to McClellan, 3, 4, and 6 Nov; Gov. W. Dennison (Ohio) to McClellan, 4 Nov 1861. McClellan Papers, A-30, A-31. See Map 8 for this chapter.

10. *ORA*, IV, 342.

11. *ORA*, IV, 356; V, 38–39.

12. Buell to McClellan, 22 and 27 Nov; McClellan to Buell, 25 Nov 1861. *ORA*, 433–44, 447, 450–52.

13. McClellan to Buell, 28 Nov 1861. *ORA*, 457–58.

14. See McClellan to Buell, 3 and 5 Dec 1861. *ORA*, 468, 473–74.

15. McKeever (AAG) to Maj-Gen Frémont, 9 Nov 1861. *ORA*, LIII, 507. James M. Merrill, *Battle Flags South: The Story of the Civil War Navies on Western Waters* (Rutherford, Vt., 1970) p. 46. Cmdr R. Perry to Foote, 7 Nov; Foote to Welles, 9 Nov; Report of Brig-Gen Grant, 17 Nov; Report of Brig-Gen G. Pillow (CSA) 10 Nov 1861. *ORN*, 398, 400, 404, 412–17.

16. John G. Nicolay and John Hay, *Abraham Lincoln*. 10 vols. (New York, 1917) IV, 434. Lincoln to McClellan, 21 Nov; Lincoln to Halleck, 2 Dec 1861. *Lincoln Works*, V, 27, 35.

17. *ORA*, 480.

18. Buell to McClellan, 23 Dec 1861. *ORA*, 511–12.

19. McClellan to Buell, 29 Dec 1861. *ORA*, 926.

20. Buell to McClellan, 29 Dec; Lincoln to Halleck and Buell, 31 Dec 1861; Lincoln to Buell, 4 Jan 1862. *ORA*, 521, 530, 534. Lincoln to Halleck, 1 and 7 Jan 1862. *Lincoln Works*, V, 87, 92.

21. Thomas to Buell, 30 Dec 1861; Buell to Lincoln, 1 and 5 Jan 1862. *ORA*, 524, 526, 530–31.

22. Halleck to Lincoln, 1 Jan 1862. *Lincoln Works*, V, 84. Halleck to Lincoln, 6 Jan 1862. *ORA*, 532–33.

23. See Lincoln's endorsement on dispatch cited *supra*, Lincoln to Buell, 6 Jan 1862. *Lincoln Works*, V, 91. McClellan to Buell, 6 Jan 1862. *ORA*, 531.

24. McClellan to Halleck, 3 Jan, and reply 9 Jan 1862. *ORA*, 527–28, 539–40.

25. Report of Brig-Gen McClernand, 24 Jan 1862. *ORA*, 68–72. C. F. Smith to Thomas (AG) 8 Nov 1861; Phelps to Foote, 11 and 18 Jan 1862. *ORN*, 427–28, 497, 507. Stanley F. Horn, *The Army of Tennessee* (Norman, Okla., 1952) pp. 80–81.

26. C. F. Smith to Halleck, 23 Nov 1861. *ORA*, 445–46. Phelps to Foote, 10 Dec 1861. *ORN*, 457–58.

27. A. S. Johnston to Cooper (AG); Johnston to Benjamin 27 Nov 1861. *ORA*, IV, 478–79; VII, 707. This warning was repeated with even greater urgency to the Tennessee governor on 25 December. *Ibid.*, 794–95.

28. A. S. Johnston to Cooper (AG) 22 Jan 1862. *ORA*, 844–45. Horn, *Army of Tennessee*, p. 72.

29. C.F. Smith to AAG Cairo. *ORA*, 561. Foote to Halleck, 28 Jan 1862. *ORN*, 524. Encouraged by Fox, who was always anxious to obtain credit for the Navy, Foote later claimed on the basis of this telegram, dated one day earlier than Halleck's order for the movement, that the attack on Fort Henry was his idea and that he persuaded both Grant and Halleck to approve it. After carefully verifying the date with the telegraph office, Fox actually circulated copies of the telegram to influential Congressmen and reporters after the fort was taken. His propaganda was so effective that historians persist in crediting Foote and, to a lesser extent, Grant with initiating and devising operations in the West. See Fox to Foote, 1 Mar 1862. *ORN*, 648–49.

30. Halleck to C. F. Smith, 24 Jan; McClellan to Halleck, 29 Jan 1862. *ORA*, 571, 930. Halleck to Foote, 29 Jan 1862. *ORN*, 525. Brig-Gen W. S. Hancock to McClellan, 29 Jan 1862. McClellan Papers, A-38. Beauregard did not bring his command but came in person to confer with Johnston, survey the river defenses, and eventually take charge at Columbus. He arrived at Bowling Green just after Fort Henry fell.

31. McClellan to Halleck, 29 Jan; Halleck to McClellan, 30 Jan 1862. *ORA*, 930–31, 571–72.

32. Halleck to McClellan, 30 Jan; Halleck to T. Scott, 5 Feb; Buell to McClellan, 30 Jan and 1 Feb; Buell to Halleck, 5 Feb 1862. *ORA*, 572, 585, 932–33.

33. Lincoln to Buell. *Lincoln Works*, V, 98. McClellan to Buell. *ORA*, 547.

34. For a detailed account of the battle, see Report of Maj-Gen Crittenden, 13 Feb 1862. *ORA*, 105–110.

35. G. Thomas to Buell, 23 Jan; Buell to L. Thomas (AG), 27 Jan; Buell to McClellan, 30 Jan 1862. *ORA*, 564, 568, 572–73.

36. McClellan to Buell and reply ,5 Feb; Buell to Halleck, 5 Feb; Buell to Thomas, 6 Feb; Buell to McClellan, 6 Feb 1862. *ORA*, 583–84, 585, 587–88, 589, 936.

37. Halleck to McClellan, 15 Feb 1862. *ORA*, 617.

38. McClellan to Halleck, 15 Feb 1862. *ORA*, 617–18.

39. See Halleck to McClellan, 16 Feb 1862. *ORA*, 624.

40. Maynard to Thomas, 4 Feb; McClellan to Buell, 6 Feb 1862. *ORA*, 582, 586.

41. Halleck to McClellan, 5 Feb; Halleck to Buell, 5 and 6 Feb; Stanton to Buell, 9 Feb 1862. *ORA*, 583, 583–84, 588, 937–38.

42. Halleck to McClellan, 30 Jan 1862. *ORA*, 572. Foote to Halleck, 7 and 17 Dec 1861; Phelps to Foote, 7 Jan; Foote to Fox, 11 Jan 1862. *ORN*, 454–55, 500, 685–86, 513–14, 492–94.

43. Report of Rear-Adm Foote, 13 Nov 1862; Foote to Welles, 23 Oct; Foote to Meigs (QMG) 7 and 20 Nov 1861. *ORN*, 314, 376, 395–96, 438. Foote to Fox, 2 Nov 1861. *Fox Correspondence*, II, 9–11.

44. Meigs to Foote, 1 Nov; Foote to Welles, 2 Nov 1861. *ORN*, 390.

45. Foote to McClellan, 6 and 7 Dec 1861. *ORN*, XXII, 453, 455.

46. Foote to McClellan, 6 Dec; Foote to Meigs, 14 Dec; Halleck to Foote, 17 Dec; Fox to Foote, 17 and 30 Dec; Foote to Fox, 19 and 30 Dec 1861. *ORN*, 453, 462, 463, 464, 467–68, 477–78. Also see Foote to Welles, 22 Jan and reply 23 Jan 1862. *ORN*, 516.

47. Foote to Halleck and reply, 3 Feb 1862. *ORN*, 530–31. McClellan eventually supplied the rest of the men from the Army of the Potomac. McClellan Papers, A-40.

48. Reports of Flag-Off Foote, Brig-Gen L. Tilghman (CSA, cmdg Ft. Henry), Col A. Heiman (CSA), and Lt-Col J. Gilmer (CS Eng). *ORN*, 537–43, 553–61, 564, 603–04. James L. Nichols, *Confederate Engineers* (Tuscaloosa, Ala., 1957) pp. 45–46.

49. Grant to McClernand, 7 Feb; Grant to Foote, 10 Feb 1862. John Y. Simon (ed.) *The Papers of Ulysses S. Grant.* 5 vols. (Carbondale, Ill., 1967–73) IV, 164, 182. Grant, *Memoirs*, p. 154.

50. Cullum (COS) to Halleck, 9 Feb 1862. *ORN*, 577–78. Report of Flag-Off Foote in U.S. Navy Department, *Report of the Secretary of the Navy in relation to Armored Vessels* (Washington, D.C., 1864) pp. 359–60. Hereafter cited as *Armored Vessels*.

51. Halleck to Cullum (COS) 9 and 10 Feb; Halleck to Buell, 13 Feb

1862. *ORA*, 598, 603–04, 609. Foote to Phelps, 10 Feb; Halleck to Foote, 11 Feb 1862. *ORN*, 582, 583–84.

52. Report of Flag-Off Foote. *ORN*, 537–38.

53. Halleck to Buell, 14 Feb; Halleck to McClellan, 15 Feb 1862. *ORA*, 616, 938–39.

54. Halleck to McClellan, 16 Feb 1862. *ORA*, 625.

55. Beauregard to Hardee (Memorandum) 7 Feb 1862. *ORA*, 861–62. Pollard, *First Year of the War*, p. 239. T. Harry Williams, *P.G.T. Beauregard: Napoleon in Gray* (Baton Rouge, La., 1954) pp. 118–19.

56. Reports of Brig-Gen G. Pillow (CSA) and Lt-Col Gilmer. *ORN*, 598–600, 604–08. Floyd to A. S. Johnston, 15 Feb 1862. *ORA*, LII, Pt. II, 815.

57. McClellan to Buell and reply, 7 and 15 Feb; Buell to Halleck, 15, 17, 18, and 19 Feb 1862. *ORA*, 593, 620, 621–22, 630, 632, 639.

58. Buell to Halleck and reply, 15 Feb; Halleck to McClellan, 15 and 16 Feb; Halleck to Buell, 19 Feb; T. Scott to Halleck, 19 Feb 1862. *ORA*, 617, 621–22, 625, 632, 635.

59. *ORA*, Ser. III, Vol. I, 875; Kenneth P. Williams, *Lincoln Finds a General.* 5 vols. (N.Y., 1952) III, Appendix, 451; Thomas and Hyman, *Stanton*, pp. 172–73; T. Scott to McClellan, 19 Feb 1862. *ORA*, 635.

60. Halleck to McClellan, 17 Feb 1862. *ORA*, 635. He had proposed this to McClellan as early as 8 February. *Ibid.*, pp. 594, 595; Stephen E. Ambrose, *Halleck: Lincoln's Chief of Staff* (Baton Rouge, La., 1962) p. 34.

61. Halleck to McClellan, 20 and 21 Feb 1862. *ORA*, 641, 647.

62. Stanton to Buell, 20 Feb; Stanton to Halleck, 22 Feb 1862. *ORA*, 646, 652. McClellan to Halleck, in Samuel Rickey Kamm, *The Civil War Career of Thomas A. Scott* (University of Pennsylvania, 1940) p. 111.

63. Halleck to Cullum, 18 Feb 1862. *ORA*, 633.

64. Cullum to Halleck, 19 Feb 1862. *ORA*, 942–44. Report of Rear-Adm Foote, 13 Nov 1862; Foote to Wells, 17 and 20 Feb 1862. *ORN*, 584, 618–19, 624–25.

65. Halleck to Cullum, 20 Feb; McClellan to Halleck, 24 Feb; Buell to C. F. Smith, 25 Feb; Stanton to T. Scott, 8 Mar 1862. *ORA*, 641, 661, 944–45; X, Pt. II, 20. McClellan to Cullum, 20 Feb; Foote to Welles, 22 and 24 Feb 1862. *ORN*, 621, 624–25.

66. McClellan to Buell, 24 and 25 Feb 1862. *ORA*, 660, 664.

67. Scott to Stanton, 3 Mar; Buell to McClellan, 1 and 6 Mar 1862. *ORA*, 680, 945; X, Pt. II, 11. The Confederates had sent all the stores and equipment in Nashville to Chattanooga. A. S. Johnston to Benjamin, 27 Feb 1862. *ORA*, 911.

68. Buell to McClellan, 6 Mar 1862. *ORA*, X, Pt. II, 11.

69. Halleck to McClellan, 19 Feb; Halleck to T. Scott, 21 Feb; Scott to Stanton, 6 Mar 1862. *ORA*, 636, 648; X, Pt. II, 12–13. Halleck to McClellan, 8 Mar 1862. McClellan Papers, A-44.

70. Nicolay and Hay, *Lincoln*, V, 306–310, 314–15.

71. Kamm, *Thomas Scott*, p. 119.

72. 10 Mar 1862. *ORA*, X., Pt. II, 24–25.

73. *Lincoln Works*, V, 155.

74. Report of E. H. Tunnicliff, U.S. Police, 22 Jan; Halleck to McClellan, 2 Feb 1862. McClellan Papers, A-37, A-39. *Lincoln Works*, V, 106.

75. In December, Confederate Secretary of War Benjamin told General Braxton Bragg that the government had been worried about losing Missouri until saved by the appointment of Frémont, "whose incompetency, well known to us, was a guarantee against immediate peril." 27 Dec 1861. *ORA*, VI, 788.

76. Lincoln to Frémont, 16 Jun 1862. *Lincoln Works*, V. 273–74.

CHAPTER 4

1. For typical examples, see reports from E. J. Allen (Pinkerton) to McClellan dated 20 and 25 Dec 1861, 14 and 28 Jan 1862. McClellan Papers, A-33, A-34, A-36, A-38. Confederate sources paint an even gloomier picture. As early as 1 October, Major General G. W. Smith and Beauregard warned Davis that unless the Army was permitted to take the offensive, its morale and condition would be so poor by spring that it would be unable to defend Richmond. For details, see Report of Maj-Gen Smith. *ORA*, V. 884-86.

2. Draft Memorandum dated November 1861; General Orders, Army of the Potomac, 17 Feb 1862. McClellan Papers, A-31, A-41.

3. Henry Adams to C. F. Adams, Jr., 25 Oct 1861 and 22 Jan 1862; C. F. Adams to C. F. Adams, Jr., 10 Jan 1862. Worthington Chauncey Ford (ed.) *A Cycle of Adams Letters, 1861–1865.* 2 vols. (London, 1931) I, 61, 99, 105. Charles Francis Adams Sr. was the U.S. ambassador to the United Kingdom; his son, Henry, was his secretary and assistant.

4. See Maps 8 and 10. McClellan to Lincoln, 1 Dec 1861. *Lincoln Works*, V, 34–35. Testimony of Brig-Gen Barnard, 25 Feb 1863. *JCR* (1863), I, 387–88.

5. Memorandum from Barnard for McClellan, 28 Nov 1861. *ORA*, V, 667–68.

6. Cf. the most recent theoretical work on combined operations, Thomas M. Molyneux's *Conjunct Expeditions* published in 1759 (London, Dodsley) based on lessons drawn from British operations on the French coast during the Seven Years War.

7. Joinville to McClellan, 15 Dec 1861. McClellan Papers, A-33.

8. Nicolay and Hay, *Lincoln*, IV, 467. Senator Benjamin F. Wade of Ohio, the future chairman of the Joint Committee, told Lincoln and McClellan in October that even certain defeat was better than doing nothing. H. L. Trefousse, *Benjamin Franklin Wade: Radical Republican from Ohio* (New York, 1963) p. 154.

9. Testimony of G. V. Fox, 19 Mar 1862. *JCR* (1863) III, 417.

10. Report of Brig-Gen Meigs, 28 Jan 1862. *ORA*, Ser. III, Vol. I, 866-68. For the fiscal year ending 1 June 1862, the Federal government borrowed 530 million dollars. President's Annual Message to Congress,

1 Dec 1862. *Lincoln Works*, V, 523; J. G. Randall, *Lincoln: The President*. 4 vols. (London, n.d.) II, 75.

11. Peter Smith Michie, *General McClellan* (New York, 1901) pp. 177–78. This is probably the best biography of McClellan; the author was a regular in the Engineer Corps and served with McClellan in the Peninsula.

12. Testimony of Maj-Gen McDowell, 30 Jun 1862. *JCR* (1863) I, 270. *Military Historical Society of Massachusetts Papers*, I, (1902) 20.

13. Comte de Paris, *Civil War in America*, I, 608–09. Malcolm Ives to G. Bennett, 15 Jan 1862, "Bennett Correspondence," *AHR* 39:285–90 (Oct 1933). The reporter promised not to publish this information until after the campaign.

14. Henry Adams to C. F. Adams, Jr., 10 and 22 Jan 1862. *Adams Letters*, I, 100, 105. Two days later, the consul in Liverpool, Thomas Dudley, reported that the shipping interests, through the press, were loudly clamouring for intervention. Owsley, *King Cotton Diplomacy*, p. 210.

15. See draft memorandum, 31 Jan 1862. McClellan Papers, A-39.

16. E. J. Allen to McClellan, 27 and 30 Jan 1862. McClellan Papers, A-38. Emphasis in original.

17. McClellan to Stanton, 31 Jan 1862. McClellan Papers, A-39; or see same memorandum dated 3 February in *ORA*, V, 42–45.

18. McClellan to Stanton, 3 Feb 1862. George B. McClellan, *Report on the Organization and Campaigns of the Army of the Potomac* (New York, 1864) pp. 104–05. See Map 1.

19. See Lincoln to McClellan, 9 May 1862. *Lincoln Works*, V, 208.

20. JCR (1863) V, 5. Trefousse, *Wade*, pp. 159–60.

21. Myers, *McClellan*, pp. 256–57. Testimony of Brig-Gen Franklin, 26 Dec and Brig-Gen F. J. Porter, 28 Dec 1861. *JCR* (1863) I, 122–30, 170–78.

22. Testimony of Brig-Gen Lander, 27 Dec; Brig-Gen Rosecrans, 31 Dec.; Maj-Gen McDowell, 26 Dec; Brig-Gen Hooker, and Brig-Gen Heintzelman, 24 Dec 1861. *Ibid.*, pp. 119–21, 131–44, 163–64, 204–05.

23. Burton J. Hendrick, *Lincoln's War Cabinet* (Boston, 1946) pp. 298–99.

24. JCR (1863) I, 75; 6 Jan 1862. *Chase Diaries*, p. 56. Trefousse, *Wade*, p. 167. On 15 February, at the insistence of the committee, Stanton questioned McClellan about his progress in opening the B & O at which time the general outlined his plan. Thomas and Hyman, *Stanton*, p. 177.

25. Jackson to Rhett (AAG) 24 Dec 1861. *ORA*, V, 1005. John B. Jones, *A Rebel War Clerk's Diary*, ed. by Earl Schenck Miers (N.Y., 1958) p. 61; Kamm, *Thomas Scott*, pp. 65–66; Testimony of Brig-Gen Lander, 27 Dec 1861. JCR (1863) I, 163. Festus P. Summers, *The Baltimore and Ohio in the Civil War* (N.Y., 1939) 102–03; Garrett to Chase, 6 Jan; Garrett to McClellan, 6 Feb 1862. McClellan Papers, A-35, A-43. Turner, *Victory Rode the Rails*, pp. 57–61, 90–92, 111–115.

26. McClellan to Lander, 15 Jan 1862. McClellan Papers, A-36.

Lander to McClellan, 18 Jan 1862. *ORA*, V, 702–03, 704. Comte de Paris, *Civil War in America*, I, 610–11.

27. Barnard to McClellan, 24 Jan 1862. McClellan Papers, A-37. See Map 9.

28. Michie, *McClellan*, pp. 199–200. See Map 10. Hooker had suggested such an operation as early as 30 October 1861. See McClellan Papers, A-29. Lincoln to McClellan and reply, 8 Feb 1862. *Lincoln Works*, V, 130.

29. McClellan to Hooker, 20 Jan; Williamson to S. Williams (AAG) 20 Jan; E. J. Allen to McClellan, 25 Jan; and unsigned report on the Potomac defenses dated 1 Feb 1862. McClellan Papers, A-37, A-39.

30. Hooker to Williams, *ORA*, V, 709–11.

31. Wyman to Fox, 10 Feb; Marcy (COS) to Hooker, 15 Feb 1862. *ORN*, V, 20–21; *ORA*, LI, Pt. I, 532.

32. Wyman to Fox, cited *supra*; Hooker to S. Williams. *ORA*, V, 724.

33. Hooker to McClellan (confidential) 20 Feb 1862. McClellan Papers, A-41.

34. Barnard to Colburn (AAG) 1 Feb 1862. *ORA*, V, 712. Banks to McClellan, 5, 9, 14, 23 and 25 Feb; W. P. Smith to McClellan, 14 Feb; Capt J. C. Duane (US Eng) to Marcy (COS) 21 Feb; McClellan to Stanton, 27 and 28 Feb; Stanton to McClellan, 27 Feb 1862. McClellan Papers, A-39, A-40, A-41, A-43.

35. General Orders, 26 Feb 1862. McClellan Papers, A-42. McClellan to Marcy 27 Feb (two telegrams); Barnard to McClellan, 27 Feb 1862. *ORA*, V, 727, 728; LI, Pt. I, 542. Wyman to Fox, 28 Feb 1862. *Fox Correspondence*, I, 429. Testimony of Maj-Gen McClellan, 28 Feb 1863. *JCR* (1863) I, 420–21.

36. Davis was shocked by Johnston's sudden decision to retreat which meant abandoning most of his stores. Davis to Johnston, 6 and 28 Feb; Johnston to Davis, 22, 23, and 28 Feb 1862. *ORA*, V, 1063, 1079, 1083, 1084. Jones, *War Clerk's Diary*, p. 68.

37. Report of Maj-Gen McClellan; McClellan to Marcy, 27 Feb 1862. *ORA*, V, 50, 728. Testimony of G. V. Fox, 31 Mar 1863. *JCR* (1863) V, 628–29.

38. Testimony of Col Frank Fiske. *JCR* (1863) III, 622. Hooker to S. Williams, 11, 15, 22 Nov, 13 Dec 1861, 12 Jan 1862. *ORA*, V, 663, 648–49, 652–53, 686, 698. Hooker was far more worried that the Potomac might be closed by ice. See Hooker to Williams, 15 Dec 1861, *Ibid.*, 687; also Wyman's reports in *ORN*, V, 3–23.

39. Johnston to Pres Davis, 22 Nov 1861; Johnston to Whitney, 11 and 12 Nov 1861, 12 Feb 1862; Trimble to Johnston, 16 Nov; Davis to Johnston, 18 Nov 1861; Johnston to Davis, 23 Feb 1862. *ORA*, LI, Pt. II, 1072–73; I, 797, 948–49, 949–50, 959–60, 963, 1069, 1079.

40. McClellan to Wool, 21 Feb 1962. *ORA*, IX, 15–16.

41. Daniel J. Carrison, *The Navy from Wood to Steel* (New York, 1965) p. 63; Welles to Paulding (Cmdg N.Y. Navy Yard) 6 Mar 1862, 4:10 P.M. *ORA*, IX, 17. 7 Mar 1862. *ORN*, VI, 686.

42. Welles to Marston. *ORN*, VI, 687. In view of the above orders, it is extraordinary that the *Virginia* was able to take the *Cumberland* and *Congress* by surprise on the afternoon of the 8th, or that these ships should have been stationed off Newport News at all. The Union Navy's predilection for the old methods, instead of conferring by telegraph, caused many such foul-ups in the war.

43. Wyman to Welles, 9 Mar 1862. *ORN*, V, 23.

44. Testimony of the Maj-Gen Keyes, 26 Mar 1863. *JCR* (1863) 597–98. Like most good generals, McClellan had never held a council of war, nor did he approve of them.

45. McClellan had suggested this himself in December 1861, but dropped the idea when he discovered he could not select his own commanders in violation of seniority. See Testimony of Brig-Gen Meigs, 27 Dec 1861. *JCR* (1863) I, 159.

46. Report of Maj-Gen McClellan. *ORA*, V, 49–50.

47. Lincoln to Buell, 10 Mar 1862. *ORA*, X, Pt. II, 612

48. See McClellan to Burnside, 21 May 1862. *ORA*, IX, 392.

49. Stanton's view that wars could only be won by an "aggressive fighting general" prepared to take risks and lose men is typical of the time and has been echoed by absent-minded historians and amateur critics ever since. See Thomas and Hyman, *Stanton*, p. 174. On 3 September 1862, Welles complained in his diary that McClellan "wishes to outgeneral the Rebels, but not to kill and destroy them." Gideon Welles, *Diary of Gideon Welles, Secretary of the Navy under Lincoln and Johnson.* 3 vols. (Boston, 1909–1911) I, 107.

50. Report of divisional commanders, 5 Mar 1862. McClellan Papers, A-43; Comte de Paris, *Civil War in America*, I, 615.

51. McClellan wanted to organize the army into six corps, assigning Franklin, Fitz John Porter, and Andrew Porter to corps commands in addition to Sumner, McDowell, and Heintzelman. Keyes was not to be included. He intended placing the best units under command of the first three generals. Memorandum, March 1862. McClellan Papers, A-50.

52. Hooker to Williams, 5 Mar 1862. McClellan Papers, A-43; Hooker to Marcy (COS) 13 Mar 1862. *ORA*, V, 753. Wyman to Welles, 13 Mar 1862. *ORN*, V, 25.

53. Joinville to McClellan, 15 Dec 1861. McClellan Papers, A-33. Shields to McClellan, 10 Jan 1862. *ORA*, V, 700–2.

54. McClellan to Stanton, *ORA*, V, 45.

55. *ORA*, V, 55–56.

56. Stanton to McClellan, 13 Mar 1862. *ORA*, V, 750.

57. Fox to McClellan, 13 Mar 1862. *JCR* (1863) I, 629. Stanton to McClellan, 13 Mar 1862. *ORA*, V, 56.

58. Report of Maj Palmer, December 1861 based on topographical survey of Virginia by the constructor of the Fredericksburg and Potomac R.R. McClellan Papers, A-34. The roads also contained viaducts requiring six weeks to rebuild. Prince de Joinville, *The Army of the Potomac* (New York, 1862) p. 28.

59. For a report on this establishment and the types of guns manufactured, see E. J. Allen to McClellan, 26 Dec 1861. McClellan Papers, A-34.

60. Joinville, *Army of the Potomac*, p. 26.

61. General Order, 17 Mar; McClellan to Stanton, 5 Apr 1862. McClellan Papers, A-47, A-50. Testimony of Maj-Gen McDowell, 27 Jun 1862, and Maj-Gen Franklin, 28 Mar 1863. *JCR* (1863) I, 261, 621. Maj-Gen McDowell's Special Orders #5, 23 Mar 1862. *ORA*, XI, Pt. III, 50.

62. *ORN*, VII, 125, 167–68.

63. Testimony of G. V. Fox, 31 Mar, and Rear-Adm Goldsborough, 1 Apr 1863. *JCR* (1863) I, 628–34.

64. Keyes to Harris, in McClellan, *Report on the Organization and Campaigns of the Army of the Potomac*, pp. 166–67; also see testimony of Brig-Gen Keyes, 26 Mar 1862. *JCR* (1863) I, 597–98.

65. *ORA*, LI, Pt. I, 554; McDowell to Marcy, 18 and 20 Mar 1862. McClellan Papers, A-47.

66. McDowell to McClellan, 21 Mar; Stanton to McClellan, 22 Mar 1862. McClellan Papers, A-47, A-48.

67. *ORA*, V, 57–58.

68. Barnard to McClellan, 20 Mar 1862. McClellan Papers, A-47.

69. This suspicion was confirmed by a dispatch from his ADC Lieutenant Colonel D. P. Woodbury who also discussed the matter with Goldsborough on the 19th. *ORA*, XI, Pt. III, 22–24.

70. Confidential memorandum, 22 Mar 1862. McClellan Papers, A-48. He asked that a siege train comprising twenty 10-inch mortars, twenty 8-inch mortars, twenty 8-inch howitzers, twenty 4.5-inch wrought iron siege guns, twenty 24-pounder siege guns, and forty 20-pounder Parrott rifles be shipped immediately to Fort Monroe. McClellan to Marcy, 22 Mar 1862. *Ibid.*

71. Fox to Goldsborough, 24 Mar 1862. *Fox Correspondence*, I, 251. Barnard to McClellan, 28 Mar 1862. McClellan Papers, A-49.

72. Testimony of Brig-Gen Barnard, 25 Feb 1863. *JCR* (1863) I, 388–94.

73. Comte de Paris, *Civil War in America*, I, 580; Bache, Notes on the Coast of the United States, Sect. III, Pt. 2, 16–17; McClellan, *Report on the Organization* . . . , p. 155.

74. Report of Maj-Gen McClellan, 4 Aug 1863. *ORA*, XI, Pt. I, 7. Bache's Coast Survey maps indicated the position of the mouth of the Warwick River but not its course. Since it entered the James from the northwest, it seemed to confirm Cram's maps.

75. "Narrative of Rear-Admiral Goldsborough, U.S. Navy," *U.S. Naval Institute Proceedings*, 59:1023–31 (July 1933) p. 1026.

76. McClellan to Stanton, 19 Mar 1862. *Report on the Organization* . . . , pp. 132–34. McClellan to Gen Winfield Scott, 11 Apr 1862. McClellan Papers, A-51. Magruder was reported to have 15,000 men at Yorktown and Gloucester and Huger 18,000 at Norfolk. Wool to McClellan, 17 Mar 1862. McClellan Papers, A-47.

CHAPTER 5

ORA references to Volume XI, *ORN* references to Volume VII, unless otherwise indicated.

1. Davis to Lee, 3 Mar; General Orders #6, 4 Mar; Lee to Magruder, 9 Apr 1862. *ORA*, XI, Pt. III, 398–99, 400, 401, 433–34.

2. Lee to J. E. Johnston, 28 Mar 1862. *Ibid.*, pp. 408–09. Johnston, *Narrative*, p. 112; Comte de Paris, *Civil War in America*, II, 7–8.

3. See Map 11. Reports of Maj-Gen Magruder, 3 May and Col H. C. Cabell (Ch of Arty) 10 May 1862. *ORA*, Pt. I, 405–07, 411–13. Davis, *Confederate Government*, II, 83.

4. Report of Brig-Gen Barnard, 26 Jan 1863. *ORA*, Pt. I, 126.

5. Lincoln to Stanton, 3 Apr; Lincoln to McClellan, 9 Apr 1863. *Lincoln Works*, V, 179, 184. McClellan, *Report on the Organization . . .*, pp. 161–62. Wadsworth to Stanton; Thomas (AG) and Hitchcock to Wadsworth, 2 Apr 1862. *ORA*, Pt. III, 60–62.

6. Keyes said McClellan considered it his best division, and Fitz John Porter described Franklin's command as "one of the best divisions of the army." Testimony of Brig-Gen Keyes, 27 Mar 1863. *JCR* (1863), I, 614. Porter, "Hanover Court House and Gaines's Mill," *B & L*, II, 335.

7. D. H. Hill to Johnston, 26 Apr 1862. *ORA*, Pt. III, 465; McClellan, *Own Story*, p. 288. Only two guns in the upper works bore on the river.

8. McClellan, *Report on the Organization . . .*, p. 128.

9. Testimony of Cmdr J. M. Brooke (CSA). Confederate States of America, Congress. *Report of the evidence taken before a Joint Special Committee to both Houses of the Confederate Congress, to investigate affairs of the Navy Department* (Richmond, 1863) p. 412. Hereafter cited as *Report of the Joint Special Committee*. A 68-pound shell from one of these guns broke the nine-inch-thick forged iron slab on top of the pilot house and another of the same weight left a 2¼-inch bulge on the inside of the turret. Chief Engineer A. Stimers to Commo Smith, 17 Mar 1862. *ORN*, 27.

10. Testimony of Cmdr Brooke. *Report of the Joint Special Committee*, p. 414.

11. John Taylor Wood, "The First Fight of the Ironclads," *B & L*, I, 704–09. Goldsborough to COs of naval vessels in Hampton Roads, 12 Apr 1862. *ORN*, 228. Thomas (AG) to Welles, 13 Mar 1862. *ORA*, V, 751.

12. Fox to McClellan, 9 and 13 Mar 1862. *Fox Correspondence*, I, 435, 438. Lincoln to Welles, 10 Mar; Fox to Blair, 11 Mar 1862. *Lincoln Works*, V, 154.

13. See Goldsborough to Fox, 1 Mar 1862. *Fox Correspondence*, I, 245–47. As early as 15 December 1861, Goldsborough was worried about being passed over for promotion and retired without a pension. See *Ibid.*, pp. 218–20.

14. Lincoln to Wool, 1 Nov 1861. McClellan Papers, A-30. In 1861, Scott was 76, Wool was 80, and McClellan only 35.

15. Lincoln to McClellan, 1 Nov 1861. *Lincoln Works*, V, 9–10. Stanton to Wool, 26 Mar 1862. *ORA*, Pt. III, 38–39.

16. Brig-Gen W. B. Franklin to McClellan, 7 Apr 1862. McClellan Papers, A-50. Thomas and Hyman, *Stanton*, pp. 176, 188–89. Stanton to Wool, 6 Apr 1862. *ORA*, Pt. III, 72.

17. Report of Maj-Gen McClellan, 4 Aug 1863; Thomas (AG) to Wool and McClellan, 3 Apr; Stanton to Wool, 7 Apr 1862. *ORA*, Pt. I, 7; Pt. III, 76.

18. "Narrative of Rear Admiral Goldsborough," p. 1025; Richard S. West, Jr., *Gideon Welles: Lincoln's Navy Department* (Indianapolis, 1943) pp. 154, 180–82. Testimony of Rear-Adm Goldsborough, 1 Apr 1863. *JCR* (1863) I, 631.

19. See Map 10. Report of Capt Marston on the defenses of Norfolk, 21 Feb; Huger (CSA) to Benjamin, 8 Mar 1862. *ORA*, VI, 659; XI, 59. Welles to Fox, 10 Mar 1862. *Fox Correspondence*, I, 436–37.

20. Goldsborough to Welles, 22 Apr 1862. *ORA*, Pt. III, 123.

21. McClellan to Burnside, 20 Apr 1862. *Ibid.*, pp. 114–15; also see Testimony of Gen G. B. Randolph (Sec of War) 5 Feb 1863. *Report of the Joint Special Committee*, pp. 325–28.

22. McClellan to Stanton, 19 Mar 1862; Testimony of Maj-Gen McClellan, 28 Feb 1863. *JCR* (1863) I, 425.

23. Fox to Goldsborough, 19 Apr 1862. *Fox Correspondence*, I, 256. Davis to Mrs. Davis, 30 Nov 1862. *Charles Henry Davis*, pp. 288–89.

24. Welles to Capt W. Hudson (Cmdg Boston Navy Yard), 1 Mar 1862. *ORA*, IX, 25. Carrison, *Navy from Wood to Steel*, p. 25. These vessels were part of a crop of "90-day wonders" built as quickly and cheaply as possible to ease the Navy's acute ship shortage.

25. Missroon to McClellan, 5 Apr 1862. *ORA*, Pt. III, 80–82. Same to same, 6 Apr 1862. McClellan, *Own Story*, p. 291.

26. See Lincoln to McClellan, 9 Apr, and Blair to McClellan, 12 Apr 1862. McClellan Papers, A-51.

27. This report confirmed that of Fitz John Porter's balloon reconnaissance of the 7th. Porter to Colburn (ADC) 7 Apr 1862. *Ibid.*, A-50.

28. Goldsborough to McClellan, 6 Apr; McClellan to Thomas (AG), 6 Apr; Missroon to McClellan, 13 Apr 1862. *ORA*, Pt. III, 70, 74, 95.

29. McClellan to Stanton, 7 Apr 1862. *Report on the Organization* . . . p. 163. McClellan to Gen Scott, 11 Apr 1862. McClellan Papers, A-51. McClellan to Rodgers, 6 Apr; McClellan to Fox, 20 Apr 1862. *ORA*, Pt. III, 75, 115.

30. McClellan to Rodgers, 11 Apr 1862. *ORA*, Pt. III, 90. Testimony of Maj-Gen Franklin, 28 Mar 1863. *JCR* (1863) I, 621.

31. See Map 11. McClellan to Stanton, 10 Apr; McClellan to Goldsborough, 12 Apr 1862. *ORN*, 215, 229. Missroon to McClellan, 12 and 14 Apr 1862. *ORA*, Pt. III, 92–93.

32. Missroon to McClellan, 9 and 11 Apr; McClellan to Goldsborough, 13 Apr 1862. *ORN*, 212–13, 226, 232.

33. Missroon to McClellan, 11 and 14 Apr 1862. *ORN*, 213–32, 234–35. Twenty Confederate guns actually bore on the river.

34. Badger to McClellan and Missroon to McClellan, 16 Apr 1862. *Ibid.*, 240, 241.

35. McClellan to Fox, 14 Apr 1862. *Fox Correspondence*, II, 288–89.

36. Magruder to Randolph, 11 Apr 1862. *ORA*, Pt. III, 436. McClellan to Stanton, 15 Apr 1862. *ORN*, 238. Johnston with the rest of his army, about 28,000 men (aggregrate 55,000) arrived in Yorktown and took command on the 18th. McClellan had approximately 100,000 effectives.

37. Report of Brig-Gen Barnard, 6 May 1862. *ORA*, Pt. I, 318–19. Comte de Paris, *Civil War in America*, II, 11.

38. Fox to Goldsborough, 23 Apr 1862. *Fox Correspondence*, I, 262.

39. "Narrative of Rear Admiral Goldsborough", p. 1026; Thomas and Hyman, *Stanton*, p. 151.

40. McClellan to Stanton, ca. 20 Apr 1862, in McClellan, *Own Story*, pp. 281–83.

41. Report of Brig-Gen Barnard, 26 Jan 1863. *ORA*, Pt. I, 127.

42. Report of Brig-Gen Barnard, 6 May 1862. *Ibid.*, p. 327.

43. Alexander himself was responsible for selecting this boat over the newer and much lighter inflatable rubber pontoons preferred by General Barnard. The batteau's endurance and versatility justified Alexander's choice.

44. Report of Lt. Col Alexander, 28 Jan 1863. *ORA*, Pt. I, 134–39.

45. For a more detailed description of Alexander's preparations, see his very interesting report cited *supra*.

46. See McClellan to Gen Scott, 11 Apr 1862. McClellan Papers, A-51.

47. Tattnall (CSN) to Mallory, 21 Apr 1862. *ORN*, VI, 769–70.

48. Welles to Goldsborough, 17 Apr 1862. *Ibid.*, VII, 244.

49. Lee to Mallory, 8 Apr; Magruder to Randolph, 12 Apr 1862. *ORA*, Pt. III, 429–30, 437. Tattnall to Mallory, 12 Apr 1862. *ORN*, 223–34. Jefferson Davis, *The Rise and Fall of the Confederate Government* (London, 1881). Johnston was given command of both military and naval forces in Norfolk and the Peninsula. Special Order #6. *ORA*, Pt. III, 428.

50. See Map 11. Goldsborough to Welles, 15 Apr 1862. *ORN*, 236.

51. Lawrence to Welles and reply, 18 Apr; Badger to Naval Ordnance Bureau, 27 Apr; Wise to Badger, 30 Apr 1862. *ORN*, 248–49, 285–86, 294.

52. The locks were finally destroyed by Lt Cmdr Flusser's flotilla on 26 April. *Ibid.*, pp. 250–51, 260.

53. Fox to Goldsborough, 19 and 23 Apr; Goldsborough to Welles, 20 and 22 Apr; Welles to Stanton, 24 Apr 1862. *Fox Correspondence*, I, 256–57, 262; *ORN*, 250, 255–56, 263–64; *ORA*; Pt. III, 123.

54. Missroon to McClellan, 17 Apr 1862, in McClellan, *Own Story*, pp. 293–94.

55. *ORN*, 243.

56. Goldsborough to Capt A. A. Harwood, 18 Apr 1862. *ORA*, Pt. III, 109.

57. See Map 11. McClellan to his wife, 18 Apr 1862, in McClellan, *Own Story*, p. 311. The road from Yorktown to Williamsburg passed through a ravine exposed to enfilade from the river. *ORA*, Pt. I, 320.

58. Goldsborough to Fox, 20 and 24 Apr 1862. *Fox Correspondence*, I, 263, 257–59. The *Galena*'s armor was 2½ inches thick.

59. Goldsborough to Fox, 28 Apr 1862. *Ibid.*, pp. 263–65.

60. *ORN*, 256–57.

61. By 4 May, about seventy heavy guns and mortars had been positioned in front of Yorktown. Report of Maj A. Doull, *ORA*, Pt. I, 254–58.

62. Smith to Goldsborough, 1 May 1862. *ORN*, 299.

63. McClellan to Goldsborough, 1 May and reply 3 May 1862. *ORN*, 299, 305.

64. After examining the river defenses, Fox expressed his disgust with Missroon, remarking that "the water batteries on both sides were insignificant and according to all our naval conflicts thus far, could have been passed at night with impunity." Fox to Goldsborough, 7 May 1862. *Fox Correspondence*, I, 266.

65. Nichols, *Confederate Engineers*, p. 19. Report of Brig-Gen Barnard, 6 May, and Lt C. B. Comstock, 5 May 1862 with Barnard's endorsement. *ORA*, Pt. I, 337, 338–39. McClellan's infamous intelligence agent, Allen Pinkerton, while sometimes overestimating enemy troop concentrations, was surprisingly accurate when describing the number, type, and location of the York River batteries. See his report of 1 Feb 1862 in the McClellan Papers, A-39, and two reports dated 29 Mar 1862 in *ORA*, Pt. I, 264–68.

66. For reference to the effectiveness of this gun, see Magruder to Lee, 14 Apr 1862. *ORA*, Pt. III, 441.

67. Hill to Randolph, 15 and 24 Apr, and reply 25 Apr 1862. *ORA*, Pt. III, 440, 461, 464.

68. Hill to Johnston. *Ibid.*, p. 465.

69. Randolph to Hill, 25 Apr; Davis to Johnston, 1 May 1862. *Ibid.*, pp. 464, 484–85. Jones, *War Clerk's Diary*, p. 74.

70. Johnston, *Narrative*, p. 118; Johnston to Lee, 27 and 29 Apr 1862. *ORA*, Pt. III, 469, 473.

71. Brig-Gen W. F. Barry to S. Williams (COS) 30 Apr 1862. McClellan Papers, A-55. McClellan to Stanton, 30 Apr 1862. *ORA*, Pt. III, 129. Cmdr Smith to Goldsborough, 1 May 1862. *ORN*, 299.

72. Report of the Chief Signal Officer, 21 Oct 1862. *ORA*, Pt. I, 233. This very thorough report is one of the most valuable sources for the Peninsular campaign.

73. McClellan to Smith and reply, 4 May 1862. *ORN*, 309; *ORA*, Pt. III, 138.

74. For detailed reports of this engagement, see *ORA*, Pt. I, 423–613.

75. Report of Ch Sig Off, 21 Oct 1862. *Ibid.*, pp. 234–35.

76. The order was sent at 9:30 P.M. on the 5th. McClellan to Franklin, *ORA*, Pt. III, 143.

77. Report of Lt Col Alexander, 28 Jan 1863. *ORA*, Pt. I, 136.

78. Report of Cmdr Smith, 7 May 1862. *ORN*, 312.

79. Reports of Lt Col Alexander, Brig-Gen Franklin, and Capt Arnold. *ORA*, Pt. I, 137–38, 614–15, 618.

80. Johnston to Lee, 8 May 1862. *ORA*, Pt. III, 500.

81. Report of Maj-Gen G. Smith, 12 May 1862. *ORA*, Pt. I, 626–27.

He attacked against orders from Johnston who warned him not to bring on a battle.

82. Report of Maj-Gen McClellan, 4 Aug 1863. *Ibid.*, p. 23.

83. Johnston recognized this clearly. In a letter to Lee on 30 April advocating an immediate invasion of the North to regain the initiative, he wrote: "We can have no success while McClellan is allowed, as he is by our defensive, to choose his own mode of warfare." *ORA*, Pt. III, 477.

CHAPTER 6

ORA references to Volume XI, *ORN* to Volume VII, unless otherwise indicated.

1. Burnside to Stanton, 3 May; McClellan to Stanton, 10 May 1862. *ORA*, IX, 383–84; XI, Pt. III, 160.

2. McClellan to Goldsborough, 4 May 1862. *ORN*, 309. McClellan to Fox, 4 May; Wm Sprague to Stanton, 6 May; McClellan to Stanton, and reply, 7 May 1862. *ORA*, LI, Pt. I, 596; XI, Pt. III, 146–47, 148 "Narrative of Rear Admiral Goldsborough," p. 1027. Lincoln to Goldsborough, 7 May 1862. *Lincoln Works*, V, 207. Testimony of Gen Randolph. *Report of the Joint Special Committee*, pp. 326–27; Goldsborough to Welles, 13 May; Report of Maj-Gen Wool, 12 May 1862. *ORA*, Pt. III, 169; Pt. I, 634.

3. See Map 11. Lee to Huger, 7 and 8 May 1862. *ORA*, Pt. III, 497, 499. Cmdr J. R. Tucker to Mallory, 8 May 1862. *ORN*, 786. South of the James, the Confederate forces in eastern Virginia and North Carolina pulled back to their second line covering the Wilmington and Weldon R.R.

4. Colston to Tucker and reply, 23 Feb 1862. *ORN*, 744–76.

5. Testimony of Dr. Dinwiddie B. Philips and A. L. Rives, Asst Chief of the Engineer Bureau. *Report of the Joint Special Committee*, pp. 222, 234; also see report of Jefferson Davis to the Confederate House of Representatives, 20 Mar 1862. *ORA*, LI, Pt. II, 507–08; XI, Pt. III, 469.

6. Randolph to Provost Marshal, Petersburg, 6 May, and Pres. of R.F. & P. R.R., 9 May; Johnston to Lee, 10 May; Commissary Dept to Johnston, 13 May; Lee to Johnston, 13 May 1862. *ORA*, Pt. III, 495–96, 501–02, 506, 512–13.

7. Mallory to Lt. Cmdr C. ap R. Jones, 12 May; Mallory to Lt Eggelston, 14 May 1862. *ORN*, 799, 800. Wood, "First Fight of Ironclads," p. 711; Randolph to Huger, 14 May; Lee to Mallory, 15 May 1862. *ORA*, Pt. III, 515, 518.

8. "Narrative of Rear Admiral Goldsborough", pp. 1029–30. See Map 10.

9. Goldsborough to Rodgers, and Welles, 14 May 1862. *ORN*, 352–53; *ORA*, Pt. III, 172.

10. McClellan to Stanton, 12 May 1862. *ORA*, Pt. III, 167.

11. *ORN*, 355.

12. Reports of Cmdr Rodgers and Lt. Neuman (Ex-Off) 16 May 1862. *ORN*, 357, 359.

13. Report of Cmdr Farrand (CSN) 15 May 1862. *ORN*, 269–70. W. H. Taylor (AAG) to Johnston, 15 May 1862. *ORA*, Pt. III, 518.

14. Reports of Asst Surgeon Gieson, Lt Jeffers, and Lt Morris, 16 May 1862. *ORN*, 358–59, 362, 363.

15. Reports of Cmdr Rodgers and Lt Jeffers, *supra*. Goldsborough to Fox, 21 May 1862. *Fox Correspondence*, I, 271–72.

16. McClellan to Stanton and Goldsborough. *ORA*, LI, Pt. I, 615.

17. McClellan to Stanton, 17 and 18 Mar 1862. *ORA*, Pt. III, 177, 180.

18. Seward to Stanton; McClellan to Stanton, 18 May; Report of reconnaissance by Brig-Gen H. M. Naglee, 23 May 1862. *ORA*, Pt. III, 178–80; Pt. I, 648–49. Goldsborough to Fox, 21 May 1862. *Fox Correspondence*, I, 273. Comte de Paris, *Civil War in America*, II, 32–33; McClellan, *Own Story*, p. 343. See Map 12.

19. Stanton to McClellan, 18 May; McClellan to Lincoln, 21 May; Report of Maj-Gen McClellan; Lincoln to McClellan, 21 May 1862. *ORA*, Pt. I, 27, 28–29; Pt. III, 184.

20. McClellan to Rodgers, 24 June 1862. *ORA*, Pt. III, 250. Davis had urged Johnston to keep McClellan's army away from the James at all cost, even if it meant attacking from a disadvantageous position. 17 May 1862. *Ibid.*, pp. 523–24.

21. Testimony of Rear Adm Goldsborough, 1 Apr 1863. *JCR* (1863) I, 633. Lincoln to McClellan, 24 May; Report of Maj-Gen McClellan; Marcy (COS) to Stanton, 28 May; Anderson to Maj-Gen L. O'B. Branch (CSA) 25 May 1862. *ORA*, Pt. I, 30; Pt. III, 195–96.

22. See Map 12. For an inside view of the Richmond government's discouragement, see Jones, *War Clerk's Diary*, p. 78.

23. A. Long to R. S. Ewell, 15 May; Lee to Jackson, 16 May 1862. *ORA*, Pt. III, 891, 892–93.

24. For a good account of this confused action, see Fred Harvey Harrington, *Fighting Politician: Major General N. P. Banks* (Philadelphia, 1948) pp. 66–67.

25. See Map 8. Lincoln to McClellan, 24 May 1862. *Lincoln Works*, V, 232–33. J. W. Garrett to Stanton, 18 May; Lincoln to McDowell, 24 May 1862; Brig-Gen J. H. Bradley to Maj-Gen G. Thomas. *ORA*, XII, Pt. III, 201–02, 219; Ser. III, Vol. II, 91. Randall, *Lincoln*, II, 91; Testimony of Maj-Gen McClellan, 28 Feb 1863. *JCR* (1863) I, 427–28.

26. "The roaring, howling gun-boat shells," wrote D. H. Hill, "were usually harmless to flesh, blood, and bones, but they had a wonderful effect upon the nervous system." "McClellan's Change of Base and Malvern Hill," *B & L*, II, 390.

27. Report of Maj-Gen McClellan, 4 Aug 1863. *ORA*, Pt. I, 30–31. Joinville, *Army of the Potomac*, p. 70.

28. McClellan exaggerated the risk himself, apparently on the correct assumption that the government would send reinforcements only if they thought the army in imminent danger of being destroyed. See his dispatch to Lincoln and Stanton in his report cited *supra*.

29. Report of Maj-Gen Keyes, 13 Jun 1862. *JCR* (1863) I, 614–16.

Report of Maj-Gen Johnston, *Narrative*, pp. 129–30; Douglas Southall Freeman, *R.E. Lee*, 4 vols. (New York, 1934) pp. 60–61; Davis, *Confederate Government*, II, 120.

30. Cf. Porter's handling of V Corps during the battles north of the Chickahominy a month later.

31. Testimony of Maj-Gen Heintzelman, 17 Feb 1863; Report of Maj-Gen Keyes. *JCR* (1863) I, 351, 616–20.

32. On 1 June, the three Federal corps south of the river numbered approximately 50,000. Johnston gives his force on 31 May as 74,000. Deducting the 6,000 Confederate casualties of the 31st and adding 8,000 reinforcements which arrived on the 1st, Lee had 76,000 men.

33. Lee to Maj W. H. Stevens (Ch Eng) 3 Jan 1862. Report of Gen Lee, 6 Mar 1863. Clifford Dowdey (ed.) *The Wartime Papers of R. E. Lee* (Boston, 1961) #186, #229.

34. McClellan to Stanton, 16 Jun; Report of Brig-Gen Barnard, 15 Aug 1862. *ORA*, Pt. III, 231; Pt. I, 116.

35. *Lee's Wartime Papers*, #188; also see Lee to Davis, 10 Jun 1862. *Ibid.*, #195.

36. Lee to Jackson, 8, 11, and 16 Jun 1862. *ORA*, Pt. III, 907, 910, 913.

37. Report of Maj-Gen McClellan; McClellan to Stanton, 12 Jun; Lincoln to McClellan, 20 Jun 1862. *ORA*, Pt. I, 31; Pt. III, 225, 236.

38. McClellan to Porter, 17 Jun 1862. *ORA*, LI, Pt. I, 679. Testimony of Maj-Gen McClellan, 2 March 1863. *JCR* (1863) I, 434; Joinville, *Army of the Potomac*, p. 84.

39. Testimony of Maj-Gen Franklin, 28 Mar 1863. *JCR* (1863) I, 622. Freeman, *Lee*, p. 66; Harrison Strode, *Jefferson Davis* (New York, 1959) p. 252. Marcy to Porter, 23 June 1862. *ORA*, Pt. III, 247. Fitz John Porter, "Hanover Court House and Gaines's Mill," and "The Battle of Malvern Hill,"; Daniel H. Hill, "Lee's Attacks North of the Chickahominy," in *B & L*, II, 327, 406, 359.

40. Keyes to S. Williams (AAG) 15 Jun; S. Van Vliet (QMG) to Goldsborough, 23 Jun; McClellan to Rodgers, 24 Jun; McClellan to Goldsborough, 27 Jun 1862. *ORA*, Pt. III, 229, 250, 258, 267. Testimony of Maj-Gen Keyes, 27 May 1863. *JCR* (1863) I, 610–11.

41. See report of General Lee, 6 Mar 1863. *Lee's Wartime Papers*, #229. Strode, *Davis*, pp. 269–70. On 18 July, Lee wrote Davis: "I think it is certain that heavy reinforcements are reaching McClellan, and that they will leave no stone unturned to capture Richmond. I fear they will draw upon their western army, leaving a force to mask ours, and thus render it unavailable to us." *ORA*, LI, II, 1075. This, of course, is what the Lincoln administration should have done.

42. Report of Brig-Gen John Peck. *ORA*, Pt. III, 293. The Confederate mounted troops approaching White House watched in frustration as the last of 400 Union transports moved down the Pamunkey out of range. R. Ingalls (Asst QMG) to Meigs, 29 Jun 1862. *Ibid.*, p. 273.

43. Goldsborough to Fox, 16 Jun 1862. *Fox Correspondence*, I, 287–88. Same to same, 27 Jun 1862. *ORA*, Pt. III, 263.

44. Goldsborough to Welles, 4 Jul 1862. *ORA*, Pt. III, 295. Entry of 10 Aug 1862. *Welles Diary*, I, 73. *ORN*, 548. Goldsborough rightly interpreted this novel command arrangement as lack of confidence in his professional ability. Although he asked to be relieved on 15 July, he was not actually replaced by Rear Admiral Samuel P. Lee until 2 September.

45. Wilkes to Welles, 15 Jul 1862. *ORN*, 574–75.

46. Lincoln to Seward, 30 Jun 1862. *ORA*, Pt. III, 276.

47. *ORA*, Pt. III, 278.

48. Stanton to Seward, 30 Jun; McClellan to Thomas (AG) 1 Jul 1862. *ORA*, Pt. III, 277, 281. Lincoln telegraphed the Union governors on 3 July: "If I had fifty thousand additional troops here *now*, I believe I could substantially close the war in two weeks." *Lincoln Works*, V, 304.

49. Lincoln to Burnside, 28 Jun 1862. *Lincoln Works*, V, 288. Stanton to McClellan, 1 Jul; McClellan to Lincoln, 3 Jul 1862. *ORA*, Pt. III, 281, 292. Marcy (COS) to McClellan, 4 Jul 1862. McClellan Papers, A-72.

50. McClellan to Lincoln, 4 Jul 1862. McClellan Papers, A-72.

51. "Throughout this campaign," wrote D. H. Hill, "we attacked just when and where the enemy wished us to attack." *B & L*, II, 395.

52. Lee to Davis, 4, 6, and 9 Jul 1862. *Lee's Wartime Papers*, #226, #227, #230.

53. *ORA*, XII, Pt. III, 333–47. Major General Shields, whose advanced brigade was defeated at Port Republic on 12 June because of inability to bring up supports or induce General Frémont to launch a simultaneous attack, begged McDowell to quiet the Washington alarmists, "or we will defeat ourselves without the presence of an enemy." Shields to Col Scriver (COS) 18 Jun 1862. *Ibid.*, p. 406.

54. Executive Order, 26 Jun 1862. *ORA*, XII, Pt. III. 435. John Pope, "The Second Battle of Bull Run", *B & L*, II, 449–50; *Chase Diaries*, pp. 91–92; Thomas and Hyman, *Stanton*, p. 204.

55. Pope, *op cit.*, p. 450; Pope to McClellan, and reply 7 Jul 1862. *ORA*, Pt. III, 295–97, 306–07.

56. Pope to McClellan, 4 Jul 1862. *ORA*, Pt. III, 295–97. Testimony of Maj-Gen Pope, 8 Jul 1862. *JCR* (1863) Pt. I, 276–82.

57. Thomas and Hyman, *Stanton*, p. 214.

58. Lincoln to Halleck, 6 Jul; Halleck to W. T. Sherman, 16 Jul; Halleck to McClellan, 30 Jul 1862. *ORA*, Pt. III, 302, 343; Pt. II, XVII, 100. Entry of 3 Sep 1862. *Welles Diary*, I, 108. Lincoln ignored Scott's advice about operations which was to support McClellan and go all out for an attack on Richmond by the river lines even if it meant "uncovering Washington." See Scott's memorandum dated 23 Jun 1862. *Lincoln Works*, V. 284.

59. Memorandum of interview between Lincoln and officers of the Army of the Potomac, 8–9 Jul 1862. *Lincoln Works*, V, 309–12. Testimony of Maj-Gen Burnside, 19 Mar 1863. *JCR* (1863) I, 638. Keyes to Meigs (referred to Halleck) 21 Jul 1862. *ORA*, Pt. III, 331–33; Barnard to Fox, 24 Jul 1862. *Fox Correspondence*, II, 330–31.

60. McClellan to Lincoln, 7 Jul; Welles to Farragut, 5 Jul 1862. *ORA*, Pt. III, 305; XV, 517. Rodgers to Goldsborough, 30 Jun and 4 Jul;

Mansfield to McClellan, 26 Jul; Welles to Goldsborough, 25 Jul; Cmdr M. Woodhull to Wilkes, 9 Aug; Goldsborough to Welles and reply, 1 Aug; Wilkes to Welles, 7 Aug 1862. *ORN*, 529–30, 541, 594, 595, 609, 639, 634.

61. The others were abandoned on the beach at Norfolk. Wilkes to Welles; Wilkes to Commo Paulding; Cmdr B. J. Totten to Goldsborough, 1 Aug 1862. *ORN*, 610–11, 609.

62. McClellan to Pope, 7 Jul 1862. *ORA*, Pt, III, 306.

63. Sen A. Johnson to Halleck, 5 Jun; Lincoln to Halleck, 8 Jun 1862. *ORA*, X, 261, 277. McClellan had earlier suggested such a movement himself. See McClellan to Lincoln, 5 June and reply 7 Jun; also Lincoln to Halleck, 5 Jun 1862. *Lincoln Works*, V, 260–61, 263.

64. Lincoln to Halleck; Stanton to Halleck and reply, 30 Jun; Halleck to Stanton, 1 Jul; Stanton to Maj-Gen D. Hunter; Lincoln to McClellan, 3 Jul; Lincoln to Halleck, 4 Jul 1862. *ORA*, Pt. III, 279–80, 285, 291, 294; Halleck to Lincoln, 5 Jul 1862. McClellan Papers, A-72.

65. Testimony of Maj-Gen Halleck, 11 Mar 1863. *JCR* (1863) I, 452.

66. Halleck's memorandum to the secretary of War, 27 Jul 1862. *ORA*, Pt. III, 337–38.

67. *Ibid.*

68. Michie, *McClellan*, p. 375.

69. McClellan to Mrs. McClellan, 30 Jul 1862, in *Own Story*, p. 438; Entry of 31 Aug 1862. *Welles Diary*, I, 97. H. J. Eckenrode and Bryan Conrad, *George B. McClellan: The Man Who Saved the Union* (Chapel Hill, N.C., 1941) p. 128. Burnside declined the command.

70. Keyes to Lincoln, 25 Aug 1862. *ORA*, Pt. III, 382–83.

71. Halleck to McClellan, 5 Aug 1862. McClellan Papers, A-73. Halleck to McClellan, 7 Aug 1862. *ORA*, Pt. III, 359–60. Testimony of Maj-Gen Halleck, 11 Mar 1863. *JCR* (1863) Pt. I, 452.

72. Wilkes to Welles, 17 and 18 Aug; Wilkes to Goldsborough, 7 Aug. *ORN*, 629–30, 653–54, 655–56. Entry of 25 Aug 1862. *Welles Diary*, I, 92.

73. Fitz John Porter was court-martialed and dismissed from the service; Franklin was arrested after the Fredericksburg campaign, deprived of his corps, and sent to the fever-ridden Mississippi valley. Burnside, promoted to command the Army of the Potomac after McClellan's failure to follow up his victory at Sharpsburg to the government's satisfaction, was discredited at Fredericksburg and returned to a corps command for the remainder of the war.

CHAPTER 7

ORN references are to Volume XVIII unless otherwise indicated.

1. For this chapter, see Maps 14, 15, 16, and 17.

2. Butler to Stanton, 13 Apr 1862. *Butler Correspondence*, I, 410–11; also see Welles to Farragut (confidential) 20 Jan 1862. *ORN*, 7–8. Farragut's instructions regarding the Gulf blockade, issued by Welles on 25 January, were incompatible with any offensive operations. Farragut was advised not to concentrate his ships at any one point but to spread them

out along the whole coast from St. Andrews Bay, Florida to the Rio Grande. *Ibid.*, pp. 9–10.

3. Farragut to Cmdr Bell, 17 Apr; Detailed report of Cmdr Porter, 30 Apr 1862. *ORN*, 133, 361–74. W. B. Robertson (CSA) "The Water-Battery at Fort Jackson," *B & L*, II, 100. Butler to Stanton, 1 Jan; Report of Lt Weitzel, 5 May 1862. *ORA*, XV, 450; LIII, 525–26. West, *Butler*, p. 119.

4. Farragut to Porter, 24 Apr; Farragut to Welles, 25 Apr; General Order of Flag-Off Farragut, 20 Apr 1862. *ORN*, 142, 153, 160.

5. See Report of Lt J. Palfrey (US Eng) to Weitzel (Ch Eng) 16 May; Weitzel to Gen J. G. Totten, 5 May 1862. *ORA*, XV, 433; LIII, 524–25.

6. L. James (ADC) to Lovell (CSA) 27 Apr 1862, 260. Testimony of Col E. Higgins (CSA) 24 Apr 1862, Confederate States of America, War Department. *Proceedings of the Court of Inquiry Relative to the Fall of New Orleans* (Richmond, 1864) p. 592.

7. See Lovell to Randolph, 15 Apr; Report of Brig-Gen M. L. Smith, Aug 1862; Beauregard to Capt Harris (CS Eng) 21 Apr 1862. *ORA*, VI, 877; XV, 6–12, 812.

8. Farragut to Welles, 29 Apr; Farragut to Fox, 26 Apr 1862. *ORN*, 148, 155. Journal entry of 29 Apr 1862, in Loyall Farragut, *The Life of David Glasgow Farragut* (New York, 1879) p. 261. Report of Maj-Gen Butler, 29 Apr 1862. *ORA*, VI, 505.

9. Farragut to Capt T. Craven, 3 May 1862. *ORN*, 465. The wide flood plain and erratic course of the Mississippi made it difficult to detect the channel during high water. Ships able to pass over the numerous shoals were therefore likely to become stuck in the mud when the water level suddenly dropped, which it frequently did during the late spring and early summer.

10. *Butler Correspondence*, I, 428.

11. Butler to Stanton, 8 May 1862. *ORA*, VI, 507.

12. Farragut to Butler, 6 May 1862. *ORN*, 470; Farragut to Fox, 7 May 1862. *Fox Correspondence*, I, 311–12.

13. Farragut to Welles, 6 May 1862, in Farragut, *Life of Farragut*, p. 250; *ORN*, 473. West, *Butler*, p. 163; Butler to Stanton, 16 May 1862. *ORA*, XV, 422–24.

14. Farragut to Capt H. Morris, 10 May; Cmdr S. P. Lee to Authorities at Vicksburg, 18 May 1862, and reply. *ORN*, 477, 491–92. Report of Brig-Gen M. Smith (CSA) August 1862. *ORA*, XV, 6–12.

15. Extract from Private Diary of Cmdr H. H. Bell (Fleet Capt) 19 May 1862. *ORN*, 703–04. Charles Lee Lewis, *David Glasgow Farragut* (Annapolis, 1943) pp. 81–82.

16. Weitzel to Maj G. Strong (AAG) 27 May 1862. *ORN*, 514. Merrill, *Battle Flags South*, p. 175; Brennan to Butler, 21 May 1862. *Butler Correspondence*, I, 546–47.

17. Farragut to Butler, 22 May 1862. *ORA*, XV, 457–58. Extract from Diary of Cmdr Bell, 25 May 1862. *ORN*, 705–06.

18. Capt T. Craven to Mrs. Craven, 3 Jun 1862. *ORN*, 528–35.

19. Williams to Strong (AAG) 29 May 1862. *Butler Correspondence,* I, 529–43.

20. 30 May 1862. *ORN,* 519–21. Also see Farragut to Welles, 3 Jun 1862. *Ibid.,* pp. 577–79.

21. Stanton to Butler, 14 Jun 1862. *Butler Correspondence,* I, 628. From 12 May, when Lincoln declared New Orleans an open port, until 1 September 1862, a huge trade with the Confederacy developed through this point, as well as through Memphis. John Christopher Schwab, *The Confederate States of America, 1861–1865.* Reprint ed. (New York, 1968) pp. 259–63.

22. The fall of Forts Henry and Donelson further spurred the Confederate policy of abandoning the seacoast to defend interior lines. On 18 February Confederate Secretary of War Judah P. Benjamin ordered Bragg to strip Mobile and Pensacola of troops, to reinforce A. S. Johnston in Tennessee. Benjamin recognized that they could not be brought back in time if the Federals moved quickly against Mobile. *ORA,* VI, 828.

23. Testimony of Maj-Gen M. L. Smith, 23 Apr 1863. *Proceedings of the Court of Inquiry re the Fall of New Orleans,* p. 585. Lovell to Beauregard, 25 May 1862. *ORN,* 850. Report of Brig-Gen M. Smith, August 1862. *ORA,* XV, 6–12.

24. Farragut to Welles, 3 Jun 1862, in Farragut, *Life of Farragut,* pp. 266–68. Porter to Fox, 3 Jun 1862. *Fox Correspondence,* II, 199–21. Butler to Stanton, 31 May 1862. *ORA,* XV, 447.

25. See Porter to Welles, 10 May 1862. *ORN,* 478–79. Fox to Porter, quoted in West, *Porter,* p. 149.

26. *Fox Correspondence,* I, 313; also see Fox to Farragut, 15 May 1862. *ORN,* 245.

27. Welles to Farragut, 16 May, also 19 May 1862. *ORN,* 498, 502. Fox to Farragut, 17 May 1862. *Fox Correspondence,* I, 314–15.

28. *ORN,* 707–08; Farragut to Fox, 12 Jun 1862. *Fox Correspondence,* I, 315–16. Farragut to Welles, 16 Jun 1862. *ORN,* 561. Butler to Stanton, 1 Jun 1862. *Butler Correspondence,* I, 536.

29. Butler to Porter, 1 Jun; Butler to Williams, 6 Jun 1862. *Butler Correspondence,* I, 549–50, 562–63. Porter to Butler, 9 Jun; Butler to Williams, 6 Jun; Williams to R. S. Davis (AAG) 12 Jun; Butler to Stanton, 17 Jun 1862. *ORA,* XV, 25–26, 26, 464, 478–79.

30. Porter to Fox, 30 Jun 1862. *Fox Correspondence,* II, 122–23. Van Dorn to Pres Davis, 28 Jun 1862. *ORN,* 651.

31. Farragut to Davis; Davis to Welles, 28 Jun 1862. *ORN,* 231–32.

32. Farragut to Capt J. DeCamp, 25 Jun; Farragut to Welles, 28 Jun; Farragut to Davis, 28 Jun 1862; Reports of Capt Craven, Lt J. H. Russel, and Lt Preble. *ORN,* 585–86, 588, 589, 599–602.

33. *ORA,* XV, 515–16.

34. See H. Wager Halleck, *Elements of Military Art and Science.* Reprint ed. (Westport, Conn., 1971) pp. 40–41. This work, first published in 1846, was reissued in 1854 and 1862. It was the standard work on strategy carried by Civil War officers.

35. Halleck to McClellan, 8 Mar 1862. *ORA,* X, Pt. II, 20–21. See Map

1. See Halleck, *Elements*, pp. 46, 52, 54; also Baron de Jomini, *The Art of War*. Reprint ed., trans. by G. H. Mendell and W. P. Craighill (Westport, Conn., n.d.) pp. 63, 104. The first American edition of this 1838 French work was published in English in 1862.

36. Foote to Welles, 4 Mar and 20 Mar 1862. *ORN*, XXII, 651, 697. Sherman to Halleck, 5 Mar 1862. *ORA*, X, Pt. II, 7. Foote to Fox, 9 Mar 1862. *Fox Correspondence*, II, 44–50.

37. See Halleck to Cullum (COS) 1 Mar 1862. *ORA*, X, Pt. II, 93. Lincoln to Johnson, 27 Apr 1862. *Lincoln Works*, V, 200.

38. Ambrose, *Halleck*, pp. 45–48.

39. Foote to Welles, 15 Apr 1862. *ORN*, XXIII, 10.

40. See Halleck to Foote, 13 May 1862. *Ibid.*, p. 94.

41. Halleck to Foote, 15 Apr; Halleck to Pope, 16 Apr; Pope to Foote, 16 Apr; Foote to Welles, 17 Apr 1862. *Ibid.*, pp. 5–8. This cautious method of proceeding was approved by Lincoln who warned him, on 11 May, to "be sure to sustain no reverse in your Department." *Lincoln Works*, V, 210.

42. Pollard, *First Year of the War*, pp. 293–94. Henry Walke, "The Western Flotilla," *B & L*, I, 439–40.

43. Foote to Welles, 23 and 30 Apr 1862. *ORN*, XXIII, 11–12, 62.

44. Report of Capt Montgomery (CSN) 1 Jul 1862. *ORA*, XII, Pt. II, 37–40.

45. Davis to Welles, 21 and 24 May; Report of Brig-Gen I. F. Quinby, 24 May; Quinby to Davis, 3 Jun; Col. T. H. Rosser (cmdg Memphis) to Brig-Gen Ruggles (CSA) 3 Jun; Report of Col C. Ellet (USA) 5 Jun; Detailed report of Capt Davis, 6 Jun 1862. *ORN*, XXIII, 25, 28–29, 30–31, 48–49, 58–59, 113–14, 119–21.

46. Breckinridge's division from Tupelo and Ruggles' command from Jackson arrived on 22 June. General Earl Van Dorn took command on the 28th. Report of Brig-Gen M. L. Smith, August 1862. *ORA*, XV, 6–12.

47. Journal entry of 2 Jul 1862, in Farragut, *Life of Farragut*, pp. 282–83.

48. Williams, *Beauregard*, pp. 152–54; Charles Bertrand Lewis, *Field, Fort and Fleet* (Detroit, 1885) pp. 181–83.

49. A. Johnson to Halleck, 5 Jun; Lincoln to Halleck, 8 Jun 1862. *ORA*, X, Pt. II, 261, 277. Statement of Gen Buell before the "Buell Commission," 5 May 1863. *ORA*, XVI, Pt. I, 30–31.

50. Halleck to Stanton, 31 May and 17 Jun 1862. *ORA*, X, Pt. I, 668; Pt. II, XII, 12. *Personal Memoirs of U.S. Grant*. 2 vols. (New York, 1895) I, 326–27.

51. In a letter to Stanton on 25 June, Halleck argued that Corinth lacked water and was unhealthy in the summer, thus preventing its use as a base for a further concentrated offensive and necessitating the breakup of his army. See *ORA*, XXIII, 62–63. This excuse, offered after the fact, was obviously designed to justify his failure of initiative and his entanglement in sideshow operations. If Corinth was a bad base, he could have used Memphis or Decatur. That he did not actually consider it unsuitable, however, is demonstrated by his own orders to fortify the

place and rebuild the railroads.

52. This thinking would have been consistent with Halleck's strategic theory. See *Elements*, p. 51.

53. Brig-Gen E. Barksdale (CSA) to Pres Davis, 6 Jun 1862. *ORN*, 854. Bragg to Cooper (AG) 23 Jun 1862. *ORA*, XVII, Pt. II, 655–56.

54. See testimony of Gen Buell before the "Buell Commission," 5 May 1863; Bragg to Beauregard, 22 Jul; Halleck to Stanton, 9 Jun; Report of Maj-Gen Mitchel, 10 Jun; Maj-Gen E. K. Smith (CSA) to Capt W. Taylor (AAG) 9 Jun 1862. *ORA*, XVI, Pt. I; LII, Pt. II, 330–31; X, 671, 919, 921–22. Benson J. Lossing, *The Civil War in the United States of America*. 2 vols. (Hartford, Conn., 1868) I, 290–91.

55. Morgan to Stanton, 19 Jul; Rosecrans to Col J. Kelton (COS) 28 Jun; Halleck to Grant, 1 Jul 1862. *ORA*, X, 56; LII, Pt. II, 43; XII, Pt. II, 60.

56. Strong to Davis, 12 Jun 1862. *ORN*, XXII, 160–61.

57. Stanton to Halleck, 27 Jun 1862. *ORA*, XII, Pt. II, 40.

58. Stanton to Brig-Gen C. Ellet, 25 Apr 1862. *ORA*, Ser. III, Vol. II, 25–26. Stanton to Col A. W. Ellet, 20 Jun; Welles to Senator Preston King, 30 Jun 1862. *ORN*, 218, 247.

59. C. Ellet to Davis and reply, 11 Jun; Davis to Col G. N. Fitch (USA) 14 Jun 1862. *ORN*, XXII, 162–63, 164.

60. Davis to Grant, 26 Jun 1862. *Ibid.*, p. 182.

61. Halleck to Sherman, 21 Jun; Stanton to Halleck, 23 Jun; Halleck to Grant, 29 Jun and 1 Jul 1862. *ORA*, XII, Pt. II, 22, 26, 46, 60.

62. Grant to Halleck, 25 June 1862; *Grant Papers*, V, 155. Lt J. Shirk (USN) to Davis; *ORN*, XXII, 188–89. Hindman actually had only a thousand men and a few field guns at the bluff and considered his own situation desperate. See his report in *Ibid.*, pp. 197–98.

63. Davis to Welles, 5 Jul 1862. *ORN*, XXIII, 251. Robert L. Kerby, *Kirby Smith's Confederacy: The Trans-Mississippi South, 1863–1865*. (New York, 1972) pp. 32–33.

64. On 16 July, Curtis warned Halleck that Price's whole army had crossed the river, and to look out for him. *ORN*, XXIII, 260.

65. Stanton to Halleck, 14 Jul, and reply 15 Jul; Halleck to Grant, 31 Jul 1862. *ORA*, XII, Pt. II, 97, 142; XV, 518–19. Welles to Stanton, 29 Jul 1862. *ORN*, XIX, 95–96.

66. Spears, *Farragut*, pp. 253–54; Farragut to Welles, 8 Jul; Welles to Davis, 14 Jul 1862. *ORN*, XVIII, 670; XXIII, 235–36. Also Welles to Farragut, 14 and 18 Jul 1862. *ORN*, XVIII, 682, XIX, 19.

67. *ORA*, XV, 531.

68. 18 Jul 1862. *ORN*, XIX, 75.

69. A. Ellet to Stanton, 2 Jul 1862. *ORN*, 590–91.

70. Farragut to Bell, 13 Jul; Davis to Welles, 16 Jul 1862. *ORN*, XVIII, 635; XIX, 6–7.

71. Report of Flag-Off Farragut, 17 Jul 1862. *ORN*, XIX, 4.

72. Lewis, *Farragut*, pp. 113–18.

73. For discussion of this whole matter, and arrangements, see Farragut to Davis, 15, 16, 17, 18, 19, 20, 21, and 22 Jul, and replies 17, 20,

21, and 22 Jul 1862. *ORN*, XIX, 7–18.

74. Ellet to Stanton, 23 Jul; Phelps to Foote, 29 Jul; Davis to Welles, 12 Sep; Report of Cmdr W. D. Porter, 1 Aug; Farragut to Welles, 11 Sep 1862. *Ibid.*, pp. 45–46, 55–59, 59–60, 60–62, 62–63.

75. 29 Jul 1862. *Ibid.*, pp. 96–98.

76. A. T. Mahan, *The Navy in the Civil War: The Gulf and Inland Waters* (New York, 1905) p. 104; Farragut to Davis, 22 Jul; Williams to Davis, 23 Jul 1862. *ORN*, XIX, 17, 50.

77. Report of Maj-Gen Breckinridge (CSA); Weitzel to Capt R. S. Davis (AAG) 8 Aug 1862. *ORA*, XV, 76–81, 545. Reports of Lt F. A. Roe (USN) and Lt G. M. Ransom (USN) 6 Aug 1862. *ORN*, XIX, 118–19.

78. Farragut to Welles, 5 Aug 1862. *ORN*, XIX, 115–17.

79. Isaac N. Brown (CSN) "The Confederate Gun-Boat 'Arkansas'," *B & L*, III, 758–79.

80. Farragut to Welles, 11 and 21 Aug; Welles to Farragut, 19 Aug; Lt-Cmdr Roe to Farragut, 23 Aug; Farragut to Cmdr H. W. Morris, 23 Aug; Farragut to Butler, 31 Aug 1862. *ORN*, XIX, 146–172.

81. Phelps to Foote, 29 Jul 1862. *Ibid.*, p. 58.

82. Niven, *Welles*, p. 453.

83. Grant to Halleck, 17 Jul; Price to Van Dorn, 4 and 27 Aug; Bragg to Price 12 Aug 1862. *ORA*, XII, Pt. II, 114; XVII, Pt. II, 663–64, 687, 677. Wise to Foote, 21 Jul; Curtis to Halleck, 6 Aug 1862. *ORN*, 266–67, 286.

84. Report of Brig-Gen G. Granger, 28 Aug; J. T. Boyle (USA) to Maj-Gen Lew Wallace, 20 Aug 1862. *ORA*, XVII, Pt. I, 40; LII, Pt. I, 272–73.

85. *Fox Correspondence*, I, 335.

CHAPTER 8

1. Farragut to Welles, 30 Sep and 23 Oct. 1862. *ORN*, XIX, 242–43, 312. Farragut, *Life of Farragut*, p. 297.

2. Entry of 28 Jun 1863. *Welles Diary*, I, 230; Lewis, *Farragut*, pp. 135–47.

3. Farragut to Welles, 14 Nov 1862, in Farragut, *Life of Farragut*, pp 297–98. The Confederate garrison at Mobile was still unprepared to resist even a small-scale combined operation. On 4 November, in response to urgent requests from the commander at Mobile, one of the best Confederate engineers, Brigadier General Daniel Leadbetter, arrived in the city. He reported the defenses inadequate against both land and naval attack. There were no obstructions between Forts Morgan and Gaines to hold enemy ships under the guns; no mines on the approaches or in the inner harbor; the land defenses of the city were very weak and incomplete. Leadbetter to Cooper (AG), 14 Nov 1862. *ORA*, XV, 867.

4. Farragut to Butler, 23 Oct and reply 25 Oct 1862. *ORN*, XIX, 313, 315–16.

5. Annual Report of the U.S. Army QMG, 18 Nov 1862. *ORA*, Ser. III, Vol. II, 808. Lt-Cmdr T. McK. Buchanan to Farragut, 9 Nov 1862. *ORN*, XIX, 326–29.

6. West, *Butler*, pp. 187–89.

7. Farragut to Butler, 23 Oct; Fox to Farragut, 1 Nov; Lincoln to Farragut, 11 Nov 1862. *ORN*, XIX, 313, 338, 342.

8. Acting Master F. Crocker to Farragut, 12 Oct; Butler's confidential instructions to the officers of the Blockading Squadron, 24 Sep; Farragut to Welles, 28 Oct; Stanton to Butler, 11 Nov; Welles to Farragut, 21 Sep 1862. *ORN*, XIX, 226, 227, 230, 231, 237.

9. Banks to Cullum (COS) 27 Oct; Lincoln to Banks (two letters) 22 Nov 1862. *ORA*, Ser. III, Vol. II, 712–13, 862, 863. Harrington, *General Banks*, p. 54.

10. Halleck to Banks, 9 Nov 1862. *ORA*, XV, 590–91.

11. Ambrose, *Halleck*, pp. 30–31.

12. See McClernand to Stanton, 10 Nov 1862, *ORA*, LIII, Pt. II, 332–34, in which McClernand repeats the arguments he had used with Lincoln and the Cabinet during conversations in August and September.

13. 7 Oct 1862. *Chase Diaries*, p. 170; Entry of 12 Jan 1863. *Welles Diary*, I, 220.

14. Halleck to A. W. Ellet, 11 Nov 1862. *ORA*, Ser. III, Vol. II, 761–62; Welles to Porter, 1 Oct; Porter to Welles, 21 Oct; Welles to Stanton, 31 Oct 1862. *ORN*, XXIII, 388, 428, 430–31. Entry of 10 Oct 1862. *Welles Diary*, I, 167; John D. Milligan, *Gunboats Down the Mississippi* (Annapolis, 1965) pp. 94–95.

15. Porter to Welles, *ORN*, XXIII, 428. Stanton to McClernand (confidential), 29 Oct; Porter to Welles, 29 Oct 1862. *ORA*, XII, Pt. II, 302, 321.

16. McClernand to Lincoln, 28 Sep 1862. *ORA*, XVII, Pt. II, Appendix, 849–53.

17. Memorandum regarding the operations of the Mississippi Squadron. *ORN*, XXIII, 397.

18. Ambrose, *Halleck*, pp. 109, 113; ORA, XVIII, 468–69, 469.

19. Curtis to Halleck, 6 Aug 1862. *ORA*, XXIII, 286–87. Halleck to Curtis, 7 Aug 1862. U.S. Army, *Telegrams Sent by Maj-Gen H. W. Halleck*. 10 vols. (Washington, D.C., 1877) I, 390.

20. Sherman to Rawlins (COS) 18 Oct; Col W. S. Hillyer to Sherman, 29 Oct 1862. *ORA*, XII, Pt. II, 280–307.

21. Grant to Halleck, 29 Oct 1862. *Ibid.* pp. 302–03; W. T. Sherman, *Memoirs of General William T. Sherman.* 2 vols in 1, reprinted. (Bloomington, Indiana, 1957) I, 279–280; Francis Vinton Greene, *The Mississippi* (New York, 1903) pp. 64–65.

22. *ORA*, XVII, Pt. I, 467.

23. Sherman to Porter, 12 Nov 1862. *ORA*, XVII, Pt. II, Appendix, 862–63. Grant to Porter, 22 Nov; Grant to Sherman, 8 Dec; Sherman to Porter, 8 Dec 1862. *ORN*, XXIII, 496–97, 539, 539–40. Sherman's instructions to his divisional commanders dated 23 Dec 1862, in Sherman, *Memoirs*, I, 287.

24. Davies to Halleck, 20 and 27 Dec; Grant to Maj-Gen J. H. McPherson, 19 and 20 Dec 1862. *ORA*, XVII, Pt. II, 436, 441, 445, 494.

25. Stanton to McClernand, 15 and 17 Dec; McClernand to Halleck,

16 Dec, and Stanton, 17 Dec; Halleck to Grant; Grant to McClernand, 18 Dec 1862. *Ibid.*, pp. 413, 415, 420, 425.

26. Flag-Off W. F. Lynch (CSN) to Brig-Gen D. Ruggles (cmdg Miss. Dist.) 9 Oct 1862. *Ibid.*, p. 725.

27. Detailed report of Rear-Adm Porter, 17 Dec 1862. *ORN*, XXIII, 545–46.

28. Earl Schenck Miers, *The Web of Victory: Grant at Vicksburg* (New York, 1955) pp. 64–67; Lossing, *Civil War*, I. 576.

29. Davies to Halleck, 20 Dec; Col L. B. Parson (ADC) to Halleck, 26 Dec 1862. *ORA*, 441, 497. Sherman, *Memoirs*, I, 279–95. Also see Porter to Welles, 27 Dec 1862. *ORN*, XXIII, 580.

30. Porter to Lt-Cmdr E. K. Owen, 27 Dec 1862. *ORN*, XXIII, 579.

31. For Confederate preparations to meet the assault, see John C. Pemberton, *Pemberton, Defender of Vicksburg* (Chapel Hill, N.C., 1942) pp. 66–67.

32. Thomas L. Livermore, *Numbers and Losses in the Civil War in America, 1861–65* (Bloomington, Ind., 1957) p. 96. On 5 January Sherman advised Halleck that the gunboats could not injure the Yazoo batteries and that an assault on the upper defenses of Vicksburg could not possibly succeed except in overwhelming force; greater than three to one. *ORA*, XVII, Pt. I, 613.

33. Grant to Halleck, 9 Jan 1863. *ORA*, XVII, Pt. II, 549. The Lincoln administration never recognized that appointing political generals to command important expeditions alienated the professional Army establishment and thus practically ensured that these expeditions would run into serious problems or fail altogether for lack of cooperation.

34. One of the best examples is J. F. C. Fuller's, *The Generalship of Ulysses S. Grant* (London, 1929) pp. 132–45. In his adulation for Grant's supposed strategic genius, Fuller goes so far as to claim that Grant purposefully fumbled around with approaches he knew would fail, for the sake of confusing Pemberton—a fantastic notion not supported by a shred of evidence.

35. *ORN*, XIX, 536–57.

36. Cmdr W. Smith to Farragut, 3 Feb; Farragut to Lt-Cmdr H. A. Adams, 4 Feb; Farragut to Commo R. B. Hitchcock, 4 Feb; Farragut to Capt H. Bell, 7 Feb 1863. *ORN*, XIX, 600, 600–1, 605–606.

37. Farragut, *Life of Farragut*, pp. 309–10.

38. Farragut to Bell, 15 Dec 1862; Farragut to Lt-Cmdr A. P. Cooke, 5 Feb 1863. *ORN*, XIX, 409, 602. Farragut to Fox, 23 Dec 1862. *Fox Correspondence*, I, 322–23. Halleck to Banks, 9 Nov 1862, 4 and 18 Jan 1863; Butler to Lincoln, 18 Dec 1862. *ORA*, XV, 590–91, 636, 656, 1096–97. Lincoln to Stanton, 23 Jan 1863. *Butler Correspondence*, II, 587.

39. Farragut to Capt J. Alden. *ORN*, XIX, 536–37. Maj-Gen R. Taylor (CSA) to Brig-Gen Ruggles, 20 Aug; P. Pond. Jr. to Cooper (AG, CSA) 21 Sep 1862. *ORA*, XV, 802, 808–09.

40. Weitzel to Banks, 14 Jan; Weitzel to Lt-Col R. B. Irwin (AAG), 18 Jan; Banks to Halleck, 24 Jan 1863. *ORN*, XIX, 516, 539–40, 578–79.

41. Halleck to Banks, 24 Jan 1863. *Ibid.*, pp. 518–19; Ambrose, *Halleck*, p. 146.

42. Farragut to Welles, 3 Feb; Farragut to Cooke, 5 Feb; Banks to Halleck, 12 Feb 1863. *ORN*, XIX, 597–98, 602, 610.

43. Report of Col C. R. Ellet; Porter to Ellet, 8 Feb; Porter to Welles, 4 Feb 1863. *ORN*, XIV, 219–24, 374, 375–76.

44. *ORN*, XXIV, 379, 392, 402.

45. Memo re operations of the Mississippi Squadron. *ORN*, XXIII, 404.

46. Porter to Welles, 22 Feb 1863. *ORN*, XIV, 382–83.

47. Porter to Sen J. W. Grimes, 24 Jan 1863. *ORN*, XIV, 194–95.

48. Fox to Porter; also see Welles to Porter, 19 Jan 1863. *Ibid.*, pp. 181, 242–43.

49. Porter to Welles, 7 Feb 1863. *Ibid.*, p. 322.

50. Farragut to Fox, 7 Mar 1863. *Fox Correspondence*, I, 328. Banks to Halleck, 28 Feb 1863. *ORA*, XV, 1105–06. Farragut to Banks, 2 Mar 1863. *ORN*, XIX, 644.

51. See Banks to Halleck, 13 Mar; Report of Maj-Gen Banks, 21 Mar 1863. *ORN*, XX, 5–6; XIX, 697–98.

52. Reports of Rear-Adm Farragut, Capt Alden, and Capt M. Smith, 16 Mar; Report of Maj-Gen F. Gardner (CSA), 18 Mar 1863. *ORN*, XIX, 665–88, 704–05. Carrison, *Navy from Wood to Steel*, p. 102.

53. *ORN*, XX, 8, 15.

54. Grant to Sherman, 22 Mar 1863. *ORN*, XIV, 489. Grant to Banks, 22 Mar 1863. *ORA*, XXIV, Pt. III, 125–26.

55. *ORN*, XIV, 479. Also Porter to Farragut, 26 Mar, and Porter to Grant, 29 Mar 1863. *ORA*, XXIV, Pt. II, 152; *ORN*, XX, 11.

56. Ellet to Farragut, 22 Mar; Ellet to Walke, 23 Mar; Walke to Porter, 23 Mar; Grant to Farragut, 23 Mar; Ellet to Stanton, 13 Apr 1863. *ORN*, XX. 12–18, 27.

57. Walke to Porter, 25 Mar; Porter to Ellet and reply, 25 Mar 1863. *ORN*, XX, 20–24. On 2 April Porter demanded that the Mississippi Marine Brigade be broken up, the men incorporated into Grant's army, the vessels turned over to him. Welles tried persuading the War Department to satisfy Porter, but Halleck advised Stanton to refuse. Lincoln finally settled the question on the grounds that the change would be politically unpopular. *Ibid.*, 523–24. On 5 April Porter sent Ellet to operate with Rosecrans on the Tennessee.

58. Farragut to Porter, 25 Mar 1863. *ORN*, XX, 25.

59. Greene, *Mississippi*, p. 107. Fox to Farragut, 2 Apr 1863. *Fox Correspondence*, I, 331. Grant to Porter, 29 Mar; Welles to Porter (confidential) 2 Apr 1863. *ORN*, XIV, 517, 522.

60. Porter to Welles, 1 Apr 1863. *Ibid.*, pp. 519–20.

61. Grant to Porter, 2 Apr 1863. *ORA*, XXIV, III, 168.

62. Porter to Grant, 11 Apr 1863. *Ibid.*, p. 186; Welles to Farragut; also Welles to Porter (confidential) 15 Apr 1863. *ORN*, XX, 121–22; XIV, 552.

63. Fox to Porter, 6 Apr; Fox to Commo Rowan, 6 Apr 1863. *ORN*, XIV, 533; XX, 123.

64. *Fox Correspondence*, II, 172. Sherman to Col J. H. Rawlins (COS) 8 Apr 1863. *ORA*, XXIV, Pt. III, 179–80.

65. Grant to McClernand, 12 Apr 1863. *Ibid.*, pp. 188–89; Porter to Welles (confidential) 12 Apr 1863. *ORN*, XIV, 544–45.

66. Grant to Farragut (for Banks). *ORN*, XX, 14. Greene, *Mississippi*, pp. 221–22.

67. *ORN*, XX, 73.

68. Banks to Grant, 10 Apr; Banks to Farragut, 18 and 23 Apr; E. K. Smith (CSA) to Lt-Gen T. H. Holmes (Cmdg Trans-Miss. Dept.) 24 Apr 1863. *ORA*, XXIV, Pt. III, 182; XV, 704, 707–08, 1054.

69. Banks to Halleck, 29 Apr; Banks to Grant (2 disptches) 30 Apr 1863. *ORA*, XV, 117–18, 711; XXIV, Pt. III, 247, 265.

70. Farragut to Grant, 1 May 1863. *ORA*, XXIV, Pt. III, 259–60. Banks to Farragut, 3 May 1863. *ORN*, XX, 74.

71. Porter to McClernand, 22 Apr; McClernand to Grant, 24 Apr 1863. *ORA*, XXIV, Pt. III, 222, 229.

72. Grant to Sherman, 24 Apr; Grant to McClernand, 27 Apr 1863. *Ibid.*, pp. 231, 237–38; Grant, *Memoirs*, I, 396–97.

73. Detailed report of Rear-Adm Porter, 29 Apr; Brig-Gen J. S. Bowen (CSA) to Pemberton, 29 Apr 1863. *ORN*, 611, 632–33. Porter to Fox, 1 May 1863. *Fox Correspondence*, II, 178–82. Milligan, *Gunboats Down the Mississippi*, p. 156.

74. C. L. Stevenson (CSA) to Pemberton. *ORN*, XIV, 598. Sherman *Memoirs*, I, 319. Also Grant to Sherman, 24 Apr 1863. *ORA*, XXIV, Pt. III, 231.

75. See McClernand to Grant, 26 Apr 1863, suggesting that Grant land the whole army down river at Hard Times. *ORA*, XXIV, Pt. III, 234.

76. Grant to Col W. S. Hillyer, 5 May 1863. *Ibid.*, p. 275.

77. *ORN*, XIV, 607. Also see Porter to Fox, 25 Apr 1863. *Fox Correspondence*, II, 172–75.

78. 10 May 1862. *ORA*, XXIV, Pt. III, 289.

79. Grant to Sherman, 9 May; Steele to Porter, 19 May; Porter to Grant, 23 May 1863. *Ibid.*, pp. 285–86, 328, 342–43.

80. Banks to Grant, 12 May 1863. *Ibid.*, pp. 298–99. Everywhere Union forces had come to a standstill or suffered defeat. Du Pont's repulse at Charleston in April was followed, on 4 May, by Hooker's crushing defeat at Chancellorsville, Virginia. After the battle of Murfreesborough at the beginning of the year, Rosecrans' army had hardly progressed at all toward Chattanooga and still sat facing Bragg on the Tennessee; no amount of prodding would induce Rosecrans to move until Vicksburg fell and Grant's troops were available for his offensive.

81. *ORA*, XXVI, Pt. I, 494.

82. Halleck to Capt Pennock. *ORN*, XIV, 13–14. The request was referred to Breese, and finally to Porter who refused on the grounds of low water in the Arkansas. Undoubtedly, Banks learned about it through Porter. See Porter to Welles and Halleck, 25 May 1863. *Ibid.*, p. 138. As late as 4 June, when the issue of the siege at Vicksburg was still in doubt, Halleck advised Major General John Schofield, command-

ing the Department of Missouri, not to send Grant any more reinforcements because he intended to send an expedition up the Arkansas. *ORA*, XXIV, Pt. III, 384.

83. *ORA*, XXIV, Pt. II, 12–13; Kerby, *Trans-Mississippi South*, pp. 115–18.

84. E. K. Smith to Cooper (AG) 14 Jun 1863. *ORA*, XXIV, Pt. II, 32. Cmdr Palmer to Porter, 3 Jun; Palmer to Banks, 4 Jun 1863. *ORN*, XX, 221–23.

85. Carroll Storrs Alden, *George Hamilton Perkins, Commodore U.S.N.: His Life and Letters* (Boston and New York, 1914) p. 154.

86. Smith to Taylor, 9 Jun 1863. *ORA*, XXIV, Pt. II, 41–42.

87. Taylor to Col J. L. Logan, 15 Jun; Smith to Taylor, 12 Jul; Taylor to Maj E. Surget (AAG) 14 Jul 1863. *ORA*, XXVI, Pt. II, 53; XXIV, Pt. II, 109, 110–11.

CHAPTER 9

1. Entry of 26 Jun 1863. *Welles Diary*, I, 384.
2. Merrill, *Battle Flags South*, p. 109.
3. See Pollard, *First Year of the War*, pp. 323–24.
4. See Chapter 7.
5. See Chapter 6.
6. Nicolay and Hay, *Lincoln*, V, 235; *Du Pont Letters*, II, 96–97. Testimony of G. V. Fox, 19 Mar 1862. *JCR* (1863) IV, Pt. III, 420–21. *Fox Correspondence*, I, 115–16.
7. Welles to Goldsborough, 13 May 1862. *ORN*, VII, 348–49. Fox to Goldsborough, 3 Jun; Fox to Lee, 7 Nov and reply, 30 Nov; Fox to Lee, 15 Dec 1862. *Fox Correspondence*, I, 281–82; II, 230–31, 244–45.
8. Lee to Fox, 2 Dec 1862. *Ibid.*, II, 233–34.
9. Fox to Du Pont, 3 Apr, 12 May, and 3 Jun 1862. *Ibid.*, I, 115–16, 119, 126. In the last letter, Fox wrote: "I feel that my duties are two fold; first to beat our Southern friends; second, to beat the Army. We have done it so far and the people acknowledge and give us the credit."
10. Du Pont to Fox, 25 and 31 May; Drayton to Du Pont, 2 Jul (enclosure); Du Pont to Fox, 9 Jul 1862. *Fox Correspondence*, I, 120–21, 122–23, 136–37. Du Pont to Mrs. Du Pont, 19 May and 22 Jun; Du Pont to Fox, 31 May; Du Pont to Welles, 31 May 1862. *Du Pont Letters*, II, 61, 91, 129; III, 154–55. Rosecrans to McClellan, 19 Nov 1861. *ORA*, V, 657.
11. 7 Oct 1862. *Chase Diaries*, p. 169; *ORA*, X, 290–95; XIV, 380–90. Mitchel to Halleck, 20 Sep 1862. *ORA*, XIV, 383.
12. Entry of 26 Sep 1862. *Welles Diary*, I, 153. Fox to Farragut, 9 Sep 1862. *Fox Correspondence*, I, 317–18.
13. Du Pont to Mrs. Du Pont, 12 and 23 Sep 1862. *Du Pont Letters*, II, 223, 229.
14. Du Pont to Fox, 20 Sep 1862. *Fox Correspondence*, I, 156. In June, he had aptly described the harbor as like "a porcupine's hide and quills turned outside in and sewed up at one end." *Ibid.*, p. 129.

15. "Fort Sumter was regarded in the public mind, North and South, as the citadel of the fortress, the incarnation of rebellion, and as such it was attacked and defended." Ammen, *Atlantic Coast*, p. 5.

16. Du Pont to Mrs. Du Pont, 20 Oct 1862. *Du Pont Letters*, II, 250. Niven, *Gideon Welles*, p. 427.

17. U.S. Congress. Joint Committee on the Conduct of the War. *Report on Heavy Ordnance* (Washington, D.C., 1865) pp. 72, 76. Hereafter cited as *Heavy Ordnance*; Journal Letter #1, 22 Oct 1862. *Du Pont Letters*, II, 258–59.

18. Du Pont to Mrs. Du Pont, 16 Oct 1862. *Du Pont Letters*, II, 247. Du Pont to Fox, 23 Oct and reply, 7 Nov 1862. *Fox Correspondence*, I, 163, 165.

19. See Dahlgren to Welles, 1 and 11 Oct 1862. *ORN*, XIII, 353–54, 377–78. Entry of 1 Oct 1862. *Welles Diary*, I, 158. Du Pont to Fox, 8 Oct 1862. *Fox Correspondence*, I, 160–61. Welles to Du Pont, 26 Jun; Du Pont to J. W. Grimes, 8 Aug 1863. *Du Pont Letters*, III, 185, 222.

20. Du Pont to Fox, 23 Oct 1862. *ORN*, XIII, 408–09. Du Pont to Welles, 25 Oct 1862. *Du Pont Letters*, II, 267. Also see Du Pont to Fox, 10 Jan 1863. *Fox Correspondence*, I, 174–75.

21. Drayton to Du Pont. *Du Pont Letters*, II, 280.

22. Du Pont to Welles, 1 Dec 1862, and 24 Jan 1863. *ORN*, XIII, 487, 535. Journal Letter #22, 27 Dec 1862; Du Pont to C. H. Davis, 4 Jan 1863. *Du Pont Letters*, III, 324, 340. Welles to Du Pont, 4 Nov 1863. *Armored Vessels*, pp. 53, 263–70.

23. For correspondence and reports of this expedition, see *ORA*, XVIII, 53–122, 494–536; Comte de Paris, *Civil War in America*, II, 615; J. Lewis Stackpole (Maj-USV) "The Department of North Carolina Under General Foster, July, 1862 to July, 1863." *Military History Society of Massachusetts Papers*, IX (1912) 90–94.

24. Drayton to A. Hamilton, 5 and 9 Dec 1862. *Naval Letters from Captain Percival Drayton, 1861–1865* (New York, 1906) pp. 20–22. Entry of 5 Jan 1863. *Welles Diary*, I, 216. Fox to Du Pont, 11 Mar 1863. *Fox Correspondence*, I, 191.

25. Foster to Halleck, 30 Jan and 2 Feb 1863; Naglee to Halpine (AAG) 11 Feb 1863, *ORA*, XVIII, 530, 533; XIV, 399.

26. Fox to Du Pont, 6 Jan 1863. *Fox Correspondence*, I, 173. Hunter to Halleck, 26 Jan and 7 Feb 1863. *ORA*, XIV, 393, 394.

27. Stackpole, "Department of North Carolina," pp. 87–110.

28. *Ibid.*

29. Foster to Halleck, 13 Feb 1863. *ORA*, XIV, 400.

30. West, *Welles*, p. 226; Entry of 16 Feb 1863. *Welles Diary*, I, 236–37.

31. See Hunter to Halleck, 11 Feb 1863. *ORA*, XIV, 396.

32. Naglee to Foster; Naglee to Halpine (AAG) 11 Feb 1863. *Ibid.*, 397, 398–400.

33. General Orders #13, HQ Dept. of the South; Hunter to Halleck, 11 Feb, and reply, 15 Feb; Brig-Gen E. Potter (COS) et al. to Stanton, 2 Mar 1863. *ORA*, XIV, 396, 397, 400–01, 417.

34. *Ibid.*, pp. 404–08; also Halleck to Foster, 18 Feb 1863. *Halleck Telegrams*, I, 554.

35. Foster to Halleck; Col E. Townsend (AAG) to Stanton, 16 Feb 1863. *ORA*, XIV, 402–03.

36. Halleck to Foster, 16 and 17 Feb, and reply, 18 Feb; Townsend (AAG) to Stanton, 17 Feb 1863. *ORA*, XIV, 402, 403, 408.

37. Stackpole, "Department of North Carolina," pp. 95–99.

38. Seymour to Naglee,. 28 Feb 1863. *ORA*, XIV, 414–15.

39. *ORA*, XIV, 415–16, 419.

40. Hunter to Halleck; Special Orders #127, HQ, Dept. of the South, 5 Mar 1863. *Ibid.*, pp. 417–18, 420.

41. See Halleck to Dix, 9 Feb and 27 Mar 1863. *Halleck Telegrams*, I, 492.

42. Du Pont to Welles (confidential) 24 Jan 1863. *Du Pont Letters*, II, 377.

43. Jones, *War Clerk's Diary*, p. 158. New York *Tribune*, and New York *World*, 29 Jan 1863.

44. Fox to Du Pont, 16 Feb 1863. *Fox Correspondence*, I, 180.

45. *Du Pont Letters*, II, 399–400; *ORN*, XIII, 571; *Armored Vessels*, pp. 53–54.

46. Reports of Lt-Col J. Yates (CSA) and Maj J. Brown (CSA) 1 Feb 1863. *ORN*, XIII, 567–79. John Johnson, *The Defense of Charleston Harbor, 1863–1865.* Reprint ed. (Freeport, N.Y., 1970) pp. 26–28.

47. Ammen, *Atlantic Coast*; Du Pont to Capt J. Worden, 5 Feb 1863. *ORN*, XIII, 644. Fox to Du Pont, 12 Feb 1863. *Fox Correspondence*, I, 179.

48. John Ericsson, "The Building of the 'Monitor'," *B & L*, I. 730–44. The turret mechanism was inferior to that designed by Captain Cowper Coles of the Royal Navy which revolved on circumferential rollers, because the monitor turret jammed much more easily without being struck. See Cowper P. Coles, *A Comparison Between Iron-Clad Ships with Broadside Ports and Ships with Revolving Shields* (Portsea, England, 1863); S. Eardley-Wilmot, *The Development of Navies During the Last Half-Century* (N.Y., 1892) p. 79.

49. Prior to the invention of armor-piercing shell, the best tactics against ironclad ships were to fire very heavy projectiles at point-blank, which forced the plates inward and sprung the bolts at their outer edges. This caused them to fall off, exposing the wooden hull. U.S. Navy Department. *Report of the Chief of the Bureau of Ordnance, November 1864* (N.Y., 1864).

50. *Heavy Ordnance*, pp. 7, 13, 40, 72, 74, 76, 80, 123; *Armored Vessels*, pp. 3–7; Edward Simpson (Lt, USN) *A Treatise on Ordnance and Naval Gunnery.* 2nd rev. ed. (New York, 1863) pp. 364, 414–15.

51. Ammen, *Old Navy and New*, p. 370; Bureau of Naval Ordnance Memorandum #6, 5 Jan 1863, in *Heavy Ordnance*, p. 127; *Du Pont Letters*, III, 224; Davis, *Charles Henry Davis*, pp. 137–38; James Phinney Baxter, *The Introduction of the Ironclad Warship* (Cambridge, Mass., 1933) pp. 245–47. The problem of producing accurate fire with smoothbore artillery was compounded in the monitors because their

excessive stability on the water made them highly unstable gun platforms.

52. Report of Rear-Adm Du Pont, 28 Jan 1863. *ORN*, XIII, 543–44. Journal Letter #31, 28 Jan 1863. *Du Pont Letters*, II, 390–91. Drayton to A. Hamilton, 11 Feb, and L. Hoyt, 28 Feb 1863. *Drayton Letters*, pp. 26, 29–30. Du Pont, *Samuel Francis Du Pont.* p. 182; Ammen, *Atlantic Coast*, 89–90.

53. *Du Pont Letters*, II, 387.

54. *Fox Correspondence*, I, 179–81.

55. Du Pont to Fox, 2 Mar 1863. *Ibid.*, p. 187.

56. See Journal Letter #55, 10 Apr 1863. *Du Pont Letters*, III, 14.

57. Report of Capt J. McCrady (CSA) 8 Mar 1863. *ORN*, XIII, 730–33. Ammen, *Atlantic Coast*, p. 87; *Old Navy and New*, pp. 370–71.

58. Confidential Memo for Mr. Fox. *Fox Correspondence*, I, 190–91.

59. *Du Pont Letters*, II, 510–11; U.S. National Archives. Confederate Documents. Dispatches relative to engagement between Ft. McAllister and Union ironclads, 1863.

60. *ORA*, XIV, 424–25.

61. *Ibid.*, p. 431.

62. *Du Pont Letters*, II, 533–34.

63. *Ibid.*, pp. 544–45, (emphasis in original). Fox to Du Pont, 26 Mar 1863. *Fox Correspondence*, I, 196.

64. Circular instructions from General Ripley, 26 Dec 1862. *ORN*, XII, 102–05. See Map 18.

65. Johnson, *Defense of Charleston Harbor*, pp. 49–58; Jones, *Siege of Charleston*, p. 188.

66. 4 Apr 1863. *ORN*, XIV, 8–9.

67. Journal Letter #55; Du Pont to Mrs. Du Pont, 6 Apr 1863. *Du Pont Letters*, III, 17; II, 552. *Heavy Ordnance*, p. 96. The *Ironsides's* broadside batteries consisted of eight 11-inch Dahlgrens on each side. These were augmented by two 8-inch pivot guns.

68. For a detailed description of this raft, see Ammen, *Atlantic Coast*, p. 92, note 1. Du Pont disliked and ridiculed these devices before he had even examined or tested them. Informing his wife on 17 February that one of the rafts had just arrived at Port Royal, the other three sent from New York having been lost at sea, he thought it "a pity the fourth did not follow, for I have no more idea that we can use them than we can fly." *Du Pont Letters*, II, 439.

69. Report of Capt J. Rodgers, 20 Apr 1863. *Armored Vessels*, pp. 96–97.

70. See Journal Letter #53, 8 Apr 1863. *Du Pont Letters*, III, 3. Ammen, *Atlantic Coast*, pp. 102–03.

71. Cf. Farragut's orders for the naval attack on the Mobile forts in August 1864. Farragut chose the flood tide so disabled vessels would be carried past the forts into the bay. Mahan, *Gulf and Inland Waters*, p. 228. The average height of the tide at Charleston was 5.1 feet, compared to 1 foot at Mobile. Tide Tables for the Use of Navigation, in Bache, Notes on the Coast, Sect. III, Pt. I, Appendix #33.

72. Testimony of Rear-Adm Du Pont. *Heavy Ordnance*, pp. 94, 97. The *Keokuk*'s armor was only 2½ inches on the two fixed turrets, ¾ inch on the hull. Because her hull was iron instead of wood like the monitor's, it was easily penetrated and crushed in, causing the vessel to founder during the night. Ammen, *Atlantic Coast*, p. 116.

73. A slight dent near the base of the turret deranged the alignment of the track and prevented rotation, while the port stoppers jammed by being bent in only ½ inch. Because the turret had no wood backing, a moderate concussion sheared off the iron bolts and sent the nuts catapulting across the inside of the turret. Almost all of the fleet casualties were caused in this manner. After the bombardment of Sumter, the turrets were lined with boiler iron. Although this expedient eliminated casualties, the bolts still broke, loosening the turret armor and making it more vulnerable to penetration at the joints. Ammen, *Atlantic Coast*, p. 87.

74. Ripley to T. Jordon (COS) and Col A. Rhett to Jordan, 12 Oct 1863. *ORN*, XIV, 107–08, 109–110. Although most Federal reports claim that the ships approached much closer and only turned back upon encountering the obstructions, the Confederate reports, based on pre-measured ranges and knowledge of the depth of water at various points are more reliable; but see Drayton to A. Hamilton, 15 Apr 1863. *Drayton Letters*, p. 34.

75. George E. Belknap, "Reminiscence of the Siege of Charleston." *Military History Society of Massachusetts Papers*, XII (1902) 170. For details of the engagement, see reports in *ORN*, XIV, 3–112; *Armored Vessels*, pp. 57–80, 193–97, 263–70; Ammen, *Old Navy and New*, pp. 379–81; Johnson, *Defense of Charleston*, pp. 49–54.

76. However, Jones points out that one round from the fleet was heavier in weight of metal than one round from all of the land batteries. *Siege of Charleston*, p. 180.

77. The Southerners used a new cogwheel system invented by Colonel Yates of the C.S. Artillery which permitted rapid traverse of the guns to keep them trained on moving targets. *Fremantle Diary*, p. 144.

78. Testimony of Rear-Adm Du Pont. *Heavy Ordnance*, pp. 94–95; Reports of Maj Echols (CSA) 9 Apr, with drawings, and Col Rhett, 13 Apr 1863. *ORN*, XIV, 85–95, 95–98. For a similar opinion, see the testimony of Captain B. J. Sullivan (RN) and Rear Admiral A. Cooper Key (RN) Director of Naval Ordnance, in *British Parliamentary Papers*. Report of the Fortifications Board (1869), Minutes of Evidence, pp. 528–29, 574.

79. Extract from letter by F. H. Thralston dated 26 April 1863 found on blockade-runner re bombardment of Ft. Sumter, 7 Apr 1863. *Armored Vessels*, p. 85.

CHAPTER 10

ORN references are to Volume XIV, *ORA* to Volume XXVIII, unless otherwise indicated.

1. *Armored Vessels*, pp. 87–89.

2. Entry of 25 May 1863. *Welles Diary*, I, 312; Report of Rear-Adm Du Pont, 24 Apr; Rodgers to Welles, 2 May 1863. *ORN*, XIV, 45–48, 58. Du Pont to H. W. Davis, 3 May 1863. *Du Pont Letters*, III, 76.

3. Lincoln to Du Pont, 13 Apr 1863. *Lincoln Works*, VI, 170. Halleck to Hunter, 13 Apr 1863. *Halleck Telegrams*, II, 484. Journal Letter #57, *Du Pont Letters*, III, 42. Lincoln to Hunter, 14 Apr; Welles to Du Pont, 11 Apr 1863. *ORN*, 123–24, 132–33.

4. Although the British Fortification Board recommended mutually supporting fortified systems in depth for the new English coast defenses in 1860, none of these systems were completed before 1870. See *British Parliamentary Papers*. Report and Minutes of Evidence of the Fortifications Board, 1860.

5. *Field, Fort, and Fleet*, p. 163; also see U.S. War Dept., Engineer Bureau. Report of the Board of Engineers appointed to consider modifications in United States seacoast defenses, submitted to the secretary of War, 31 May 1864. AGO, S.O., 41.

6. Confederates States of America. *Correspondence Relating to Fortification of Morris Island and Operations of Engineers* (Charleston, S.C., 1863), 43 pp.

7. Halleck to Banks, 18 Apr 1863. *ORA*, XV, 702.

8. 31 Aug 1863. *Chase Diaries*, pp. 180–83. Robert Greenhalgh Albion and Jennie Barnes Pope, *The Sea Lanes in Wartime*. 2nd ed. (Archon Books, 1968) pp. 150–73.

9. The monitors' inability to carry troops or Marines was another serious deficiency for operations against coastal batteries. See Du Pont to Wm. Whetten, 17 Mar 1863. *Du Pont Letters*, II, 489.

10. Fox to D. D. Porter, 16 Jul 1863. *Fox Correspondence*, II, 186.

11. Entries of 23 May and 6 Jun 1863. *Welles Diary*, I, 309, 324. Halleck to Banks, 9 Apr and 11 May; Halleck to Foster, 9 May 1863. *ORA*, XV, 700–01, 736; XVIII, 711. Fox to Du Pont (unofficial) 2 Apr 1863. *Du Pont Letters*, II, 538.

12. *ORA*, XIV, 459.

13. Hunter to Lincoln, 22 May 1863. *ORN*, 33; *ORA*, XIV, 455–57.

14. Jones, *Siege of Charleston*, p. 193.

15. Entry of 23 May 1863. *Welles Diary*, I, 309–10. Du Pont to Welles, 3 Jun 1863; *Du Pont Letters*, III, 158–59; *ORN*, 68–73.

16. Halleck to Gillmore, 28 Jul; Special Orders #249 (HQ, US Army) 3 Jun 1863. *ORA*, XIV, 464; XXVIII, Pt. II, 29–30.

17. Quincy A. Gillmore, *Engineer and Artillery Operations Against the Defences of Charleston Harbor in 1863* (New York, 1863) pp. 15–17. Gillmore to Halleck, 11 Oct 1863. *ORA*, Pt. II, 105.

18. Nichols, *Confederate Engineers*, p. 68. Beauregard's force had been reduced by half between 7 April and 10 July to reinforce other threatened points. Of the 5,861 infantry available for defending Charleston, 1,184 were stationed on James Island, 204 on Sullivan's Island, 612 on Morris Island, and 462 in the city. Johnston, *Defense of Charleston Harbor*, pp. 85–86. Reinforcements could be brought by rail from Savannah in a few hours. Gillmore based his calculations on this

fact and not on the number of troops permanently stationed on James Island. Report of Maj-Gen Gillmore, 28 Feb 1864. *ORA*, Pt. I, 4–5.

19. See Map 18.

20. Report of Cmdr P. Drayton, 17 Jun 1862. *ORN*, XIII, 104–05; *ORA*, XIV, 42–104; Hazard Stevens, "Military Operations in South Carolina in 1862," *Military History Society of Massachusetts Papers*, IX (1912) 134–54.

21. See Report of Maj-Gen Gillmore, 28 Feb 1864. *ORA*, Pt. I, 9. The evidence concerning this and other details of Gillmore's initial plan for seizing Morris Island is sketchy and somewhat confusing.

22. Journal Letter #73, 24 Jan 1863. *Du Pont Letters*, III, 183. Most of the ironclad captains shared Du Pont's view. See Drayton to A. Hamilton, 15 Apr 1863. *Drayton Letters*, p. 36; Ammen, *Atlantic Coast*, p. 115.

23. Journal Letter #74, 28 Jun 1863. *Du Pont Letters*, III, 187–88. Welles to Du Pont, 6 Jun and reply 29 Jun 1863. *ORN*, XIV, 298–99. Gillmore to Halleck, 30 Jun 1863. *ORA*, Pt. II, 7.

24. Gillmore to Du Pont, 26 Jun 1863. *ORN*, 298–99.

25. Report of Gen Beauregard, 18 Sep 1863. *ORA*, Pt. I, 69–71. Williams, *Beauregard*, pp. 185–86; G. T. Beauregard, "The Defense of Charleston", *B & L*, IV, 14. Johnson, *Defense of Charleston Harbor*, Appendix lxxvi; Jones, *War Clerk's Diary*, p. 261.

26. Robert C. Gilchrist, *The Confederate Defence of Morris Island* (Charleston, S.C., 1884) pp. 8–9.

27. *ORN*, 307; Journal Letter #73, 25 Jun 1863. *Du Pont Letters*, III, 183.

28. Dahlgren to Welles, 6 Jul 1863. *ORN*, 311.

29. See Map 20.

30. Dahlgren's instructions for the attack dated 9 Jul 1863. *ORN*, 317–18. Reports of Lt F. E. Town (Ch Sig Off) and Lt T. L. Hatfield, 11 Sep 1863. *ORA*, Pt. I, 45, 340.

31. Reports of Lt A. S. MacKenzie and Lt Cmdr F. M. Bunce, 12 Jul 1863. *ORN*, 327–28, 329–30. Reports of Lt-Col Meeker, 23 Feb 1864 and of Col R. F. Graham (CSA), 18 Jul 1863. *ORA*, Pt. I, 357, 413–14.

32. Report of Rear-Adm Dahlgren, 10 Jul 1863. *ORN*, 319–21. Report of Col Graham (CSA, Cmdg Morris Island) in Johnson, *Defense of Charleston Harbor*, Appendix, lxxi–lxxii. Reports of Brig-Gen R. S. Ripley (CSA) 22 Jul, and Lt-Col J. A. Yates (CSA, Cmdg Morris Is.) 17 Jul and 27 Nov 1863. *ORA*, Pt. I, 370–71, 527, 530.

33. Report of Brig-Gen Seymour, 1 Nov 1863. *ORA*, Pt. I, 344. Dahlgren to Welles, 28 Jul 1863, in U.S. Navy Dept., *Report of the Secretary of the Navy* (Washington, D.C., 1864) p. 269. Gillmore had made no arrangements with the fleet for fire support. Dahlgren knew nothing of the intended assault until two hours after it began, when he received the general's note asking the Navy to prevent enemy reinforcements reaching Wagner by shelling the ground in rear of the battery. *ORA*, Pt. II, 17.

34. Gillmore, *Engineer and Artillery Operations*, p. 35.

35. Reports of Brig-Gen Seymour, 10 Nov, and Brig-Gen W. B. Talia-

ferro (CSA, Cmdg Batty Wagner) 21 July 1863. *ORA*, Pt. I, 417–19. Q. A. Gillmore, "The Army Before Charleston in 1863," *B & L*, IV, 59; Johnson, *Defense of Charleston Harbor*, pp. 101–03; Report of Rear-Adm Dahlgren, 19 Jul 1863, in *Armored Vessels*, pp. 221–222. Wagner's garrison of 1,190 men sustained 181 casualties. The ten Federal regiments engaged (5,000 men) lost 246 killed, 880 wounded, and 389 taken prisoner. They attacked in battalion column and had been ordered to use only the bayonet. Report of Lt J. C. Abbott, 16 Aug 1863. *ORA*, Pt. I, 364–65.

36. Reports of Brig-Gen Turner (Ch of Arty) 8 Sep and 3 Nov 1863. *Ibid.*, pp. 212–19, 219–24.

37. Gillmore, *Engineer and Artillery Operations*, pp. 44–45.

38. Dahlgren to Welles, 21 Jul 1863. *ORN*, 380.

39. Welles to Dahlgren, 24 and 28 Jul, and reply 6 Aug; Instructions for the Marine Regiment, 7 Aug 1863. *ORN*, 395, 401, 428, 428–29. Report of Col L. M. Keitt (CSA) 8 Aug 1863. *ORA*, Pt. I, 446.

40. Dahlgren to Gillmore, 20 Jul 1863. *ORA*, Pt. II, 466; Same to same, 8 Aug; Report to Maj Zeilin (Cmdg Marine battalion) 13 Aug 1863. *ORN*, 430, 439–40.

41. Gillmore to Halleck, 30 Aug; Report of Col A. Rhett (CS Arty, cmdg Ft. Sumter) 4 Sep 1863. *ORA*, Pt. I, 601–02, 621. Seventy-five percent of the 7,180 projectiles fired struck the wall at some point. Tabular statement of shots fired against Fort Sumter, 17 Aug to 1 Sep 1863. *ORA*, Pt. I, 648.

42. G. J. Rains (CSA) to Jones, 2 Sep 1863, in Jones, *War Clerk's Diary*, p. 268. These land mines were invented by General Rains and were first used in the defense of Yorktown in April 1862. For a detailed account of the siege of Battery Wagner, see reports and Journal of Maj Thomas Brooks (USA), Asst Engineer. *ORA*, Pt. I, 264–335.

43. Gillmore, *Engineer and Artillery Operations*, pp. 53–56, 67–70; Report of Capt C. E. Chichester (CSA, Ch of Arty) 16 Aug; Gillmore to Dahlgren, 5 and 23 Aug 1863. *ORA*, Pt. I, 515–16; Pt. II, 37, 56. Alfred P. Rockwell, "The Operations Against Charleston", *Miltary History Society of Massachusetts Papers*, IX, 182–83. Viktor von Scheliha in his *Treatise on Coast-Defense* (London, 1868, pps. 32–33 points out that *Ironsides* 11-inch smoothbores did most of the damage. Of the 2,864 shot and shell fired from the rifled land batteries on 5 and 6 September, 1,200 struck the bombproof; 1,400 struck the parapet and traverses, but these structures remained intact.

44. Report of Gen Beauregard, 18 Sep; Report of Ordnance at Fort Sumter and where shipped, dated 5 Sep; Beauregard to Cooper (AG, CSA) 6 Sep 1863. *ORA*, Pt. I, 88, 622; Pt. II, 342. Williams, *Beauregard*, p. 190; Johnson, *Defense of Charleston Harbor*, pp. 108–111. Dahlgren to Gillmore, 27 Aug 1863. *ORN*, 446–47.

45. Dahlgren to Du Pont, 12 Mar 1863. *Du Pont Letters*, II, 505, note 4; Rbt. Danby (Fleet Eng) to Cmdr Wm. Reynolds, 22 Aug; Dahlgren to Welles, 8 and 24 Sept 1863. *ORN*, 471, 592, 596–97, 671–72.

46. *ORN*, 468; Gillmore to Dahlgren (signals), 10 A.M. and 2:35 P.M., 22 Aug 1863. *ORA*, Pt. II, 54.

47. Report of Brig-Gen Jordan, Addenda #2, 12 Jul; T. Jordan (COS) to Taliaferro (CSA) 24 Jul 1863. *ORA*, Pt. I, 60–62; Pt. II, 394–95.

48. Dahlgren to Welles, 6 Aug 1863. *ORN*, 428. There were no mines on the obstructions in 1863. For a detailed description of the barrier, see Johnson, *Defence of Charleston Harbor*, pp. 29–30. Commander Ammen in the monitor *Patapsco* reconnoitered these obstructions in a rowboat on the night of 22 September, cutting a piece away for further examination. Although Ammen found no contact mines and told Dahlgren the fleet could go in safety at any time, he thought the Confederates had probably laid electric mines in the channel. Ammen. *Old Navy and New*, pp. 376–77. On 21 August the Confederate engineers laid two rows of mines in the inner harbor between Castle Pinckney and Fort Ripley but none between Sumter and Moultrie. Lt G. T. Cox (CSA) to Jordan (COS). *ORA*, Pt. II, 300.

49. *Du Pont Letters*, III, 3, 14, 17, 28; Dahlgren to Gillmore, 29 Aug 1863. *ORA*, Pt. II, 69–70. Dahlgren to Welles, 21 Jul and 2 Sep 1863. *ORN*, 380, 532.

50. Ensign M. L. Johnson to Dahlgren, 7 Sep 1863. *ORN*, 548.

51. Beauregard to Cooper (AG), telegram, 9 Sep; Report of Gen Ripley, 22 Sep 1863. *Ibid.*, pp. 636, 760; Thomas H. Stevens, "The Boat Attack on Sumter," *B & L*, IV, 50. Captain Belknap, *Ironsides'* executive officer, pointed out that the Federal boats filled with sailors and Marines crossed the bar before dark in full view of Sumter's garrison, further alerting the enemy. George E. Belknap, "Reminiscences of the Siege of Charleston," *Military History Society of Massachusetts Papers*, XII (1902) pp. 188–89.

52. Extract from Dahlgren diary, dated 8 Sep; Reports of Maj Elliott (CSA, Cmdg Ft. Sumter) 9 and 12 Sep 1863. *ORN*, 635–39. Report of Lt-Cmdr Williams (USN) 27 Sep 1863. *Report of the Secretary of the Navy* (1864) pp. 236–37.

53. See signals exchanged between Gillmore and Dahlgren, 8 Sep 1863, in Gillmore, *Engineer and Artillery Operations*, Appendix G, 339.

54. *Ibid.*

55. Halleck to Gillmore, 13 Sep; General Order of 15 Sep 1863. *ORA*, Pt. II, 28, 94: S. W. Preston to Du Pont, 3 Aug 1863. *Du Pont Letters*, III, 215–16. Gillmore's Chief of Artillery, Brigadier General J. W. Turner, thought that the object of the campaign had been simply to close the port and that, having accomplished this by commanding the city wharves with artillery, the Federals had rendered Charleston of no further strategic value to the Confederacy. Turner to Butler, 18 Sep 1863. *Butler Correspondence*, III, 114.

56. Report of Rear-Adm Dahlgren, in *Report of the Secretary of the Navy* (1864) p. 242.

57. Gillmore to Halleck, 12 Nov 1863. *ORA*, Pt. I, 604–05. Dahlgren

to Gillmore, 26 and 29 Sep, and replies, 27 and 30 Sep 1863. Gillmore, *Engineer and Artillery Operations*, Appendix G, 339–46.

58. Gillmore to Halleck, 15 Oct and 17 Dec 1863. *ORA*, Pt. II, 107, 130.

59. For an account of this operation, see E. Milby Burton, *The Siege of Charleston, 1861–1865* (Columbia, S.C., 1970) pp. 285–87.

60. Dahlgren to Welles, 6, 11, 12, 22, and 26 Aug; 10, 11, 12, 28 and 29 Sep 1863. *ORN*, 428, 435–36, 470, 523, 641, 643–44, 679, 680–81. Ammen, *Atlantic Coast*, p. 160.

61. Ammen, *Old Navy and New*, p. 377.

62. Entries of 10 Jun, 19 Jul, and 17 Aug 1864. *Welles Diary*, II, 52–53, 81–82, 108. Shipyard strikes that winter contributed to the delay. Lincoln to Stanton (private) 21 Dec 1863. *ORA*, Pt. II, 134.

CHAPTER 11

1. West, *Welles*, p. 289; Seymour to Sen Ira Harris, 12 Jan 1864. *ORA*, LIII, 95–98; *Butler's Book*, pp. 582–83; *JCR* (1863) I. 65.

2. Banks to Halleck, 30 Jul and 1 Aug 1863. *ORA*, XXVI, Pt. I, 661, 666; Long, *Grant Memoirs*, pp. 303, 310–11, 360.

3. Harrington, *Fighting Politician*, p. 151; Thomas and Hyman, *Stanton*, p. 284. Entries of 9 and 23 Jun 1863. *Welles Diary*, I, 387–89. Halleck to Banks, 24 and 31 Jul, 10 and 12 Aug; Lincoln to Stanton, 29 Jul; Lincoln to Grant, 9 Aug 1863. *ORA*, XXVI, Pt. I, 652–53, 659, 664, 673, 675; XXIV, Pt. III, 584

4. Halleck to Banks, 10 Aug; Banks to Halleck, 15 and 26 Aug; Banks to Porter, 28 Aug and reply, 4 Sep 1863. *ORA*, XXVI, Pt. I, 673, 682–83, 695–97, 699, 715–16.

5. Halleck to Banks, 30 Sep and 7 Dec 1863; Banks to Halleck, 16 Oct (two letters); Banks to Meigs, 3 Nov; 1863. *Ibid.*, pp. 742, 767–68, 785, 834–35.

6. Porter to Fox, 26 Oct 1863. *Fox Correspondence*, II, 193–94. Porter to Welles, 2 Dec 1863. *Report of the Secretary of the Navy* (1864) p. 543.

7. For the extensive correspondence exchanged between the principals of this expedition, see *JCR* (1865) II, xvii–xxxii; also pp. 127–56.

8. The best source for the details of this expedition is *Ibid.*, pp. 175–401. The official records are incomplete.

9. Entry of 9 May 1864. *Welles Diary*, II, 27. Trefousse, *Wade*, pp. 207–08.

10. Sherman to Comstock (ADC) 5 Apr 1864. *JCR* (1866) I, 25–26; *ORA*, Atlas, Plate CXXXV-A. For some reason, this map has been universally interpreted to claim that, even at this early date, Grant intended, or at least foresaw, Sherman's famous "march to the sea." More than a cursory glance at it, however, reveals that Atlanta (circled), not Savannah, was the objective and that the line must represent movement in the opposite direction, *away* from the coast. The other lines on this map are rarely discussed, apparently on the assumption that they mean

nothing. On 19 January 1864 Grant told General Thomas that he was opposed to marching an army on Richmond from Washington, preferring to throw 60,000 men on Raleigh via Suffolk, opening communications with the coast further south through Wilmington and New Berne. The same day he advised Halleck that, were he given command of the Army of the Potomac as rumored, he would base it on Fort Monroe, striking Wilmington and New Berne directly by seaborne operations. *ORA*, XXXII, Pt. II, 143; XXXIII, 394–95.

11. Ambrose, *Halleck*, pp. 160–61.

12. Sherman to Grant, 10 Mar 1864. *JCR* (1866) I, 15.

13. West, *Butler*, p. 229. The government could hardly say no to the enterprising Butler who, once again, had practically raised his own army, enlisting and outfitting Negro regiments, Southern deserters, even prisoners of war. Although only ordered to seize a base on the James, Butler and Grant hoped this army might take Richmond quickly while Lee opposed Grant north of the city. A month before Grant's appointment, Butler had opposed Halleck's plan to move the Army of the Potomac from Fredericksburg upon Richmond, instead advocating the James River line for both armies. On 11 February he wrote Representative George Boutwell that he could see no sense in landing any army at Aquia "to march over a land route intersected by five rivers—150 miles—necessitating a land carriage of supplies that distance for the purpose of getting within twenty miles of the swamp side of Richmond," when this same army could disembark "without opposition on the James within 20 miles of Richmond, with a water carriage which allows them to be brought from New York without transshipment to a high, dry, cultivated land" between Fort Monroe and Richmond. "Until I am instructed on this point by the forthcoming work on military science by the General-in-Chief of the Army [Halleck]," he sarcastically remarked, "I shall remain unconvinced of the superior feasibility of the present [overland] route to Richmond." *Butler Correspondence*, III, 405–06.

14. Grant to Sherman, 4 Apr 1864. *JCR* (1866) I, 26–27. Halleck to McClellan, 13 Sep 1862. *ORA*, XIX, Pt. I, 280.

15. Report of W. W. Wright (Ch. Eng, US Mil. RRs) 24 Apr 1866. *ORA*, Ser. III, Vol. V, 952; Turner, *Victory Rode the Rails*, pp. 353–54.

16. Butler referred to a plan of Grant's to move his whole force against Wilmington instead of Richmond in a letter to the Lieutenant General dated 15 April 1864, but mentioned no details. This plan was apparently squelched by Halleck. *Butler Correspondence*, IV, 76.

17. Ambrose, *Halleck*, pp. 176–78.

18. Farragut and Major General E. R. S. Canby, who succeeded Banks at New Orleans, planned to move 20,000 men against the city in October. But again, Halleck got his way and Canby's force was dispatched to Missouri to repel an "invasion" by General Price. Grant, his hands full with his own operations, did not attempt to "interfere." Thus, the port intended to supply Sherman's army once it had reached Atlanta remained in Confederate hands until after Lee's surrender.

19. For details of the combined operations against Mobile, see *ORA*, XXXIX, Pt. I, 402–57; *ORN*, XXI, 397–601; *B & L*, IV, 379–413; Mahan, *Gulf and Inland Waters*, pp. 218–251.

20. Report of Lt-Cmdr W. B. Cushing of Reconnaissance of Wilmington Harbor dated 23 Jun 1864. *Report of the Secretary of the Navy* (1864) p. 213; Lee to Welles, 6 Aug and 8 Sep; Welles to Lee, 3 and 17 Sep; Seddon to Lee (CSA), 23 Sep; Whiting to Gov Vance (N.C.) 26 Sep; Whiting to Mallory, 6 Oct; Mallory to Davis, 22 Oct 1864. *ORA*, LI, Pt. II, 1042–43; *ORN*, X, 338–39, 419, 441–44, 467, 750–51, 774–75, 793–94.

21. Whiting to Beauregard, 31 Aug; Seddon to Whiting, 5 Sep; Whiting to Lee, 26 Sep, endorsed by Lee 5 Oct to Seddon, 6 Oct; Whiting to Mallory, 27 Sep 1864. *ORA*, XLII, Pt. I, 1212–13, 1236–37, 1294–95, 1297; Don C. Seitz, *Braxton Bragg, General of the Confederacy* (Columbia, S.C., 1924) pp. 462–66.

22. Welles to Lincoln, 25 Oct; Halleck to Stanton, 6 Jan 1864. *ORN*, XI, 4; IX, 386–87. Merrill, "Strategy Makers in the Union Navy Department," p. 30; Jones, *Civil War at Sea*, III, 263–68. Entry of 30 Aug 1864. *Welles Diary*, II, 127–28. Stanton to Grant, 1 Sep 1864. *ORA*, XLII, Pt. I, 624. Halleck to Grant, 1 Sep 1864. *Halleck Telegrams*, II, 273; Ambrose, *Halleck*, p. 179.

23. Fox to Grant, 4 Jan 1865. *Butler Correspondence*, V, 465–66. Gillmore to Halleck, referred to Grant on 10 Sep 1864. *ORA*, XLII, Pt. I, 731–34.

24. Grant to Fox, 19 Sep 1864; Testimony of Maj-Gen Weitzel, 7 Feb 1865. *JCR* (1865) II, 67, 216.

25. Fox to Grant, 3 Sep; Welles to Farragut, 5 Sep; Farragut to Welles, 22 Sep and reply, 1 Oct 1864. *ORN*, X, 418, 430–31; XXI, 655–56. Grant to Fox, 3 Sep 1864. *ORA*, XLII, Pt. I, 674. Spears, *Farragut*, pp. 346–47.

26. Porter to Fox (private) 15 Oct 1864. Merrill, "Fort Fisher and Wilmington Campaign," pp. 464–65; Grant to Butler, 30 Nov 1864. *Butler Correspondence*, V, 371. Testimony of Maj-Gen Butler, 17 Jan 1865. *JCR* (1865) II, 6.

27. Grant to Butler, 6 Dec; J. W. Turner (COS) to Weitzel, 6 Dec 1864. *ORA*, XLII, Pt. I, 971–73. The expedition carried only field rations and 160 rounds of small arms ammunition per man.

28. Grant's instructions to Butler, 6 Dec 1864. *Ibid.*; *Butler's Book*, p. 782; For Butler's instructions to Weitzel, see *JCR* (1865) II, 9.

29. West, *Porter*, p. 279. It was otherwise with Weitzel. This dour engineer had been on the outs with the flamboyant Porter since the New Orleans operations, which was one reason Butler went in personal command. See testimony of Maj-Gen Butler, 17 Jan 1865. *JCR* (1865) II, 11.

30. Butler to Porter, 6 Dec 1864. *Butler Correspondence*, V, 383. Testimony of Capt J. Alden (*Brooklyn*) 23 Jan 1865. *JCR* (1865) II, 64; Porter to Fox (private) 19 Oct 1864 and 7 Jan 1865. Merrill, "Fort Fisher and Wilmington Campaign," pp. 465–69.

31. Contrast this system with that used at Charleston and Mobile, which were important industrial and communications centers in addition to their value as ports of entry.

32. *ORA*, XLVI, Pt. I, 406–09; Barrett, *Civil War in North Carolina*, pp. 265–66.

33. Detailed report of Col Lamb (Cmdg Ft. Fisher) 27 Dec 1864. *ORN*, XI, 369. Johnson Hagood (CSA), *Memoirs of the War of Secession* (Columbia, S.C., 1910) p. 322.

34. *Lyman Letters*, p. 284.

35. Philip Van Dorn Stern, *The Confederate Navy: A Pictorial History* (Garden City, New York, 1962) p. 203. Testimony of Lt-Gen Grant, 11 Feb 1865. *JCR* (1865) II, 51–56. Report of Major T. L. Casey (US Eng) 29 Dec 1864. *ORA*, XLII, Pt. I, 993. The latter explosion levelled everything for twenty acres around.

36. Fox to Porter, 16 Nov 1864. *ORN*, XI, 68. From a careful examination of the records, it would seem that Porter initiated the project to compensate for the absence of troops and probably suggested it to Fox immediately after a conference at Grant's HQ on 12 November, during which Grant again refused to detach troops for an expedition against Wilmington. *Ibid.*, 79,

37. Porter to Fox, 20 Nov; Fox to Butler, 22 Nov; Porter to Cmdr W. H. Macomb, 23 Nov 1864. *ORN*, XI, 79, 81, 83. Butler to Porter and reply, 26 Nov 1864. *ORA*, XLVII, Pt. III, 715.

38. Delafield to T. Casey, 8 Dec 1864. *Ibid.*, pp. 863–64; Report of Gen R. Delafield, 18 Nov 1864. *JCR* (1865) II, 217–23.

39. Fox to Butler, 24 Nov; Porter to Butler, 25 Nov, and reply 26 Nov 1864. *ORN*, XI, 90, 95, 96. Maj J. G. Benton to Wise, 18 Nov; Jeffers to Wise, 23 Nov; Memorandum of discussion dated 23 Nov 1864. *JCR* (1865) II, 223–26.

40. Grant to Porter, 30 Nov and 2 Dec; Porter to Grant, 30 Nov 1864. *ORA*, XLVII, Pt. III, 750, 767. Porter to Fox, 2 Dec 1864. *ORN*, XI, 119.

41. Grant to Butler, 30 Nov, 4, 7, and 11 Dec; Butler to Porter and reply, 6 Dec 1864. *ORA*, XLVII, Pt. III, 760, 799, 836–37, 973, 974. Grant to Butler, 4 and 6 Dec 1864. *Butler Correspondence*, V, 379, 382. Butler to Porter, 4 Dec 1864. *ORN*, XI, 135. Testimony of Maj-Gen Butler, 17 Jan 1865. *JCR* (1865) II, 30.

42. *JCR* (1865) II, 229.

43. Testimony of Capt Wise. *Ibid.*, pp. 228–242.

44. Porter to Butler, 13 and 16 Dec 1864. *ORN*, XI, 191, 196. Porter to Butler, 13 Dec 1864. *Butler Correspondence*, V, 410. Testimony of Maj-Gen Weitzel, 7 Feb 1865. *JCR* (1865) II, 69.

45. Porter to Butler, 18 Dec 1864. *JCR* (1865) II, 18.

46. Testimony of Bvt Brig-Gen Comstock. *Ibid.*, pp. 82–87.

47. Porter to Rhind, 19 Dec; Porter to Cmdr Watmough, 23 Dec 1864. *ORN*, XI, 224, 225.

48. Porter to Rhind, 17 Dec 1864. *Ibid.*, pp. 222–223.

49. Report of Maj T. L. Casey, 29 Dec 1864. *ORA*, XLII, Pt. I, 988–91. Porter to Rhind, 17 and 23 Dec 1864. *ORN*, XI, 222–23, 225–26.

50. Report of Cmdr Rhind. *ORN*, XI, 226–27. Letter of Gen Whiting. *JCR* (1865) II, 106–07.

51. Maj T. J. Rodman (US Army Ordnance) to Capt Wise, 27 Jan 1865. *ORN*, XI, 236–37. Memorandum of W. N. Jeffers, Inspector of Ordnance, to Rear-Adm Porter, 14 Feb 1865. *JCR* (1865) II, 255.

52. Lamb to Maj Hill (ADC) 24 Dec 1864. *ORN*, XI, 362. Lee to Seddon, 24 Dec 1864. *ORA*, XLII, Pt. III, 1301. Whiting to Butler, 28 Feb 1865. *JCR* (1865) II, 105–06.

53. The Confederates thought this the most practicable alternative for the Federals. In fact, Whiting expected not only an attempt to run vessels into the river, but a night landing from small boats in the rear of Fisher, a contingency which, he claimed, would have led to the immediate surrender of the fort. *ORN*, XI, 360–61.

54. Porter to COs *Monadnock, Canonicus,* and *Mahopac,* 17 Dec 1864; Report of Acting Master C. Pettit, 24 Jan 1865. *ORN*, XI, 197, 198. Butler to Grant, 20 Dec 1864. *ORA*, XLVII, Pt. III, 1049

55. Report of Rear-Adm Porter, 27 Dec; Porter to Welles, 21 Dec 1864. *ORN*, XI, 261, 266–67.

56. Testimony of Rear-Adm Porter, 7 Mar 1865. *JCR* [1865] II, 87–104.

57. General Orders #40, NABSq, 10 Dec 1864, with fire diagram. *ORN*, XI, 245–47. The fleet consisted of the *New Ironsides*, four monitors, and about fifty other vessels, carrying a total of 619 guns. For the December attack these were organized into an ironclad division, two divisions of unarmored ships, and a reserve squadron. The 1st Division had the greatest firepower.

58. Report of Rear-Adm Porter, 26 Dec. Detailed report of Col Lamb (Cmdg Ft. Fisher) 27 Dec 1864. *ORN*, XI, 256, 366–67; Ammen; *Old Navy and New*, p. 404.

59. M. Long (Ord Sgt) to Lamb, 25 Dec 1864. *ORN*, XI, 370. Answers of Maj-Gen Whiting to questions of Maj-Gen Butler, 22 Feb 1865. *ORA*, XLII, Pt. I, 979.

60. William Lamb, "The Defence of Fort Fisher, North Carolina," *Military History Society of Massachusetts Papers*, Vol. IX (1912, pp. 349–88) pp. 365–66.

61. The compilers of the naval records give a figure of 20,271 projectiles fired during the first attack, and 19,682 during the second, but the absence of reports from many vessels and incompleteness of the logbooks make it impossible to arrive at such an exact total. See *ORN*, XI, 441, note. Lieutenant Aeneus Armstrong, manning the naval battery in Fort Fisher, remarked after the bombardment that "you can now inspect the whole works and walk on nothing but iron." *Ibid.*, p. 375.

62. Porter to Welles, 24 Dec 1964; Reports of Cmdr E. Calhoun (*Saugus*) and Capt B. Sands (*Fort Jackson*). *ORN*, XI, 253, 276–77, 332.

63. Testimony of Maj-Gen Butler, 17 Jan 1865. *JCR* (1865) II, 21.

64. Testimony of Maj-Gen Weitzel, 7 Feb 1865. *Ibid.*, pp. 70–73; Butler to Porter, 24 Dec 1864 (10 P.M.). *ORA*, XLVII, Pt. III, 1072.

65. Report of Maj-Gen Weitzel, 31 Jan 1865. *ORA*, XLII, Pt. I, 985–87.

66. Porter to Butler, 24 Dec (signal); Butler to Porter, 25 Dec 1864. *ORN*, XI, 249–50.

67. All of the naval reports mention the ammunition shortage in the fleet. Some gunboats had only enough for one hour's firing.

68. Report of Lt R. H. Lamson, 26 Dec 1864. *ORN*, XI, 345–46.

69. *Butler's Book*, p. 791; Report of Rear-Adm Porter, 26 Dec 1864. *Ibid.*, 257.

70. Detailed report of Rear-Adm Porter, 25 Dec 1864. *ORN*, XI, 258.

71. Reports of Col Lamb (CSA) 27 Dec; Lt R. Chapman (CSN, Cmdg Batty Buchanan) 29 Dec, and Lt F. Roby (CSN, Cmdg Brooke Batty) 29 Dec 1864. *ORN*, XI, 366–69, 372–73, 373–74. The Union reports do not mention damages, or even admit that the ships were fired at.

72. Report of Lt-Cmdr W. Truxton, 27 Dec 1864. *Ibid.*, p. 334.

73. Abstract log of the *Colorado* and the *Minnesota*. *Ibid.*, pp. 296–97, 303–04.

74. Testimony of Rear-Adm Porter, 7 Mar 1865. *JCR* (1865) II, 87–104. Reports of Brig-Gen Ames and Bvt Brig-Gen Curtis, 28 Dec 1864. *ORA*, XLII, Pt. I, 980–84.

75. Testimony of Bvt Brig-Gen Comstock. *JCR* (1865) II, 82–87. Adelbert Ames, "The Capture of Fort Fisher," *Military History Society of Massachusetts Papers*, IX (1912) pp. 396–97.

76. Report of Maj-Gen Weitzel, 31 Dec 1864. *ORA*, XLII, Pt. I, 985–87.

77. Testimony of Maj-Gen Butler, 17 Jan 1865. *JCR* (1865) II, 23.

78. Porter to Commo W. Radford (*Ironsides*) 25 Dec 1864. *ORN*, XI, 252. The reports reaching Butler were somewhat exaggerated. Kirkland's Brigade of this division arrived in Wilmington at midnight on the 23rd and at Sugar Loaf at 4:30 P.M. on the 24th, from which 500 men were sent into the fort that night. Hoke's other brigade, Hagood's, had left Petersburg on the 20th but, due to the broken-down condition of the railroads, did not reach Wilmington until the evening of the 26th. Report of Brig-Gen W. Kirkland (CSA) 30 Dec 1865. *ORA*, XLII, Pt. I, 1020–22. Hagood, *Memoirs*, pp. 315–16.

79. Butler to Grant, 3 Jan 1865. *Butler's Book*, Appendix pp. 1111–1116.

80. *Ibid.*, Butler to Porter, 25 Dec 1864. *Butler Correspondence*, V, 437–38.

81. Porter to Butler, 26 Dec 1864. *ORN*, XI, 250–52.

82. On 8 November, Porter had written Lieutenant Commander P. G. Watmough: "My calculations are that the explosion will wind up Fort Fisher and the works along the beach, and that we can open fire with the vessels without damage." *ORN*, XI, 217.

83. As though the delay were not sufficient to allow information to leak out, someone at Grant's HQ gave confidential details of the expedition to a free-lance correspondent who published a long article in the Philadelphia *Press* on 21 December giving the intended plan of attack

on Fort Fisher. *Welles Diary*, II, 205. Fox to Rodgers, 22 Dec 1864. *ORN*, XI, 205. Fox to Grant, 4 Jan 1865. *ORA*, XLVI, Pt. II, 29.

84. Testimony of Rear-Adm Porter, 7 Mar 1865. *JCR* (1865) II, 87–104. On 31 December he wrote Welles confidentially: "We all know very well that a fort on shore, unless attacked by troops at the same time ships are bombarding, will always hold out against the ships, that is, the enemy will leave the works (and let the ships fire away) and enter again when the ships have gone." *ORN*, XI, 277.

CHAPTER 12

1. *Lyman Letters*, pp. 296–97; Report of Brig-Gen L. C. Easton (QM), 16 Mar 1865, Annual report of the Chief Quartermaster, Mil. Div. of the Miss., 4 Oct 1864. *ORA*, Ser. III, Vol. V, 395, Ser. I, LII, Pt. I, 696–703. Bruce Catton, *Grant Takes Command* (Boston, 1968) pp. 391–92; Nicolay and Hay, *Lincoln*, X, 24–28.

2. Grant to Sherman, 6 Dec 1864. *ORA*, XLIV, 636.

3. Grant to Halleck, 15 Dec; Sherman to Grant, 16 Dec; Halleck to Sherman, 16 and 18 Dec; Sherman to Halleck, 13 Dec 1864. *ORA*, XLIV, 715, 727–28, 728–29, 741, 702. Also see James M. Merrill, *William Tecumseh Sherman* (New York, 1971) pp. 279–84.

4. Sherman to Grant, 22 and 24 Dec; Grant to Sherman, 18 Dec; Sherman to Halleck, 24 Dec 1864. *ORA*, XLIV, 6–7, 740–41, 797, 798–800.

5. See Grant to Sherman, 27 Dec 1864. *Ibid.*, pp. 820–21.

6. Stanton to Grant, 28 Dec 1864. *ORA*, XLVII, Pt. III, 1087. Fox to Grant and Welles to Grant, 29 Dec 1864. *ORN*, XI, 388, 391–92. Grant to Porter, 3 Jan 1865. *Butler Correspondence*, V, 457.

7. Ammen, *Old Navy and New*, p. 406. Ammen's views regarding the best mode of attack were reinforced by a letter from Welles on the 29th assuring Grant that "the Navy can assist in the siege of Fort Fisher precisely as it covered the operations which resulted in the capture of Fort Wagner." *ORA*, XLVII, Pt. III, 1091.

8. Grant to Porter, 3 Jan 1865. *Butler Correspondence*, V, 457. Grant to Terry, 3 Jan 1865. *ORA*, XLVI, Pt. II, 25. Grant to Terry, 3 Jan 1865. *ORN*, XI, 404.

9. Special Orders #2, HQ, US Army, 2 Jan 1865. *ORA*, XLV, Pt. II, 11. Testimony of Lt-Gen Grant, 11 Feb 1865. *JCR* (1865) II, 51–56

10. Grant to Stanton, 2 Jan 1865. *Butler Correspondence*, V, 456. Grant to Porter, 3 and 4 Jan 1865. *ORA*, XLVI, Pt. II, 19–20, 29–30. On 3 January Porter urged Grant to "send every man you can spare here, with entrenching tools and fifteen 30-pounders" because the Navy could not stop the Confederates from strengthening their defenses "without bringing the whole squadron into play and firing away all our ammunition before the time comes for work." *ORN*, XI, 405–06.

11. Comstock to Rawlins (COS) and Grant to Halleck, 9 Jan 1865. *ORA*, XLVI, Pt. II, 74, 79–80. Testimony of Lt-Gen Grant, 11 Feb 1865. *JCR* (1865) II, 51–56.

12. Porter to Grant, 3 Jan; Fox to Grant (confidential), 4 Jan 1865.

Ibid., pp. 20, 29; also see Porter to Commo H. A. Adams, 30 Dec 1864 and 6 Jan 1865; E. Mellach to Porter, 31 Dec 1864; General Orders #77, NABSq, 1 Jan 1865; Fox to Grant, 2 Jan; Grant to Terry, 3 Jan; Capt. J. M. Berrien to Porter, 5 Jan 1865. *ORN*, XI, 392, 398, 401, 403, 404, 411, 442, 443.

13. This judgment was based on the 1861 coast survey report. See Bache, "Notes on the Coast . . .," Sect. IV, 37, 45.

14. Report of Maj-Gen Terry. *ORA*, XLVI, Pt. I, 394–400.

15. Report of Brig-Gen Paine, 20 Jan 1865. *Ibid.*, pp. 423–24. Terry to Rawlins (COS), 13 Jan 1865. *Butler Correspondence*, V, 484.

16. Bragg to Hoke, 13 Jan (1 A.M.); Bragg to Lee, 13 Jan (2 P.M.) 1865. *ORA*, XLVI, Pt. II, 1044, 1046. William Lamb, "The Defense of Fort Fisher," *B & L*, IV, 649.

17. Terry to Brig-Gen H. L. Abbott (US Arty), 13 Jan; Bragg to Lee, 14 Jan 1865. *ORA*, XLVI, Pt. II, 123, 1053.

18. Report of Lt-Col Comstock. *Ibid.*, Pt. I, 406–07.

19. Grant to Terry, 3 Jan; Porter to Grant, 14 Jan 1865. *ORN*, XI, 404, 432.

20. Porter to Grant, 14 Jan 1865. *Ibid.*, p. 432.

21. von Scheliha, *Treatise on Coast-Defence*, pp. 164–165; General Orders #75 and #81, NABSq,. 30 Dec 1864 and 4 Jan 1865. *ORN*, XI, 252–53, 427. Porter to Fox, 7 Jan 1865. Merrill, "Fort Fisher and Wilmington Campaign", pp. 467–68; Thomas O. Selfridge, Jr., "The Navy at Fort Fisher", *B & L*, IV, 658.

22. Report of Maj-Gen Terry, 25 Jan 1865. *ORA*, XLVI, Pt. I, 394–400.

23. Orders of Rear-Adm Porter, 15 Jan 1865; Reports of Lt L. E. Fagan (USMC) and Capt L. L. Dawson (Cmdg Marine battalion). *ORN*, XI, 430, 516, 576–77.

24. See Maps 22 and 23.

25. Report of Lt-Col Comstock, 27 Jan 1865. *ORA*, XLVI, Pt. I, 407.

26. Report of Maj-Gen Terry. *Ibid.*, pp. 394–400.

27. Porter to Welles, 15 Jan 1865. *Ibid.*, Pt. II, 165–66. Detailed Report of Rear-Adm Porter, Porter to Welles, 17 Jan 1865. *ORN*, XI, 436–42, 445.

28. Report of Lt-Col Comstock, 27 Jan 1865. *ORA*, XLVI, Pt. I, 406–07. Reports of Cmdr E. G. Parrott (*Monadnock*), Lt-Cmdr G. E. Belknap (*Canonicus*), Capt James Alden (*Brooklyn*), and Lt-Cmdr R. Chandler (*Maumee*). *ORN*, XI, 462, 464, 468, 484.

29. Report of Cmdr J. C. Beaumont (*Mackinaw*). *ORN*, XI, 522.

30. Report of Lt-Cmdr Breese, 16 Jan 1865. *Ibid.*, p. 446.

31. Report of Lt Fagan, 15 Jan 1865. *Ibid.*, pp. 514–16.

32. Letter of Lt John Bartlett, 18 Jan 1865. *Ibid.*, p. 527.

33. Report of Lt-Cmdr Breese, 16 Jan; Report of Lt Fagan, 15 Jan 1865. *Ibid.*, pp. 446–48, 514–15.

34. Reports of Capt Dawson, Acting Ensigns G. C. Williams and G. H. Wood, 15 Jan 1865. *Ibid.*, pp. 576–77, 474–75, 552–54.

35. Report of Cmdr Breese, 16 Jan 1865. *ORN*, XI, 446–48.

36. Terry to Abbott, 14 Jan 1865. *ORA*, XLVI, Pt. II, 129.

37. Report of Col R. Daggett (117th N.Y.), 17 Jan 1865. *Ibid.*, Pt. I, 418–19.

38. Report of Maj-Gen Terry. *Ibid.*, pp. 394–400.

39. Report of Cmdr J. C. Howell (*Nereus*). *ORN*, XI, 488–89.

40. Report of Maj-Gen Terry, 15 Jan 1865. *Ibid.*, pp. 587–91.

41. *Ibid.*

42. Report of Lt-Cmdr Breese, 16 Jan 1865. *ORN*, XI, 446–48.

43. Reports of Lt-Cmdr Parker and Act Esgn Williams, 15 Jan 1865. *Ibid.*, 498, 474–75.

44. Lamb, "Defense of Fort Fisher," p. 650; Porter to Fox (confidential), 21 Jan 1865. Merrill, "Fort Fisher and Wilmington Campaign," p. 472.

45. Reports of Rear-Adm Porter, 15 and 17 Jan; Cmdr E. G. Parrott; Lt-Cmdr F. Sicard; Lt-Cmdr Parker; Lt-Cmdr Cuchman and Cmdr S. D. Trenchard (*Rhode Island*), 15 Jan 1865. *ORN*, XI, 434–35, 436–42, 462–63, 485, 495–99, 551–54, 557–58; Selfridge, "Navy at Fort Fisher," p. 658.

46. Lt R. H. Lamson to Cmdr A. C. Rhind, 16 Jan 1865; Report of Lt-Cmdr T. O. Selfridge. *Ibid.*, 450–51, 476–77.

47. Report of Lt Fagan; Report of Capt Dawson, 17 Jan 1865. *Ibid.*, pp. 516, 577–80. Another 500 arrived later that evening, the remainder of the survivors and wounded having returned to the ships.

48. See Lamb, "Defense of Fort Fisher," p. 650.

49. Report of Commo Radford (cmdg Ironclad Div.), 15 Jan; Minutes of O.B. McCurdy (Capt's Clerk, *Minnesota*), 15 Jan 1865. *ORN*, XI, 461–62, 492–93.

50. General Orders #78; 2 Jan; Special Orders #8, 3 Jan 1865. *Ibid.*, pp. 425–27, 427.

51. Detailed Report of Rear-Adm Porter, 17 Jan 1865; Reports of Capt J. Alden and Lt-Cmdr D. L. Braine (*Pequot*); Abstract log of *Unadilla*. *Ibid.*, pp. 436–42, 468, 476, 479; Ammen, *Atlantic Coast*, p. 231; Ames, "Capture of Fort Fisher", p. 402; Report of Maj Wm Saunders (CSA, Ch of Arty, 18 Jan 1865. *ORA*, XLVI, Pt. I, 437.

52. Report of Capt H. B. Essington, 17 Jan 1865. *Ibid.*, pp. 420–21. Lamb, "Defense of Fort Fisher," p. 651.

53. Letter from Col Comstock to Maj-Gen Rawlins (COS) dated 3 A.M., 16 Jan 1865. U.S. National Archives, R.G. 108; Reports of Brig-Gen Ames, 16 Jan, and Maj Saunders (CSA), 18 Jan 1865. *ORA*, XLVI, Pt. I, 416, 438.

54. Lamb, "Defense of Fort Fisher," p. 652; Report of Maj-Gen Whiting, 18 Jan 1865. *ORA*, XLVI, Pt. I, 399–400.

55. Detailed report of Rear-Adm Porter, 17 Jan; Porter to Commo Radford, 17 Jan 1865. *ORN*, XI, 436–42, 660.

56. Report of Brig-Gen Abbott, 17 Jan 1865. *ORA*, XLVI, Pt. I, 410. Lamb, "Defense of Fort Fisher", p. 652.

57. Report of Lt-Col G. T. Gordon (CSA), 17 Jan 1865. *ORA*, XLVI, Pt. I, 436. Reports of Capt D. B. Ridgley (*Shenandoah*) and Lt-Cmdr W. B. Cushing, 15 Jan 1865. *ORN*, XI, 539, 560.

58. Report of Col A. Rockwell (6th Conn.), 17 Jan; and Maj Saunders, 18 Jan 1865. *ORA*, XLVI, Pt. I, 411, 439.

59. See reports of Maj-Gen Whiting, 18 and 19 Jan 1865. *Ibid.*, pp. 440–41, 441–42; Bragg to Lee, 8 P.M., 14 Jan 1865, in Seitz, *Bragg*, p. 489.

60. Reports of Maj-Gen Whiting, 30 Dec 1864, and Brig-Gen L. Hébert, 3 Jan 1865. *ORA*, XLII, Pt. I, 993–97, 1000.

61. Dispatch quoted in Seitz, *Bragg*, pp. 490–91; also see Lee to Pres Davis, 15 Jan 1865. *Lee's Dispatches*, #179, pp. 316–18.

62. Report of Lt-Cmdr Cushing. *ORN*, XI, 560; Hagood, *Memoirs*, pp. 323–25.

63. Bragg to Gov Vance (N.C.), 8 P.M., 15 Jan; Reports to AAG Petersburg, 8 P.M., 15 Jan 1865. *ORA*, LXVI, Pt. II, 1061, 1062; Ammen, *Atlantic Coast*, pp. 236–37.

64. Report of Lt-Cmdr J. H. Upshur (*A. D. Vance*); Abstract logs of the *Aries, Wilderness,* and *Governor Buckingham. ORN*, XI, 568, 565, 566, 575. Report of Gen Bragg, 15 Jan 1865. *ORA*, XLVI, Pt. I, 431–35.

65. *Civil War Times Illustrated*, 3:5–9, 31–35 (August 1964). This is an excellent account of the second attack on Fisher, despite the omission of some important details discussed in this chapter.

66. Testimony of Rear-Adm Porter, 5 Mar 1865. *JCR* (1865) II, 87–104. Carrison, *Navy from Wood to Steel*, p. 134.

67. Halleck to Grant, 9, 16, and 25 Jan 1865. *Halleck Telegrams*, II, 328, 323, 339; Porter to Fox (confidential), 20 and 21 Jan 1865. Merrill, "Fort Fisher and Wilmington Campaign," pp. 469–71; Grant to Schofield, 31 Jan 1865. *ORA*, XLVI, Pt. I, 44–45. Grant to Ammen (personal), 4 Feb 1865, in *Old Navy and New*, Appendix, pp. 532–33.

68. Reports of Lt-Col J. E. Remington, 1 Jul, and Capt H. M. Whittelsey (QM), 21 Mar 1865. *ORA*, Ser. III, Vol. V, 413–20, 427–30. Hagood, *Memoirs* p. 333.

69. *ORA*, XLVI, Pt. I, 44–45.

70. Davis, *Confederate Government*, II, 630–31.

71. *Ibid.*, pp. 648–55; Bragg to Beauregard, 25 Feb 1865, in Seitz, *Bragg*, p. 518. In his report of 22 July 1865, General Grant wrote: "At this time [March] the greatest source of uneasiness to me was the fear that the enemy would leave his strong lines about Petersburg and Richmond for the purpose of uniting with Johnston, before he was driven from them by battle or I was prepared to make an effectual pursuit." *ORA*, XLVI, Pt. I, 50.

72. L. B. Northrop (CSA, Comm-Gen) to Seddon, 11 Jan 1865. *ORA*, XLVI, Pt. II, 1035. Edward Younger (ed.), *Inside the Confederate Government: The Diary of Robert Garlick Hill Kean* (New York, 1957), p. 204.

73. Davis, *Confederate Government*, II, 648.

74. *Kean Diary*, pp. 213–15. As early as the summer of 1863, the eastern railroads were too worn-out and inefficient to transport the abundant food and stores in the Carolinas, Georgia, and Tennessee to Lee's army. By December 1864, it took almost as long for troops to move

over these roads than if they marched the same distance with wagon transport. Turner, *Victory Rode the Rails*, pp. 267, 343–44, 368–70.

75. Reports of Brig-Gen D. C. McCallum (Mgr, US Mil RRs), 8 Feb, and W. W. Wright (Ch Eng), 24 Apr 1866. *ORA*, Ser. III, Vol. V, 589, 970.

76. Johnston, *Narrative*, pp. 378–81. Report of Col. M. C. Garber, (QM), 10 Jul 1865. *ORA*, LIII, 49–59. Seitz, *Bragg*, pp. 509–10; Hagood, *Memoirs*, p. 355.

77. The Southerners expected Grant to employ Sherman's army as a waterborne force. P. W. Alexander warned General Bragg on 2 December 1864 that the Federals seemed to be adopting a new and far more dangerous strategy against which the Confederacy had no defense. "For four years the enemy has tried to penetrate the Confederacy from the north and east by land. He reached Atlanta it is true but found it impossible to keep open his communications, since the further he advanced the longer and more difficult of defense became his base and line of communication. This policy, it now appears, has been changed. Hereafter he will operate from the sea or some of its tributaries. This makes his lease safe, and renders it easy to protect his short communications." He also warned Bragg not to allow the garrisons of Savannah and Charleston to be cut off from the army in Virginia. *ORA*, XLVI, 923–24.

SELECTED BIBLIOGRAPHY

The last three sections of the following list include publications not cited but especially useful to students of Civil War combined operations. Standard theoretical works are listed for nonspecialists. Only a few of the large number of general histories of the war provide a satisfactory introduction to the subject and most of those are non-analytical. The early books do contain information based on personal interviews and observations not found elsewhere. Reference volumes in Section VI are of high quality and of constant benefit to researchers in all areas of Civil War history. A fairly extensive grasp of the technology of the period is indispensable to an accurate assessment of operations or operational capability. A selection of the best technical books, manuals, and treatises—neglected by historians—has therefore been included. Because the number of Civil War sources, both primary and secondary, is so enormous, no attempt has been made to compile a balanced list. Except for the special categories indicated, this bibliography contains only works referred to in the notes.

I. DOCUMENTS AND OFFICIAL RECORDS

Agassiz, George R., ed. *Meade's Headquarters, 1863–1865; Letters of Colonel Theodore Lyman.* Boston: Massachusetts Historical Society, 1922.

Basler, Roy P., ed. *The Collected Works of Abraham Lincoln.* 10 vols. New Brunswick, N.J.: Rutgers University Press, 1953.

"Confidential Correspondence of James Gordon Bennett." *American Historical Review.* 39:284–91 [October 1933].

Confederate States of America. *Correspondence Relating to Fortification of Morris Island and Operations of Engineers.* Charleston, S.C., 1863.

Confederate States of America. *Statutes at Large of the Provisional Government of the Confederate States of America.* Volume I. Richmond: R. N. Smith, 1864.

Confederate States of America. Congress. *Report of evidence taken before a joint special committee of both Houses of the Confederate Congress, to investigate affairs of the Navy Department.* P. Kean, reporter. Richmond: G. P. Evans and Co., 1863.

Confederate States of America. War Department. *Proceedings of the*

Court of Inquiry Relative to the Fall of New Orleans. Richmond, 1864.

Donald, David, ed. *Inside Lincoln's Cabinet: The Civil War Diaries of Salmon P. Chase.* New York: Longmans, Green, and Co., 1954.

Dowdey, Clifford, ed. *The Wartime Papers of R. E. Lee.* Boston: Little, Brown and Co., 1961.

Drayton, Percival. *Naval Letters from Captain Percival Drayton, 1861–1865.* New York: Public Library, 1906.

Ford, Worthington Chauncey, ed. *A Cycle of Adams Letters, 1861–1865.* 2 vols. London: Constable, 1931.

Fremantle, James A. L. *The Fremantle Diary.* ed. by Walter Lord. Boston: Little, Brown and Co., 1854.

Goldsborough, Louis M. "Narrative of Rear Admiral Goldsborough, U.S. Navy." *United States Naval Institute Proceedings.* 59:1023–31 [1933].

Great Britain. *Parliamentary Papers.* Reports of the Fortifications Board, 1860 and 1869, with Minutes of Evidence.

Hayes, John D., ed. *Samuel Francis Du Pont: A Selection from his Civil War Letters.* 3 vols. Ithaca, N.Y.: Cornell University Press, 1969.

Jones, John B. *A Rebel War Clerk's Diary.* ed. by Earl Schenck Miers. New York: Sagamore Press, 1958.

Lee, Robert E. *Lee's Dispatches, 1862–1865.* ed by Douglas Southall Freeman: new edition by Grady McWhiney. New York: Putnam's, 1957.

McClellan, George B. *Report on the Organization and Campaigns of the Army of the Potomac.* New York: Sheldon and Company, 1864.

Marshall, J. A. copyrighter. *Private and Official Correspondence of Gen. Benjamin F. Butler.* 5 vols. Norwood, Mass.: Privately Printed, 1917.

Merrill, James M. "The Fort Fisher and Wilmington Campaign: Letters from Rear Admiral David D. Porter." *North Carolina Historical Review.* 35:461–75.

Simon, John Y., ed. *The Papers of Ulysses S. Grant.* 5 vols. Carbondale: Southern Illinois University Press, 1967–1973.

Thompson, Robert Means, ed. *Confidential Correspondence of Gustavus Vasa Fox, Assistant Secretary of the Navy, 1861–1865.* 2 vols. New York: Naval History Society, 1919.

United States Army. *Telegrams Sent by Major Gen. H. W. Halleck.* 10 vols. Washington, D.C.: Government Printing Office, 1877.

United States. Congress. *Report of the Joint Committee on the Conduct of the War.* 3 vols. Washington, D.C.: Government Printing Office, 1863.

United States. Congress. *Report of the Joint Committee on the Conduct of the War.* 3 vols. and Supplement [1866]. Washington, D.C.: Government Printing Office, 1865.

United States. Congress. *Reports of the U.S. Military Commission to Europe, 1855–1856.* Washington, D.C.: Government Printing Office, 1857–60.

United States. Congress. Joint Committee on the Conduct of the War. *Report on Heavy Ordnance.* Washington, D.C.: Government Printing Office, 1865.

United States. Department of Commerce. *Military and Naval Service of the United States Coast Survey, 1861–1865. Official Letters and Documents.* Washington, D.C.: Government Printing Office, 1916.

United States. Library of Congress, Manuscript Division. George B. McClellan, Sr. Papers, Series A.

United States. National Archives, R.G. 23 A.D. Bache. Notes on the Coast of the United States, 1861, with charts.

United States. National Archives, R.G. 23. Records of the Headquarters of the Army. Letters from Col. C. B. Comstock to Maj-Gen Rawlins Relating to the Occupation of Fort Fisher, Dec 1864–Jan 1865.

United States. National Archives. Confederate Documents. Despatches relative to engagement between Ft. McAllister and Union ironclads, 1863.

United States. National Archives. Confederate Documents. Testimony taken by the Congressional Committee to investigate the Roanoke Island defeat. 3rd Ad. Sess., 1862.

United States. Navy Department. *Report of the Chief of the Bureau of Ordnance,* November, 1864. New York: D. Van Nostrand, 1864.

United States. Navy Department. *Report of the Secretary of the Navy.* Washington, D.C.: Government Printing Office, 1864.

United States. Navy Department. *Report of the Secretary of the Navy in relation to armored vessels.* Washington, D.C.: Government Printing Office, 1864.

United States. Navy Department. Office of Naval War Records. *Official Records of the Union and Confederate Navies in the War of the Rebellion.* 30 vols and Index. Washington, D.C.: Government Printing Office, 1894–1922.

United States. War Department. *The War of the Rebellion: A Compilation of Official Records of the Union and Confederate Armies.* 70 vols in 128. Washington, D.C.: Government Printing Office, 1880–1901.

United States. War Department. Engineer Bureau. R.G. 77. Report of the Board of Engineers appointed to consider modifications in United States seacoast defenses, submitted to the Secretary of War 31 May 1864. (Also called "Report on Fortifications, 1864"), AGO S.O. 41.

Welles, Gideon. *Diary of Gideon Welles, Secretary of the Navy under Lincoln and Johnson.* 3 vols. Boston: Houghton Mifflin, 1909–1911.

Younger, Edward, ed. *Inside the Confederate Government: The Diary of Robert Garlick Hill Kean.* New York: Oxford University Press, 1957.

II. MEMOIRS AND PARTICIPANT ACCOUNTS

Ammen, Daniel. *The Atlantic Coast* ("The Navy in the Civil War," Vol. II). New York: Chas. Scribner's Sons, 1883.

Ammen, Daniel. *The Old Navy and the New.* Philadelphia: J. B. Lippincott, 1891.

Battles and Leaders of the Civil War. 4 vols. New York: The Century Co., 1887.

Butler, Benjamin F. *Butler's Book: Autobiographical and Personal*

Reminiscences of Major-General Benjamin F. Butler. Boston: A. M. Thayer, 1892.

Davis, Jefferson. *The Rise and Fall of the Confederate Government*. 2 vols. London: Longmans, Green and Co., 1881.

Gilchrist, Robert C. *The Confederate Defence of Morris Island*. Charleston, S.C.: The News and Courier Book Presses, 1884.

Gillmore, Quincy A. *Engineer and Artillery Operations against the Defenses of Charleston in 1863*. New York: D. Van Nostrand, 1865.

Grant, Ulysses S. *Personal Memoirs of U. S. Grant*. 2 vols. New York: The Century Company, 1895.

Hagood, Johnson. *Memoirs of the War of Secession*. Columbia, S.C.: The State Company, 1910.

Johnson, John. *The Defense of Charleston Harbor, 1863–1865*. Reprint ed. (1st ed., 1890) Freeport, N.Y.: Books for Libraries Press, 1970.

Johnston, Joseph E. *Narrative of Military Operations*. Bloomington: Indiana University Press, 1959.

Joinville, Prince de. *The Army of the Potomac*. New York: D. F. Randolph, 1862.

Jones, Samuel. *The Siege of Charleston*. New York: Neale Co., 1911.

Long, E. B., ed. *Personal Memoirs of U. S. Grant*. Cleveland: World Publishing Co., 1952.

McClellan, George B. *Own Story: The War for the Union, the Soldiers Who Fought It, the Civilians Who Directed It, and His Relation to It and to Them*. New York: C. L. Webster and Company, 1887.

Military Historical Society of Massachusetts Papers. Vols I, 1902, and IX, 1912.

Parker, William Harwar. *Recollections of a Naval Officer, 1841–1865*. New York: Chas. Scribner's Sons, 1883.

Pollard, Edward A. *The First Year of the War*. 2nd rev. ed. New York: Richardson, 1864.

Seward, Frederick W. *Reminiscences of a War-Time Statesman and Diplomat*. New York and London: G. P. Putnam's Sons, 1916.

Sherman, W. T. *Memoirs of General William T. Sherman*. 2 vols in 1. Reprint ed. Bloomington: Indiana University Press, 1957.

Southern Historical Society Papers. Volume I, February 1876.

III. BIOGRAPHY

Alden, Carroll Storrs. *George Hamilton Perkins, Commodore, U.S.N.: His Life and Letters*. Boston and New York: Houghton Mifflin Co., 1914.

Ambrose, Stephen E. *Halleck: Lincoln's Chief of Staff*. Baton Rouge: Louisiana State University Press, 1962.

Davis, Charles H. *Life of Charles Henry Davis, Rear Admiral, 1807–1877*. Boston: Houghton Mifflin, 1899.

Du Pont, H. A. *Rear Admiral Samuel Francis Du Pont*. New York: National Americana Society, 1926.

Eckenrode, H. J. and Bryan Conrad. *George B. McClellan: The Man Who*

Saved the Union. Chapel Hill: University of North Carolina Press, 1941.

Farragut, Loyall. *The Life of David Glasgow Farragut.* New York: D. Appleton and Co., 1879.

Freeman, Douglas Southall. *R. E. Lee: A Biography.* 4 vols. New York: Scribner's, 1934–35.

Harrington, Fred Harvey. *Fighting Politician: Major General Nathaniel P. Banks.* Philadelphia: University of Pennsylvania Press, 1948.

Hassler, Warren W. *George B. McClellan.* Baton Rouge: Louisiana State University Press, 1957.

Holtzman, Robert S. *Stormy Ben Butler.* New York: Macmillan Company, 1834.

Kamm, Samuel Rickey. *The Civil War Career of Thomas A. Scott.* Published Ph.D. thesis, University of Pennsylvania, 1940.

Lewis, Charles Lee. *David Glasgow Farragut.* Annapolis: United States Naval Institute, 1943.

Michie, Peter Smith. *General McClellan.* New York: D. Appleton and Co., 1901.

Merrill, James M. *William Tecumseh Sherman.* New York: Rand McNally & Company, 1971.

Myers, William Starr. *General George Brinton McClellan.* New York: D. Appleton-Century, 1934.

Nicolay, John G. and John Hay. *Abraham Lincoln.* 10 vols. New York: The Century Company, 1917.

Niven, John. *Gideon Welles: Lincoln's Secretary of the Navy.* New York: Oxford University Press, 1973.

Pemberton, John C. *Pemberton: Defender of Vicksburg.* Chapel Hill: University of North Carolina Press, 1942.

Randall, James G. *Lincoln: The President.* 4 vols. London: Eyre & Spottiswoode, n.d.

Seitz, Don C. *Braxton Bragg: General of the Confederacy.* Columbia, S.C.: The State Company, 1924.

Spears, John Randolph. *David G. Farragut.* Philadelphia: Jacobs, 1905.

Strode, Harrison. *Jefferson Davis: Confederate President.* New York: Harcourt, Brace, 1959.

Tate, Allen. *Jefferson Davis: His Rise and Fall.* Reprint ed. New York: Kraus Reprint Co., 1969.

Thomas, Benjamin P. and Harold M. Hyman. *Stanton: The Life and Times of Lincoln's Secretary of War.* New York: Knopf, 1962.

Trefousse, H. L. *Benjamin Franklin Wade: Radical Republican from Ohio.* New York: Twayne Publishers, 1963.

West, Richard S., Jr. *Gideon Welles: Lincoln's Navy Department.* Indianapolis: Bobbs-Merrill Co., Inc., 1943.

West, Richard S., Jr. *Lincoln's Scapegoat General: A Life of Benjamin F. Butler, 1818–1893.* Boston: Houghton Mifflin, 1965.

West, Richard S., Jr. *The Second Admiral: A Life of David Dixon Porter.* New York: Coward-McCann, Inc., 1937.

Williams, Harry. *P. G. T. Beauregard: Napoleon in Gray*. Baton Rouge: Louisiana State University Press, 1954.

Wright, Marcus. *General Scott*. New York: A. Appleton, 1894.

IV. OTHER BOOKS AND ARTICLES

Albion, Robert Greenhalgh and Jennie Barnes Pope. *The Sea Lanes in Wartime*. 2nd ed. n.p.: Archon Books, 1968.

Barrett, John G. *The Civil War in North Carolina*. Chapel Hill: University of North Carolina Press, 1963.

Black, Robert C., III. *The Railroads of the Confederacy*. Chapel Hill: University of North Carolina Press, 1952.

Bright, Samuel R. *Confederate Coast Defense*. Ph.D. thesis, Duke University, 1964.

Buttgenbach, Walter J. "Coast Defense in the Civil War." *Journal U.S. Artillery*, 39:210–16, 331–338 [Mar–May]; 205–215, 306–313 [Jul–Nov] 1913; 41:19–47, 191–211, 317–336 [Jan–May]; 42:68–83, 185–213 [Jul–Sep] 1914.

Carrison, Daniel J. *The Navy from Wood to Steel, 1860–1890*. New York: Franklin Watts, 1965.

Catton, Bruce, *Grant Takes Command*. Boston: Little, Brown and Company, 1968.

Cauthern, Charles E. *South Carolina Goes to War, 1860–1865*. ("The James Sprunt Studies in History and Political Science," Volume 32.) Chapel Hill: University of North Carolina Press, 1950.

Copeland, Melvin Thomas. *The Cotton Manufacturing Industry in the United States*. Cambridge, Mass.: Harvard University Press, 1923.

Daly, Robert W. "Burnside's Amphibious Division." *Marine Corps Gazette*, December 1951.

Fuller, J. F. C. *The Generalship of Ulysses S. Grant*. London: John Murray, 1929.

Greene, Francis Vinton. *The Mississippi* ("Campaigns of the Civil War," Volume III.) New York: Chas. Scribner's Sons, 1903.

Hendrick, Burton J. *Lincoln's War Cabinet*. Boston: Little, Brown and Co., 1946.

Horn, Stanley F. *The Army of Tennessee*. Norman: University of Oklahoma Press, 1952.

Kerby, Robert L. *Kirby Smith's Confederacy: The Trans-Mississippi South, 1863–1865*. New York and London: Columbia University Press, 1972.

Lewis, Charles Bertrand. (M. Quad, pseudo.) *Field, Fort, and Fleet*. Detroit: Free Press Publishing Co., 1885.

Luvaas, (Morton) Jay. "The Fall of Fort Fisher." *Civil War Times Illustrated*, 3:5–9,31–35 (August 1964).

Mahan, Alfred T. *The Navy in the Civil War: The Gulf and Inland Waters*. New York: Chas. Scribner's Sons, 1905.

Merrill, James M. *Battle Flags South: The Story of the Civil War Navies on Western Waters*. Rutherford, N.J.: Fairleigh Dickinson University Press, 1970.

Miers, Earl Schenck. *The Web of Victory: Grant at Vicksburg*. New York: Alfred A. Knopf, 1955.

Milligan, John D. *Gunboats Down the Mississippi*. Annapolis: United States Naval Institute, 1965.

Nichols, James Lynn. *Confederate Engineers*. Tuscaloosa, Ala.: Confederate Publishing Co., 1957.

Owsley, Frank Lawrence. *King Cotton Diplomacy*. 2nd ed. Chicago: University of Chicago Press, 1959.

Schwab, John Christopher. *The Confederate States of America, 1861–1865: A Financial and Industrial History of the South During the Civil War*. Reprint ed. (1st ed., 1901) New York: Burt Franklin, 1968.

Summers, Festus Paul. *The Baltimore and Ohio in the Civil War*. New York: Putnam's Sons, 1939.

Turner, George Edgar. *Victory Rode the Rails: The Strategic Place of Railroads in the Civil War*. Indianapolis: Bobbs-Merrill, 1953.

Williams, Kenneth P. *Lincoln Finds a General*. 5 vols. New York: Macmillan, 1952.

V. GENERAL HISTORIES AND THEORY

Anderson, Bern. *By Sea and By River: A Naval History of the Civil War*. New York: Alfred A. Knopf, 1962.

Boynton, C. B. *The History of the Navy During the Rebellion*. 2 vols. New York: D. Appleton and Co., 1867–68.

Callwell, C. E. *Military Operations and Maritime Preponderance: Their Relation and Independence*. Edinburgh and London: William Blackwood, 1905.

Carse, Robert. *Blockade: The Civil War at Sea*. New York: Rinehart and Co., 1958.

Colomb, Philip H. *Naval Warfare: Its Ruling Principles and Practice*. 3rd ed. rev. London: W. H. Allen & Co., 1899.

Corbett, Julian S. *Some Principles of Maritime Strategy*. 2nd ed. London: Longman's, Green, 1938.

Eardley-Wilmot, S. *The Development of Navies During the Last Half-Century*. New York: Chas. Scribner's Sons, 1892.

Halleck, H. Wager. *Elements of Military Art and Science*. Reprint ed. Westport, Conn.: Greenwood Press, 1971.

Hittle, James Donald. *The Military Staff: Its History and Development*. Rev. ed. Harrisburg, Pa.: Military Services Publishing Co., 1949.

Heinl, Robert Debs Jr. *Soldiers of the Sea: The United States Marine Corps, 1775–1962*. Annapolis: United States Naval Institute, 1962.

Ingersoll, L. D. *A History of the War Department*. Washington, D.C.: Government Printing Office, 1880.

Jomini, (Henri Antoine) Baron de. *The Art of War*. trans. by G. H. Mendell and W. P. Craighill. Reprint ed. Westport, Conn.: Greenwood Press, n.d.

Jones, Virgil Carrington. *The Civil War at Sea*. 3 vols. New York: Holt, Rinehart & Winston, 1960.

Lossing, Benson J. *The Civil War in the United States of America.* 2 vols. Hartford, Conn.: T. Belknap, 1868.

Mahan, Alfred Thayer. *The Influence of Sea Power Upon History.* 12th ed. Boston: Little, Brown and Company, n.d.

Molyneux, Thomas M. *Conjunct Expeditions.* London: Dodsley, 1759.

Nash, Howard P. *A Naval History of the Civil War.* South Brunswick and New York: A. S. Barnes and Company, 1972.

Orleans, Louis d', Comte de Paris. *History of the Civil War in America.* 4 vols. Philadelphia: Porter and Coates, 1876–88.

Paullin, Charles Oscar. "A Half Century of Naval Administration, 1861–1911." Parts I and II—"The Navy Department during the Civil War, 1861–1865." *United States Naval Institute Proceedings.* 38: 1309–36 (December 1912); 39:165–95 (March 1913).

Potter, E. B. and Chester W. Nimitz, eds. *Sea Power: A Naval History.* Englewood Cliffs, N.J.: Prentice-Hall, Inc., 1960.

Rogers, W. L. "A Study of Fortified Harbors." *United States Naval Institute Proceedings.* 30:708–744 (December 1904).

Scharf, J. T. *History of the Confederate States Navy.* New York: Rogers and Sherwood, 1887.

Shannon, Fred A. *The Organization and Administration of the Union Army, 1861–1865.* 2 vols. Cleveland, 1928.

Stern, Phillip Van Dorn. *The Confederate Navy: A Pictorial History.* Garden City, N.Y.: Doubleday & Co., 1962.

United States. Marine Corps. General Headquarters, Historical Branch, G-3 Division. *The United States Marines in the Civil War.* Washington, D.C.: Marine Corps Historical Reference Series, No. 2, Revised 1961.

United States. War Department. *The Military Policy of the United States, by Bvt. Major Gen. Emory Upton, United States Army.* 4th impression. Washington, D.C.: Government Printing Office, 1917.

Vagts, Alfred. *Landing Operations.* Harrisburg, Pa.: Military Services Publishing Co., 1946.

VI. REFERENCE

Amann, William F., ed. *Personnel of the Civil War. Volume I, The Confederate Armies. Volume 2, the Union Armies.* New York, 1961.

Atlas to Accompany the Official Records of the Union and Confederate Armies in the War of the Rebellion. Washington, D.C.: Government Printing Office, 1891–95.

Callahan, Edward W. *List of Officers of the Navy of the United States and of the Marine Corps from 1775 to 1900.* New York: Haskell House, 1969.

Dyer, Frederick H. *A Compendium of the War of the Rebellion.* 3 vols. Des Moines, 1908.

Esposito, Vincent J. *The West Point Atlas of American Wars.* Volume I: 1689–1900. New York: Frederick A. Praeger, 1959.

Hammersley, Lewis Randolph. *The Records of Living Officers of the U.S.*

Navy and Marine Corps; with a history of naval operations during the Rebellion of 1861–5, and a list of the ships and officers participating in the great battles. Philadelphia: J. B. Lippincott, 1870.

Heitman, Francis B. *Historical Register and Dictionary of the United States Army from Its Organization, September 29, 1789, to March 2, 1903.* 2 vols. Urbana: University of Illinois Press, 1965.

Livermore, Thomas L. *Numbers and Losses in the Civil War in America, 1861–65.* Bloomington: Indiana University Press, 1957.

Long, E. B., with Barbara Long. *The Civil War Day by Day: An Almanac, 1861–1865.* Garden City, N.Y.: Doubleday & Company, 1971.

Meneely, A. Howard. *The War Department, 1861.* New York: Columbia University Press, 1928.

Neeser, Robert W. *Statistical and Chronological History of the United States Navy, 1775–1907.* 2 vols. New York: Macmillan, 1909.

Osbon, Bradley Sillick, comp. *Handbook of the United States Navy: Being a Compilation of all the Principal Events in the History of Every Vessel of the United States Navy.* From April, 1861, to May, 1864. New York: D. Van Nostrand, 1864.

United States. Coast and Geodetic Survey. *Charts, Nos. 55* (1873), *1240* (1939), *1001* (1947), *1007* (1947). Washington, D.C.: Cartographic Branch, National Resources Records Division, National Archives.

United States. Navy Department, Naval History Division. *Civil War Naval Chronology, 1861–1865.* Washington, D.C.: Government Printing Office, 1971.

United States. Navy Department, Office of Naval War Records. *List of U.S. Naval Vessels, 1861–1865, including the Ellet Ram Fleet and Mississippi Marine Brigade; Appendix, List of U.S. Coast Survey Vessels, 1861–1865.* Office Memorandum #4. Washington, D.C.: Printing Office, 1891.

United States. Navy Department, Office of Naval War Records. *Register of Officers of the Confederate States Navy, 1861–1865.* Washington, D.C.: Government Printing Office, 1931.

Upton, Francis H. *The Law of Nations affecting Commerce during War.* New York: D. Appleton Co., 1861.

Walton, William. *The Army and Navy of the U.S. from the Revolution to the present day.* 2 vols. Boston: G. Barrie & Sons, 1889–95.

VII. TECHNICAL STUDIES AND MANUALS

Anderson, Bern. "The Impact of Rapid Communications on the Employment of Naval Forces". *United States Naval Institute Proceedings.* 77:1156–67 (Nov 1951).

Barnard, John G. *Notes on Seacoast Defense.* New York: D. Van Nostrand, 1861.

Baxter, James Phinney. *The Introduction of the Ironclad Warship.* Cambridge, Mass.: Harvard University Press, 1933.

Bennett, F. M. *The Steam Navy of the United States: A History of the*

Growth of the Steam Vessel of War in the United States and of the Naval Engineer Corps. Pittsburgh, Pa. 1896.

Boxer, Edward M. *Remarks on the System of Ordnance Likely to Prove Most Effective against Iron-clad Ships and Batteries.* Woolwich, England, 1862.

Brialmont. A. *Etudes sur la défense des états et sur la fortification.* 3 vols. Bruxelles, 1863.

Brown, J. Willard. *The Signal Corps, U.S.A., in the War of the Rebellion.* Boston: Houghton Mifflin, 1896.

Canfield, Eugene B. *Notes on Naval Ordnance of the American Civil War, 1861–1865.* Washington: American Ordnance Association, 1960.

Clark, George Sydenham. *Fortification.* 2nd ed. (1st ed., 1890). London: John Murray, 1907.

Coles, Cowper P. *A Comparison Between Iron-Clad Ships with Broadside Ports and Ships with Revolving Shields.* Portsea, England: James Griffin, 1863.

Confederate States of America. Army. *The Ordnance Manual for Use of the Confederate States Army.* Richmond, 1863.

Dahlgren, John A. *Shells and Shell-Guns.* Philadelphia: King & Baird, 1856.

Greene, Albert S. *Organization of the Engineer Corps of the Navy and Education of its Officers.* Washington, D.C.: Government Printing Office, 1864.

Holley, Alexander L. *A Treatise on Ordnance and Armor; Embracing Descriptions, Discussions, and Professional Opinions Concerning the Material, Fabrication . . . of European and American Guns . . . and their Rifling, Projectiles, and Breech-Loading. . . .* New York: D. Van Nostrand, 1865.

Jeffers, William N. *A Concise Treatise on the Theory and Practice of Naval Gunnery.* New York: D. Appleton & Co., 1850.

Lemly, Henry R. *Changes Wrought in Artillery in the Nineteenth Century and their Effect upon the Attack and Defense of Fortified Places.* Fort Monroe, Va., 1886.

Lewis, Berkeley R. *Notes on Ammunition of the American Civil War.* Washington, D.C.: American Ordnance Association, 1959.

Lott, A. S. *Most Dangerous Sea: A History of Mine Warfare.* Annapolis: United States Naval Institute, 1959.

Mahan, Dennis Hart. *Treatise on Field Fortification.* 3rd ed. New York: John Wiley, 1862.

Myer, Albert J. *A Manual for Signals: For Use of Signal Officers in the Field.* Washington, D.C.: Government Printing Office, 1866.

Parker, William A. *Instructions for Naval Light Artillery, Afloat or Ashore.* Annapolis: R. F. Bonsall, 1861.

Paulding, J. N. *The Cannon and Projectiles Invented by Robert Parker Parrott.* New York: J. N. Paulding, 1874.

Plum, William R. *The Military Telegraph during the Civil War in the United States.* 2 vols. Chicago, 1882.

Ripley, Warren. *Artillery and Ammunition of the Civil War*. New York: Van Nostrand Reinhold Company, 1970.

Scott, Winfield. *The Infantry Tactics*. 3 vols. New York: D. Van Nostrand, 1859.

Simpson, Edward. *A Treatise on Ordnance and Naval Gunnery*. 2nd rev. ed. New York: D. Van Nostrand, 1863.

Smith, Edgar. *A Short History of Naval and Marine Engineering*. Cambridge, England, 1938.

Totten, Joseph G. *Report on the Effects of Firing with Heavy Ordnance from Casemate Embrasures: and also the Effects of Firing against the same Embrasures*. Washington, D.C.: Government Printing Office, 1857.

United States. Army. *Instructions for Heavy Artillery: Prepared by a Board of Officers for the Use of the Army of the United States*. Charleston, S.C., 1861.

United States. Navy Department, Bureau of Ordnance. *System of Boat Armament in the U.S. Navy*, by John A. Dahlgren. 2nd ed. Philadelphia: King & Baird, 1856.

Vandiver, Frank Everson. *Ploughshares into Swords: Josiah Gorgas and Confederate Ordnance*. Austin: University of Texas Press, 1952.

Ward, James Harman. *A Manual of Naval Tactics: Together with a Brief Critical Analysis of the Principal Modern Naval Battles*. New York: D. Appleton & Co., 1859.

von Scheliha, Viktor E. K. R. *A Treatise on Coast-Defence*. London: E. & F. N. Spon, 1868.

INDEX